*Proceedings*

# International Conference on Software Engineering

# *ICSM-2000*

# Proceedings

# International Conference on Software Engineering

San Jose, California, USA
October 11 – 14, 2000

**Sponsored by**
IEEE Computer Society Technical Council on Software Engineering

IEEE
COMPUTER
SOCIETY

Los Alamitos, California

Washington   •   Brussels   •   Tokyo

IEEE Computer Society Order Number PR00753
ISBN 0-7695-0753-0
ISBN 0-7695-0754-9 (case)
ISBN 0-7695-0755-7 (microfiche)
ISSN Number 1063-6773

*Additional copies may be ordered from*:

| IEEE Computer Society | IEEE Service Center | IEEE Computer Society |
|---|---|---|
| Customer Service Center | 445 Hoes Lane | Asia/Pacific Office |
| 10662 Los Vaqueros Circle | P.O. Box 1331 | Watanabe Bldg., 1-4-2 |
| P.O. Box 3014 | Piscataway, NJ 08855-1331 | Minami-Aoyama |
| Los Alamitos, CA 90720-1314 | Tel: + 1-732-981-0060 | Minato-ku, Tokyo 107-0062 |
| Tel: + 1-714-821-8380 | Fax: + 1-732-981-9667 | JAPAN |
| Fax: + 1-714-821-4641 | http://shop.ieee.org/store/ | Tel: + 81-3-3408-3118 |
| E-mail: cs.books@computer.org | customer-service@ieee.org | Fax: + 81-3-3408-3553 |
| | | tokyo.ofc@computer.org |

Editorial production by Bob Werner
Cover art production by Joe Daigle/Studio Productions
Printed in the United States of America by The Printing House

# Table of Contents

## International Conference on Software Maintenance — ICSM 2000

## Reverse Engineering II

## Re-Engineering

## Empirical Studies I

## Empirical Studies II

# Program Analysis

# Management I

# Management II

# Welcome

**D**ear Colleagues,

Welcome to Silicon Valley and to the International Conference on Software Maintenance 2000! This year we present a different type of ICSM. The major change is our close collaboration with the International Symposium on Software Reliability Engineering (ISSRE), chaired by Allen Nikora. ISSRE and ICSM are appearing back-to-back with our joint Industry Day between the two conferences on Wednesday, featuring software reliability and maintenance panels and case studies. Participants in Industry Day include: IBM, Sun, NASA, Agilent, Cisco, Raytheon, Swedish School of Economics, University of Corona, Xenium, Naval Postgraduate School, Carleton University, Software Reliability Engineering and Testing Courses, Jet Propulsion Laboratory, Colorado State University, OAO Corp., Air Force Materiel Command, Reliable Software Technologies, and Netsiel. The record of these sessions has been published in the Industry Day Proceedings. To top off the industry theme, we will visit the Technical Museum of Innovation in San Jose on Wednesday evening to partake of the technical exhibits and dinner.

We have included as much industry material, including sessions on Silicon Valley companies, as feasible consistent with presenting a solid research program, which has been published in the ICSM Proceedings. ICSM and ISSRE have also collaborated on our Technology Fair. This event is not limited to the traditional tools exhibits; in addition, it includes project reports and demonstrations and book displays. In addition to the collaboration with ISSRE, the International Workshop on Empirical Studies of Software Maintenance, chaired by George Stark, follows ICSM on Saturday.

This year we are fortunate to have as our keynoters Ray Kammer, Director of the National Institute of Standards and Technology; Lou Blazy, NASA Headquarter, Former Director of NASA IV&V Center; and Tom McCabe, McCabe Technology.

In addition to participating in the technical program, we want you to have fun in San Jose. To meet that goal, Ned Chapin has identified a number of interesting social activities in the area, including museums, historical sites, universities, and musical and sporting events. Please see Ned for additional information.

There were many colleagues — too numerous to mention in this limited space — who made outstanding contributions to this conference. Three people stand out: Lionel Briand, Jeff Voas, and Ryan MacMichael. As Program Co-Chair, Lionel did a marvelous job of organizing the Program Committee (PC), running the PC meeting, and getting the papers reviewed and published. Jeff Voas wore two hats: Co-Program Chair for ICSM and Publicity Chair for ICSM and ISSRE. In the latter role, he exercised great initiative in obtaining maximum exposure for both conferences through various media and in providing the Reliable Software Technologies web sites. As Webmaster, Ryan was innovative and proactive in getting the web sites implemented, updating them with new information as program planning evolved, and in providing links to conference and hotel registration. I also want to thank Allen Nikora for his high degree of professionalism in collaborating to make this week not two isolated conferences but a truly integrated conference event.

**Norman Schneidewind**
**General Chair, ICSM 2000**

# Conference Committee

**General Chair**
Norm Schneidewind, Naval Postgraduate School

**Program Co-Chairs**
Lionel Briand, Dept. of Systems and Computer Engineering, Carleton University
Jeffrey M. Voas, Reliable Software Technologies

**Tutorial Co-Chairs**
Shawn Bohner, META Group, Inc.
Giuliano Antoniol, I.R.S.T.

**Tools Exhibition Co-Chairs**
William Farr, NSWCDD
Hongji Yang, Computer Science Department, De Montfort University

**Industry Co-Chairs**
George Stark, IBM Global Services
Linda Rosenberg, Software Assurance Technology Center, NASA GSFC

**Webmaster**
Ryan A. MacMichael, Reliable Software Technologies

**Activities Chair**
Ned Chapin

**Local Arrangements Chair**
Norman F. Schneidewind, Naval Postgraduate School

**Program Committee**
Giuliano Antoniol, I.R.S.T.

Pearl Brereton, Keele University

Gerardo Canfora, University of Sannio

Ned Chapin, InfoSci Inc.

Aniello Cimitile, University of Sannio

Sasa Dekleva, DePaul University

Khaled El Emam, National Research Council

Keith Brian Gallagher, Loyola College in Maryland

Jean-Francois Girard, Fraunhofer Institute for Experimental, Software Engineering (IESE)

David R. Harris, The MITRE Corporation

Rudolf K. Keller, Université de Montréal

Taghi M. Khoshgoftaar, Florida Atlantic University

Sebastian Kutscha, xenium AG, Sustainable Software Systems

Bruno Lague, Bell Canada

Filippo Lanubile, University of Bari

Paul J.Layzell, UMIST

Chung-Horng Lung, Nortel Networks

Anneliese von Mayrhauser, Colorado State University

Ettore M. Merlo, Ecole Polytechnique

Audris Mockus, Lucent Technologies, Bell Laboratories

Sandro Morasca, Politecnico di Milano

Dr. Hausi A. Muller, University of Victoria

Malcolm Munro, University of Durham

John C. Munson, University of Idaho

Paolo Nesi, Associate Professor, University of Florence

Allen P. Nikora, Autonomy and Control Section, Jet Propulsion Laboratory

Thomas M. Pigoski, TECHSOFT, Inc.

Vaclav Rajlich, Wayne State University

Dr. Linda H. Rosenberg, Software Assurance Technology Center, NASA GFC

Gregg Rothermel, Oregon State University

Robert W. Schwanke, Siemens Corporate Research, Inc.

Raj Sood, Primary Automation Systems, Process Automation Department, BFCF Dofasco Inc.

George Stark, IBM

William M. Thomas, The MITRE Corporation

Giuseppe Visaggio, Department of Informatics

Lee White, Case Western Reserve University

Dr F.G. Wilkie, The University of Ulster

Dr. Hongji Yang, De Montfort University

Nicholas Zvegintzov, Software Management Network

# Keynotes

# Software Maintenance in the New Millennium: Issues and Challenges

Ray Kammer, Director of NIST

As we approached the year 2000, concerns about the Y2K "bug" focused attention on the importance of high quality, reliable software in supporting the economic foundation of the US and world economy. Additionally, security attacks against systems have been escalating, as hackers exploit known software vulnerabilities that have not been patched. Public attention on the quality of software is increasing – and demand is increasing for solutions.

The responsibility of a vendor does not end once a product is released. Likewise, user responsibilities do not end one that software has been installed. If software is not properly maintained, a well documented, cleanly designed product can decay into a poorly documented, difficult to maintain headache. The more difficult it is to maintain a software product, the greater the likelihood that software patches will not be correctly installed by users in a timely manner – and that additional vulnerabilities may be introduced during software maintenance. In a network environment, a bug in system software has ramifications beyond just poor operation or lost functionality. A bug is often an avenue of access pursued by a hostile intruder.

According to Business Week: "More than 75% of the [security] incidents...are the direct result of bugs." "[M]ore real testing -- not 'beta testing' in the marketplace -- will yield programs that are less vulnerable to attack." (Business Week, February 28, 2000, "Locking Out the Hackers") A significant number of bugs are introduced during maintenance – but this does not have to be. There is a large body of knowledge and relevant standards to provide guidance for the maintenance process. One challenge is to disseminate that information in a easy-to-use, timely manner – accompanied by enhanced development and use of automated software testing.

Over the past seventeen years since the first software maintenance conference, we have learned a great deal about software maintenance. However, each new generation often repeats the same mistakes and has to relearn the same lessons. This is unfortunately true in many other arenas. We must do a better job of learning from our past mistakes.

Technology is not standing still. We talk not of Vacuum tubes and punch cards but the Internet age. Many software problems can be fixed by downloading and installing software patches. Often systems can be configured so that this happens automatically. Interactive television, with its capability to easily deliver software for entertainment and electronic commerce to a mass audience, is around the corner. Devices for pervasive computing are already in widespread use. What comes next might be based on quantum phenomena. It might be something else. We will not know until it arrives. What we do know is that we will continue to need to maintain high quality software. This most difficult challenge can be addressed, but requires diligence and perseverance. We must integrate what we know with new research to preserve and enhance software that we maintain so that we can all benefit from high quality, reliable, secure software.

# Software Life Cycles for e-Commerce Businesses

## Tom McCabe, McCabe Technology

The new, growing, and changing forms of electronic business have demanded a radical change to our notion of the software lifecycle. In addition to dealing with the usual software development issues managers of Web businesses are now faced with numerous requests and changes from many diverse domains including the following:

Software development, content development, advertisements, news, announcements, message boards, database, related links, FAQ's, prices, products...

These Web domains are different in nature, overlap in time, and each requires a distinct lifecycle. This talk will describe groupware maintenance coordination of projects, policies, and people to many concurrent Web domains.

Not only has the rate of change accelerated beyond our classical lifecycles capability but also the demands of high quality and low cost are beyond our past capabilities — how to leverage specific outside tools to meet these demands will be presented. This presentation will focus on a spirit of collaboration and cooperation expressed in Web lifecycles and compare that with the traditional lifecycles that were characterized by command and control. The synergy of workflow management, knowledge management, and collaboration tools will be applied to the highly volatile e-business environment.

The following topics will be included:

- Software infrastructure tools for building, running, and improving a Web based business.
- Web maintenance request arbitration — the domains, policies, and automated workflow.
- Project, People, and Policy Collaboration as the backbone.

# Notes

# Panel 1: Trends in Preserving and Enhancing the Value of Software

# Trends in Preserving and Enhancing the Value of Software

Ned Chapin
Information Systems Consultant
InfoSci Inc., Box 7117
Menlo Park CA 94026–7117, USA
NedChapin@acm.org

## Abstract

*This position paper on the ICSM 2000 conference theme reviews five key questions about determining software value. Afterward it groups some major trend issues relevant to software value into four clusters. Then drawing upon existing practices, it notes trends in seven value-preserving and enhancing groups of processes. In conclusion, it points to the critical role of management in preserving and enhancing the value of software.*

## ICSM 2000 Conference theme

"Preserving and enhancing the value of software" is the announced theme of this year 2000 International Conference on Software Maintenance, held in San Jose in California. This broad theme invites a variety of viewpoints, some of which are championed by some of the panel participants. Since the panel participants have been invited to supply position papers on trends in this theme, this position paper by the panel chair does not summarize their positions but instead takes a general overview position. This position paper looks first at some key clarifying questions. It then reviews four clusters of issues. It closes by pointing to a few trend highlights after noting some value-preserving processes and their connections to trends in preserving and enhancing the value of software.

## Key questions

*Who and what determines software value?* One man's treasure is another man's trash, as the old saying goes. For example, the user preserves software that meets the user's needs. But the software historian preserves software regarded as representing significant steps or states in the evolution of ideas or technology. And the software vendor preserves software that generates lots of sales of licenses. As organizations and people become more dependent upon software, more perspectives are involved in determining software value.

*When is software value determined?* Sometimes it is retrospective, as in "Why have we not retired that software yet?" Sometimes it is prospective, as in "Shall we convert to this new enterprise management system?" Sometimes it is current, as in "We need to enhance this system to make the new reporting cover all of the product lines." What happens as software ages?

*How is the value of software determined?* Even as a question of economics, different possible "customers" assign different values depending upon their economic situations (the "demand curve"). Yet economics is not the only determinant and often not the dominant determinant. Some of the determinants arise from esthetics, organizational politics, support quality, personnel skills, security, organizational procedures and practices, regulations, fit with other software, public image, competition, and personal taste. As more people become affected by the use of software, the trend is for more variety in determining the value of software.

*How does preserving the value of software differ from preserving the software?* For example, to what extent does migrating a system to a new platform preserve both? Is re-engineering a system a process that preserves the software, or the value of the software, or neither? To what extent does adding an enhancement preserve the software, or the value of the software, or neither? What does software evolution do to software and to the value of the software? Where is the trend?

*What happens when the value of software changes?* The things that happen to software are either accidents (like corruption of the object file) or actions by people. Ignoring the accidents, the actions by people may be to do nothing, or to modify the software, or to modify the environment in which the software operates. Because the two modify alternatives can become complex, one simplifying approach is to ask first the other major questions, and subsequently turn to this one. Diversity and dependences make the trends unclear.

## Four clusters of issues affecting trends

The first issue cluster concerns the relationships between stakeholders and software. Where there is no relationship seen by the stakeholders, they recognize no value. Where the stakeholders see a tight and direct relationship, and especially a dependence, the stakeholders recognize value in the software, be it positive or negative. An example is a cashier using a computer-operated cash register. Where the relationship is loose or indirect, assessing the value can be uncertain. An example is a shop-floor supervisor who is asked by a young journeyman machinist about her pension vesting achieved to date.

The second issue cluster concerns the software itself. Some issues are its form (such as embedded), its application domain (such as euro transactions), its location (such as geographically dispersed), its robustness or reliability (such as fails about twice a week), its age (such as 16 years), its relative cost to modify (such as average), its structure or composition (such as unstructured with COTS components), its documentation quality (such as obsolete or missing), its main language of implementation (such as assembly), its platform (such as emulated), etc. Some of these may affect the value of the software.

The third issue cluster concerns software maintenance processes and their management. The effective location of the management of maintenance may be anywhere in the organization (such as anywhere from a vice president to a junior programmer), and differ for different systems. The processes may range from repeatable and consistent, to ad hoc and idiosyncratic, and be with or without effective quality assurance. The value of software can rise or fall depending upon the maintenance done and how it is done.

The fourth issue cluster concerns the drivers for change. Excepting accidents, software does not deteriorate, but lives out its life span in an environment of sticky change. Stakeholders change, competition changes, fashions change, operating environments change, platforms change, regulations change, and technology changes. The changes come irregularly with some periods of stability interspersed. The changes and the organization's responses to them give rise to changes in the value of software.

## Some value-preserving/enhancing processes

*Train the personnel.* For decades, we have known that the more the personnel know about the software, the more highly the personnel typically value it, whether as users, managers or maintainers [1]. Knowledge of existing software is lost to the organization as personnel turnover occurs, and as the normal forgetting occurs as time passes. Hence, providing refresher training periodically can be an effective process for preserving and enhancing software

value. The current mild upward trend appears to fall short of what could be done.

*Favor software evolution over new development.* Personnel in an organization typically regard the organization as better managed when software is evolved rather than replaced [2]. Partly this seems to come from more continuity in the way the organization works, with less chaos from having to unlearn a familiar system while trying to learn a new system. Partly it seems to come from enhancing systems to meet current needs as they change, instead of waiting until the gap between needs and system capabilities is so large that "junk and replace" starts to appear reasonable. Since software evolution can provide better support for meeting the needs of the organization, favoring software evolution over new development can be an effective process for preserving and enhancing software value. The trend here appears to be flat, resulting in missed opportunities.

*Migrate, application mine and reuse, or re-engineer the system.* When the declining value of a system appears to come primarily from it loss of fit with its environment, the question arises, "Can we migrate this software [3], or extract what can be reused, or do we have to re-engineer?" Reuse of software replicates software and fits it into new systems [4]. Especially for technology changes, migrating, mining, reuse or re-engineering the software of a system can be an effective process for preserving and enhancing software value. The trend here appears to be upward.

*Keep the documentation current and trustworthy.* Too often the documentation is allowed to get out of step with the running object code as the software is maintained. As the documentation content becomes gradually more obsolete, personnel confidence in the system declines and the cost rate to do a maintenance project on the software rises [5]. If management does not care enough about the system to have the documentation kept current, then the other personnel come to believe that the system must not be worth as much to the organization as it used to be. Keeping the documentation current and trustworthy can be an effective process for preserving and enhancing software value. The trend in this neglected area continues to be barely flat or slightly down.

*Modernize the system interface.* When people's expectations have changed about how they are to interact with the system, GUI interfaces as via screen scraping and Internet access can be inserted. Facilitating the human interface with the software can be an effective process for preserving and enhancing software value, and takes up an increasing proportion of the software. The trend appears to be strongly upward.

*Use emulators, translators and wrappers.* Emulators, translators and wrappers keep much of the original software intact, but change how the environment sees the software. Wrappers add an encompassing modified interface, emulators make the environment adapt to the software's characteristics, and translators retain the functionality but change the form of the software. All can be effective processes for preserving and enhancing software value. This trend continues to be upward.

*Apply CRM with respect to the software's stakeholders.* Customer relationship management (CRM) involves listening to the software's stakeholders rather than ignoring their self-perceived needs [6]. It also makes the stakeholders feel more in the ownership or driver position with respect to any changes in software and the timing of those changes, especially those that might affect the externally seen functionality of the system. People typically value more highly what they feel they have an ownership interest in or exercise some control over. Hence, applying CRM with respect to the software's stakeholders can be an effective process for preserving and enhancing software value. This largely overlooked area is ripe for the initiation of an upward trend.

## Conclusions

In conclusion, the key actor in preserving and enhancing the value of software appears to be management. It plays the gatekeeper role. Because management has to sift through the Babel of increasing information overload to see the value of software, the overall trend appears flat currently.

## References

1. Lientz BP, Swanson EB. *Software Maintenance Management.* Addison-Wesley Publishing Co.: Reading MA, 1980; 214 pp.
2. Chapin N. Software maintenance characteristics and effective management. *Journal of Software Maintenance* 1993, **5**(2):91–100.
3. Brodie ML, Stonebraker M. *Migrating Legacy Systems.* Morgan Kaufmann Publishers: San Francisco CA, 1995; 210 pp.
4. Karlsson E-A (ed.). *Software Reuse.* John Wiley & Sons, Inc.: New York NY, 1995; 510 pp.
5. Chapin N. Software maintenance: a different view. In *AFIPS Proceedings of the National Computer Conference*, Volume 54. AFIPS Press: Reston VA, 1985; 507–513.
6. Brown SA. *Customer Relationship Management: Linking People, Process, and Technology.* John Wiley & Sons, Inc.: New York NY, 2000; 384 pp.

# Preserving the Value of Software -- A CIO Perspective

Tama H. Olver
Vice President Information Services and CIO
Quantum Corporation
500 McCarthy Blvd.
Milpitas, CA 95132

## Abstract

*This paper outlines a management perspective of software quality based on a portfolio management approach. It outlines how an assessment of quality and strategic importance can be used to develop strategy for applications maintenance.*

## Context

Within Information Services at Quantum, we take a straightforward view of Value as the difference between benefit and cost. Value is determined at many places in the lifecycle of an information asset. Senior management who fund activities related to creating and preserving value ultimately determines it

## Portfolio Approach to Software Asset Management

A time-tested method for prioritizing investments in information technology is to assess all of the assets as a portfolio with varying degrees of strategic value and quality. Strategic value is measured by criticality to revenue generation, customer satisfaction, key skills acquisition and retention, product introduction, velocity of operations, business transformation, and other strategic goals. Quality is measured by criteria such as: alignment with the functional needs of the organization and its business processes, reliability, availability, supportability, and cost of maintenance.

By viewing each application on a 2 by 2 grid of strategic value and quality, it is possible to select among four maintenance strategies: Invest or replace to assure high quality for strategic assets; maintain or limp along to avoid over investment in assets of low strategic value.

## Relevance of the Approach in 21$^{st}$ Century Business Conditions

The most significant current business conditions affecting this approach are
- Rate of change in business
- Rate of change in technology
- Cost and value of upgrades
- Risks of vendor support
- Talent shortage

It has become more complex to assess and provide quality; although the principles remain the same.

At the same time, the tried-and-true portfolio management approach can be adapted to provide insight into software quality investment decisions in light of the new challenges:

A high rate of change in business suggests that strategic applications of low quality will be come replaced, perhaps sooner than later. This implication may affect capitalization, depreciation, and sourcing strategies.

A high rate of change in technology suggests a framework or middleware strategy. At Quantum we have chosen an aggressive middleware strategy to provide a platform for operating at the speed of business and adopting new technologies quickly.

The relative cost and value of upgrades suggests adoption of an ASP sourcing strategy or other emerging services models.

Risks of vendor support suggest a multiple-sourcing model, which is not affordable by most of us; however, is being adopted by some leading edge services suppliers.

Last and far from least, the talent shortage suggests multiple responses including replacement of software, self-service support, and sourcing from service providers.

# Notes

# Panel 2: Preventive Maintenance!
# Do We Know What It Is?

# Preventive Maintenance!  Do we know what it is?

Mira Kajko-Mattsson
Software Maintenance Laboratory
Department of Computer and Systems Sciences
Stockholm University/Royal Institute of Technology
Electrum 230
SE-164 40  KISTA
mira@dsv.su.se

## Abstract

*Inconsistency exists within the software community surrounding the understanding of and the adherence to the IEEE definition of preventive maintenance, due to congruence between the IEEE definitions of **perfective** and **preventive** maintenance. A panel debate is advocated to discuss the definition and current state of preventive maintenance practice.*

## 1   Introduction

Close scrutiny reveals inconsistency in the way the software community interprets and applies the IEEE definition of preventive maintenance [13, 14]. Analysis contrasting current practice with the IEEE definition of maintenance and its categories (see Table 1) [13, 14], reveals overlap between preventive and perfective maintenance. This paper advocates a panel debate to discuss the following:

1.   *What is preventive software maintenance?*

2.   *What is the current state of preventive software maintenance practice within research and industry?*

3.   *Why does preventive maintenance mean different things to different people?*

4.   *Is there any <u>overlap</u> between preventive maintenance and other categories such as perfective, adaptive or corrective maintenance?*

5.   *Should preventive software maintenance concern safety critical systems only?*

6.   *Can we as software engineers learn anything from preventive hardware maintenance?*

---

**IEEE 94, Std 610.12-1990 [13]**

**Maintenance:** (1) The process of modifying a software system or component after delivery to correct faults, improve performance or other attributes, or adapt to a changed environment. (2) The process of retaining a hardware system or component in, or restoring it to, a state in which it can perform its required functions. *See also*: **preventive maintenance**.

**Corrective maintenance:** Maintenance performed to correct faults in hardware or software.

**Adaptive maintenance:** Software maintenance performed to make a computer program usable in a changed environment.

**Perfective maintenance:** Software maintenance performed to improve the performance, maintainability, or other attributes of a computer program.

**Preventive maintenance:** Maintenance performed for the purpose of preventing problems before they occur.

**IEEE 94, Std 1219-1998 [14]**

**Software Maintenance:** Modification of a software product after delivery to correct faults, to improve performance or other attributes, or to adapt the product to a modified environment.

**Corrective maintenance:** Reactive modification of a software product performed after delivery to correct discovered faults.

**Adaptive maintenance:** Modification of a software product performed after delivery to keep a computer program usable in a changed or changing environment.

**Perfective maintenance:** Modification of a software product after delivery to improve performance or maintainability.

**Preventive maintenance:** IEEE Std 1219-1998 does not define preventive maintenance.

**Table 1.** IEEE definitions of maintenance categories.

## 2   Current state of practice

Maintenance means working with ageing software. Two types of software ageing have been identified: *software product ageing* and *software process execution ageing*. Software product ageing is degradation in software code and documentation quality by continual maintenance. Software process execution ageing is manifest as degradation in performance or transient failures in continuously running software systems.

### 2.1   Software product ageing

Improving maintainability is one method suggested for combating software product ageing. Maintainability is "the ease with which a software system or a component can be modified ...." [13]. According to the IEEE [13, 14], maintainability is included in perfective maintenance. Some authors adhere strictly to this definition [9, 21, 23, 25, 26], while others claim that maintainability is a feature of preventive maintenance [6, 8, 11].

In order to provide an early evaluation of system maintainability, models have been proposed that predict change difficulty in the maintenance process [4]. Various reverse engineering and reengineering technologies have been suggested for improving maintainability [3, 17, 19]. According to Pearse [21], the reengineering process should run concurrently with the general maintenance process. One should periodically monitor system "health" and prevent system "illness" by checking the system maintainability level. The frequency of applying the reengineering process should not be linked to the modification rate but to the maintainability level [17].

Using programming style guidelines has been suggested as a method for improving preventive maintenance. Good programming style can reduce the impact of change and thereby reduce maintenance costs [18]. Writing reusable software has also been proposed for promoting preventive maintenance [18]. Reusing well-tested software increases efficiency during the corrective maintenance phase.

Issuing corrected release announcements is also seen by industry as a form of preventive maintenance. Reporting a recurring software problem is costly for both the maintainer and user, especially when the product has a large usership [1]. The cost of preparing and distributing the corrected product to all users must always be weighed up against the resources needed to reactively manage software problems for the individual user at the upfront and execution maintenance process levels [15].

Swanson claims that not only software, but also user knowledge of particular systems should be maintained [25]. Most organisations today view this as a preventive measure. Significant resources can be saved at the upfront maintenance process level [15] through providing (a) ongoing user training in relevant systems and their operation, (b) written recovery/restart instructions [5], and (c) notification about known problems.

## 2.2    Software process execution ageing

The performance characteristics of a software system are degraded over time through continuous running. The effects become manifest in reduced service performance and/or failures (system crashes or hangs). Other problems such as data inconsistency, memory leakage, unreleased file-locks, data corruption, storage space fragmentation and an accumulation of round-off errors may also occur.

"Software rejuvenation" has been advocated as a preventive maintenance measure    [2, 10, 12]. The software is periodically stopped and restarted in order to refresh its internal state.   This prevents, or at least postpones the occurrence of failures. Though software rejuvenation implies overheads, it prevents more severe (and therefore more costly) failures.

## 3    Final remarks

How did maintainability become a property of either perfective or preventive maintenance?    Investigation suggests that maintainability came under the umbrella of perfective maintenance when the IEEE [13] took over Swanson's original categorisation of maintenance types [24] which did not include preventive maintenance. Preventive maintenance was added subsequently by the IEEE [13] without the overall revision of the existing maintenance categories and their definitions. This has led to the overlap between perfective and preventive maintenance, thereby causing some degree of confusion within the software community.

When scrutinising IEEE definitions of the other maintenance categories, it becomes apparent that the IEEE definition of perfective maintenance does not explicitly express its objectives. Enhancements for example are not stated explicitly as a constituent, though can be implicitly understood by inference from "improved performance" [13, 14] and "other attributes" [13] (see Table 1).

Acquiring an understanding of preventive maintenance requires the reader's immersion in the pertinent literature on maintenance and its various categories. This reveals that disagreement not only exists regarding defining preventive maintenance, but also in defining software maintenance, its categories and scope, and the dividing line between software development and software maintenance [26]. Given the disagreements, it is of little wonder that software maintenance costs vary between 40%-90% of total software life cycle costs.

The majority of the maintenance categories are today covered by generic maintenance process models. Unfortunately these generalised models do not help us in acquiring an objective understanding of the scope of each maintenance category. One remedy would be to agree on a single classification system for maintenance categories and their inherent activities. There have already been some attempts made in this direction [7, 16, 20]. One common, detailed classification system would substantially aid the creation of specialised process models for each maintenance category. This would provide good opportunity for scrutinising the definition of each category and its respective name, aims and most importantly would lead us towards a common and objective understanding.

## Acknowledgements

I wish to thank the Swedish National Board for Industrial and Technical Development (NUTEK) for making this study possible.

## References

[1]    Adams, E., N., Optimising Preventive Service of Software Products, IBM/Research and Development, vol. 28, no. 1, pp. 2-14, January 1984.

[2]     Avritzer A., Weyuker, E., J., Monitoring smoothly degrading systems for increased dependability, Journal of Empirical Software Engineering, 2(1), 1997.

[3]     Bennet, K., H., Do Program Transformations Help Reverse Engineering, Proceedings for International Conference on Software Maintenance, Bethesda, Maryland, USA, November 16-20, 1998, pp. 247-254.

[4]     Briand, L., C., Measuring and Assessing Maintainability at the End of High Level Design, Proceedings for International Conference on Software Maintenance, Montreal, Quebec, Canada, September 27-30, 1993, pp. 88-97.

[5]     Calow, H., Maintenance Productivity Factors – A Case Study, International Conference on Software Maintenance, Sorrento, Italy, 1991, October 15-17, 1991, pp. 250-253.

[6]     Capretz, M., A., M., Munro M., CONFORM – A Software Maintenance Method Based on the Software Configuration Management Discipline, Proceedings for International Conference on Software Maintenance, Orlando, Florida, November 9-12, 1992, pp. 183-192.

[7]     Chapin, N., The job of software maintenance. In Proceedings Conference on Software Maintenance, 1987, Los Alamitos CA, 1987; 4–12.

[8]     Colbrook A., Smythe C., The Retrospective Introduction of Abstraction into Software, Proceedings for International Conference on Software Maintenance, Miami, Florida, October 16-19, 1989, pp. 166-173.

[9]     Cote, V., St-Pierre, D., A Model for Estimating Perfective Software Maintenance Projects, Conference on Software Maintenance, San Diego, California, November, 26-29, 1990, pp. 328-334.

[10]    Garg S., Puliafito S., Telek M., Trivedi K., S., Analysis of Preventive Maintenance in Transaction Based Software Systems, IEEE Trans. On Computers, 47(1), pp. 96-107, 1998.

[11]    Harjani, D.-R., Queille, J.-P., Proceedings for International Conference on Software Maintenance, Orlando, Florida, November 9-12, 1992, pp. 127-136.

[12]    Huang, Y., Kintala C., Kollettis N., Software rejuvenation: Analysis, module and applications. In Proc. of 25th Int. Symposium on Fault-Tolerance Computing (FTCS-25), Pasadena, CA, USA, June 1995.

[13]    IEEE Standard Glossary of Software Engineering Terminology, IEEE Std 610.12-1990 (1991 Corrected Edition). The Institute of Electrical and Electronics Engineers, Inc., 1994.

[14]    IEEE Standard for Software Maintenance, IEEE Std 1219-1998. The Institute of Electrical and Electronics Engineers, Inc. 1998.

[15]    Kajko-Mattsson, Mira, Maintenance at ABB (I): Software Problem Administration Processes, Proceedings, Conference on Software Maintenance, Oxford, Sept, 1999.

[16]    Kitchenham B., et al., Toward an Ontology of Software Maintenance. Journal of Software Maintenance 1999, 11 (6):365–389.

[17]    Lanubile, F., Visaggio, F., Iterative Reengineering to Compensate for Quick-Fix Maintenance, Proceedings for International Conference on Software Maintenance, Opio (Nice), France, October 17-20, 1995, pp. 140-146.

[18]    Lieberherr, K., J., Holland I., M., Tools for Preventive Software Maintenance, Proceedings for International Conference on Software Maintenance, Miami, Florida, October 16-19, 1989, pp. 174-178.

[19]    von Mayrhauser, A., Wang, J., Experience with Reverse Architecture Approach to Increase Understanding. Proceedings for International Conference on Software Maintenance, Oxford, England, August 30 - September 13, 1999, pp. 131-138.

[20]    Parikh G. The several worlds of software maintenance - a proposed software maintenance taxonomy. ACM SIGSOFT Software Engineering Notes 1987, 12(2):51–53.

[21]    Pearse, T., Maintainability Measurements on Industrial Source Code Maintenance Activities, Proceedings for International Conference on Software Maintenance, Opio (Nice), France, October 17-20, 1995, pp. 295-303.

[22]    Pigoski, T., M., Practical Software Maintenance, John Wiley & Sons, 1997.

[23]    Schneidewind, N., F., Setting Maintenance Quality Objectives and Prioritising Maintenance Work by Using Quality Metrics, International Conference on Software Maintenance, Sorrento, Italy, 1991, October 15-17, 1991, pp. 240-249.

[24]    Swanson, B., The dimensions of maintenance, Proceedings of the 2nd International Conference on Software Engineering, IEEE Computer Society Press, Los Alamitos CA, pp. 492-497.

[25]    Interview with E. Burton Swanson, Software Maintenance: Research and Practice, Vol. 7, 303-315, 1995.

[26]    Swanson, B., E., IS Maintainability: Should It Reduce the Maintenance Effort? SIGCPR 1999, New Orleans LA, USA.

# Do We Know What Preventive Maintenance Is?

Ned Chapin
Information Systems Consultant
InfoSci Inc., Box 7117
Menlo Park CA 94026–7117, USA
NedChapin@acm.org

## Abstract

*After setting the context with a brief review of some history, this paper places preventive maintenance in that context, as brought up to date. It closes by pointing out a link between scheduled maintenance and preventive maintenance.*

## A bit of history

While the literature of the field before 1976 recognized various types of software maintenance (e.g., [1]), the definitions were implicit. In the fall of 1976, E. Burton Swanson offered an explicit typology of software maintenance [2]. He viewed software maintenance as "...activities toward organizational ends..." [2] and based the typology on the "...causes and choices which motivate..." [2] software maintenance. His typology grouped maintenance activities into three mutually exclusive and exhaustive categories based upon the purpose or intention (the 'why' or "...basis..." [2]) for doing them: corrective maintenance, adaptive maintenance, and perfective maintenance. In summary and with the examples paraphrased from [2], the distinctions among them are as follows:

- *Corrective maintenance.* These are reactive activities, intended to correct detected processing or function defects (e.g., to fix a bug reported by a user), to correct detected performance defects that impair usefulness (e.g., to make too slow software perform faster), and to correct detected implementation defects (e.g., to make the source code conform to the local software standard).
- *Adaptive maintenance.* These are anticipative activities because "...changes [in the environment of a program] may be anticipated..."

[2]. The intended adaption may be to anticipated changes in the data environment (e.g., the data organization in a file or database is to be changed), or to anticipated changes in the processing environment (e.g., the software is to run under a new release of the operating system or on a different platform).

- *Perfective maintenance.* These also are anticipative activities but to "...better serve the needs of ...users..." [2] and often done in response to "...initiatives of user and maintenance personnel..." [2]. The intended increase in perfection to the software may be to improve the performance (e.g., use a superior algorithm in place of a satisfactory existing one), or to improve the functionality to include meeting a new need expressed by the user (e.g., add new data items to a report), or to improve maintainability (e.g., rewrite some of the documentation).

Swanson also proposed gathering objective data to measure quantitatively the maintenance work done of each of the three types, but not for the purpose of determining the type [2]. Also in 1976, Swanson did not list 'preventive' as a type of software maintenance. In 1995, he added some examples of these three types of software maintenance, but declined to list 'preventive' as a type of maintenance [3], probably because his typology offers "...mutually exclusive and exhaustive..." types (page 153 in [4]).

## Preventive maintenance

The introduction of 'preventive' as a type of software maintenance has often been attributed to Lientz's and Swanson's 1980 book [4], or sometimes even to Swanson 1976 paper, as for example in a major text on software engineering [5]. Yet Swanson has pointed out that the software maintenance types in the Lientz and Swanson book were founded upon Swanson's 1976 paper [3]. Since a 4% figure for preventive maintenance has been attributed to the Lientz and Swanson book, this may be because that book's figure 5.2 on "problem areas" lists as item 'g' "Recoding for efficiency in computation 4.0" [4]. Yet anyone who has carefully read and applies Swanson's 1976 paper will classify recoding for efficiency in computation as corrective maintenance if it is intended to correct a detected defect in performance, or as perfective maintenance if it is intended to improve performance not detected as defective [2].

The four parts of the 1998 *IEEE Standard for Software Maintenance*, like the three clauses of the 1993 version, make no mention of preventive maintenance, but do recognize three types (implicitly exhaustive) of software maintenance: corrective, adaptive, and perfective [6]. While the *Standard's* terminology copies Swanson's terminology, the *Standard* does not use Swanson's definitions of the types—a very common situation as noted elsewhere [7]. Further, the *Standard* recasts (rather than copying exactly) the definitions in the IEEE glossary [6, 8]. Also, the *Standard's* Annex A on "Maintenance guidelines" is not part of the *IEEE Standard* for compliance purposes, but is appended only for "...information..." [6]. Thus, Annex A mentions 'preventive maintenance' and in its section A.1.7 defines it as an intention-based type of maintenance " ...performed for the purpose of preventing problems before they occur...." [6, 8].

The 1991 revision of the *IEEE Standard Glossary of Software Engineering Terminology* includes on page 57 an entry for 'preventive maintenance' as just quoted above [8]. Comparing that entry with its entry for 'maintenance' reveals that 'preventive maintenance' is not defined as a member of an exhaustive set of types of maintenance; rather, it is defined as a type that co-exists with or overlaps other types. Thus, the *Glossary* implies that an instance of software maintenance can be simultaneously both 'perfective' and 'preventive' (not either or), since both are there defined as intentions-based anticipative types.

While other literature mentions 'preventive maintenance' as a type of software maintenance, most authors either cite the Lientz and Swanson book [4] or the IEEE glossary [8] as the source. A few do not. Some offer their own definitions of 'preventive maintenance', some directly such as Perry's book *Managing Systems Maintenance* [9] or Garg *et al.* in their paper on transaction software maintenance [10]. Others use the term or close to it in what appears to be their own way but without defining it, such as Lieberherr and Orleans [11], or just talk about the situation without using the term, such as Slaughter *et al.* [12].

Finally, we must remind ourselves that if we hew to the Swanson typology, then there is no place for preventive maintenance as a primary type, on an equal footing with corrective, adaptive, and perfective. Since both the adaptive and perfective types are anticipatory (not reactive to detected defects), either or both of these primary types are the logical place for 'preventive maintenance' as a subtype, since it is anticipatory [3]. But should it be a subtype under both? If not, should it be a subtype only under adaptive or only under perfective maintenance? Sound reasons exist for each alternative.

Swanson's typology has been influential, especially among researchers [3]. However, as noted earlier, it has been the nomenclature that has been adopted, not the meaning or the actual definitions that distinguish the types of maintenance. Perhaps putting emphasis on 'preventive maintenance' would allow us to appreciate better the real contributions of the Swanson typology.

## Conclusion

Applying to software the IEEE's definition of 'preventive maintenance' as "...preventing problems before they occur..."[8] puts us in the forecasting business. If we take 'preventive maintenance' to mean improving software's future maintainability, we are still in the forecasting business. Forecasting either "problems" or what will improve maintainability is very difficult to do, to achieve overall economic success from the consequences. The successes have to outweigh the failures, and a dollar near term has more value than a dollar long term.

The main reason is that forecasting software situations requires making a longer term forecast of the future than is the typical response time for most instances of anticipatory types of maintenance. For example, if a contract is signed today for the installation of a new operating system seven months from now, then the organization has about seven months in which to do adaptive maintenance. Thereafter some of the uncompleted maintenance will become corrective maintenance.

That forecast is fairly easy. But forecasting the organization's competitive environment, user demands, and regulatory changes, for example, becomes increasingly inaccurate as the forward reach of the forecast lengthens. Furthermore, maintainers have a very poor track record in making accurate forecasts even when the forecasts are imprecise and involve software they know intimately [13]. The question is, how far do we have to look ahead to have 'preventive maintenance' pay off?

In my observation the most successful looking ahead is done when software maintenance (other than 'emergency maintenance') is done on a scheduled basis. Scheduled maintenance is not a new idea, and typically is not introduced or continued primarily to do preventive maintenance per se but to reduce maintenance cost and improve the quality of the maintenance service (for an early report, see [14]; see also [3]). If managed toward that end and after time to get the processes settled down, the preventive (sub)type of maintenance can become part of the software maintenance work done in scheduled maintenance.

## References

1. Canning RG. That maintenance "iceberg". *EDP Analyzer* 1972. **10**(10):1–14.

2. Swanson EB. The dimensions of maintenance. In *Proceedings of the 2nd International Conference on Software Engineering*. IEEE Computer Society Press: Los Alamitos CA, 1976; 492–497.

3. Swanson EB, Chapin N. Interview with E. Burton Swanson. *Journal of Software Maintenance* 1995. **7**(5):303–315.

4. Lientz BP, Swanson EB. *Software Maintenance Management: a Study of the Maintenance of Computer Application Software in 487 Data Processing Organizations*. Addison-Wesley Publishing Company: Reading MA, 1980.

5. Pressman RS. *Software Engineering (5th edition)*. McGraw-Hill Companies: New York NY, 2001.

6. IEEE. *IEEE Standard for Software Maintenance, IEEE Std 1219-1998*. The Institute of Electrical and Electronic Engineers, Inc.: New York NY, 1998.

7. Chapin N. Software maintenance types—a fresh view. In *Proceedings International Conference on Software Maintenance*. IEEE Computer Society Press: Los Alamitos CA, 2000; in press.

8. IEEE. *IEEE Standard Glossary of Software Engineering Terminology, IEEE Std 610.12-1990 (1991 Corrected Edition)*. The Institute of Electrical and Electronic Engineers, Inc.: New York NY, 1991.

9. Perry WE. *Managing Systems Maintenance*. Q.E.D. Information Sciences, Inc.: Wellesley MA, 1981.

10. Garg S, Puliafito A, Telek M, Trivedi K. Analysis of preventive maintenance in transactions based software systems. *IEEE Transactions on Computers* 1998. **47**(1):96–107.

11. Lieberherr KJ, Orleans D. Preventive program mainten-ance in Demeter/Java. In *Proceedings of the 1997 International Conference on Software Engineering*. Association for Computing Machinery: New York NY, 1997; 604–605.

12. Slaughter SA, Harter DE, Krishnan MS. Evaluating the cost of software quality. *Communications of the ACM* 1998. **41**(8):67–73.

13. Weissman L. Psychological complexity of computer programs: an experimental methodology. *ACM SIGPLAN Notices* 1974. **9**(6):25–36.

14. Lindhorst WM. Scheduled maintenance of applications software. *Datamation* 1973. **19**(5):64, 67.

# What Is Preventive Software Maintenance?

Risto Vehvilainen
Swedish School of Economics and Business Administration
P.O. Box 479, FIN-00101 Helsinki, Finland
Tel: +358-50 5544 722
risto.vehvilainen@kolumbus.fi

## 1    Introduction

In this talk, I will approach software maintenance from the service point of view. I will particularly emphasize co-operation with the client. My definition of software maintenance is: *Software maintenance refers to all the actions that are needed to keep software in such a running order that it achieves all its objectives from the beginning until the end of the usage.* The ideas I will present are based on several software maintenance development projects that I have been involved in as a consultant. I will answer to the title question by describing 'preventive software maintenance' in connection with classification factors.

## 2    IEEE 94, Std 610,12-1990

The IEEE definition of software maintenance categories provides [1] four different categories:
1. Corrective
2. Adaptive
3. Perfective
4. Preventive

This definition is not sufficient or usable from the service point of view because
1. it doesn't cover all activities connected to service: advise, settlement or study, planning, and so on
2. it includes several types of logic: process, influence on software and reason for change
3. it has only a limited operational or management usage
4. it is general and permanent, whereas classification needs are deeper and wider, and they vary case by case.

## 3    Classification Factors

Software maintenance simply means preparing and implementing software changes, but it can be classified according to various classification factors. The following Table 1 includes a selection of classification factors, an example for each factor, as well as comments on the importance of each factor and, finally, the connection between the factor and preventive maintenance.

| Classifi-cation Factor | Classification Example | | Importance | Preventive Mainte-nance |
|---|---|---|---|---|
| Process | 1. | Fault correction | An important instruction and therefore needed | Study and maintenance project |
| | 2. | Small change | | |
| | 3. | Large change | | |
| | 4. | Maintenance project | | |
| | 5. | Advise | | |
| | 6. | Study | | |
| Priority | 1. | Immediately | An important instruction and therefore needed | Planned schedule |
| | 2. | Soon | | |
| | 3. | Planned schedule | | |
| | 4. | On suitable situation | | |
| Compul-sion | 1. | Compulsory | A rather important but controversial factor | Optional |
| | 2. | Compulsory, but with a flexible schedule | | |
| | 3. | Optional | | |
| Change Target | 1. | Code | Will be specified carefully within the request. | Anything |
| | 2. | Specifications | | |
| | 3. | Procedures | | |
| | 4. | Instructions | | |
| | 5. | Descriptions | | |
| Request Size | 1. | Very small, not registered as a separate request | Obvious factor which may be interesting for the reporting purposes | At least moderate |
| | 2. | Small, registered as | | |

1063-6773/00 $10.00 © 2000 IEEE

| Classification Factor | Classification Example | Importance | Preventive Maintenance |
|---|---|---|---|
| | a separate request 3. Moderate 4. Large | | |
| Influence on Software | 1. Corrective 2. Changing functionality 3. Changing capacity or performance 4. Improving quality 5. Applying to new environment | Interesting as an additional information from a reporting point of view | Anything except corrective |
| Reason of the Change | 1. Error: software doesn't work according to the specifications 2. Need to improve software = cost/benefit analysis 3. Changes in business of the client 4. Need to change technological environment | Interesting as an additional information from a reporting point of view | Anything except error |
| Initiator of the Change | 1. User 2. User liaison 3. User management 4. IT management 5. Maintainer 6. Other IT person | Interesting as an additional information from a reporting point of view. Can be concluded from other factors. | IT management or maintainer |
| Role of the Maintainer | 1. Reactive 2. Proactive 3. Co-operation | Interesting as an additional information from a reporting point of view. Can be concluded from other factors. | Co-operation |

| Classification Factor | Classification Example | Importance | Preventive Maintenance |
|---|---|---|---|
| Planning Scope | 1. Immediate 2. Short range, few months 3. Year | Not very interesting because can be concluded from other factors. | Year |
| Preparation before implementation | 1. Not needed 2. On request level 3. On application level | Not very interesting because can be concluded from other factors. | On application level |
| Risks | 1. Minor 2. Moderate 3. Major | Useful as an additional information | At least moderate risks |
| Importance for Business | 1. No special importance 2. A moderate importance 3. Critical 4. Strategic | Useful as an additional information | At least a moderate importance |

**Table 1:** Software Maintenance Classification and Preventive Software Maintenance

## 4    Preventive software maintenance

"Preventive maintenance" is not a classification factor. However, preventive software maintenance is an important activity that should be defined in each organization, taking into account the local planning and working procedures. Thus, the practical definition is: *Preventive software maintenance refers to all activities that are prepared and decided upon regularly, for example annually, in co-operation between the client and the maintainer organizations, and are based on the joint analyses of the present condition as well as the forecasted needs of the software.*

## 5    References

[1]    Mira Kajko-Mattsson: Preventive Maintenance! Do we know what it is? Conference proceedings for ICSM 2000, San Jose, CA October 11-14.2000

# Notes

# Reverse Engineering I

# Bridging Program Comprehension Tools by Design Navigation

Sébastien Robitaille          Reinhard Schauer          Rudolf K. Keller

*Département IRO*
*Université de Montréal*
*C.P. 6128, succursale Centre-ville*
*Montréal, Québec H3C 3J7, Canada*
*+1 (514) 343-6782*
*{robitais, schauer, keller}@iro.umontreal.ca*

## Abstract

*Source code investigation is one of the most time consuming activities during software maintenance and evolution, yet currently available tool support suffers from several shortcomings. Browsing is typically limited to low-level elements, investigation is only supported as a one-way activity, and tools provide little help in getting an encompassing picture of the system under examination. In our research, we have developed tool support for design navigation that addresses these shortcomings. A Design Browser allows for flexible browsing of a system's design level representation and for information exchange with a suite of program comprehension tools. The browser is complemented with a Retriever supporting full-text and structural searching. In this paper, we detail these tools and their integration into a reverse engineering environment, present three case studies, and put them into perspective.*

## 1. Introduction

Understanding source code plays a prominent role during software maintenance and evolution. It is a time consuming activity, especially when dealing with large-scale software systems, and it can rapidly turn into a major bottleneck for software evolution. Zawinski, for instance, attributed one of the main causes for the development slow-down of the *Netscape Communicator* project to the fact that "it takes a long time for a new developer to dive in and start contributing" [29].

Singer et al. define *Just In Time Comprehension* as the source code exploration activity performed by software engineers that leads to software understanding [20].

Software engineers are doing *Just In Time Comprehension* by repeatedly searching for source code artifacts and navigating through their relationships. According to Sim et al., this activity can be split into the two navigation styles normally used for the purpose of information retrieval [19]: *Browsing*, an exploratory and unstructured activity with no specific goal, and *searching*, a planned activity with a specific goal.

Keeping the information retrieval perspective, any collaboration of elements of a software system can be viewed as an *information space*. For example, both physical subsystems, such as files or directories, and logical subsystems, such as class collaborations, are information spaces. These spaces are subsets of the global information space, which represents the whole system. *Information views* are the means to represent information spaces to the software engineer. They normally illustrate information spaces as class diagrams, collaboration diagrams, dependency diagrams, and alike. According to [19], browsing of information views aims at exploring high-level elements of the underlying information space, and searching focuses on retrieving low-level details. Using a combination of these two navigation styles, software engineers can investigate source code and build up a mental model of the system. However, currently available tool support for source code investigation suffers from three major shortcomings.

First, the browsing functionality of current tools is restricted to few high-level elements. However, most high-level elements are of interest during investigation, and hence design level querying and navigation should be supported. Furthermore, browsing should be extensible in the sense that customized queries can be defined. Current tools fail to provide such flexibility.

Second, source code investigation is typically supported as a *one-way trip* from one information view to the source code of the system, which prevents the software engineer from bringing the acquired knowledge back to

This research was supported by the SPOOL project organized by CSER (Consortium for Software Engineering Research) which is funded by Bell Canada, NSERC (National Sciences and Research Council of Canada), and NRC (National Research Council of Canada).

the information view where the navigation started. Thus, proceeding in an *iterative* manner by using the acquired knowledge in subsequent investigations is precluded. Furthermore, as an investigation normally comprises many little steps of browsing and searching, failing to preserve such knowledge may distract the software engineer from the original goal of the investigation and thus add significant overhead to program comprehension [23].

Third, current tools provide little help in getting an encompassing picture of the system under examination. They fail to join the knowledge acquired from different investigations done in different contexts, that is, from browsing different information views. Consider a puzzle where all the pieces put together at the right positions lead to the complete picture. Tools should not only support browsing and searching for software artifacts and identifying the relevant pieces of the puzzle, but they should also allow for the rapid and easy navigation between different views describing the system at different abstraction levels, and thus reduce the time needed to put the pieces of the puzzle to the right place.

In our research, we have developed tool support for design navigation that addresses these shortcomings. A *Design Browser* allows for browsing the source code *model* of a given system, that is, the system's design level representation, and for exchanging information with a suite of program comprehension tools. The browser is complemented with a *Retriever* supporting full-text and structural searching. These two tools allow for bridging the various information views describing the system, and thus joining the different pieces of the puzzle. The tools have been implemented as part of the SPOOL reverse engineering environment. Preliminary experience within our research team and at Bell Canada, our industrial partner, suggests that these tools and the underlying technology substantially ease the task of source code investigation.

Section 2 of this paper describes the SPOOL environment, the testbed in which this research was conducted. In Section 3, the Design Browser and the Retriever are detailed. Section 4 illustrates and assesses these tools, by presenting three case studies where design navigation helped bridging different information views. Section 5 discusses implementation and experience, performance, and related work. Section 6 concludes the paper and provides an outlook into future work.

## 2. SPOOL environment

The purpose of the SPOOL reverse engineering environment is to help software engineers understand, maintain, and assess software. It has been designed to support software investigation at various levels of abstraction; yet, it emphasizes the design level, in order to

complement and bridge architecture and source code level investigation.

The environment has at its core a *repository* that stores *source code models* (see Figure 1). The environment comprises tools to populate the repository, to execute queries on the elements contained in the repository, and to extract and visualize information from these elements. *Source code capturing* can be achieved using *Datrix* [3], *GEN++* [5], or *SNiFF+* [21], and the parsed code is stored in an intermediate, ASCII-based file format. An *importer* is used to parse the *intermediate format* and to provide the repository with the relevant source code elements, that is, the information that is required to support the various levels of source code investigation (for the list of elements contained in the repository, refer to [14]). The schema of the repository is based on the UML metamodel 1.1 [27], which we extended to support the specifics of C++, such as friendship, unions, and enumerations [12]. The object-oriented database management system *Poet 6.0* [15] serves as the repository backend, and the schema is represented as a Java class hierarchy. Given this repository architecture, the elements in the database can be accessed like normal Java objects and used to build graphical representations in form of diagrams (information views).

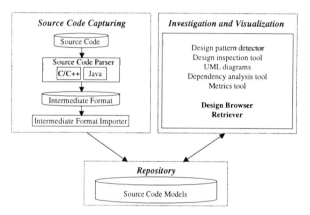

**Figure 1: SPOOL architecture**

The SPOOL environment provides a number of tools for *investigation and visualization*. At the design level, the *design pattern detector* allows for the identification of implemented design patterns in the system, and the *design inspection tool* supports the visualization of the participants of the recovered patterns within collaboration diagrams [14]. At the architecture level, different *UML diagrams* are provided for the exploration of the system's architecture, and the *dependency analysis tool* allows for the visualization of dependencies between packages, files and classes (such as generalizations, instantiations, operation calls, friendships, and alike). At the source code level, via an integration mechanism enabling communication between SPOOL and external tools, source code inspection is supported by providing access to the *SNiFF+* source code engineering environment [21]. Furthermore, the *metrics tool* is available for the computation and visualization of metrics. Finally, the *Design Browser* and the *Retriever* provide support for design navigation.

## 3. Support for design navigation

Design navigation is supported by two tools: the *Design Browser*, which allows for browsing the source code model and exchanging results with the different SPOOL tools, and the *Retriever*, which supports full-text and structural searching. They are described in the sections below.

### 3.1. SPOOL Design Browser

The user interface of the browser is separated into the three sections *Starting Point, Queries,* and *Results* (see Figure 2). The first and the last of these sections may contain each a list of *ModelElements*[1], characterized by their names and by different colored icons that represent their kind (such as *C* for class, *F* for file, and *M* for method). Selecting a *ModelElement* in the *Starting Point*

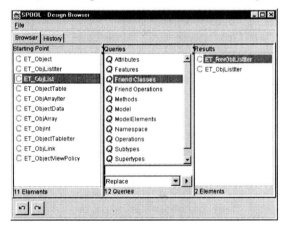

**Figure 2: The SPOOL Design Browser**

section starts browsing, whereupon the browser displays in the *Queries* section a predefined list of queries for that *ModelElement*. After the query is executed, the result is shown as a new list of *ModelElements* in the *Results* section. For example, Figure 1 shows the browser after the execution of a query that retrieves all the friend classes of *ET_ObjList*, a class from the system *ET++* [9].

---

[1] A *ModelElement*, as described in the UML documentation, is "An element that is an abstraction drawn from the system being modeled" [27]. Accordingly, a *ModelElement* can represent object-oriented concepts such as class or method, as well as files, utilities, and alike.

To make querying more flexible and to support bridging the browser with the other tools of the environment, the Design Browser comprises a Drag and Drop (DnD) mechanism. For one thing, this mechanism allows the user to move *ModelElements* back and forth between the Results and the Starting Point sections of the browser, and, in case more than one browser is active, between any pair of browsers. In this way, the result elements of a previous query may serve as the starting point of a new query. Note that there is also an integrated history mechanism that allows the retrieval of previous states of the browser using back and forward buttons (Figure 2). Furthermore, the DnD mechanism makes it possible to move elements between the browser and any other SPOOL tool. In the target of the DnD operation, be it another SPOOL tool or a SPOOL Design Browser, the user is asked via a popup menu to specify the *drop action* that should be performed with the elements being moved.

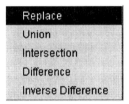

**Figure 3: Drop actions in the browser**

Possible actions include copy, move, and visualize. In the case of a DnD operation inside a browser or between two browsers, the popup menu shown in Figure 3 appears. The drop actions are *set operations* such as union, intersection, and difference, to be executed on the set of elements being moved and the set of elements in the target section. Note that the entries of both the *Starting Point* and the *Results* sections are internally represented as sets.

The SPOOL Design Browser is query-based. The underlying query mechanism relies on the internal representation of the *ModelElements* of the SPOOL repository. Since the source code model of a parsed system is represented as an object-oriented class hierarchy, many elements for querying are already built-in as Java methods and attributes of the classes that represent the source code elements. As an example, consider *UmlClass, UmlAttribute,* and *UmlMethod,* the Java classes in the schema that represent the corresponding UML *ModelElements*. Instances of these classes represent the elements of the system being studied. Suppose *aClass* is an instance of *UmlClass,* and *aMethod* is an instance of *UmlMethod,* then:

- `aClass.getFeatures()` returns the set of all *UmlOperation, UmlMethod* and *UmlAttribute* instances contained in that class.
- `aMethod.getCalledOperations()` returns the list of *UmlOperation* that are called by that method.

The predefined queries provided by the SPOOL Design Browser are all based on these and other methods of the SPOOL repository schema.

Browsing exclusively via predefined queries is not sufficient in many cases, and more specific queries may be needed. Therefore, the SPOOL Design Browser allows for the easy addition of new queries which must be written in Java and which must implement a simple predefined interface. Of course, users who want to write custom queries must know about the SPOOL schema. Yet, since the schema follows closely the UML metamodel, this requirement should not be a major obstacle.

The steps to add a new query are simple. As a first step, the user must implement an abstract *execute* method of a predefined *Query* class which is provided by the SPOOL environment. The second step is to add this new query to the browser. The user must provide the query name, its Java package name, and the kind of elements on which the query can be executed, by editing a simple configuration file. Finally, the browser uses Java's reflection mechanisms [10] to instantiate, visualize, and execute the new query.

## 3.2. SPOOL Retriever

The SPOOL Retriever allows the user to search for a string of characters in the names of the *ModelElements* that are contained in a namespace. A namespace, as described in the UML metamodel documentation, is "a part of the model in which the names may be defined and used. Within a namespace, each name has a unique meaning" [27]. Accordingly, a namespace class can be found in the SPOOL schema, allowing the Retriever to

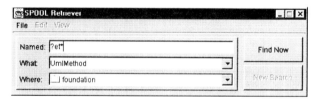

**Figure 4: The SPOOL Retriever**

search elements that are contained inside other elements such as the whole system, or packages, directories, files, and classes.

Before starting a search, the user specifies in a dialog box (see Figure 4) the search string (*Named*), as well as the kind of element (*What*) and the container (*Where*) of the search. Note that the specification of the search string is optional, and that the Retriever allows the use of wildcards like * and ? to find elements in the system. As an example, Figure 4 shows how *get/set* methods can be retrieved from a particular container (directory, file, class, and alike). This combination of full-text search and structural search is a feature that is typically absent in

search tools that are entirely text-based, such as the family of Unix *grep* tools. The structural search capability provided by the SPOOL Retriever is quite powerful and is

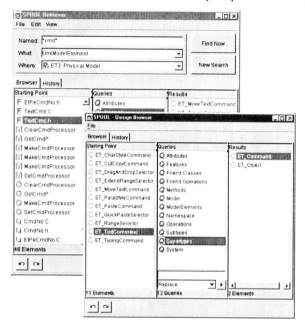

**Figure 5: Use of retriever and browsers in concert**

due, similarly to the case of the SPOOL Design Browser, to the expressiveness of the schema of the underlying source code models.

The results of a search are displayed in the *SPOOL Design Browser,* to allow for further investigation of the result elements. As an example, in Figure 5 a search for all the *UMLModelElements* in the *ET3:PhysicalModel* that contain the substring *cmd* in their names has been launched, by pressing the *Find Now* button. The results are displayed in the Starting Point section of the top left browser. From there, navigation is continued, by querying about *Classes* and by spawning the button right browser.

The *SPOOL Retriever* can also be applied to recover design concepts, such as design patterns. For instance, in ET++ [9] we found many instances of the *Iterator* [8] pattern just by searching for the expression *iter\** in method names. As another example, instances of the *Observer* pattern may be identified by looking for method names containing *\*observ\**, *\*updat\**, or *\*notif\**. Note, however, that for general pattern recovery a more systematic and human-controlled approach is needed [14]. Nevertheless, this simple method can lead to many instances and provide a good starting point for further pattern-based investigations.

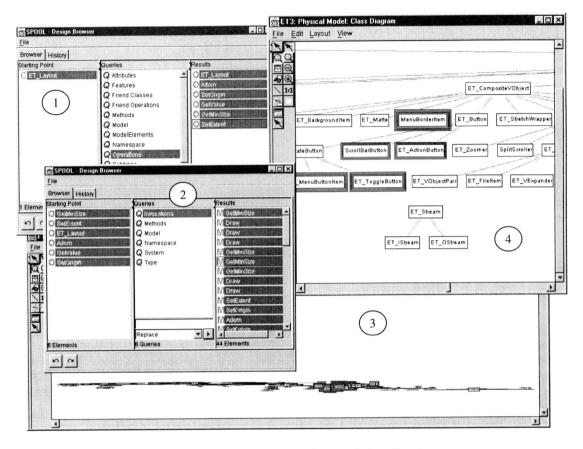

**Figure 6: Context investigation and visualization**

## 4. Case studies

In the previous section we described how the SPOOL design navigation tools support browsing and searching the elements and relationships of a system and set the stage for further investigation. In this section, we present three case studies that demonstrate how the SPOOL Design Browser and the SPOOL Retriever can be used to bridge the different investigation tools of the environment and how program comprehension is supported. The case studies address context investigation and visualization, namespace dependency analysis, and design pattern recovery and analysis.

### 4.1. Context investigation and visualization

The investigation and visualization of contexts is key to program comprehension. This is supported by the tool integration mechanism of the SPOOL environment, which enables tools to communicate without being tightly coupled. The design of SPOOL is event-based, allowing the tools to send events to each other through established event channels [4]. Any SPOOL tool can request from the SPOOL *tool factory* the instantiation of another tool, and send it an event with a set of *ModelElements* as the

starting point for further investigation. From the user's point of view, such event-based communication is triggered by using the *drag and drop (DnD)* mechanism described in Section 3.1.

Figure 6 illustrates a typical investigation and visualization scenario. In this example, the user launches the browser to retrieve all the methods that are calling the operations defined in the class *ET_Layout* (windows 1 and 2). Then, the user requests from the tool factory the instantiation of a class diagram and drags the methods into that new diagram. Upon selection of the *visualize* action in the popup menu of the class diagram, these methods (*ModelElements*) are visualized by drawing bounding boxes around the classes in which they are defined (window 3). It is then possible to zoom-in and zoom-out the diagram in order to investigate each of the retrieved classes. For instance, window 4 shows a zoomed part of the cluster of retrieved classes found in the center of window 3. The browser may be used again to go further in the investigation of the system, by starting from one or several classes shown in windows 3 or 4.

26

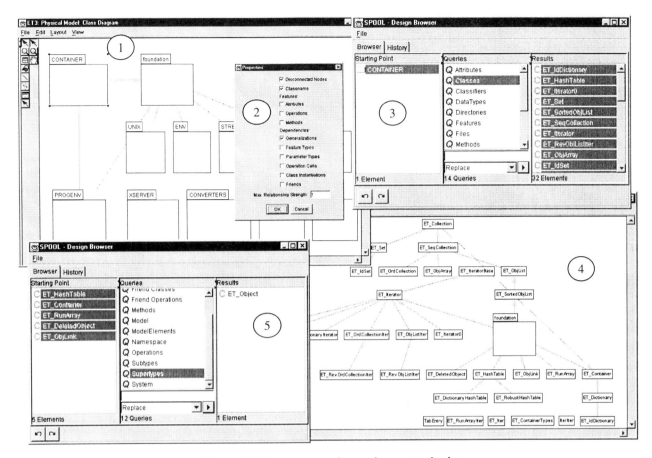

**Figure 7: Namespace dependency analysis**

## 4.2. Namespace dependency analysis

Another important activity of program comprehension is the investigation of dependencies among a program's constituent parts. To this end, the SPOOL environment comprises a dependency analysis tool (Figure 7, windows 1 and 4), which visualizes mutual dependencies among namespaces, such as directories, files, classes, and unions. It is quite an intuitive tool that helps understand both desirable and undesirable dependencies among the elements of the system being studied. Particular types of dependencies, such as those based on generalization, operation call, or class instantiation relationships, may be displayed or hidden, according to the settings specified in the diagram's property sheet (Figure 7, window 25). The Design Browser enhances the capabilities of the dependency analysis tool in that it can serve as the data feed as well as the data sink during dependency analysis.

As an example, assume that the user retrieves all directories from ET++ using the Design Browser. Then, he or she selects a few of these directories and drags them over into a dependency analysis diagram (Figure 7,

window 1) where they are displayed in form of UML package symbols. The diagram automatically loads the dependencies among these directories from the repository, and visualizes them as uni- or bi-directional lines, respectively. In window 1, only generalization dependencies are shown, according to the specification provided via the property sheet (window 2). Then, the user selects in the dependency analysis diagram the directory *CONTAINER* and invokes a Design Browser from this symbol (window 3). Thereafter, he or she executes a query on that directory to retrieve all the contained classes, and drags the result elements into another dependency analysis tool (window 4) containing initially only the *foundation* directory. By putting these elements together, the user can investigate the bi-directional inheritance relationships between the classes of the *CONTAINER* directory and the classes contained in *foundation*. From the set of five classes that inherit from the classes contained in *foundation*, a further browser is started (window 5), where the user queries the superclasses of the set of classes. The only superclass is *ET_Object*, which is the root class of the foundation package.

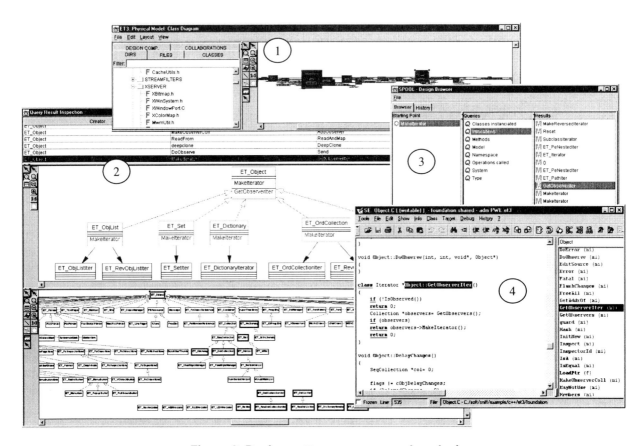

**Figure 8: Design pattern recovery and analysis**

## 4.3. Design pattern recovery and analysis

In many object-oriented software systems, the key design decisions are implemented based on well-known design patterns, such as those of Gamma et al. [8], Buschmann et al. [4], and Schmidt [18]. In [14,17], we have reported on automated support for the recovery and analysis of some of these patterns. In this section, we present parts of the functionality implemented to this end, and discuss how design navigation fits in.

As an example, window 1 of Figure 8 illustrates the occurrences of the *Factory Method* pattern [8] in ET++. The recovered pattern instances are visualized by bounding boxes that are incrementally drawn around their so-called reference class, which can be selected by the user. In the example, the reference class chosen by the user is the class that owns the *Creator* role in the *Factory Method* pattern. The size of the outermost bounding box of a class indicates the number of *factory methods* that are implemented in that class. As a second step, the user inspects the recovered pattern instances by starting the design inspection tool (window 2). This diagram shows in its upper part the list of recovered Factory Method patterns, identified by the Creator class and the factory method. The middle part shows the selected Factory

Method as a collaboration diagram. The example shows the class *ET_Object* with the method *GetObserverIter* calling the factory method *MakeIterator*[2] (top row). This method is overridden in five subclasses of ET_Object (middle row). Each of these implementations of MakeIterator instantiates different *Products* (bottom row). The lower part of the window shows the recovered classes in the context of the overall class hierarchy. This example presents the case where the design patterns Factory Method and Iterator are combined to provide for a flexible traversal mechanism of ET++ containers, such as lists, sets, dictionaries, collections, and arrays. Recall that the SPOOL Design Retriever might have been used to hint at instances of the Iterator pattern (cf. Section 3.2).

The content of the design inspection diagram was automatically generated by one of the SPOOL design recovery queries for the Factory Method pattern. The diagram provides precious information for program comprehension as it presents in a concise way all the classes that take on some role in a pattern-based

---

[2] MakeIterator is defined in the class *ET_Container* which is a subclass of ET_Object and a superclass of the classes redefining MakeIterator.

collaboration. Note that in the physical file structure, these classes may be spread out over many directories and subsystems. Yet, the diagram falls short in conveying all the information a user might wish to obtain about the design fragment being studied. He or she might want to know, for instance, the classes and methods that invoke MakeIterator, or get information about the semantics of the method GetObserverIter, whose name alludes to its purpose of creating an Iterator of the Observers of a view element. A visual design inspection tool can never answer all of these questions.

The SPOOL Design Browser together with the SPOOL mechanism for integrating external tools provides the flexibility to obtain detailed knowledge as well as context information about the constituents of a recovered, pattern-based design. For example, the browser of window 3 shows all the methods from which MakeIterator is invoked, including the GetObserverIter method already identified in window 2. By invoking the *SNiFF+* environment, the user can then investigate and edit the retrieved elements directly in the *SNiFF+* source code editor (window 4). This provides invaluable context information about how, in our example, a Factory Method is used.

## 5. Discussion

In this section, we first report on the implementation and our experience with the SPOOL design navigation tools. Then, performance issues are discussed. Finally, we provide an overview on related work.

### 5.1. Implementation and experience

The SPOOL Design Browser and Retriever have been implemented in Java, using the *JFC/Swing* components [11]. The implementation consists of some 80 classes and 4,100 lines of code (LOC; comment lines not counted). The complete SPOOL environment comprises currently 640 Java classes and 60,8K LOC; to run the navigation tools stand-alone, the SPOOL framework and repository classes are needed, making up for 240 classes and 17,1 K LOC.

The SPOOL environment, including prototype versions of the navigation tools presented in this paper, has been used extensively as a vehicle for doing joint research with Bell Canada. It played an important role in our research on hot spot recovery [17] and on method replacement inspection and analysis [12]. For example, the capability to display only selected elements of a system in a dependency tool, the possibility to run customized queries on these elements to navigate through their relationships, and the support for visualizing the result elements in known context views were all features that have proven invaluable in the investigation of the large-scale industrial

systems that we are considering in our work. Recently, a prototype stand-alone browser has been made available to Bell Canada's quality assessment team, our industrial partner group. Preliminary experience suggests that the browser is indeed useful for the team's daily work.

### 5.2. Performance

Tool performance is critical for the success of source code investigation. Each step in the investigation process should be fast enough in order to avoid confusion and disorientation with the user. In the following, we present two anecdotal experiments in which the performance of SPOOL queries was measured. The experiments were done on a 350MHz Pentium II machine with 256Mb of RAM running Windows NT 4.0.

The first experiment consisted in measuring the times needed to execute a built-in query, that is, a query that is not directly supported by the metamodel schema. Table 1 shows the data for such a query, that is, the times needed to retrieve all the *ModelElements* (directories, files, classes, C++ structures, C++ unions, C++ enumerations, operations, methods, and attributes), for three industrial C++ software systems. ET++ 3.0 and ACE [25] are both well-known application frameworks. System A is a large-scale system from the telecommunications domain provided by Bell Canada (for confidentiality reasons we cannot disclose the real name of the system).

| C++ Systems | # Elements | Duration 1 (seconds) | Duration 2+ (seconds) |
|---|---|---|---|
| ET++ | 20868 | 22 | 2 |
| ACE | 21577 | 49 | 3 |
| System A | 47834 | 47 | 6 |

**Table 1: Performance for a built-in query**

The table shows that the first time the browser runs a query, it takes longer (*Duration 1*) because, first, Poet needs to recreate the persistent objects that are stored on disk and, second, when loading a system, SPOOL caches some of the objects in internal hash tables. As soon as an element is "touched" by a query, it becomes available in memory, and the next time any query is accessing it, the execution is much faster *(Duration 2+).*

| C++ Systems | Total number of template methods found | Duration (seconds) |
|---|---|---|
| ET++ | 371 | 15 |
| ACE | 21 | 23 |
| System A | 364 | 360 |

**Table 2: Performance for the *Template Method* query**

|  |  | Discover | Visual Age for Java | SNiFF+ | Source-Navigator | SPOOL |
|---|---|---|---|---|---|---|
| **Browsing** | Built-in queries | + | - | - | - | + |
|  | Customized queries | - | - | - | - | + |
|  | Bridging | - | - | - | - | + |
| **Searching** | Full-text | + | + | + | + | + |
|  | Structural | + | +- | +- | +- | + |

**Table 3: Feature comparison of commercial tools and SPOOL**

The above experiment shows that the retrieval of elements that are already referenced in the database is pretty fast. The execution of more complicated (not built-in) queries may take considerably longer. As a second experiment, we measured the time needed to retrieve all occurrences of the Template Method [8] pattern in the three systems. This query basically consists of the following five steps::

1. retrieve all classes in the system,
2. for each class, retrieve all methods,
3. for each method, retrieve all call actions,
4. for each call action, get the receivers,
5. for each receiver, look if the call action is defined in the same class and implemented in a subclass.

Table 2 shows the times needed to execute this query for the first time, assuming that all the *ModelElements* are already cached (a query that retrieves all *ModelElements* in the system was executed previously). These numbers are quite good considering that a very high number of relations must be crossed in order to retrieve the desired information. The time needed to run a particular query may be higher, but these experiments suggest that only the complexities of the query and of the system are susceptible to increase execution time, whereas the access time to the *ModelElements* of the repository is relatively constant (mainly due to the use of hash tables).

## 5.3. Related work

Many tools have been developed for program comprehension, especially in academia. Some interesting academic tools in respect to browsing and searching include *SHriMP* [24], the *Searchable Bookshelf* [19], and *tksee* [20]. *SHriMP* is a tool that allows navigation of source code using hyperlinks and provides some support for context navigation. Browsing is quite limited in that there are few built-in queries and query customization is not supported. The *Searchable Bookshelf* is a system that provides advanced capabilities for generating and navigating software structure diagrams (called landscapes). It comprises a query language for searching and browsing a system's fact base. The presentation of query results is purely textual, and DnD-style bridging of tools is not supported. *Tksee*, finally, is a representative of the tools that are designed to allow software browsing and searching, but only at the source code level.

On the commercial side, several tools are available that exhibit capabilities for software comprehension. Typically, they provide, beyond these capabilities, support for software development in general. We conducted an informal comparison between the SPOOL navigation tools and four of these tools that we consider most representative for the state-of-the-art, namely, *Discover* [7], *Visual Age for Java* [28], *SNiFF+* [21], and *Source-Navigator* [22]. At the time of the writing of this paper, the comparison is based on practical experience with a professional license of *SNiFF+*, evaluation licenses of *Visual Age for Java* and of *Source-Navigator*, and on the study of the documentation of *Discover* that was made available to us [1,2,26]. A more comprehensive comparison has been incepted and will be described in [16]. The informal comparison considers three browsing features and two searching features (see Table 3): availability of built-in query lists, capability of specifying customized queries, and possibility of bridging browsing with other software comprehension tools as well as support of full-text searching and of structural searching. For each tool, the support of these features was weighted as strong (+), medium (+-), or weak (-).

Table 3 summarizes the results of the comparison. The SPOOL navigation tools, which were especially designed to support the considered features, naturally stand out with strong support of all the features. Three observations are worth mentioning. First, the comparison suggests that the commercial tools have limited browsing capabilities, since except for Discover, they provide little support of built-in querying permitting the navigation of the system relationships and because none of them supports the customization of queries. Second, mechanisms for the bridging of browsing and other software investigation techniques are not present either (in the case of Discover, no such mechanism is described in the available documentation). We believe that support for these browsing features is of invaluable help for program comprehension, especially if it is integrated into a development environment. Third, full-text searching is well supported by all the tools, whereas structural searching is strongly supported by Discover, with the remaining three commercial tools lacking full support of these capabilities. Recall that the SPOOL Design Browser together with the SPOOL DnD mechanism supports the creation of user-defined views or diagrams, which is an additional important feature that is absent from the commercial tools we considered.

## 6. Conclusion

Mechanisms for context searching and browsing in a development or maintenance environment are key to help software engineers investigate large-scale software systems. We presented various tools that we consider useful for software comprehension, and we detailed the SPOOL Design Browser and Retriever, two tools developed for the purpose of bridging the other comprehension tools. We showed that it is possible to navigate across various information views, that is, the representations of information spaces, by using the query-based mechanism of the browser and the searching capabilities of the Retriever. The three case studies of this paper demonstrated the usefulness of the tools and the underlying communication mechanism for tool integration. Finally, we presented statistics about the performance of the tools to assess their usability, and we compared some of their features with other well-known, considered "state-of-the-art" development environments.

In the future, we intend to formalize the source code investigation model based on context navigation and bridging, for better synchronization of the knowledge acquired from investigations and the tool-provided information views. We also plan to complement the SPOOL tools with mechanisms allowing for on-the-fly construction of context views, and to extend the Design Browser with "query suites" supporting specific analysis tasks, such as dependency analysis, change impact analysis [5] or component-based reverse engineering [14]. We believe that by using this model and the corresponding tools, software engineers will understand large-scale systems faster and more easily, and will get less lost when browsing such systems. Finally, we wish to assess the usability of such tools. In the first place, we aim to collect further feedback from the quality assessment team at Bell Canada, our industrial partner, concerning their work experience with the tools. Moreover we plan to carry out a controlled experiment about this issue.

## Acknowledgement

We would like to thank the following organizations for providing us with licenses of their tools, thus assisting us in the development part of our research: *Bell Canada* for the source code parser *Datrix*, *Lucent Technologies* for their C++ source code analyzer *GEN++* and the layout generators *Dot* and *Neato*, and *TakeFive Software* for their software development environment *SNiFF+*.

## References

[1] Barr, J., Product Review "Reengineer/SET", Software Development Magazine, August 1996. On-line at <*http://www.sdmagazine.com/breakrm/products/reviews/s968r2.shtml*>.

[2] Barr, J., Product Review "DISCOVER 3.0", Software Development Magazine, March 1996. On-line at <*http://www.sdmagazine.com/breakrm/products/reviews/s963r2.shtml*>.

[3] Bell Canada. DATRIX abstract semantic graph - reference manual. Montreal, Quebec, Canada. January 1999. Available on request from <*datrix@qc.bell.ca*>.

[4] Buschmann, F., Meunier, R., Rohnert, H., Sommerlad, P., and Stal, M., Pattern-Oriented Software Architecture – A System of Patterns. *John Wiley and Sons*, 1996.

[5] Chaumun, A., Kabaili, H., Keller, R. K. and Lustman, F., A Change Impact Model for Changeability Assessment in Object-Oriented. In *Proceedings of the Third Euromicro Working Conference on Software Maintenance and Reengineering*, pages 130-138, Amsterdam, The Netherlands. March 1999.

[6] Devanbu, P. T. GENOA – a customizable, language and front-end independent code analyzer. In *Proceedings of the 14th International Conference on Software Engineering (ICSE'92)*, pages 307-317. Melbourne, Australia. 1992.

[7] Discover online documentation, Software Emancipation Technology. On-line at <*http://www.setech.com/*>.

[8] Gamma, E., Helm, R., Johnson, R. and Vlissides, J., Design Patterns: Elements of Reusable Object-Oriented Software. *Addison-Wesley*. Menlo Park, CA. 1995.

[9] Gamma, E. and Weinand, A., ET++: A Portable C++ Class Library for a UNIX Environment. Tutorial notes. *OOPSLA '90*. Ottawa, ON, Canada. October 1990.

[10] Java documentation, Sun Microsystems Inc. On-line at <*http://java.sun.com/*>.

[11] Java Foundation Classes (JFC) documentation, Sun Microsystems Inc. On-line at <*http://www.javasoft.com/products/jfc/index.html*>.

[12] Keller, R. K., Knapen, G., Lague, B., Robitaille, S., Saint-Denis, G., and Schauer, R., The SPOOL design repository: Architecture, schema, and mechanisms. In *Hakan Erdogmus and Oryal Tanir*, editors, *Advances in Software Engineering. Topics in Evolution, Comprehension, and Evaluation.* Springer-Verlag, 2000. 28 pages. To appear.

[13] Keller, R. K., and Schauer, R., Towards a Quantitative Assessment of Method Replacement. In *Proceedings of the Fourth Euromicro Working Conference on Software Maintenance and Reengineering*, pages 141-150, Zurich, Switzerland, February 2000. IEEE.

[14] Keller, R. K., Schauer, R., Robitaille, S., and Pagé, P., Pattern-Based Reverse Engineering of Design Components In *Proceedings of the 21st International Conference on Software Engineering (ICSE'99)*, pages 226-335, Los-Angeles, CA, USA. May 1999.

[15] POET Java ODMG Binding documentation. Poet Software Corporation. San Mateo, CA, USA. On-line at *<http://www.poet.com>*.

[16] Robitaille, S. Tool support for understanding industrial-sized, object-oriented software systems. *Master's thesis*, Université de Montréal, Montreal, Quebec, Canada, April 2000. French title: Support informatique à la compréhension des logiciels orientés objet de taille industrielle.

[17] Schauer R., Robitaille S., Keller, R. K. and Martel, F., Hot Spot Recovery in Object-Oriented Software with Inheritance and Composition Template Methods. In *Proceedings of the International Conference on Software Maintenance (ICSM'99)*, pages 220-229. Oxford, England. August 1999.

[18] Schmidt, D., Design patterns for concurrent, parallel, and distributed systems. On-line at *<http://siesta.cs.wustl.edu/~schmidt/patterns-ace.html>*.

[19] Sim, S. E., Clarke, C. L. A., Holt, R. C. and Cox, A. M., Browsing and Searching Software Architectures. In *Proceedings of the International Conference on Software Maintenance (ICSM'99)*, pages 381-390. Oxford, England, August 1999.

[20] Singer, J., Lethbridge, T., Vinson, N. and Anquetil N., An Examination of Software Engineering Work Practices. In Proceedings of CASCON'97, pages 209-223. Toronto, ON, Canada. 1997.

[21] SNiFF+ documentation set. On-line at *<http://www.takefive.com>*.

[22] Source-Navigator documentation set. On-line at *<http://www.cygnus.com/sn/>*.

[23] Storey, M.-A. D., Fracchia, F. D. and Müller, H. A., Cognitive design elements to support the construction of a mental model during software exploration. Journal of Systems and Software, 44(3):171-185, January 1999.

[24] Storey, M.-A. D. and Müller, H. A., Manipulating and documenting software structures using SHriMP views. In Proceedings of the International Conference on Software Maintenance (ICSM'95), pages 275-284. Opio (Nice), France. October 1995.

[25] Syyid, U., The Adaptative Communication Environment: "ACE". Hughes Network Systems. On-line at *<http://www.cs.wustl.edu/~schmidt/PDF/ACE-tutorial.pdf.gz>*.

[26] Tilley, S. R., Discovering DISCOVER. Technical report CMU/SEI-97-TR-012. Pittsburgh, PA, Oct.1997. On-line at *<http://www.sei.cmu.edu/publications/documents/97.reports/97tr012/97tr012title.htm>*.

[27] UML, Documentation set version 1.1. September 1997. On-line at *<http://www.rational.com>*.

[28] Visual Age for Java online documentation, IBM Corporation. On-line at *<http://www.ibm.com>*.

[29] Zawinsky, J., resignation and postmortem, 1999. On-line at *<http://www.jwz.org/gruntle/nomo.html>*.

# TraceGraph: Immediate Visual Location of Software Features

Kazimiras Lukoit, Norman Wilde[1], Scott Stowell, Tim Hennessey
The University of West Florida
Pensacola, Florida, U. S. A.

## Abstract

*Software engineers often need to locate where particular features of a program are implemented in order to fix a bug or introduce an enhancement. This paper describes a tool called TraceGraph to support this task, particularly for large, long-running or interactive software. TraceGraph provides a simple visual display of the program's trace which allows changes in execution to be easily distinguished. A software engineer can run the feature he or she is interested in, and immediately view how program execution varies. Case studies on two large systems show how TraceGraph may be applied to different kinds of traces. Displays similar to TraceGraph would be good candidates for inclusion in software monitoring or debugging systems.*

## 1. Introduction

One of the more difficult problems for the maintainer of unfamiliar software is the location of the code that needs to be understood and changed. While in principle a maintainer should understand the entire system before making changes, in practice it is essential to use an "as-needed" strategy [KOEN.91]. The maintainer must first locate the code components that are needed for the specific change and then understand how they function in the context of the larger system.

Location is more difficult because it often involves contrasting views of the system. A programmer sees software as a collection of interacting *components*: source files, subroutines, data objects, lines of code, etc. However the end user sees the system as a provider of many different *features*. The features of a word processor, for example, might include loading files, cutting and pasting text, spell checking, etc. Program change requests are often given in terms of the features to be changed, which may not map clearly onto the code. Requirements traceability documentation should provide this mapping, but it is costly to keep up to date and thus is rarely present in maintenance situations.

## 2. The Software Reconnaissance Technique

One technique that has been developed to help locate features in code is *Software Reconnaissance* [WILD.95]. Software Reconnaissance is based on a comparison of traces from different test cases. The target program is instrumented to produce a trace of components executed as each test is run. Then test cases are run, some "with" and some "without" the desired feature. For example to locate the spell checker of a word processor, the programmer would run several tests that include a spell check and several others that do not. The "marker" components for the spell check feature are found by taking the set of components executed in the "with" tests and subtracting the set of components executed in the "without" tests.

Software Reconnaissance has been tried in case studies on a number of systems of different sizes, both in an academic setting and in industry [WILD.96, AGRA.98]. Results have generally been quite favorable:

1.  The marker components are generally only a small fraction of the target program, and so help the maintainer to focus quickly on code that is likely to be important for the desired feature.
2.  While the marker components are by no means *all* the code that the maintainer needs to study, they usually are *close to* the needed code and so provide good "places to start looking" for the as-needed strategy.
3.  Generally only a few test cases are needed if they are well chosen. It is important to make the test cases "with" the feature as similar as possible to the test cases "without" the feature to avoid accidentally including irrelevant components in the trace.
4.  The technique often provides insights into the target program that are surprising, even to programmers who have considerable experience with it.

---

[1] Address correspondence to: Norman Wilde, Department of Computer Science, University of West Florida, 11000 University Parkway, Pensacola, Florida 32514, U. S. A., Tel. 850-474-2542, Fax 850-857-6056, E-mail nwilde@uwf.edu

Tools for Software Reconnaissance are now available, including the freeware Recon2 tool from the University of West Florida (http://www.cs.uwf.edu/~wilde/recon) and commercial testing and program comprehension tools such as χSuds™ from Telcordia (http://xsuds.argreenhouse.com).

However these case studies have also revealed problems with the usability of the Software Reconnaissance technique as currently implemented. A maintainer using the technique goes through a cycle such as the one shown in Figure 1. The maintainer has to switch back and forth between running tests, keeping track of trace files, setting up the analysis program so that it will know which traces exhibit each feature, and running the analysis program. While this process may be marginally adequate for batch programs, it is particularly awkward for long running or interactive programs such as a word processor or a web server. It takes considerable time to start up and terminate each test case, so the test-analyze cycle is quite time consuming.

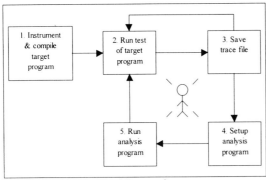

**Figure 1**
**Locating Features Using Software Reconnaissance**

## 3. Visual Location of Features

Our conversations with practicing software engineers have clearly established that ease of use is an indispensable quality for program comprehension tools. Maintainers working under time pressure will fall back on easy to use text search tools such as grep unless more precise methods are made equally user friendly. Accordingly we have been developing a visually oriented feature location tool called TraceGraph that combines two concepts:

**1. Immediate feedback from a running program**
TraceGraph monitors the program as it executes; trace files are written and analyzed continuously. The maintainer of, for example, the word processor would only need to start it once. To locate the code for, say, the spell check feature, he would simply do the spell check operation in one window and immediately

check the TraceGraph window to see what was executed. (Figure 2)

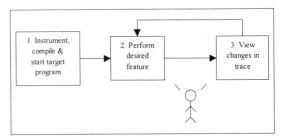

**Figure 2**
**Locating Features Using TraceGraph**

**2. Graphic display of results**
TraceGraph uses a display somewhat like an oscilloscope trace which slowly extends to the right as the program executes (see Figure 3). Each vertical column corresponds to a time period, say 5 seconds of execution. Each horizontal row corresponds to one software component. Each small rectangle is grey if the component was executed in that time period or blank if it was not. Black rectangles are used for emphasis the first time the component is executed.

Just as an engineer uses an oscilloscope to see how a circuit responds to different inputs, a maintainer will be able to use TraceGraph to view how the program responds to different actions. TraceGraph will provide *immediacy*, with a rapid visual response to the maintainer's operations. TraceGraph also takes advantage of the human's ability to distinguish texture in images. It is easy for the eye to pick out a change in the execution of a component, even if it is represented only by a color change in a few pixels.

To explore the usability of the TraceGraph concept on real software, we have tested a user interface prototype in case studies of two, very different, large systems. The studies were not done in "real-time" since we needed to experiment with different colors and parameters in the TraceGraph display. Instead, a sequence of trace files was generated and stored for each target system. TraceGraph then read these files in order and painted out the display as if they were being generated in real-time. The results of these case studies are described in the next sections.

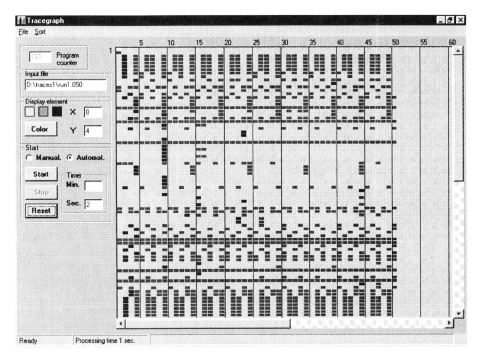

**Figure 3**
**A TraceGraph Display from the *Joint STARS* Case Study**

## 4. The *Joint STARS* Case Study

The first case study was intended to evaluate if TraceGraph could provide insight into features of a large real-time system. The study used trace data from the *Joint Surveillance Target Attack Radar Subsystem* (Joint STARS) developed by Northrop Grumman for the United States Department of Defense.

Joint STARS is an airborne targeting and battle management system which includes an EC-8 aircraft, a multi-mode radar system, mobile ground station modules, voice and data communications, control computers and workstations and a self-defense suite. The version of the Joint STARS software used in this study consisted of 7692 units totaling 363 K lines of code and divided into 233 processes running on a variable number of processors. The processes communicate by message passing.

In systems such as Joint STARS, understanding the process interactions is vital for understanding overall system design. In a previous study, we had used a variant of the Software Reconnaissance technique to recover *design threads*, data flow diagrams showing how the processes interact for a particular system feature [WILD.98]. That study used traces of inter-process messages collected in the Joint STARS test bed, which is a mockup of the interior of the EC-8 aircraft. Three test

runs were made, each including tests of five Joint STARS features plus periods of system idle time. The start and stop times for each feature were noted. The result was approximately 8.2 M bytes of message trace data with 67,605 messages representing about 30 minutes of system operation.

We used part of this same message trace data for the TraceGraph case study. The trace was broken up into segments corresponding to about 5 seconds of Joint STARS execution. Each of these trace segments generated one vertical column on the TraceGraph display of Figure 3. Each horizontal row of rectangles represents a distinct message between two processes. As previously described, a rectangle is black the first time the message occurred, grey for each subsequent occurrence, and blank if the message did not occur.

Figure 3 shows a TraceGraph display covering two features of Joint STARS. Feature A is quite brief and executed completely within the 5 second period of column 9. The new messages are clearly visible as the black rectangles in that column. Feature B runs more slowly and its execution is spread across columns 15 to 23. Again, some new messages are shown by black rectangles while other gray rectangles represent messages that might be part of the feature or part of background processing.

35

The TraceGraph display seems to be effective for feature location in Joint STARS. It clearly identifies some messages that need to be investigated (the black rectangles) since they do not appear until the feature was executed. The maintainer can also visually identify other potentially interesting messages which cluster in the time period of the feature, even though they are sometimes executed at other times. Finally, the maintainer may eliminate many other messages that occur all the time.

The TraceGraph display also allows quick insight into other aspects of Joint STARS messaging. Many messages are periodic, and occur at a fixed interval. These provide the regular patterns across the screen which can be seen in Figure 3. The display provides a quick feel for the system's background periodic processing.

Note that the TraceGraph display allows the human eye to replace the Software Reconnaissance set difference operation to locate a feature. The differences between components executed "with" and "without" the feature can be easily distinguished by the pattern of the rectangles. The eye can also identify more complicated patterns, such as the periodic messages.

## 5. The *Mosaic* Case Study

The second case study evaluated the usability of the TraceGraph display on a more detailed trace of each decision point in the code. In earlier studies we have found that detailed traces are often needed to locate features in old code since higher-level traces, can lose too much information [WILD.92]. Unfortunately, low level traces may be very large, so display techniques need to be carefully chosen.

The target system used was *NCSA Mosaic*, which is famous as one of the first web browsers to be widely distributed and used. Source code for the X Windows version is publicly available from www.ncsa.uiuc.edu and has been used in other case studies of program comprehension techniques (e.g. [JERD.97B, CHEN.00]). The version we studied consisted of approximately 86 K lines of C code.

Mosaic was instrumented at the decision level using the Recon2 instrumentor, so that a trace record was generated each time the program executed a branch statement such as an "if" or a "while". The initial trace files were very large, over 94 MB of trace being generated just during Mosaic start up. However most of the trace records were duplicates generated by just a few inner loops. Recon2 functions to suspend and resume tracing were inserted at 11 points, thus reducing the trace file to just over 36 MB, which proved to be manageable when chopped into 5 second chunks for the display. One of the lessons for future versions of TraceGraph is that the maintainer should be provided with convenient facilities for eliminating tracing of such tight loops.

Figure 4 shows how TraceGraph displays the detailed traces from Mosaic. As can be seen from the size of the scroll bar, only a fraction of the trace is visible at once since there are many more components (rows) in a detailed trace. (Compare to the scroll bar of Figure 3.) However the newly executed components (black rectangles) are very easy to see so the maintainer can quickly scroll up or down to find them.

The display of Figure 4 shows TraceGraph when trying to locate the Mosaic feature "display a GIF image". Up to column 13 we have the traces for starting up Mosaic and navigating to a web page that has no images. Then at column 14 the maintainer has entered the URL for a page that does contain a GIF. The black rectangles show the code executed for the first time at that point.

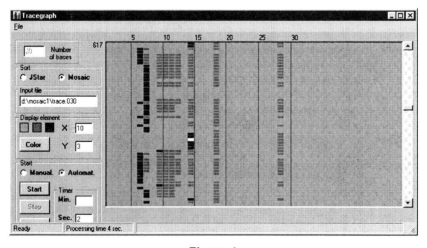

**Figure 4**
**A TraceGraph Display from the *Mosaic* Case Study**

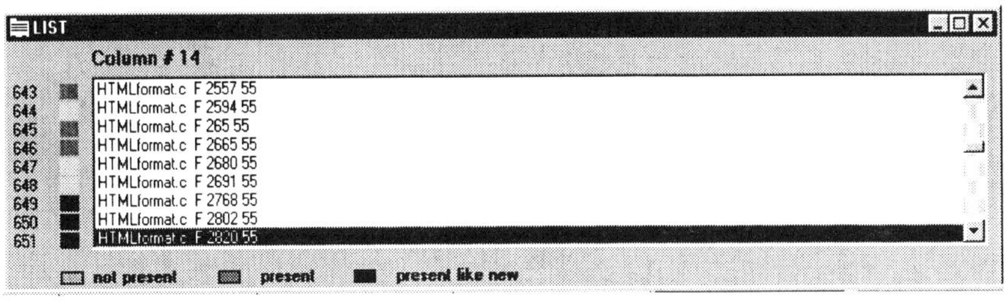

**Figure 5**
**A TraceGraph Pop-Up Display**

To help in analysis, the maintainer can mouse on any of the rectangles to get a more detailed pop-up display as shown in Figure 5. (The selected rectangle is white in Figure 4). The pop-up display shows the actual records from the trace file. As can be seen the selected rectangle corresponds to taking the False branch of a decision on line 2820 of source file `HTMLformat.c`. A look at the code shows that that line is in a function called `ImagePlace` which, as its name indicates, draws an image on the page. This would clearly be one of the functions a maintainer would need to study to understand the "display a GIF image" feature. TraceGraph seems to be effective in locating important code for a feature relatively quickly, even for very large and detailed traces.

## 6. Related Work

The literature on software visualization is now quite large, ranging from graphic techniques for animating algorithms as a teaching tool to systems for visualizing performance bottlenecks in large commercial programs. A good survey and taxonomy of the field is given by Price, Baecker and Small [PRIC.98]. In their classification, TraceGraph would probably be categorized as a `General/Scalable` system providing a `Graphical` view of `Control Flow`. (Unfortunately it would also be classified as `Intrusive`, since the production of a trace almost always has some impact on system performance.)

Pixel level displays, such as those used in TraceGraph, have been proposed in several software visualization systems, notably by Ball and Eick to visualize code statistics or the changes in a system between one version and another [BALL.96].

Numerous tools have been proposed for visualizing software to aid maintainers. Most such tools use static analysis, which parses the code and displays software structure without execution, for example [RAJL.88, CLEV.89, LINO.94]. A few more recent tools also use dynamic analysis for program comprehension. For example De Pauw, Kimelman and Vlissides describe a dynamic system for understanding object-oriented software that allows, among other things, visualization of inter-class calls and tracking of the number and parameters of object instances [DEPA.94].

The year 2000 problem generated several ideas for dynamic analysis of legacy software. Reps, Ball, Das and Larus [REPS.97] developed a "path spectrum" approach, in which each loop-free path is instrumented and the program is executed using different date inputs. The path spectrum is a bar graph with one bar for each path showing if it has been executed or not in the test. Comparison of pre-2000 and post-2000 path spectra may indicate the presence of year 2000 faults. Wilde, Justice, Blackwell and Wong [WILD.99] used a similar approach in which the number of executions of a basic block was either graphed or analyzed using Fourier analysis to identify program plans such as leap year computations.

Jerding, Stasko and Ball [JERD.97A] have described several tools that they call "Execution Murals". These tools also involve instrumentation and visualization, especially of the messages (calls) in an object oriented system. They describe several different kinds of displays, one of which is rather similar to the TraceGraph scrolling display in that it has time on one axis and classes on the other. A vertical bar is drawn to indicate a message passed from one object to another. The most recent tool from this group is *ISVis* described by Jerding and Rugaber [JERD.97B]. This tool provides visualizations using both static and dynamic analysis. After extraction of static information, such as a call graph and symbol table, the target system is instrumented and executed through several user defined scenarios to generate event traces, which are read into ISVis for analysis. ISVis allows for the definition of "actor" code components and for displays of the interaction events between actors. Jerding and Rugaber show how they have applied ISVis to the problem of locating where to insert a modification into a large system.

There are few other papers that address explicitly the problem of using visualization tools to locate the needed code for "as-needed" program comprehension. The general assumption seems to be that the maintainer will be able to identify some starting point, such as a variable or subroutine, and that the visualization tools will then let him or her navigate to the rest of the code that needs to be understood. This may not be a bad assumption in some cases. A maintainer will often have some prior knowledge about the program that can provide a starting point or, in the worst case, he or she can start at the main program and work down, a strategy that has been formalized by Chen and Rajlich [CHEN.00]. However prior knowledge may not be available, and top down exploration can be very time consuming, especially in poorly written code.

The main advantage of TraceGraph is that it should provide convenient answers to one specific problem: finding quick starting points for locating features in large, unfamiliar systems. Our experience with the similar Software Reconnaissance technique shows that it may also often provide insights and starting points that are unexpected, even for maintainers who are familiar with the target program.

## 7. Conclusions

Software maintainers are notoriously short of time to carry out the many tasks required to keep modern software in service. TraceGraph is intended to make it faster for them to locate code in large, long-running programs that need to be modified. The tool takes advantage of the human eye's ability to identify patterns in large amounts of information presented graphically. It also emphasizes quick feedback so that the maintainer can try different program inputs and get an immediate picture showing the target program's response.

We believe that the two case studies indicate that displays like TraceGraph can provide an effective means of locating features in programs, and that the results should be comparable with those of the slower Software Reconnaissance approach. The technique should be usable on a wide variety of traces produced by many different tools. Displays of this kind are good candidates to be included in software monitoring and debugging tools.

It is important to note the limitations that TraceGraph shares with Software Reconnaissance. First, it may only be used to locate features which the program's user can control. Most programs contain a significant amount of common code that is *always* executed on every non-trivial test. While a maintainer may need to locate some specific part of this common code, such as the symbol table handler in a compiler, neither TraceGraph nor Software Reconnaissance can help. Second, as for any dynamic analysis technique, the results depend to some extent on the test cases used. If a feature is sometimes handled one way and sometimes another, neither technique will find all of it unless the maintainer supplies inputs that cover

both cases. On the other hand, both techniques will identify unwanted code components if the "with" tests accidentally include functionality that is absent in the "without" cases. Finally, both techniques only provide *starting points* for the exploration of code. The maintainer still needs to do the hard work of studying each identified component and understanding how it fits into the rest of the target system. Other analysis tools, such as those mentioned in the previous section, may then be very useful.

The current version of TraceGraph is still an early user interface prototype, but we plan to include a more finished tool as part of the Recon3 system currently under development.

## References

[AGRA.98]  Agrawal, Hira; Alberi, James L.; Horgan, Joseph R.; Li, J. Jenny; London, Saul; Wong, W. Eric; Ghosh, Sudipto; Wilde, Norman, "Mining System Tests to Aid Software Maintenance", *IEEE Computer*, Vol. 31, No. 7 (July 1998), pp. 64 - 73.

[BALL.96]  Ball, T. and Eick, S. "Software Visualization in the Large", *IEEE Computer*, Vol. 29, No. 4, April 1996, pp. 33-43.

[CHEN.00]  Chen, Kunrong and Rajlich, Vaclav, "Feature Location Using Dependency Graph", *Proc. International Workshop on Program Comprehension 2000*, IEEE Computer Society, June, 2000.

[CLEV.89]  Cleveland, Linore, "A Program Understanding Support Environment", *IBM Systems Journal*, Vol. 28, No. 2, 1989, pp. 234 - 344.

[DEPA.94]  De Pauw, Wim; Kimelman, Doug; Vlissides, John, "Modeling Object-Oriented Program Execution", *Proc. ECOOP'94, The Eighth European Conference on Object-Oriented Programming*, Springer Verlag, 1994, pp. 163 - 182.

[JERD.97A] Jerding, Dean; Stasko, John; Ball, Thomas, "Visualizing Interactions in Program Executions", *Proc. 1997 International Conference on Software Engineering*, pp. 360 - 370, IEEE Computer Society, May, 1997.

[JERD.97B] Jerding, D. and Rugaber, S., "Using Visualization for Architectural Localization and Extraction", *Proc. of the Fourth Working Conference on Reverse Engineering, 1997*, p. 56 - 65, IEEE Computer Society Press, October 1997.

[KOEN.91]  Koenemann, Jurgen and Robertson, Scott, "Expert Problem Solving Strategies for

Program Comprehension", *Proceedings CHI'91*, p. 125 - 130, ACM Press, 1991.

[LINO.94]   Linos, Panagiotis; Aubet, Philippe, Dumas, Laurent; Helleboid, Yann; Lejeune, Patricia; Tulula, Philippe, "Visualizing Program Dependencies: An Experimental Study", *Software - Practice and Experience*, Vol 24, No. 4 (April 1944), pp. 387 - 403.

[PRIC.98]   Price, Blaine; Baecker, Ronald; Small, Ian; "An Introduction to Software Visualization", pp. 3 - 27, in *Software Visualization: Programming as a Multimedia Experience*, Stasko, Domingue, Brown and Price eds., MIT Press, 1998.

[REPS.97]   Reps, T.; Ball, T.; Das, M.; Larus, J., "The use of program profiling for software maintenance with applications to the year 2000 problem", in *Proceedings ESEC/FSE 97*, published as Vol. 1301 of *Lecture Notes in Computer Science*, Springer-Verlag, Berlin, pp. 432-449.

[RAJL.88]   Rajlich, Vaclav; Damaskinos, Nicholas; Linos, Panagiotis; Silva, Joao; Khorshid, Wafa, "Visual Support for Programming-in-the-Large", *Proc. IEEE Conference on Software Maintenance - 1988*, IEEE Computer Society, Oct. 1988, pp. 92 - 99.

[WILD.92]   Wilde, N.; Gomez, J. A..; Gust, T.; Strasburg, D., "Locating User Functionality in Old Code", *Proc. IEEE Conference on Software Maintenance - 1992*, IEEE Computer Society, November 1992, pp. 200 - 205.

[WILD.95]   Wilde, Norman and Scully, Michael, "Software Reconnaissance: Mapping Program Features to Code", *Journal of Software Maintenance: Research and Practice*, vol. 7 (1995), pp. 49 - 62.

[WILD.96]   Wilde, Norman and Casey, Christopher, "Early Field Experience with the Software Reconnaissance Technique for Program Comprehension", *Proc. International Conference on Software Maintenance*, IEEE Computer Society, November 1996, pp. 312 - 318.

[WILD.98]   Wilde, Norman; Casey, Christopher; Vandeville, Joe; Trio, Gary; Hotz, Dick, "Reverse Engineering of Software Threads: A Design Recovery Technique for Large Multi-Process Systems", *Journal of Systems and Software*, Vol 43 (1998), pp. 11-17.

[WILD.99]   Wilde, Norman; Justice, Randy; Blackwell, Kristin; Wong, W. Eric, "Dynamic Analysis Methods for the Year 2000 Problem", *Journal of Software Maintenance: Research and Practice*, Vol. 11 (1999), pp. 167 - 182.

# Information Retrieval Models for Recovering Traceability Links between Code and Documentation

G. Antoniol*, G. Canfora*, G. Casazza**, A. De Lucia*

antoniol@ieee.org {gerardo.canfora,gec,delucia}@unisannio.it

(*)University of Sannio, Faculty of Engineering - Piazza Roma, I-82100 Benevento, Italy
(**)University of Naples Federico II, DIS - Via Claudio 21, I-80125 Naples, Italy

## Abstract

*The research described in this paper is concerned with the application of information retrieval to software maintenance, and in particular to the problem of recovering traceability links between the source code of a system and its free text documentation.*

*We introduce a method based on the general idea of vector space information retrieval and apply it in two case studies to trace C++ source code onto manual pages and Java code onto functional requirements. The case studies discussed in this paper replicate the studies presented in references [3] and [2], respectively, where a probabilistic information retrieval model was applied. We compare the results of vector space and probabilistic models and formulate hypotheses to explain the differences.*

## 1. Introduction

Automated Information Retrieval (IR) systems are concerned with the retrieval of documents from (usually very large) document databases, based on user information needs [8]. They prepare the collection of documents for retrieval through an indexing process; user needs are captured by phrases which are themselves indexed and used to rank the documents.

IR has proven useful in many disparate areas, including the management of huge scientific and legal literature, office automation, and the support to complex engineering projects such as software engineering projects.

We believe that IR techniques can help software maintenance by providing a way to semi-automatically recovering traceability links between the documentation of a system and its source code. The underlying assumption is that programmers use meaningful names for code items; indeed, we believe that most of the application domain knowledge that

programmers process when writing the code is captured by the mnemonics for identifiers.

Most of the documentation that accompany large software systems consists of free text documents expressed in a natural language. Examples include requirements and design documents, user manuals, logs of errors, maintenance journals, design decisions, reports from inspection and review sessions, and also annotations of individual programmers and teams. In addition, free text documents often capture the available knowledge of the application domain, for example in the form of laws and regulations or in technical/scientific handbooks. Therefore, techniques to recover traceability links between code and free text documents are a precious aid to software maintenance as they bridge the gap between different views of a systems, and between the system's views and its domain of application.

Reference [3] highlights several scenarios of software maintenance and evolution that would benefit from the existence of such links, including program comprehension, design recovery, requirement tracing, impact analysis, and reuse of existing software. The paper also introduces an IR method to trace source code, and in particular C++ classes, onto free text documents and discusses the results obtained in a case study where the code of the LEDA library (Library of Efficient Data Types and Algorithms — available from http://www.mpi.sb.mpg.de/LEDA) was traced back onto the manual pages. The results — measured in terms of two well known IR metrics, namely precision and recall — were encouraging and, therefore, we applied the method in other scenarios, such as impact analysis [1] and requirement tracing [2]. In all cases the results were satisfactory and this enforced our believe that IR can play a useful role in maintenance.

The case studies discussed in references [3, 2] applied a probabilistic IR model. With this model, documents $D_i$ are ranked according to the probability $Pr(D_i|Q)$ of being relevant to a query $Q$ extracted from a source code component. To compute this ranking we exploited the idea of a language model, i.e. a stochastic model that assigns a probability to every string of words taken from a prescribed vocabulary [7]. We estimated a language model (actually, a unigram approximation of the model) for each document or identifiable section and used a Bayesian classifier to score the sequences of mnemonics extracted from each source code class against the models. A high score indicated a high probability that a particular sequence of mnemonics be relevant to the document; therefore, we interpreted it as an indication of the existence of a semantic link between the class from which the sequence had been extracted and the document.

In the present paper we test the hypothesis that using other IR models could also give good results. In particular, we describe a method to recover traceability links that uses a vector space IR model [10, 15]. This model treats documents and queries as vectors in an $n$-dimensional space, where $n$ is the number of indexing features (in our case, words in the vocabulary). Documents are ranked against queries by computing some distance functions between the corresponding vectors. In this paper, we use the cosine of the angle between the vectors to rank the documents [10].

The method has been applied in two case studies to trace C++ source code onto manual pages and Java code onto functional requirements. These case studies replicate the studies described in references [3] and [2], respectively. The results are in both cases satisfactory and confirm the hypothesis that IR, either probabilistic or vector space models, provides a practicable solution to the problem of semi-automatically recovering traceability links.

There are three main intended contribution of this paper:

- we present a method to recover traceability links between source code and free text documentation based on the general idea of vector space IR;

- we provide experimental results of applying the method in two case studies;

- we compare the performances of probabilistic and vector space IR models when applied to the particular problem of traceability link recovery and formulate hypotheses to explain the differences.

The reminder of the paper is organized as follows. Section 2 presents the traceability link recovery process and discusses the IR model exploited. Experimental results are presented in section 3, while section 4 discusses the performances of IR models when applied to the problem of recovering traceability links. Concluding remarks and a discussion of related and future work are given in section 5.

## 2. An IR method to recover traceability links

Our method to recover traceability links between code and free text documentation uses the identifiers extracted from a class as a query to retrieve the documents relevant to the class. In particular, we apply a vector space IR model to rank the available documents against the class.

This section describes the overall traceability link recovery process, gives background information on the IR model applied, and discusses tool support.

### 2.1 The process

Figure 1 shows the overall process of traceability link recovery using IR models. The figure highlights two paths of activities, one to prepare the document for retrieval (the lower path) and the other to extract the queries from code (the upper path).

In the first path, documents are indexed based on a vocabulary that is extracted from the documents themselves. The construction of the vocabulary and the indexing of the documents are preceded by a text normalization phase performed at three levels of accuracy:

1. at the first level all capital letters are transformed into lower case letters;

2. at the second level stop-words (such as articles, punctuation, numbers, etc) are removed;

3. at the third level a morphological analysis is used to convert plurals into singulars and to reconduct all the flexed verbs to the infinity form.

The second path builds and indexes a query for each source code class. The construction of a query consists of three steps:

1. identifier extraction, that parses class source code and extracts the list of its identifiers;

2. identifier separation, that splits into separate words the identifiers composed of two or more words (i.e. AmountDue and amount_due);

3. text normalization, that applies the three steps described above for document indexing.

Finally, a classifier computes the similarity between queries and documents and returns, for each class, a ranked list of documents.

Of course, indexing the documents and the queries and ranking the documents against a query depend on the particular IR model adopted. For example, the probabilistic model applied in references [3, 2] indexes a document by

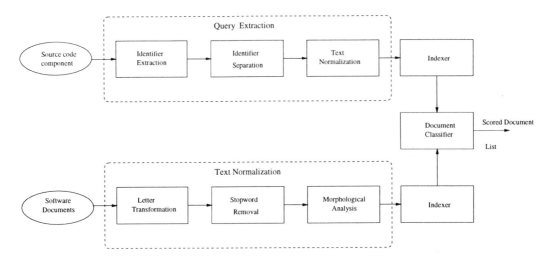

**Figure 1. Traceability Recovery Process.**

computing its stochastic language model [7], whereas the list of identifiers that define a query is not indexed at all. The similarity between a document and a query is computed as the product of the probabilities that each identifier in the query appears in the document too.

## 2.2 Vector space IR: background notions

Vector space IR models map each document and each query onto a vector [10]. In our case, each element of the vector corresponds to a word (or term) in a vocabulary extracted from the documents themselves. If $V$ is the size of the vocabulary, then the vector $[d_{i,1}, d_{i,2}, \ldots d_{i,V}]$ represents the document $D_i$. The $j$-th element $d_{i,j}$ is a measure of the weight of the $j$-th term of the vocabulary in the document $D_i$. Different measures have been proposed for this weight. In the simplest case it is a boolean value, either 1 if the $j$-th term occurs in the document $D_i$, or 0 otherwise; in other cases more complex measures are constructed based on the frequency of the terms in the documents.

We use a well known IR metric called $tf - idf$ [15]. According to this metric, the $j$-th element $d_{i,j}$ is derived from the *term frequency* $tf_{i,j}$ of the $j$-th term in the document $D_i$ and the *inverse document frequency* $idf_j$ of the term over the entire set of documents. The term frequency $tf_{i,j}$ is the ratio between the number of occurrences of word $j$-th over the total number of words contained in the document $D_i$. The inverse document frequency $idf_j$ is defined as:

$$idf_j = \frac{Total\ Number\ of\ Documents}{Number\ of\ Documents\ containing\ the\ j^{th}\ term}$$

The vector element $d_{i,j}$ is:

$$d_{i,j} = tf_{i,j} * log(idf_j)$$

The term $log(idf_j)$ acts as a weight for the frequency of a word in a document: the more the word is specific to the document, the higher the weight.

The list of identifiers extracted from a class $Q$ — that is, a query $Q$ — is represented in a similar way by a vector $[q_1, q_2, \ldots q_V]$. The similarity between a document $D_i$ and a class/query $Q$ is computed as the cosine of the angle between the corresponding vectors:

$$Similarity(D_i, Q) = s_{i,Q} =$$
$$= \frac{\sum_{j=1}^{V} d_{i,j} q_j}{\sqrt{\sum_{h=1}^{V} (d_{i,h})^2 * \sum_{k=1}^{V} (q_k)^2}}$$

Documents are ranked against a class by decreasing similarity.

## 2.3 Tool support

We have developed a toolkit that supports, and partially automates, the process shown in Figure 1.

We use top-down recursive parsers to analyze C++ and Java source code. The parse trees are traversed and each time a class is encountered the comments, if any, and the identifiers of attributes, methods, and method parameters are stored in support files. For the present study comments were disregarded: the entire traceability link recovery process relies on the mnemonics used for classes, attributes, methods and parameters.

We have integrated public domain facilities and tools developed in house to assist text processing for the English and Italian languages. Identifier separation is performed in two steps: the first step is completely automated and recognizes words separated by underscore and sequences of words starting with capital letters. The second step is semi-automatic: the tool exploits spelling facilities to prompt the software engineer with the words that might be separated. The first two steps of text normalization, namely letter transformation and stop-word removing, have also been completely automated. Finally, we have implemented a semi-automatic stemmer that uses thesaurus facilities to help users to reconduct flexed words to their roots.

The final step of cosine computation and document ranking is implemented by simple Perl scripts.

# 3. Case studies

In previous papers [3, 2], we applied a traceability link recovery method based on the probabilistic IR model in two case studies with different characteristics. The case studies have been replicated using the vector space IR model presented in the previous section, and the results are discussed in this section.

We assess the results using two widely accepted IR metrics, namely *recall* and *precision* [8].

*Recall* is the ratio of the number of relevant documents retrieved for a given query over the total number of relevant documents for that query. *Precision* is the ratio of the number of relevant documents retrieved over the total number of documents retrieved.

Recovering traceability links is a semi-automatic process. The main role of IR tools consists of restricting the document space, while recovering all the documents relevant to each source code component. Without tool support, one must analyze all the documents before discovering that a given class is not described by any document; with a restricted document space the number of documents to analyze is generally much lower. This means that high recall values (possibly 100 %) should be pursued; of course, in this case higher precision values reduce the effort required to discard false positives (documents that are retrieved but are not relevant to a given query).

It is worth noting that the recall is undefined for queries that do not have relevant documents associated. However, these queries may retrieve false positives that have to be discarded by the software engineer. To take into account such queries we used the following aggregate formulas:

$$Recall = \frac{\sum_i \#(Relevant_i \wedge Retrieved_i)}{\sum_i \#Relevant_i}\%$$

$$Precision = \frac{\sum_i \#(Relevant_i \wedge Retrieved_i)}{\sum_i \#Retrieved_i}\%$$

where $i$ ranges over the entire query set, including the queries with no associated documents. These queries do not affect the computation of the recall ($Relevant_i$ is the empty set), while they negatively affect the computation of the precision whenever $Retrieved_i$ is not the empty set. This negative influence takes into account the effort required to discard false positives.

## 3.1  LEDA case study

The first case study was a freely available C++ library of foundation classes, called LEDA (Library of Efficient Data types and Algorithms), developed and distributed by Max-Planck-Institut für Informatik, Saarbrücken, Germany. We analyzed the code and the documentation of the release 3.4, consisting of 95 KLOC, 208 Classes and 88 manual pages. The aim was to map source code classes onto manual pages.

The LEDA manual pages contain a high number of identifiers that also appear in the source code. Actually, the LEDA team generated manual pages with scripts that extract comments from the source files. A markup language was used to identify the comment fragments to be extracted. Function names, parameter names, and data type names contained in these comments appear in the manual pages, thus making the traceability link recovery task easier. For this reason, and to make the results comparable with those obtained with the probabilistic model [3], we applied a simplified version of the process shown in Figure 1. The simplification concerned the identifier separation and the text normalization activities: in particular, identifier separation only consisted of splitting identifiers containing underscores, while text normalization was performed only at the first level of accuracy, i.e. the transformation of capital letters into lower case letters.

To validate the results, we used a 208 × 88 traceability matrix linking each class to the manual page describing it. As outlined in [3], each class was described by at most one manual page, and many classes (110) were not described by any manual page. The number of links in the traceability matrix was 98. Ten manual pages did not describe LEDA classes, but basic concepts and algorithms, thus the number of relevant manual pages was 78. This means that some manual pages described more than one class: for example, very often an abstract class and its derived concrete classes were described by the same manual page.

Table 1 shows the results. The first columns (Cut) shows the number of documents retained for each query (first $N$ documents in the ranked list); the second and the third

| Cut | Retrieved | Relevant | Precision | Recall | Prob. Rel. |
|---|---|---|---|---|---|
| 1 | 208 | 52 | 25.00 % | 53.06 % | 81 |
| 2 | 416 | 71 | 17.06 % | 72.44 % | 88 |
| 3 | 624 | 79 | 12.66 % | 80.61 % | 93 |
| 4 | 832 | 82 | 9.85 % | 83.67 % | 93 |
| 5 | 1040 | 85 | 8.17 % | 86.73 % | 93 |
| 6 | 1248 | 89 | 7.13 % | 90.81 % | 93 |
| 7 | 1456 | 90 | 6.18 % | 91.83 % | 94 |
| 8 | 1664 | 93 | 5.58 % | 94.89 % | 94 |
| 9 | 1872 | 95 | 5.07 % | 96.93 % | 95 |
| 10 | 2080 | 96 | 4.61 % | 97.95 % | 95 |
| 11 | 2288 | 96 | 4.19 % | 97.95 % | 95 |
| 12 | 2496 | 98 | 3.92 % | 100.00 % | 96 |

**Table 1. LEDA results**

columns show (for each cut level) the total number of retrieved documents (for all queries) and the total number
of retrieved documents that are also relevant, respectively;
the third and fourth columns show the aggregate precision
and recall for all queries, respectively; finally, last column
shows the total number of relevant documents retrieved by
applying the probabilistic model [3].

The poor results of the precision are due to the fact that
most of the queries (110) were derived from classes without
relevant manual pages associated (these queries contribute
to the total number of retrieved documents). A moderate
number of retained candidates (12) was required to recover
all the traceability links (100 % of recall). This provides
evidence to support our hypothesis that IR models are suitable for recovering traceability links between code and documentation. A further favorable argument is the fact that the
results are not very different from those achieved in [3] with
a probabilistic model: indeed, the main difference is that the
results of the vector space model are more smoothed, while
the probabilistic model tends to retrieve very soon a high
number of relevant documents (see Figure 2). However,
both models converge to 100 % of recall with a moderate
number of retained candidates; for the probabilistic model
100 % of recall is achieved when cutting the ranked list of
retrieved documents at 17 candidates [3] (not shown in the
table), thus confirming a more irregular behavior.

### 3.2 Albergate case study

The second case study was a software system, called Albergate, developed in Java according to a waterfall process.
For this system all the documentation prescribed by the software development process was available (e.g., requirement
documents, design documents, test cases, etc.). Albergate
is a software system designed to implement all the operations required to administrate and manage a small/medium

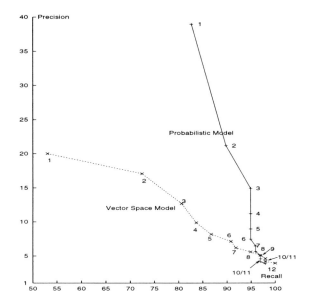

**Figure 2. LEDA Precision/Recall results.**

size hotel (room reservation, bill calculation, etc.). It was
developed from scratch by a team of final year students at
the University of Verona (Italy) on the basis of 16 functional
requirements expressed (as well as all the other system documentation) in the Italian language. Albergate exploits a
relational database and consists of 95 classes and about 20
KLOC. The aim of this case study was to trace source code
classes onto functional requirements. We focused on the
60 classes implementing the user interface of the software
system.

To validate the results, the original developers were required to provide a 16 × 60 traceability matrix linking each
requirement to the classes implementing it. Most of the
functional requirements were implemented by a low num-

44

| Cut | Retrieved | Relevant | Precision | Recall | Prob. Rel. |
|---|---|---|---|---|---|
| 1 | 60 | 29 | 48.33 % | 50.00 % | 29 |
| 2 | 120 | 34 | 28.33 % | 58.62 % | 41 |
| 3 | 180 | 46 | 25.55 % | 79.31 % | 45 |
| 4 | 240 | 51 | 21.25 % | 87.93 % | 51 |
| 5 | 300 | 54 | 18.00 % | 93.10 % | 57 |
| 6 | 360 | 55 | 15.27 % | 94.82 % | 58 |
| 7 | 420 | 58 | 13.80 % | 100.00 % | 58 |

**Table 2. Albergate results with improved process**

ber of classes: on the average, a requirement was implemented by about 4 classes with a maximum of 10. Most classes were associated to one requirement, only 6 classes were associated to two requirements, and 8 classes were not associated to any functional requirement. The total number of links in the traceability matrix was 58.

In this case study we applied the full version of the text processing steps in Figure 1 (these steps are described in section 2.1). The motivation was that the relative distance between source code and documents was higher than in the LEDA case study. Common words between requirements and classes were quite infrequent in the Albergate system: in fact unlike LEDA manual pages, Albergate functional requirements were produced in the early phases of the software development life cycle. Moreover, the Italian language has a complex grammar: verbs have much more forms than English verbs, plurals are almost always irregular, and adverbs and adjectives have irregular forms too.

Table 2 shows the results of this case study (the meaning of the columns is the same as in Table 1). Unlike the LEDA case study, the results of the vector space model are not very different than those produced by the probabilistic model [2] (see Figure 3). All the traceability links were recovered by considering the first seven documents for each class. However, the probabilistic model tends to retrieve sooner most of the relevant documents (100 % of recall was obtained by considering the first six documents for each class).

## 4. Discussion

This section analyzes and discusses the results achieved in the two case studies and draw some lessons learned. Although the limitations of the two case studies (in particular, the small size of Albergate and the fact that the LEDA documentation is extracted from comments contained in the source files) do not allow to draw definitive conclusions, some basic considerations can be already outlined. We address three points:

- how helpful is an IR model in a traceability link recovery process ?

- why the performances of the probabilistic and the vector space models are different ?

- how precision could be improved ?

The following subsections attempt to provide an answer to the questions above.

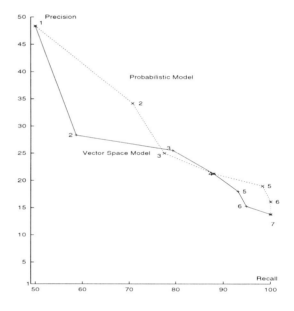

**Figure 3. Albergate Precision/Recall results with improved process.**

### 4.1 Benefits of IR

To demonstrate the benefits of using an IR model for recovering traceability links between code and documentation, we compared the results achieved in the two case studies with the probabilistic and vector space IR models with the results obtained by using the grep UNIX command, as proposed by Maarek *et al.* [12]. In fact, grep provides the simplest way to trace source code components

| | Single Code Item | | | | Code Items *or* Combined | | | |
|---|---|---|---|---|---|---|---|---|
| | #Queries | #Empty Set | Mean Size | Max Size | #Queries | #Empty Set | Mean Size | Max Size |
| Albergate | 4834 | 4575 | 5 | 14 | 60 | 0 | 11 | 13 |
| LEDA | 4670 | 451 | 20 | 88 | 208 | 1 | 75 | 88 |

**Table 3.** `grep` **results.**

(e.g., classes) onto high level documentation (e.g., manual pages and/or requirements). The search can be done at least in two ways: in the first approach each class identifier is used as the string to be searched into the files of high level artifacts while the second approach considers the *or* of the class identifiers.

Table 3 shows the results of the `grep` approach: it is worth noting that for the Albergate system 94% of the single item queries gave empty results while if items are *or* combined 94% of classed were traced onto 10 or more requirements. Empty sets are less frequent for LEDA; however, the average number of traced manual pages is quite high (20 and 75, respectively). Even worse the `grep` approach did not offer any way to rank the retrieved requirements. From a practical point of view this means that the maintainer has to examine a large number of candidates with the same priority. `grep` baseline results were thus judged quite unsatisfactory compared with IR results.

In the previous sections we have evaluated the results using the IR metrics *recall* and *precision*. To achieve an indication of the benefits of using an IR approach in a traceability link recovery process, we have also introduced a *Recovery Effort Index* (*REI*), defined as the ratio between the number of documents retrieved and the total number of documents available:

$$REI = \frac{\#Retrieved}{\#Available}\%$$

This metric can be used to estimate the percentage of the effort required to manually analyze the results achieved by an IR tool (and discard false positive), when the recall is 100 %, with respect to a completely manual analysis[1]. For a given software system, the quantity $1 - REI$ estimates the effort saving deriving from the use of an IR method to recover traceability links, with respect a completely manual analysis. The lower the REI the higher the benefits of the IR approach.

This metric also measures the ratio between the precision of the results achieved on the same software system by a completely manual process, namely $P_m$, and a semi-automatic process, namely $P_t$, that exploits IR, when the recall is 100 %:

$$\frac{Precision_m}{Precision_t} = \frac{\#(Relevant \wedge Retrieved_m)}{\#(Relevant \wedge Retrieved_t)} \frac{\#Retrieved_t}{\#Retrieved_m}$$

Note that the number of relevant documents retrieved is the same in both processes (all relevant documents) and that the documents retrieved with a manual analysis are just all documents available, then:

$$\frac{Precision_m}{Precision_t}\% = \frac{\#Retrieved_t}{\#Available}\%$$

that is the REI for the semi-automatic process.

The values of REI registered in the two case studies for the vector space IR model are rather different: Albergate requires 43.75 % REI to achieve 100 % recall, whereas LEDA only requires 13.63 % REI. A possible explanation is that the set of available documents in the Albergate case study is smaller (16 functional requirements versus the 88 manual pages of LEDA); to get the same REI as in the LEDA case study the maximum recall would have to be achieved with about 2 documents retrieved (that also means about 50 % of precision). However, this is very unlikely to be achieved with IR methods, that generally aim to retrieve a small percentage of a huge document space. Therefore, it is likely to hypothesize that greater benefits (and lower values of REI) are achieved for document spaces of greater size.

Alternatively, the REI could be computed with respect to a manual analysis supported by `grep` (queries with or combined items). In this case, the REI is computed as the ration between the number of relevant documents retrieved with an IR approach and the number of documents retrieved by `grep`[2]. For the vector space model the values for REI are 54.54 % in the Albergate case study and 16 % in LEDA.

## 4.2 Probabilistic versus vector space model

The two case studies suggest that both IR models (vector space and probabilistic) are suitable for the problem of recovering traceability links between code and documentation. The results are very similar, in particular with respect to the number of documents a software engineer needs to analyze to get high values of recall. This also means that

---

[1] At the moment we have not statistically validated the relation between this metric and the traceability link recovery effort; this will be part of future work.

[2] Of course, this requires that grep based approach achieves 100 % recall, as in our case.

| Cut | Retrieved | Relevant | Precision | Recall | Prob. Rel. |
|-----|-----------|----------|-----------|--------|------------|
| 1 | 60 | 23 | 38.33 % | 39.65 % | 15 |
| 2 | 120 | 33 | 27.50 % | 56.89 % | 17 |
| 3 | 180 | 38 | 21.11 % | 65.51 % | 20 |
| 4 | 240 | 46 | 19.16 % | 78.86 % | 23 |
| 5 | 300 | 48 | 16.00 % | 82.75 % | 28 |
| 6 | 360 | 52 | 14.44 % | 89.65 % | 30 |
| 7 | 420 | 54 | 12.85 % | 93.10 % | 32 |

**Table 4. Albergate results with simplified process**

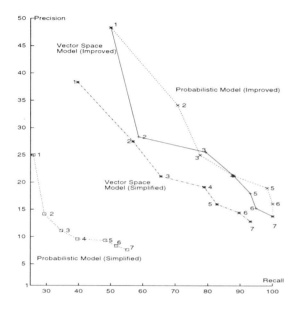

**Figure 4. Albergate Precision/Recall results.**

the two models achieve similar values of REI. However, Figures 2 and 3 show that the results of the vector space model are more smoothed than the corresponding results achieved with a probabilistic model. Moreover, the probabilistic model tends to retrieve sooner most of the relevant documents.

A possible explanation is in the nature of the two models. The probabilistic model associates a source code component (in our case studies a class) to a document based on the product of the probabilities that each code component identifier appears in the software document [3, 2]:

$$Similarity(D_i, Q) = \prod_{k=1}^{m} Pr(w_k \mid D_i) \simeq$$
$$\simeq Pr(Q \mid D_i) \simeq Pr(D_i \mid Q)$$

These probabilities are computed on a statistical basis

and code component identifiers that do not appear in the document are assigned a very low probability. Conversely, the similarity measure of a vector space model only takes into account the code identifiers that also appear in the document and weight the frequencies of the occurrences of such words in the document (code component) with respect to a measure of the diffusion of such words in other documents (code components, respectively).

Therefore, the probabilistic model is more suitable for cases where the presence of code component identifiers that do not belong to the software document is low: this is also the reason why, with respect to the best match, the probabilistic model performs better in the LEDA case study (82.65 % of recall) than in the Albergate case study (50 % of recall). It is worth noting that the probabilistic model is also used in speech recognition [7] and information theory [6] fields, where the aim is to associate a received sentence to a possible transmitted sentence, with a very low error probability. Conversely, the vector space model fits cases where each group of words is common to a relatively small number of software documents. This means that the vector space model does not aim to the best match, but rather to regularly achieve the maximum recall with a moderate number of retained documents.

This hypothesis is supported by the results obtained by applying the simplified version of the text processing steps in Figure 1 to the Albergate case study, with both the probabilistic and the vector space models. The simplified versions of the identifier separation and text normalization steps produce code components and software documents with a higher number of different words. Table 4 shows the results achieved, while Figure 4 depicts the Precision/Recall curves of the two IR models, in both simplified and improved processes. For the vector space model the results of the simplified and improved processes are not very different. Conversely, the differences are evident when applying the two versions of the text processing steps with the probabilistic model [2]. This means that unlike the probabilistic model, the vector space model is able to achieve higher recall values based on a smaller number of relevant words in a source code component.

| Percentage | Retrieved | Relevant | Precision | Recall |
|---|---|---|---|---|
| 90 % | 59 | 29 | 49.15 % | 50.00 % |
| 70 % | 101 | 38 | 37.62 % | 65.51 % |
| 50 % | 158 | 50 | 31.64 % | 86.20 % |
| 30 % | 265 | 55 | 20.75 % | 94.82 % |
| 10 % | 484 | 58 | 11.98 % | 100.00 % |
| min(10 %, best 7) | 329 | 58 | 17.62 % | 100.00 % |

**Table 5. Albergate results using a threshold**

## 4.3 Retrieving a variable number of documents per query

In our case study we have retained for each query a fixed number of documents. The results achieved for the recall can be considered good, as in both case studies we were able to achieve 100 % of recall with a moderate number of retained candidates per query.

We wondered if with a variable number of retained candidates per query we could improve precision and REI, while maintaining a maximum recall. The approach adopted to test this hypothesis consisted of using a threshold on the similarity values to prune the ranked list of documents retrieved by a query. In particular, for each query Q we computed the value of such a threshold $t_Q$ as a percentage of the similarity measure of the best match:

$$t_Q = c * [\max_i s_{i,Q}]$$

where $0 \leq c \leq 1$. A query Q returns all and only the documents $D_k$ such that $s_{k,Q} \geq t_Q$. Of course, the higher the value of the parameter $c$ the smaller the set of documents returned by a query.

Table 5 shows the results achieved with the Albergate case study using different values of the parameter $c$ (and then different thresholds). The results are not very encouraging, as the maximum recall is achieved when setting the threshold to only 10 % of the highest similarity measure. Using this percentage, the average number of retrieved documents per query is 9, while 3 documents are retrieved in the best case, and 15 documents in the worst case.

Although the results are worse than the results achieved with a fixed cut (first 7 documents in table 2), they still demonstrate the benefits of using an IR approach: indeed, when the recall is 100 % ($c = 10$ %) the REI is 50.41 %; this means that presumably about 50 % of the effort can be saved by only discarding the documents whose similarity measure is below 10 % of the best match.

Of course, the results can be improved by mixing a variable and fixed cut: each query retrieves only the documents with a similarity measure greater than a given threshold, but no more than a fixed number. As an example, last row in table 5 shows the results achieved by considering as the number of documents retrieved by each query the minimum between 7 and the number of documents whose similarity value is higher than 10 % of the best match. In this case the results are much better than the results achieved with a fixed cut (the first 7 documents in table 2): the average number of retrieved documents is 6 and the REI is 34.27 %, that means that the percentage of effort saved might be more than 65 %.

The issue of retrieving a variable number of documents per query needs further statistical investigations and this will be part of our future work.

## 5. Concluding remarks

We have presented an IR method to recover traceability links between code and free text documentation and have applied it to trace C++ and Java source classes onto manual pages and functional requirements, respectively. The method relies on a vector space IR model and ranks documents against a query (a list of identifiers extracted from a classe) by computing a distance between the corresponding vector representations.

A goal of this paper was to demonstrate that vector space IR performs as well as probabilistic IR. We have replicated the case studies presented in references [3] and [2] (which applied probabilistic IR), using a vector space model and the results support our hypothesis that IR, either probabilistic or vector space models, provides a practicable solution to the problem of semi-automatically recovering traceability links between code and documentation.

The paper has discussed the differences between the two IR models. In particular, the vector space model exhibits a behavior more regular than the probabilistic model and requires less effort in the preparation of the query and document representations. On the other hand, the probabilistic model performs better when the constraint of manually analyzing a reduced number of documents is stronger than achieving 100 % recall.

In our knowledge, the issue of recovering traceability links between code and free text documentation is not largely investigated and very few contributions appear in the

48

literature. A number of related papers are in the area of impact analysis. They assume the existence of some forms of ripple propagation graph describing relations between software artifacts, including code and documentation, and focus on the prediction of the effects of a maintenance change request on both the source code and the specification and design documents [16].

TOOR [13], IBIS [11], and REMAP [14] are a few examples of CASE tools that maintain traceability links among various software artifacts. However, these tools are focused on the development phase and either force naming conventions or require human interventions to define the links.

Reference [12] introduces an IR method to automatically assemble software libraries based on a free text indexing scheme. The method uses attributes automatically extracted from natural language IBM RISC System/6000 AIX 3 documentation to build a browsing hierarchy which accepts queries expressed in natural language.

Several software reuse environments use IR to index and retrieve the reusable assets. The RSL [5] system extracts free-text single-term indices from comments in source code files looking for keywords like "author", "date created", etc. REUSE [4] is an information retrieval system which stores software objects as textual documents in view of retrieval for reuse. Similarly, CATALOG [9] stores and retrieves C components each of which is individually characterized by a set of single-term indexing features automatically extracted from natural language headers of C programs.

Future work will be devoted to further investigate the factors that produce differences between the results achieved by the vector space and the probabilistic models. We are also working on the definition of an improved method to prune the ranked list of documents by analyzing the distribution of the similarity measures. Finally, we aim to a major improvement of the traceability link recovery process by removing the constraints that documents and code insist on the same vocabulary. In particular, our hypothesis of investigation is that for software systems available in multiple releases, a probabilistic mapping between the vocabularies of documents and source code can be statistically established.

## 6. Acknowledgements

We would like to express our gratitude to Ettore Merlo for the stimulating discussions we had during the work presented here. He also parsed the Albergate source code.

This research is supported by the project "Virtual Software Factory", funded by Ministero della Ricerca Scientifica e Tecnologica (MURST) and jointly carried out by EDS Italia Software, University of Sannio, University of Naples "Federico II", and University of Bari.

## References

[1] G. Antoniol, G. Canfora, G. Casazza, and A. DeLucia. Identifying the starting impact set of a maintenance request. In *Proceedings of the European Conference on Software Maintenance and Reengineering*, pages 227–230. Zurich, Switzerland, March 2000.

[2] G. Antoniol, G. Canfora, G. Casazza, A. DeLucia, and E. Merlo. Tracing object-oriented code into functional requirements. In *Proceedings of the 8th International Workshop on Program Comprehension*, pages 227–230. Limerick, Ireland, June 2000.

[3] G. Antoniol, G. Canfora, A. DeLucia, and E. Merlo. Recovering code to documentation links in object-oriented systems. In *Proceedings of the IEEE Working Conference on Reverse Engineering*, pages 136–144. Atlanta, Georgia, IEEE Comp. Soc. Press, October 1999.

[4] S. P. Arnold and S. L. Stepowey. The reuse system: Cataloging and retrieval of reusable software. In W. Tracz, editor, *Software Reuse: Emerging Technology*. IEEE Comp. Soc. Press, 1987.

[5] B. A. Burton, R. W. Aragon, S. A. Bailey, K. Koelher, and L. A. Mayes. The reusable software library. In W. Tracz, editor, *Software Reuse: Emerging Technology*, pages 129–137. IEEE Comp. Soc. Press, 1987.

[6] T. M. Cover and J. A. Thomas. *Elements of Information Theory*. Wiley Series in Telecommunications, John Wiley & Sons., New York, NY 10158-0012, 1992.

[7] R. DeMori. *Spoken dialogues with computers*. Academic Press, Inc., Orlando, Florida 32887, 1998.

[8] W. B. Frakes and R. Baeza-Yates. *Information Retrieval: Data Structures and Algorithms*. Prentice-Hall, Englewood Cliffs, NJ, 1992.

[9] W. B. Frakes and B. A. Nejmeh. Software reuse through information retrieval. In *Proceedings of 20-th Ann. HICSS, Kona (HI)*, pages 530–535, January 1987.

[10] D. Harman. Ranking algorithms. In *Information Retrieval: Data Structures and Algorithms*, pages 363–392. Prentice-Hall, Englewood Cliffs, NJ, 1992.

[11] J. Konclin and M. Bergen. gibis: a hypertext tool for exploratory policy discussion. *ACM Transaction on Office Information Systems*, 6(4):303–331, October 1988.

[12] Y. Maarek, D. Berry, and G. Kaiser. An information retrieval approach for automatically constructing software libraries. *IEEE Transactions on Software Engineering*, 17(8):800–813, 1991.

[13] F. A. C. Pinhero and A. G. J. An object-oriented tool for tracing requirements. *IEEE Software*, 13(2):52–64, March 1996.

[14] B. Ramesh and V. Dhar. Supporting systems development using knowledge captured during requirements engineering. *IEEE Transactions on Software Engineering*, 9(2):498–510, June 1992.

[15] G. Salton and C. Buckley. Term-weighting approaches in automatic text retrieval. *Information Processing and Management*, 24(5):513–523, 1988.

[16] R. J. Turver and M. Munro. An early impact analysis technique for software maintenance. *Journal of Software Maintenance - Research and Practice*, 6(1):35–52, 1994.

# Notes

# Reverse Engineering II

# Recovering Class Diagrams from Data-Intensive Legacy Systems

Giuseppe Antonio Di Lucca, Anna Rita Fasolino, Ugo De Carlini
dilucca/ fasolino/ decarl @unina.it

Dipartimento di Informatica e Sistemistica - Università di Napoli Federico II
Via Claudio 21, 80125 Naples, Italy

## Abstract

*Several reverse engineering methods for recovering objects from legacy systems have been proposed in the literature, but most of them neglect to identify the relationships among the objects, or recover only a part of them. This paper describes a method for recovering an O-O model together with the objects and relationships among them. The proposed approach integrates the results of reverse engineering of both the procedural code and the persistent data stores of the system, and exploits a number of heuristic criteria to obtain a class diagram. A preliminary experiment carried out to validate the method on a COBOL medium-sized system yielded encouraging results.*

## 1. Introduction

A large number of IT organisations have undertaken to migrate their legacy systems [1] towards open systems based on object-oriented technology and distributed client-server platforms. Migrating to Object-Oriented (O-O) technologies entails the definition of an O-O model of the application domain. One of the most immediate ways to obtain such a model may be based on an *ex-novo* object-oriented analysis of the domain. This model could describe all the relevant objects from the application domain, and their relationships.

Although feasible, such a solution may not be effective, as it does not take into account the domain knowledge and the expertise about the business rules, that are usually recorded only in the legacy code. Therefore, during the development of a replacement system, the knowledge encapsulated in the previous system should also be exploited.

An alternative solution to the problem of achieving an object-oriented model of the application domain is by reverse engineering the existing system. Several reverse engineering methods have been proposed for recovering objects from the code [5, 6, 7, 8, 9, 11, 12, 14, 15, 16,

17]. With these methods, objects can be searched for at different degrees of granularity: for instance, recovering coarse-grained objects can be centred around persistent data, whereas recovering fine-grained objects entails the selection of volatile data. The same methods also define approaches for recovering object operations, associating them with chunks of code at different granularity levels, such as programs, sub-routines, clusters of sub-routines, or program slices. For each of these approaches, user interaction is required to refine the initial results and assign a meaning to the objects identified.

The methods described in the literature mostly aim to recover objects from the code, but they do not usually address the problem of searching for the relationships among them and thus result in incomplete O-O models. Consequently, these methods are not effective for reverse engineering *data-intensive* systems, *i.e.* systems where much of the complexity lies in the data structures and in the relationships among them. Moreover, these approaches may not be practical when a knowledge of the relationships among objects is essential as a basis for designing the deployment of the objects on separate sites, as is usually required in a migration process towards distributed systems.

Other methods address the problem of recovering an O-O model together with the main relationships between objects. Some of them recover objects from files or database schemas, and the relationships between them are identified by analysing only the links established by the usage of key attributes and foreign keys defined in the file/database structures [3, 10]. However, such methods do not take into account data dependencies among data structures, that would have to be extracted by analysing the data-flow in the code, and so may result in incomplete O-O models.

A reverse engineering approach for recovering an object-oriented model from a non O-O legacy system is proposed in this paper. Since the approach produces the system class diagram, including both classes and their relationships, it can be successfully employed in migration processes, to obtain the initial target O-O model to be migrated towards new platforms. Analogously, the approach can be used in a replacement project to develop the preliminary requirements for a replacement system, ensuring that the features of the previous system are not overlooked or forgotten in the replacement one [2].

Recovering an O-O model from legacy systems is always a human-intensive process, where reverse engineers and their knowledge about the system and the application domain play the predominant role. The method proposed in this paper supports the work of reverse engineers by providing them with a set of *heuristic criteria*. The criteria are designed to identify candidate objects, their attributes, and relationships from *data-intensive systems*, that are strongly based on persistent data stores. The source code, the structure of the data stores, and the data flow are all analysed and taken into account by the heuristic criteria. More precisely, the criteria allow coarse-grained objects to be identified from persistent data stores, and their relationships to be defined by analysing the actual implementation strategies most commonly encountered in traditional systems for implementing relationships between related data structures. The criteria do not address the recovery of object methods, since other reverse engineering approaches described in the literature can be used for this purpose.

The method has been validated in a preliminary experiment carried out on a medium-sized COBOL system. The results of the experiment are presented in the paper.

The paper is structured as follows: section 2 illustrates the target O-O model and the data-intensive systems addressed in the paper. The proposed method is described in section 3, while section 4 illustrates the application of the method to a case study. Some conclusive remarks are made in section 5.

## 2. The Context

### 2.1. The target Object-Oriented Model

An Object-Oriented model of a given application domain includes a set of *classes*, representing the data abstractions from the application domain. Each class consists of a template to be used for instantiating *objects*, and encapsulates a set of attributes and a set of operations: the object's encapsulated attributes define the *state* of the object, while the state and the operations together define the object's *behaviour*.

An O-O model includes *associations* among classes, which describe both the structural relationships among the instances of the classes, and the usage relationships among them (client/server relationship). A peculiar characteristic of an O-O model is the *generalisation-specialisation* relationship, which is used by a class to inherit all or some of the attributes and services of a super-class, and to add more attributes and services.

Another kind of relationship among classes is the *whole-part* one, representing the structural relationship between a whole and its parts.

The O-O model to be recovered from data-intensive systems can be described by a class diagram including *classes, associations, generalisation-specialisation,* and *whole-part* relationships, according to the UML [4].

### 2.2. Data-intensive systems

A data-intensive system usually processes a large volume of persistent data, which typically correspond to the application domain elements whose values are relevant for the organisation's business goals. Such elements are usually stored in *files* in the file-system, or database *tables* from which they can be retrieved for processing.

The persistent data can be organised in data structures, such as the records of files, or the schemas of database tables. These data structures represent every single relevant element from the application domain. In the following, the term *record* will be used to refer to such data structures.

The ways the elements from the application domain interact, or are logically related, can be expressed in the code in terms of peculiar relationships among the corresponding records. Different relationships can be implemented in different ways, depending on the implementation mechanisms available, and on the specific interaction to be realised. The approach presented in this paper is based on the recovery of such interaction mechanisms.

## 3. Recovering the O-O model

The approach proposed in this paper for recovering an O-O model from a data intensive system preliminarily assumes each record description to be a candidate class, and record instances to be the objects of that class. Record fields constitute the class attributes, while programs provide the class operations, according to the method described in [7]. The relationships among candidate classes will be deduced by analysing both the record fields and their data-flow in the code. The proposed method provides a number of suitable heuristics for accomplishing this task.

Recovery of the O-O model is thus achieved by means of the following steps:

1  Identification of candidate classes;
2  Identification of associations among candidate classes;
3  Identification of generalisation-specialisation relationships;
4  Identification of whole-part relationships;
5  Validation of the model.

These steps are illustrated in the sub-sections below.

## 3.1. Identification of candidate classes

The first step in the method consists of the identification of the persistent data-stores managed by the system: each record, which is associated with a system data-store, is assumed to be a candidate class. Each class will be given the name of the associated record.

The existence of synonyms and homonyms between records compounds the difficulty of identifying candidate classes and their attributes. Two records are *synonymous* if they have different names but the same record structure, and thus correspond to the same element in the application domain. The descriptions of synonymous record structures may even be different, although such differences just consist of different levels of decomposition of the record fields. Two records are *homonymous* if they have the same name but a different record structure, and thus correspond to different elements in the application domain. In practice, homonymy is usually due to the usage of the same data store name in different programs, each of which defines a different record structure for a different data store.

During the first step, synonymous records should be associated with one and the same candidate class, as they may correspond to the same concept of the application domain. On the contrary, homonymous records should be associated with different candidate classes, as they may represent different concepts in the application domain. In both cases, a meaningful name has to be assigned to each candidate class.

The *attributes* of each candidate class can be defined as the fields of the record associated with the class. If synonymous records have been identified, and all these records have the same fields (*i.e.* the same names and structures), these fields will be assumed to be the class attributes. If, on the other hand, the number, name, and/or structure of the record fields are different, the class attributes will be defined as the record fields with the most detailed degree of granularity. In both cases, class attributes have to be given meaningful names.

A concept from the application domain should be assigned to each candidate class: this task requires the analysis of the available software documentation.

Candidate classes that do not represent meaningful abstractions from the application domain will be discarded.

## 3.2 Identification of *associations* among classes

The identification of association relationships among classes requires the analysis of both the structure of the records, and the data-flow involving their fields in the code. The aim of this analysis is to uncover those mechanisms usually employed in non-O-O programming languages to implement relationships among different records. For instance, relationships among two or more records typically take place through:

- *common fields* (particularly fields composing the record identifiers), *i.e.* the same attributes replicated in different records;
- *correspondence tables*, *i.e.* tables including the identifiers of different records;
- *data dependencies* among attributes belonging to different records.

Candidate association relationships between classes can be defined by applying the following heuristic criteria. Human intervention will then be required to validate the candidate associations, to assign them a concept, and to identify their direction and multiplicity. The knowledge about the application domain and the software engineer's expertise will be necessary for accomplishing this task.

Prior to applying these criteria, the record identifiers must be preliminarily recovered.

### Criterion A1

Identify couples of records having common fields, and define a candidate association between the classes corresponding to the records involved. Common fields that constitute record identifiers should be searched for particularly, and used to define an association. Common fields are not required to have the same name, but it is essential that they have the same meaning.

### Criterion A2

Identify each record whose fields can be partitioned into subsets, each of which corresponds to the identifiers of other records that do not have any attributes in common. A candidate association between the classes associated with the latter records can be defined.

This criterion exploits the correspondence tables mechanism used for implementing a relationship between records.

If $n$ different classes are involved in a relationship through a correspondence table, this criterion will indicate an *n-ary* association among the $n$ classes.

Of course, after applying this criterion, the class associated with the correspondence table will be discarded from the set of candidate classes.

### Criterion A3

Identify different records that are data-dependent on some fields, and define a candidate association between the classes associated with these records.

This association is more likely if the fields involved in the data dependency include those that constitute the record identifiers.

### Criterion A4

Identify different records whose fields are included in one and the same input/output form/report, and define a candidate association among the classes corresponding to these records.

The likelihood of this association depends strongly on the degree of correlation of the fields included in the form/report. In this case, human intervention is needful to decide whether the association actually exists.

### Criterion A5

Identify different records associated with the same file (*i.e.* a file with multiple records), and define a candidate association between the classes corresponding to these records.

Given an association between two classes, the association itself may have properties that can be modelled by an association class [4]. The following criterion *AC1* suggests how association classes can be identified.

### Criterion AC1

An association class between two associated classes is likely to exist if a third class, exclusively associated with the former ones, can be found. The likelihood of such an association class existing is greater if it includes attributes corresponding to the record identifiers of the other classes. The knowledge and expertise of the software engineer will be needed to decide whether the association class actually exists.

The candidate relationships obtained by applying the criteria listed above will have to be validated on the basis of the software engineer's knowledge and expertise in the application domain.

## 3.3 Identification of *generalisation-specialisation* relationships

The identification of generalisation-specialisation (Gen-Spec) relationships between a general class (the super-class) and a more specialised one (a sub-class) exploits the methods usually employed for implementing this kind of abstraction in procedural languages. For instance, these methods comprise:

- including both the super-class attributes and the sub-classes attributes in one and the same record, adding an attribute whose values discriminate among the sub-classes;

- employing as many records as there are sub-classes, and including the super-class attributes besides the sub-class attributes in each record;

- employing one record for the super-class and as many records as there are sub-classes. The record implementing the super-class will be related with each record implementing a sub-class either by common fields or by correspondence tables.

Gen-Spec relationships between classes can be defined by applying the heuristic criteria listed below. Some criteria apply to the association relationships recovered and aim to assess if they can be qualified as Gen-Spec relationships. In this case, the association must be discarded from the model and replaced with a suitable Gen-Spec relationship.

In the following criteria, the terms classes and records will be used as synonymous, as will attributes and fields.

### Criterion Gen-Spec1

Identify a class including, besides other attributes, different attribute sub-sets whose instances cannot be defined simultaneously, but assume values depending on the value of a discriminating attribute (or group of attributes). This criterion suggests defining a hierarchy with a different sub-class including each different attribute sub-set, and a super-class including the remaining common attributes.

As an example, consider a record including the generic attributes describing a publication (*i.e.* a book or a journal), book specific attributes, and journal specific ones, besides an attribute, 'type-of-publication', assuming only two values. Depending on the value of this attribute, either the book or the journal attributes will be defined in each record instance. In such a case, the criterion suggests defining a super-class (*i.e.* the publication class) including the set of generic attributes (*i.e.* the publication attributes) and a different sub-class containing the attributes for each specific type of publication (*i.e.* the book and journal classes).

*Criterion Gen-Spec2*

Identify classes that, having sets of common attributes besides disjointed ones, are linked by an association relationship (see criterion A1). This criterion suggests defining a candidate hierarchy with a super-class including the common attributes, and a different sub-class for each class that includes only the remaining attributes in each. In this case, the engineer's expertise and knowledge of the application domain will be used to establish the most adequate relationship between the Gen-Spec and the association. The set of common attributes should not only include attributes corresponding to the record identifiers (or part of them) because in such a case, an association rather than a generalisation-specialisation relationship might exist.

*Criterion Gen-Spec3*

Identify classes having all their attributes in common (*i.e.* all identical attributes): if they were not clustered previously because they were not synonymous, it will be necessary to check whether they are actually separate classes, or belong to a generalisation-specialisation hierarchy where the sub-classes have no more attributes other than those of the super-class.

In such a case, the criterion suggests defining a hierarchy, with a super-class including the set of common attributes, and a sub-class for each class including no other attributes than the super-class.

*Criterion Gen-Spec4*

Identify classes including only attributes constituting the identifiers of other classes (*i.e.* the identifiers of the records associated with these classes). This kind of class is used to implement a correspondence between other classes. In such a case, it will be necessary to check and decide, on the basis of the software engineer's expertise and knowledge of the application domain, whether the correspondence indicates only an association (see criterion A2), or a Gen-Spec relationship between classes. In the latter case, a suitable hierarchy will have to be defined.

After applying these criteria, the associations between sub-classes involved in a hierarchy should be assessed to decide whether they should be discarded or not. As a general rule, an association due to common attributes allocated in the super-class should be removed, while an association due to the attributes belonging to the sub-classes should be preserved.

## 3.4 Identification of *whole-part* relationships

Abstracting *whole-part* relationships from the code may be a difficult task, since both the association and the whole-part relationship may be implemented by the same mechanisms in the code. In this case, the software engineer's knowledge and expertise in the application domain is essential to distinguish the whole-part relationships.

The semantics of a whole-part relationship can be characterised with reference to three main features: the *lifetime dependence*, the *degree of dependence* and the *degree of sharing* among the 'whole' object and its 'part' objects [13]. The lifetime dependence indicates that the part objects are born and/or die together with the whole object; the dependence degree specifies whether the part objects may exist independently of the whole object or not; finally, the degree of sharing specifies whether the part objects are entirely owned by the whole objects, or else may be shared among other objects. The following criteria exploit this characterisation to identify whole-part relationships.

*Criterion Wp1*

Given a set of classes linked by an association relationship and the associated records, if analysis of the procedural code shows that each time a new instance of a record is created (*i.e.* written), new instances of the other records are created too, then a candidate whole-part relationship can be defined between these classes.

*Criterion Wp2*

Given a set of classes linked by an association relationship and the associated records, if analysis of the procedural code shows that each time an instance of a record is deleted, instances of the other records are deleted too, then a candidate whole-part relationship can be defined between these classes.

*Criterion Wp3*

Given a set of classes linked by an association relationship and the associated records, if analysis of the procedural code shows that each time a reference to a record instance is made, a reference to other record instances (one or more) is also executed, then a candidate whole-part relationship can be defined between these classes.

The UML subdivides the whole-part relationship into the categories of *aggregation* and *composition* relationships. The following general criteria provide an approach for recovering these.

*Criterion C1*

If two or more classes satisfy the Wp1 and Wp2 criteria simultaneously, a lifetime dependence between these classes can be deduced, and a candidate *composition* relationship between them can be defined.

### Criterion C2

If two or more classes satisfy the Wp1 and Wp3, or the Wp2 and Wp3 criteria simultaneously, a lifetime dependence between these classes can be deduced, and a candidate *composition* relationship between them can be defined.

### Criterion C3

If two or more classes satisfy at least one of the Wp1, Wp2, Wp3 criteria, so that a whole-part relationship between them has been deduced, and the 'whole' class objects are the exclusive owners of the 'part' objects (*i.e.* the part objects are not shared with other objects), a candidate *composition* relationship between the classes can be defined.

### Criterion C4

If two or more classes do not satisfy any of the C1, C2, C3 criteria, but they satisfy at least one of the Wp1, Wp2, Wp3 criteria, and the 'whole' class objects are not the exclusive owners of the 'part' objects (*i.e.* the part objects are shared with other objects), a candidate *aggregation* relationship between the classes can be defined.

### 3.5 Validation of the O-O model

The seventeen criteria illustrated above enable definition of a preliminary class diagram including candidate classes and relationships. The initial diagram should be submitted to a validation process, to assess the adequacy of each class and relationship it includes. The validation process has to verify that each recovered class, association, Gen-Spec, and whole-part relationship represents a meaningful abstraction from the application domain; moreover, association and Gen-Spec relationships must not overlap.

Both the software engineer's experience and the knowledge of the application domain will be required to validate the model.

## 4. A Case-Study

A preliminary experiment was carried out to validate the method proposed in the paper. An information system written in COBOL was used as a case study, and its class diagram was recovered using the method. The recovered diagram was validated, and the validation results were used to obtain preliminary indications about the validity of the method. In practice, the effectiveness of the method

was assessed on the basis of the number of candidate classes and relationships discarded from the initial model.

The main characteristics of the system, the tools employed during the experiment, the experimental procedure adopted, and the results obtained are described below. To conclude, the validity of the method is discussed with reference to the validation results.

### 4.1 Experimental materials and tools

An information system written in COBOL, comprising 103 programs and 90 copybooks, of an overall size of about 200 KLOC, was chosen for the experiment. The software system managed a University hall and residence and was designed by adopting a functional decomposition approach. Different functional requirements were implemented by different subsystems.

A commercial tool was used for the static analysis of the source code to extract the information required by the method. The static analyser stored the analysis results in a proprietary repository, that allowed only predefined queries and reports to be produced. To overcome this limit, the information about the data stores and the record structures provided by the tool was exported to a relational database, from which the further information required could be obtained.

### 4.2 Experimental procedure and results

The procedure for recovering the O-O model required four initial steps, during which the heuristic criteria were applied and their results were preliminarily validated. In a fifth step, the recovered class diagram was submitted to a validation process.

The description of the above steps and the results obtained are reported below.

*1. Recovering candidate classes*

In the first step, the source code was statically analysed to identify its *persistent* data stores and the associated records. The subject system employed only files as persistent data stores, which were identified by analysing both the *input-output section* of the *environment divisions,* and the *file section* of the *data divisions*. During the analysis, files assigned with mass-storage devices, such as disks, were searched for, while files assigned with other I/O devices, such as printers, were ignored. This analysis yielded 53 disk files, whose names are listed in Table 1.

Files that did not represent meaningful abstractions from the application domain were searched for in the list. Temporary files, files used only in sort/merge operations,

**Table 1: The system data stores**

| | | |
|---|---|---|
| ACCOUNTS.LIS | OUTSCR.TMP | _PROCESS.DAT |
| AHISTORY.AUD | PAYMENT.AUD | _REQUEST.DAT |
| ARCHIVE.ARC | REPAY.AUD | _RECEIPT.TMP |
| ARCHIVE.TMP | SELECT.TMP | _ROOM.DAT |
| CASH.DAT | SORT.TMP | _ROOMINV.DAT |
| CHARGES.AUD | UNSORT.TMP | _SORT.TMP |
| CHARGES.DAT | _BATCH.DAT | _USAGE.DAT |
| COLLEGE.GNT | _CITIZEN.DAT | _USER.DAT |
| CONFIG.DAT | _DAMAGE.DAT | BACKUP-FILE |
| CONIN.AUD | _DUTY.DAT | CONFIG-FILE |
| CONOUT.AUD | _DEPART.DAT | DIARY-FILE |
| CREDIT.AUD | _FACULTY.DAT | DIARY2-FILE |
| DEPOSIT.AUD | _HISTORY.DAT | ERROR-FILE |
| HARRIS.LBT | _IN.TMP | INSTALL-FILE |
| INSCR.TMP | _ITEMINV.DAT | JOURNAL-FILE |
| MASTER.DAT | _LAST.DAT | TEXT-FILE |
| NAMES.TMP | _OUT.TMP | ZLIST-FILE |
| NONCASH.DAT | _PREFER.DAT | |

**Table 2: The system data stores after synonymous/homonymous analysis**

| | | |
|---|---|---|
| ACCOUNTS.LIS | NONCASH.DAT | _PROCESS.DAT |
| AHISTORY.AUD | PAYMENT.AUD | _REQUEST.DAT |
| ARCHIVE.ARC | REPAY.AUD | _RECEIPT.TMP |
| CASH.DAT | _CITIZEN.DAT | _ROOM.DAT |
| CHARGE.AUD | _DAMAGE.DAT | _ROOMINV.DAT |
| CHARGES.DAT | _DUTY.DAT | _USER.DAT |
| CONIN.AUD | _DEPART.DAT | DIARY-FILE |
| CONOUT.AUD | _FACULTY.DAT | DIARY2-FILE |
| CREDIT.AUD | _HISTORY.DAT | JOURNAL-FILE |
| DEPOSIT.AUD | _ITEMINV.DAT | |
| MASTER.DAT | _PREFER.DAT | |

**Table 3: The classes associated with the data store records**

| | | |
|---|---|---|
| _CITIZEN-RECORD | CREDIT-RECORD | PAYMENT-RECORD |
| IN-CONTROL-RECORD | DAMAGE-RECORD | PREFERENCES-RECORD |
| OUT-CONTROL-RECORD | DEPOSIT-RECORD | PROCESSED-ROOM |
| _DEPART-RECORD | DIARY-RECORD | RECEIPT-RECORD |
| ACCOUNTS-HEADER | DUTY-RECORD | REPAY-RECORD |
| ACCOUNTS-RECORD | FACULTY-RECORD | REQUEST-RECORD |
| ARCHIVE-RECORD | HISTORY-RECORD | ROOM-RECORD |
| AUDIT-HISTORY-RECORD | ITEMINV-RECORD | ROOMINV-RECORD |
| CASH-RECORD | JOURNAL-RECORD | USER-RECORD |
| CHARGE-RECORD | MASTER-RECORD | |
| CHARGES-RECORD | NONCASH-RECORD | |

files just storing information about the system installation/configuration, and files storing the error messages were found and discarded. After this refinement step, the 31 files shown in Table 2 were obtained. Among them, the temporary file _RECEIPT.TMP was not discarded, due to its relevance in the application domain: it represented the payment receipt given to a college resident. This file was a temporary one, because it was removed from the file system once the receipts it stored had been printed.

The file list was further assessed to detect synonymous and homonymous files. Just two synonymous files, namely DIARY-FILE and DIARY2-FILE, were found (and their records were associated with a same class). Finally, a file with multiple records was identified, the file ACCOUNTS.LIS, that included the records ACCOUNTS-HEADER and ACCOUNTS-RECORD, which were associated with two distinct classes.

After these refinement steps, records associated with the resulting files were assumed to be candidate classes. The 31 identified classes are reported in Table 3 with the same names as the associated record.

At this point, record identifiers were searched for. With respect to the *indexed* and *relative* file records (13 *indexed* and 1 *relative* file were managed by the system), the fields declared as *record key*, *alternate record key*

**Table 4: The associations identified between classes**

| CLASS | CLASS | Criterion |
|---|---|---|
| ACCOUNTS-RECORD | ACCOUNTS-HEADER | A5 |
| ACCOUNTS-RECORD | CHARGE-RECORD | A3 |
| ACCOUNTS-RECORD | CHARGES-RECORD | A3 |
| ACCOUNTS-RECORD | CREDIT-RECORD | A3 |
| ACCOUNTS-RECORD | DAMAGE-RECORD | A3 |
| ACCOUNTS-RECORD | MASTER-RECORD | A1 |
| ACCOUNTS-RECORD | PAYMENT-RECORD | A3 |
| ACCOUNTS-RECORD | REPAY-RECORD | A3 |
| AUDIT-HISTORY-RECORD | USER-RECORD | A1 |
| CASH-RECORD | CHARGE-RECORD | A1 |
| CASH-RECORD | CREDIT-RECORD | A1 |
| CASH-RECORD | MASTER-RECORD | A1 |
| CASH-RECORD | REPAY-RECORD | A1 |
| CASH-RECORD | ROOM-RECORD | A1 |
| CHARGE-RECORD | CREDIT-RECORD | A1 |
| CHARGE-RECORD | JOURNAL-RECORD | A3 |
| CHARGE-RECORD | MASTER-RECORD | A1 |
| CHARGE-RECORD | REPAY-RECORD | A1 |
| CHARGE-RECORD | ROOM-RECORD | A1 |
| CHARGES-RECORD | MASTER-RECORD | A1 |
| CREDIT-RECORD | JOURNAL-RECORD | A3 |
| CREDIT-RECORD | MASTER-RECORD | A1 |
| CREDIT-RECORD | ROOM-RECORD | A1 |
| DEPOSIT-RECORD | CASH-RECORD | A3 |
| DEPOSIT-RECORD | CHARGE-RECORD | A1 |
| DEPOSIT-RECORD | CREDIT-RECORD | A1 |
| DEPOSIT-RECORD | JOURNAL-RECORD | A3 |
| DEPOSIT-RECORD | MASTER-RECORD | A1 |
| DEPOSIT-RECORD | NONCASH-RECORD | A3 |
| DEPOSIT-RECORD | REPAY-RECORD | A1 |
| DEPOSIT-RECORD | ROOM-RECORD | A1 |
| DIARY-RECORD | DUTY-RECORD | A3 |
| HISTORY-RECORD | ROOM-RECORD | A3 |
| IN-CONTROL-RECORD | ROOM-RECORD | A1 |
| ITEMINV-RECORD | ROOMINV-RECORD | A1 |
| ITEMINV-RECORD | ROOM-RECORD | A1 |
| JOURNAL-RECORD | ACCOUNTS-RECORD | A3 |
| JOURNAL-RECORD | CHARGES-RECORD | A3 |
| JOURNAL-RECORD | DAMAGE-RECORD | A3 |
| JOURNAL-RECORD | MASTER-RECORD | A3 |
| JOURNAL-RECORD | PAYMENT-RECORD | A3 |
| MASTER-RECORD | _CITIZEN-RECORD | A1 |
| MASTER-RECORD | _DEPART-RECORD | A1 |
| MASTER-RECORD | ARCHIVE-RECORD | A1 |
| MASTER-RECORD | FACULTY-RECORD | A1 |

| CLASS | CLASS | Criterion |
|---|---|---|
| MASTER-RECORD | IN-CONTROL-RECORD | A1 |
| MASTER-RECORD | PREFERENCES-RECORD | A1 |
| MASTER-RECORD | REQUEST-RECORD | A1 |
| MASTER-RECORD | ROOM-RECORD | A1 |
| NONCASH-RECORD | CHARGE-RECORD | A1 |
| NONCASH-RECORD | CREDIT-RECORD | A1 |
| NONCASH-RECORD | MASTER-RECORD | A1 |
| NONCASH-RECORD | REPAY-RECORD | A1 |
| NONCASH-RECORD | ROOM-RECORD | A1 |
| OUT-CONTROL-RECORD | ACCOUNTS-RECORD | A3 |
| OUT-CONTROL-RECORD | MASTER-RECORD | A1 |
| OUT-CONTROL-RECORD | ROOM-RECORD | A1 |
| PAYMENT-RECORD | CASH-RECORD | A3 |
| PAYMENT-RECORD | CHARGE-RECORD | A1 |
| PAYMENT-RECORD | CREDIT-RECORD | A1 |
| PAYMENT-RECORD | DEPOSIT-RECORD | A1 |
| PAYMENT-RECORD | MASTER-RECORD | A1 |
| PAYMENT-RECORD | NONCASH-RECORD | A3 |
| PAYMENT-RECORD | REPAY-RECORD | A1 |
| PAYMENT-RECORD | ROOM-RECORD | A1 |
| PREFERENCES-RECORD | PROCESSED-ROOM | A1 |
| PREFERENCES-RECORD | REQUEST-RECORD | A1 |
| PREFERENCES-RECORD | ROOM-RECORD | A1 |
| PROCESSED-ROOM | ROOM-RECORD | A1 |
| RECEIPT-RECORD | ACCOUNTS-RECORD | A3 |
| RECEIPT-RECORD | CASH-RECORD | A3 |
| RECEIPT-RECORD | DEPOSIT-RECORD | A3 |
| RECEIPT-RECORD | JOURNAL-RECORD | A3 |
| RECEIPT-RECORD | MASTER-RECORD | A1 |
| RECEIPT-RECORD | NONCASH-RECORD | A3 |
| RECEIPT-RECORD | PAYMENT-RECORD | A3 |
| RECEIPT-RECORD | ROOM-RECORD | A1 |
| REPAY-RECORD | CREDIT-RECORD | A1 |
| REPAY-RECORD | JOURNAL-RECORD | A3 |
| REPAY-RECORD | MASTER-RECORD | A1 |
| REPAY-RECORD | ROOM-RECORD | A1 |
| REQUEST-RECORD | ROOM-RECORD | A1 |
| ROOMINV-RECORD | ROOM-RECORD | A1 |
| ROOM-RECORD | DAMAGE-RECORD | A1 |
| USER-RECORD | DIARY-RECORD | A1 |
| USER-RECORD | DUTY-RECORD | A1 |
| USER-RECORD | MASTER-RECORD | A3 |
| USER-RECORD | RECEIPT-RECORD | A1 |
| USER-RECORD | ROOM-RECORD | A3 |

and *relative key* in the *select* statements from the *input-output sections* were used as record identifiers.

Finally, the methods associated with these classes were recovered using the approach described in [7].

### 2. Recovering association relationships

The five criteria illustrated in section 3.2 allowed candidate association relationships to be defined among the classes. As far as *criterion A1* was concerned, it required querying the database to search for couples of records with common fields (and in particular common fields corresponding to record identifiers). A relationship was defined between the classes involved in each couple.

This query resulted in 58 associations. No relationship was found when applying *criterion A2*, since no record implemented correspondence tables. Thanks to the facilities offered by the static analyser, data dependencies among the attributes of different classes were searched for (*criterion A3*). In this case, an association was defined between couples of classes whose attributes were linked by a data dependency. This criterion produced 30 additional associations between classes. Finally, *criterion A4* did not produce any new relationship, while another relationship was found thanks to *criterion A5*.

The final results are illustrated in Table 4, that shows 89 couples of classes linked by an association, and, for each

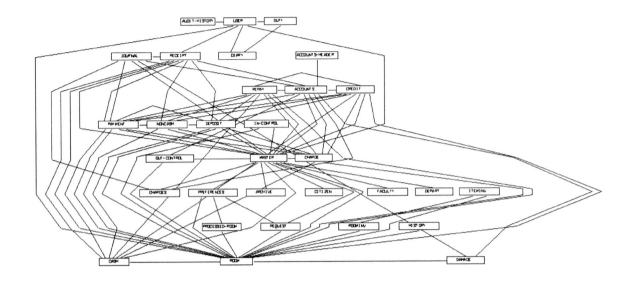

**Figure 1: The initial Class Diagram**

association, the criterion that produced it.

Figure 1 shows the initial class diagram representing all the classes and the associations found (in the diagram the suffix *–record* in each class name is not shown). The diagram shows how the system is centered on the `Master` class, which is responsible for college residents information and operations, and the `Room` class, responsible for college rooms information and operations. These classes are involved in most relationships (the `Master` class is involved in 22 relationships and the `Room` class in 19). The remaining classes are responsible for information and operations concerning:

— Room booking, confirmation, check-in and check-out (classes REQUEST, PREFERENCES, PROCESSED-ROOM, IN-CONTROL, OUT-CONTROL)

— Room decoration, inventory, charges for damage and resident housekeeping duty (classes ITEMINV, ROOMINV, DAMAGE, USER, DUTY, DIARY)

— Financial administration (classes DEPOSIT, PAYMENT, RECEIPT, CHARGES, ACCOUNTS, ACCOUNTS-HEADER, CREDIT, REPAY, JOURNAL, CHARGE, CASH, NONCASH)

— Auditing and statistics (classes AUDIT-HISTORY, HISTORY, ARCHIVE)

Other classes are responsible for general information about residents' citizenship, Faculties and Departments (classes CITIZEN, FACULTY, DEPART), while the ACCOUNTS-HEADER class is a *singleton* class and stores pointers to file records of residents' accounts.

*3. Identifying generalisation/ specialisation relationships*

*Gen-Spec2 criterion* allowed a set of common attributes among the classes Payment, Charge, Credit, Repay, Deposit, Cash and NonCash to be identified; these classes represented financial matters, such as rent charging or payment made. A Gen-spec hierarchy among these classes was introduced, by grouping together the common attributes (date, name, room, amount) in a new class named Book_Keeping that became the super-class of the hierarchy. The *Gen-Spec2 criterion* also allowed two inner Gen-Spec structures to be recognised: a first structure involved the Cash, NonCash and Payment classes, and a second one the Cash, NonCash and Deposit classes, that recorded how a payment or a deposit were made (by cash or not): in the resulting hierarchies, the class Payment, as well as the class Deposit, inherit from the classes Cash and NonCash (see Figure 2-(a)).

All the associations among the Payment, Charge, Credit, Repay, Deposit, Cash and NonCash classes, previously defined, were removed and replaced with the new Gen-Spec relationships, while all the other associations these classes had with other classes were reorganised: in particular the relationships all the

60

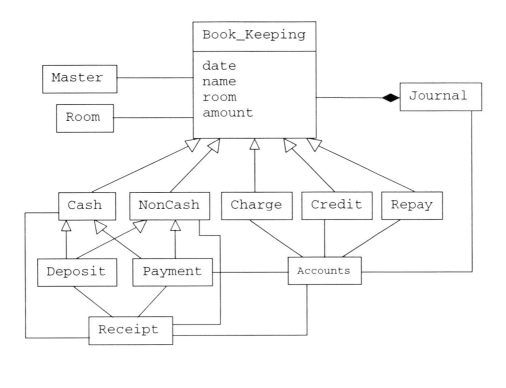

(a)

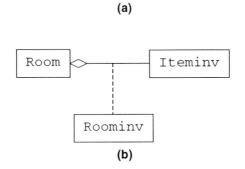

(b)

**Figure 2: The class diagram portions representing the Gen-Spec and Whole-part relationships**

61

sub-classes had with the `Master` and `Room` classes were referred to the `Book_Keeping` super-class, while the ones which were peculiar to each sub-class were left unchanged. No further Gen-Spec relationships were recognised when the remaining Gen-Spec criteria were applied.

### 4. Identifying whole-part relationships

The association relationships were then again analysed according to the criteria defined in section 3.3, , to identify potential whole-part relationships between classes.

*Wp1 criterion* allowed a composition relationship between `Book_Keeping` and `Journal` classes to be defined: the latter consisted of the financial matters represented by the `Book_Keeping` class.

*C4 criterion* allowed an aggregation relationship between the `Room` and the `Iteminv` classes to be recognised: the latter class represents the pieces of furniture belonging to the rooms, thus a `room` is considered to consist of the `iteminv` it contains.

Moreover, the class `Roominv` was recognised as an association class (*criterion A1*): it indicated the number of each `iteminv` contained in the rooms (see Figure 2-(b)).

The class diagram shown in Figure 1 was therefore modified, according to the additional relationships recovered.

### 5. Validating the class diagram

As a conclusive step of the experiment, a final concept assignment process was carried out to validate the complete class diagram. The software documentation available, including the system user guide, and the knowledge of a domain expert were used in this phase. The validation process produced the following results: four classes (AUDIT-HISTORY, HISTORY, ARCHIVE, PROCESSED-ROOM) were discarded from the model, because they did not represent meaningful abstractions from the domain. The former three classes were associated with records of files storing statistical data, while the latter was associated with a file including just summary information used for room processing. As a consequence, the relationships between these classes and the others in the diagram were also discarded.

Finally, all the remaining classes and relationships were assigned a concept belonging to the application domain.

### 4.3 Assessing the effectiveness of the method

The case study results were used for preliminary assessment of the effectiveness of the proposed method.

The effectiveness was expressed by the *adequacy* of the method, that is the method's property to recover abstractions (both classes and relationships) that can be assigned a meaningful concept from the application domain. The following simple measure of *adequacy* was used:

$$Adequacy = \frac{|N|}{|M|} \times 100\%$$

where $M$ is the set of abstractions selected by the method, $N$ is the subset of components in $M$ that can be associated with a concept of the application domain, and $|M|$ and $|N|$ denote the number of components in the $M$ and $N$ sets.

With respect to the recovered classes, the adequacy yielded a value of 87%, since 31 candidate classes were recovered by the method, while 27 were validated. As to the associations, the adequacy yielded a value of 93% (*i.e.* 89 candidate associations and 83 validated ones), while with the Gen-spec and whole-part relationships, the adequacy was equal to 100% in both cases.

The high values for adequacy obtained showed that the method was very effective. Of course, given the exploratory nature of the case study, this result cannot be generalised. A wider experiment, involving more than one system, and different application domains, should be designed and carried out to extend the validity of this experiment.

## 5. Conclusions

Recovering a class diagram from a non O-O legacy system is a preliminary step in most migration processes towards O-O distributed technologies. The relationships among the objects making up the diagram play an important role when designing the deployment of various system parts (*i.e.* the objects) in a distributed architecture, as is usually required in a migration process towards distributed platforms.

A reverse engineering method for recovering an Object-Oriented model from a non O-O legacy system has been proposed in the paper. The method focuses on data-intensive systems strongly based on persistent data stores, and employs seventeen heuristic criteria as a means for recovering the classes and relationships composing the system class diagram.

A preliminary experiment has been carried out to validate the proposed approach. A COBOL system about 200 KLOC in size was used as the case study, and its class diagram was recovered using the method. Finally, the diagram was validated by a concept assignment process, and the validation results were used to obtain preliminary indications about the validity of the method.

The method's effectiveness was assessed on the basis of the adequacy of the abstractions recovered (both classes and relationships). The high values for adequacy obtained (about 90%) show how effective the method is. However, other aspects of effectiveness, such as the completeness of the model recovered and the precision of the abstractions recovered, should be taken into account in a wider validation experiment. These will be addressed in future work.

Another point requiring further investigation is application of the approach in a migration process. The migration strategy should also aim to allocate the objects on the basis of the coupling deriving from the various relationships existing among them. Hence, the coupling between the objects of the recovered model should be assessed and exploited in the migration project. The selection of suitable metrics for evaluating this coupling, and the definition and validation a migration strategy guided by coupling measurements will also be addressed in future work.

# References

[1]     K. Bennett, "Legacy Systems: Coping with Success", IEEE Software, Jan. 1995, pp. 19- 23

[2]     Blaha, M. R., and Premerlani, W. J. (1995) 'Observed Idiosyncrasies of Relational Databases Design' Proc. of 2nd *Working Conference on Reverse Engineering*, Toronto, Canada, IEEE Computer Society Press, 116-125

[3]     M. Blaha, "An Industrial Example of Database Reverse Engineering", *Proc. of 6th Working Conference on Reverse Engineering*, IEEE CS Press, Los Alamitos, CA, 1999, pp. 196- 203

[4]     G. Booch, J. Rumbaugh, I. Jacobson, *'The Unified Modeling Language User Guide'*, Addison Wesley, 1999

[5]     P.T. Breuer, H. Haughton, and K. Lano, "Reverse-engineering COBOL via formal methods", *J. of Software Maintenance: Research and Practice*, vol. 5, 1993, pp. 13-35

[6]     G. Canfora, A. Cimitile, and M. Munro, "An improved algorithm for identifying reusable objects in code", *Software Practice and Experiences*, vol. 26, no. 1, 1996, pp. 24-48

[7]     A. Cimitile, A. De Lucia, G.A. Di Lucca, and A.R. Fasolino, "Identifying objects in legacy systems using design metrics", *The Journal of Systems and Software*, vol. 44, January 1999, pp. 199-211.

[8]     H. Gall and R. Klösch, "Finding objects in procedural programs: an alternative approach", *Proc. of 2nd Working Conference on Reverse Engineering*, Toronto, Canada, 1995, IEEE CS Press, pp. 208-216

[9]     J. George and B.D. Carter, "A strategy for mapping from function oriented software models to object oriented software models", *ACM Software Engineering Notes*, vol. 21, no. 2, March 1996, pp. 56-63

[10]    U. Kölsch, "Object-Oriented Re-engineering of Information Systems in a Heterogeneous Distributed Environment', *Proc. of 5th Working Conference on Reverse Engineering,* IEEE CS Press, Los Alamitos, CA, 1998, pp. 104- 114

[11]    S. Liu and N. Wilde, "Identifying objects in a conventional procedural language: an example of data design recovery", *Proc. of Conference on Software Maintenance*, San Diego, CA, 1990, IEEE CS Press, pp. 266-271.

[12]    P.E. Livadas and T. Johnson, "A new approach to finding objects in programs", *J. of Software Maintenance: Research and Practice*, vol. 6, 1994, pp. 249-260

[13]    R. Motschnig-Pitrik, J. Kaasboll, 'Part-Whole Relationship Categories and Their Application in Object-Oriented Analysis', IEEE Transactions on Knowledge and Data Engineering, vo. 11, no. 5, Sept/Oct. 1999

[14]    P. Newcomb and G. Kotik, "Reengineering procedural into object-oriented systems", *Proc. of 2nd Working Conference on Reverse Engineering*, Toronto, Canada, 1995, IEEE CS Press, pp. 237-249

[15]    H. M. Sneed, "Object-oriented COBOL recycling", *Proc. of 3rd Working Conference on Reverse Engineering*, Monterey, CA, 1996, IEEE CS Press, pp. 169-178

[16]    G.V. Subramaniam, E.J. Bwirne, "Deriving an object model from legacy FORTRAN code", *Proc. of International Conference on Software Maintenance*, Monterey, CA, 1996, IEEE CS Press, pp. 3-12

[17]    A.S. Yeh, D.R. Harris, and H.B. Rubenstein, "Recovering abstract data types and object instances from a conventional procedural language", *Proc. of 2nd Working Conference on Reverse Engineering*, Toronto, Canada, 1995, IEEE CS Press, pp. 227-236

# An Alternative Source Code Analysis

James E. Kimble, Jr.
*Department of Computer Science
& Information Systems
Mount Union College
Alliance, OH 44601-3993
kimbleje@muc.edu*

Lee J. White
*Department of Computer Engineering
& Science
Case Western Reserve University
Cleveland, OH 44106-7071
leew@eecs.cwru.edu*

## Abstract

*All aspects of Software Engineering strive toward guaranteeing that an implemented algorithm perform the intended tasks. This paper will describe results in investigating the relationship between specifications and re-engineered code for data processing programs in COBOL, and develop strategies for assigning significance to identified differences. A modified **F(p)** notation representation of the program will be manipulated into a standard form, from which features, called **program points**, will be used to guide complexity reduction. Finally, backbone elements called **threads** will be identified to explore the **equivalence** between the specifications and the program, where each **thread** will represent a different behavior mode of the program.*
*Keywords: Reengineering, program equivalence, testing, code analysis, legacy code.*

## 1. Introduction

Software engineering as a discipline focuses on entirely different, yet related approaches in moving between specifications and code. Forward engineering attempts to produce accurate code from concise specifications through various techniques ranging from specification-based code testing to object orientation. Re-engineering endeavors to reorganize existing systems, often during maintenance efforts, in ways that both reflect lessons learned from forward engineering and produce greater ease in modifications. Reverse engineering tries to garner understanding from existing programs and other documentation [1], [2], [9], [17].

In all of these directions, clear distinctions are made between specifications and the implementing code and between the testing methods of each. Because so much legacy COBOL exists, the time and effort put into maintenance of this code is huge [18]; simplifying the process and/or increasing the accuracy of maintenance results would be a great benefit.

Our goal is to improve maintenance by semi-automatically relating the specifications directly to the code, thereby gaining confidence that the produced code implements the specifications before stand-alone testing even begins. In order to do this, we must be able to create comparable models of both the specification and the code before analysis can be done. **Control flow diagrams** (CFDs) will be used to model the control structure of the specification and code. Each node of the control flow graph will be associated with various computational responsibilities not specifically indicated in the structure of the CFD: inputs, assignment of variables, and imposition of constraints due to predicates and other assumptions concerning variables. Section 2 will describe the overall computational model, with section 2.1 presenting our view of the **computational elements** associated with each node of the CFD. For insights into control flow, in addition to the CFD representation, we will need to use **blocks,** also described in section 2.1, as well as a linear notation for control flow developed by Canfora et. al. [7], called the **F(p) notation;** this notation is described in section 2.2, with some extensions in section 2.3.

Section 3 describes the graphical control graph model, first providing a graph theoretical analysis in section 3.1; this leads to the concept of **threads,** each of which indicate a different mode of the program or specification behavior (Jorgensen calls these feasible paths [13]). In making comparisons between the specification and the code, we will be working with different levels of abstraction; similarities and possible differences will be obtained through analysis involving a **homomorphism** between the structures of the CFD representations. These homomorphic mappings will be described in section 3.2, together with different types of equivalence we might try to show between the specification and code.

Now given two representations at the same level of abstraction, we would like to have an automatic method to decide whether the two are equivalent just based on the syntactic characteristics alone. The reason this problem is complicated is that many computations can be done in different order, and it is necessary to have a method to decide which of these differences are arbitrary and which constitute an important distinction between the two representations in that they do not accomplish the same computation. For this purpose, we present a brief description of a canonical form algorithm in section 4. It should be recognized that the equivalence of two programs cannot be established syntactically, but would require sophisticated semantic analysis. Even at that, the problem is essentially undecidable. All our canonical form algorithm can hope to do is to show that two very similar representations are computationally equivalent. If they differ in canonical form, we cannot conclude that they are necessarily nonequivalent.

In this study, a series of programs well known to the author are used, all written following a strong set of conventions and using a small set of the COBOL language. An empirical study is given in section 5, where our methods are applied to student COBOL programs, illustrating how similarities and differences between them can be detected. Limitations and lessons learned are also given, together with comments on scalability. Related work is discussed in section 6, and a summary and future work indicated in section 7.

## 2. Computational Model

This analysis relies upon both a concise set of graphical ideas (which will be described in section **3**), as well as a clear computational view. The program listing consists of a sequence of statements, each of which calls for some algebraic or operational function to be performed. Variables are given values and constraints are built in and declared by these statements.

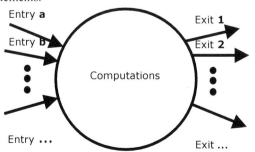

**Figure 1: Model of a Computational Element**

### 2.1. Computational Elements

A **computational element** (see Figure 1) consists of a succession of variable definitions and dynamic predicate evaluations. Computations in a computational element depend upon the path by which entry has been made, and that dependence includes a historical record of the variable values defined on that path and any constraints between those variables. A state change occurs in a computational element when variables are given new values, which could include values specified by interactive input. The computation also contains any interactive external outputs provided by the computational element. The path by which one leaves the computational element is likewise determined by the computational results and carries variables defined as part of the final state of the computational element, including all constraints appropriate for that exit path.

Although defined in the graphical framework, variable scopes are essentially computational. The demarcations of scope boundaries are performed in the content of the statements, in the assignments and inputs which are evident as part of the code itself. Nonetheless, the definition of scope will be clearer if left until the graphical section 3.1.

Program structure is often investigated with respect to blocks, and typically defined in terms of scopes. For program control structure, syntactical markers called **program points** can be identified. From these a stronger definition of a block can be stated, for creation and termination of blocks are inextricably related to the control structures that contain them.

Program points, in general, are locations in control structures at which control flow can follow multiple paths. **Initial program points** pass control to a structure, and control is passed from the structure by its corresponding **terminal program point**. For example, in Figure 2, lines 2, 5, and 10 represent initial program points of a *perform until*, an *if-then* and an *if-then-else* and the respective terminal points are contained in lines 9, 8, and 13. Occasionally, **marker program points** occur which merely designate boundaries between task lists in the alternate paths of the control structure: the line after line 11 contains no algebraic or operational function but only the marker program point *else*. Ordinarily, initial and terminal program points exist in pairs; marker program points can optionally occur within these pairs but need not be paired. For consistency, a program's code should be considered to be preceded and followed by virtual program points, functionally equivalent to attaching bookend 'no-op' operations: at the front will be a terminal program point and an initial program point will follow the program.

```
1  MOVE SPACE TO USER-FLAG,DESIRED-COLOR
2  PERFORM UNTIL USER-OK OR QUIT
3      DISPLAY "Enter desired color"
              " (or '\' to quit): "
4      ACCEPT DESIRED-COLOR
5      IF NOT QUIT
         THEN
6          DISPLAY "Is " DESIRED-COLOR
                   " correct? "
7          ACCEPT USER-FLAG
8      END-IF
9  END-PERFORM.
10 IF USER-OK
      THEN
11     DISPLAY "Color acquired."
      ELSE
12     DISPLAY "No color chosen."
13 END-IF.
```

**Figure 2 - Sample COBOL program segment**

A **block** is then defined as: a contiguous set of program statements, possible empty, bounded by two program points, one before and one after, such that any one statement is executed only when the entire set is sequentially executed. An initial program point is attached to the preceding block; a terminal program point is part of the following block. Marker program points are not part of any block. By this definition, blocks can occur with the following combinations: no program points (lines 6-7 in Figure 2), just a single initial program point (3-5, with an initial program point in line 5), just a single terminal program point (8), or exactly one each of the initial and terminal types (9-10).

### 2.2. F(p) Notation

Canfora et. al. [7] described a notation that symbolically represents procedural program structure. This form is very useful as it:
1) is linear,
2) captures the essence and important details of the program, and
3) is easily manipulated for our use.

Three main statement structures are: the sequence (represented as a block **b**), selection (**if.(b$_1$ + b$_2$)** or **if.(b$_1$ + $\phi$)** where $\phi$ represents a null path), and iteration (**w.( b$_1$ + $\phi$)** would be a **while** loop – a **repeat** loop also exists). In a program these structures are separated by a slash and subscripts are used to differentiate items of the same structure type, e.g., **b$_1$ / w$_1$.( b$_2$ + $\phi$) / b$_3$**.

### 2.3. Extensions

For purposes of analyzing COBOL programs, we have found it useful to make a number of extensions and modifications. Often, sequences need to be broken into discrete parts, e.g., a block **b$_1$** may alternatively be represented by **b$_{1a}$ / b$_{1b}$ /...** Input and output statements need to be handled separately and so are represented as **in** and **out**. Variables defined and used by a structure can be included in parentheses; for example **b$_1$(x/y)** would indicate that **x** is defined in the block and the value of **y** is used. Note that **w(x)**, **if(x)**, and **out(x)** mean that only the value of **x** is used; the "/" is unnecessary. Computational paths are enumerated by expanding on the options of the selection and iteration structures. For example, given the following program and its extended representation:

```
input c;              in_1 (c) / b_1(d) / w_2 (c).(b_2(d/d) /
d = 5;                in_3 (c) + φ) /
while(c) {            if_4 (d).(out_5 (d) + φ) / b_3(d)
  d = d + 5;
  input c;
}
if (d...)
  out d;
d = 7;
```

we can expand it to show the possible paths through the program:

in$_1$ (c) / b$_1$(d) / w$_2$ (c).(b$_2$(d/d) / in$_3$ (c) + $\phi$) / if$_4$ (d).(out$_5$ (d) + $\phi$) / b$_3$(d) =

in$_1$ (c) / b$_1$(d) / (c).(b$_2$(d/d) / in$_3$ (c)).(~c) / (d).(out$_5$ (d)) / b$_3$(d) +
    [*while* loop used; *if* is true]
in$_1$ (c) / b$_1$(d) / (c).(b$_2$(d/d) / in$_3$ (c)).(~c) / (~d) / b$_3$(d) +
    [*while* loop used; *if* is false]
in$_1$ (c) / b$_1$(d) / (~c) / (d).(out$_5$ (d) / b$_3$(d) +
    [*while* loop not used; *if* is true]
in$_1$ (c) / b$_1$(d) / (~c) / (~d) / b$_3$(d)
    [*while* loop not used; *if* is false]

## 3.  Graphical Computational Model

Control flow diagrams [11] are digraphs, consisting of nodes connected by directed arcs, and are often used to represent computer programs. In our usage, the nodes will represent statements (or groups of statements) and include the computations (see section 2.1). An arc indicates a possible control flow direction

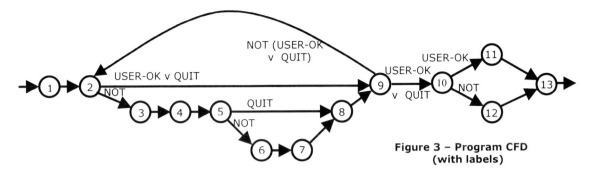

**Figure 3 – Program CFD
(with labels)**

and is labeled with conditions required to traverse it during execution.

## 3.1. Paths in the Model

A **path** is a sequence of these nodes and the arcs producing this sequence; it is topoligically feasible[13]. If the path begins with the start node and finishes with the terminal node, it is a **graph theoretical path**. A **computational path** includes node computations and arc labels. For any graph theoretical path, **P**, through some node $n_1$ and subsequently through $n_2$, an arc from $n_2$ to $n_1$ is a **backward arc** with respect to **P**. Backward arcs create loops to enable satisfying conditions in the completion of a program's behavior. The set of arcs of a computational path is partitioned into **scope**s for each variable; a scope starts with the acquisition of a value and ends with the onset of the new scope or the end of the program. Variables have **actual value**s if the initiating operation is explicit assignment, **effective value**s obtained through user or file input and defined for some arc condition in the scope to be true, or completely **unknown values**. A scope is **consistent** if no condition on any included arc is contradicted by the actual or effective value of the involved variable. If all scopes of a computational path are consistent under a single set of conditions, it is a **correct computational path**. The minimal correct computational path is a **thread**, representing a principal behavior of the program. A **contradicted subpath** is that part of a computational path which is not consistent. Subpaths which are contradicted by all computational paths in which they are included are removed, leaving either a **corrected CFD** or a non-viable program.

For examples of these defined terms, the COBOL program segment (Figure 2) has a corresponding CFD with arc labels **(Figure 3)**, where the numbers in Figure 3 represent the corresponding lines of code in Figure 2.

9->2 is a backward arc. Two simple computational paths would be 1->2->9->10->11->13 and 1->2->3->4->5->8->9->10->12->13. In the former, the actual

values assigned in line 1 of the program produce a contradiction in the arc label on 2->9; eliminating this contradicted subpath severs the path; therefore, it is not a correct computational path. In the second computational path, the 5->8 arc requires a particular value that was input in 4; the input variable has an effective value, the required one. This value is found to be consistent with the rest of the computational path and since the other variables also produce consistent scopes, this is a correct computational path.

Further, since this second path cannot be shortened, it is a thread for the program, representing the 'user decided to quit' behavior. Another thread is 1->2->3->4->5->6->7->8->9->10->11->13, representing the 'user enters a color and verifies' behavior. Additional computational paths can be generated, with and without backward arcs, but observe that i) any occurrence of the 2->9 arc is always contradicted by an assignment in node 1[1] and ii) there are only two threads.

## 3.2. Homomorphism and Equivalence

Starting with two CFDs, superimpose one over the other, with each node from the top CFD covering a group of one or more connected nodes (and connecting arcs) in the lower one. If there is a many-to-1 mapping of uncovered arcs in the lower CFD to those in the upper CFD, and the mapped sets occur between corresponding nodes and groups in the two CFD's, the CFD's are **homomorphic.**[2]

Again, the impetus for doing this is the desire to relate a program to its specifications, to try to map the specifications to the program. For example the specifications for this program could be represented by the CFD in Figure 4, which is homomorphic to the

---

[1] The existence of this arc is due to the COBOL PERFORM/END-PERFORM construct, the body of which is possibly skipped in the general case; conditions here are set to force a **repeat...until** loop.
[2] Note that the computations and arc labels do not enter into this definition.

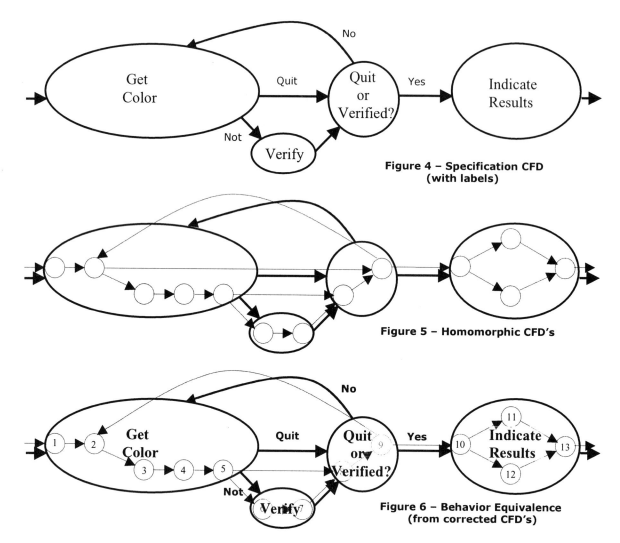

**Figure 4 – Specification CFD
(with labels)**

**Figure 5 – Homomorphic CFD's**

**Figure 6 – Behavior Equivalence
(from corrected CFD's)**

program CFD in Figure 3; both are shown superimposed in Figure 5.

Many such homomorphic relationships are possible; our selection of an appropriate one is guided by using the **corrected** CFD's, ones in which we have removed the contradicted subpaths. Given one of these homomorphisms, if the conditions on the arcs and the computations in the nodes are equivalent for corresponding features of the two corrected CFD's (as in Figure 6[3]), **behavior equivalence** exists; the program and the specifications exhibit the same behavior for corresponding threads. Stronger equivalence is based on selective restoration of contradicted subpaths. If all of the restored features: arcs and nodes, computations and labels, from the specification CFD are found in the program CFD,

specification equivalence exists; in practice this would mean that the code implements all of the specifications. Then, given specification equivalence, if the restored features in the program CFD also exist in the specification CFD, **code equivalence** exists; that is, the specifications exactly match the code. Code equivalence is welcome in a program but usually not achieved, as in our example (the specifications do not include the 2->9 arc). Specification equivalence is highly desirable, as in meeting the needs of the designer, but only behavior equivalence is required for the program to meet the specification tests.

## 4. Proposed Canonical Form

The next objective is to construct a standard form for a computational structure, whether it comes from a program or a specification. As indicated in section 1, comparing two computational models to see if they are

---

[3] Note that the contradicted 2->9 arc has been removed, but that the CFD's are still homomorphic.

equivalent is complicated by the fact that computations are in different order in the two models, and if the order of the computations can be changed, it may become clear that the two models are indeed equivalent. Instead of trying endless modifications to bring the two models into the same form, in this section we define a canonical form. Thus it is more direct to move each to a canonical form through very systematic transformations; if the two models have the same canonical form, then they are equivalent. However, as indicated in section 1, if they cannot be so converted to the same canonical form, we cannot be sure that they are still not equivalent. The best approach here is to use our approach to identify significant differences, which will show that they are not equivalent, as demonstrated in the experiments described in section 5.

The $F(p)$ extraction data of Cimitile [10] will be used to represent the control flow structure; other information will consist of definition/use pairs of variables. This information will be used to calculate a variable definition-use distance to determine the canonical form for a program.

## 4.1 Variable Definition-Use Distance

Our method depends on evaluating **variable definition-use distance**s, essentially counting program elements between the definition of variable and its use, explained here. If we consider the five program statement types that are found in COBOL, in their notations, a first measure can be stated:

| Statement Type | Size |
|---|---|
| b | 1 |
| in | 1 |
| out | 1 |
| $w(\mathbf{p}).(\mathbf{s} + \Phi)$ | $size(\mathbf{p}) + size(\mathbf{s}) + 1$ |
| $if(\mathbf{p}).(\mathbf{s_1} + \mathbf{s_2})$ | $Size(\mathbf{p}) + max(size(\mathbf{s_1}), size(\mathbf{s_2})) + 1$ |

where $\mathbf{p}$ (a predicate) is a logical expression consisting of one or more simple conditions $\mathbf{sc}$ (that is, each part evaluates to either true or false exactly), and/or functional calls, $\mathbf{fc}$, separated and connected by the logical operators **AND** and/or **OR**. The size of an $\mathbf{sc}$ is defined next; the size of an $\mathbf{fc}$ is the size of the block of code which is to be processed

$\mathbf{s}$ represents a sequence of statements, so that:

$\mathbf{s} = \mathbf{x_1} / \mathbf{x_2} / ... / \mathbf{x_n}$ where

$x_i \ni \{b, in, out, w, if, r\}$;

therefore, $size(\mathbf{s}) = \Sigma\ size(x_i)$.

An $\mathbf{sc}$ is defined by:

$<sc> = <expr> <co> <expr> | <fc> |$
$<logvar> | rue | false$

where:  $<ao> = + | - | * | /$
$<co> = = | > | < | <> | <= | >=$
$<literal> = number | string$
$<item> = <literal> | <variable> | <fc>$
$<expr> = <item> | <item> <ao> <expr>$

**Table 1: Entry Distances of Various Program Features**

| $\underline{\mathbf{x_u}}$ | $\underline{entry(\mathbf{x_u})}$ |
|---|---|
| $b_u$ | 1 |
| $out_u$ | |
| $w(\mathbf{x_u}).(\mathbf{s_2} + \Phi)$ | $entry(\mathbf{x_u})$ |
| $if(\mathbf{x_u}).(\mathbf{s_2} + \mathbf{s_3})$ | |
| $w(\mathbf{p}).(\mathbf{s_1} / \mathbf{x_u} / \mathbf{s_2} + \Phi)$ | $size(\mathbf{p}) + size(\mathbf{s_1}) + entry(\mathbf{x_u})$ |
| $if(\mathbf{p}).(\mathbf{s_1} / \mathbf{x_u} / \mathbf{s_2} + \mathbf{s_3})$ | |
| $if(\mathbf{p}).(\mathbf{s_1} + \mathbf{s_2} / \mathbf{x_u} / \mathbf{s_3})$ | $size(\mathbf{p}) + size(\mathbf{s_2}) + entry(\mathbf{x_u})$ |
| $\mathbf{fc}$ | $size(\mathbf{fc})$ |
| (**sc** variations) | |
| $\mathbf{x_u} <\mathbf{co}> <\mathbf{expr}>$ | $entry(\mathbf{x_u})$ |
| $<\mathbf{expr}> <\mathbf{co}> \mathbf{x_u}$ | $size(\mathbf{expr}) + 1 + entry(\mathbf{x_u})$ |
| $<\mathbf{fc}>$ | $size(\mathbf{fc})$ |
| $<\mathbf{logvar}>$ | 1 |
| (**p** variations) | |
| $\mathbf{x_u} <\mathbf{lo}> <\mathbf{p}>$ | $entry(\mathbf{x_u})$ |
| $<\mathbf{p}> <\mathbf{lo}> \mathbf{x_u}$ | $size(\mathbf{p}) + 1 + entry(\mathbf{x_u})$ |

69

If an **expr** has a size equal to the sum of the sizes of all **fc** contained in it (and it is possible to have a size of 0), then the size of an **sc** is the sum of the two sizes of the **expr** terms plus 1, the size of **fc**, or just 1. Now, <p> = <sc> | <fc> | <p> <lo> <p>, where <lo> = **AND** | **OR** and the size of **p** would be defined by:

| <u><p></u> | <u>Size</u> |
|---|---|
| <sc> | size(**sc**) |
| <fc> | size(**fc**) |
| <p₁> <lo> <p₂> | size($p_1$) + 1 + size($p_2$) |

For some variable **v**, whose definition occurs in $x_d$ and use exists in $x_u$, note that: $x_d$ is always of type **b** or **in**, $x_u$ can be of type **b**, **out**, **w**, or **if**, and in the latter two, the use can be either in the predicate or the contained body.

From these, the **definition-use distance** for some $x_d$ / **s** / $x_u$ is the sum of the **traverse distance**, size(**s**), and the **entry distance**, entry($x_u$), as listed in Table 1.

### 4.2. Total DU Distance

The sum of the variable definition-use distances in a program then is the **total DU distance**. By minimizing this measure we accomplish our canonical or standard form. Some important restrictions are obvious; some are not. It works best to attempt to move the explicit variable definitions first, followed by simple uses, then inputs, and finally outputs. Definitions and inputs move toward the end of the program; uses and outputs toward the beginning. However, movement of inputs and outputs is also limited by retention of their order; statements of these types must be left in the original relative order with respect to each other to retain external behavior. A secondary calculation is used to distinguish between conditions equivalent to a tie. It is of interest and importance that no movement will, or has the ability to, change the number of blocks in a program: this number is invariant for a given program.

This creation of a canonical form is makes feasible the analysis of programs and specifications which happen to include permuted independent features.

An example of the processing discussed in this paper is given in the Appendix. First an example COBOL program is presented that accepts user-entry until the user quits. Next a transformed program is given the Procedure Division has been converted to in-line code. The F(p) representation is then provided. Note that the Total DU distance is 11, and of greater interest, the first block of the program is associated with a def-use distance of 5.

The canonical program for this is given next using the techniques of this section 4. Note that the Total DU distance is now 9, obtained by moving the block beyond the output statement out(2,1), so that it can be closer to the use of its defined variable USER-ENTRY

in the while loop and in the block b(7,1,USER-ENTRY) given at the end of the program; this results in a reduced def-use distance for this first block of 3.

It is next indicated that there is only one thread possible, corresponding to the selection of one user-entry and then quitting. The corresponding CFD is also given showing this thread and behavior. A final CFD is presented in which the arc at node 3 labelled Quit is removed, as the Quit is contradicted by the initial variable value of USER-ENTRY assigned. The backward arc labelled Not appears in the final CFD, and serves to allow subsequent user-entry values before the user decides to quit.

## 5. Empirical Study

The goal of this study is to automatically identify the existence of recursion, missing functionality, extra functionality, and logical errors. If successful, this analysis method will independently recognize errors and omissions in program implementation with respect to the desired requirements, using techniques different from, but complementary to, a traditional testing process.

First, nineteen small programs were investigated, initial efforts at design and coding by students in beginning COBOL classes. The selection criterion was merely being able to compile error-free in MicroFocus COBOL, while including programs of different expected quality. The programs were written to four sets of similar requirements; for classroom purposes, the programs use the same constructs, but involve different data files and data types. The target task can be summarized in general as validation and verification of a user-entered field, done until the user verifies a valid entry or chooses to quit. These programs were compared to a program written by a Computer Information Systems professional, considered to be our gold standard; for our purposes this will act as an independently-prepared, accurate representation of the specifications. Each of these programs was subjected to the same analysis, producing opportunities for insights into identification of similarities, differences and errors.

Data processing programs in COBOL, even simple ones written to very specific requirements, can vary greatly in their structure and content. Therefore, each of the candidate programs was first parsed and massaged to fit a set of rigid conventions by an author-written Prolog tool which leaves the target in an in-line form; this aids both in the analysis and our understanding of differences between the separate versions, in turn adding to the understanding of the results from the full process. The parsing program

Table 2: Results of the Empirical Study

| | First Phase | | | Second Phase | | | | | |
| | | Failed the Parser | | | | | | | |
| | # Programs | Recur-sive | Not Recur-sive but Syntax Problems | # Programs | Failed Thread Analysis | CFD missing backward arc | Different arc condition | Non-equi-valent; but correct | Code Equi-valent |
|---|---|---|---|---|---|---|---|---|---|
| Set 1 | 8 | 4 | 4 | 5 | | 1 | 1 | 3 | |
| Set 2 | 5 | 5 | | 2 | | 1 | | | 1 |
| Set 3 | 4 | 4 | | 0 | | | | | |
| Set 4 | 2 | 0 | | 2 | 2 | | | | |
| Standard | 1 | 0 | | 1 | | | | | 1 |

produces a modified F(p) form, including extraction of definition-use information about the variables.

Next, a second move to a canonical form was made by using the algorithm to minimize the total DU distance. The F(p) notation was then analyzed from two different views: a control-flow diagram was produced and textual analysis for contradictory paths and threads was done. The latter analysis was applied to the CFD allowing for equivalence studies between programs. An example analysis of a very simple program is included in the Appendix, and was discussed in section 4.2.

## 5.1 Results

A summary of the results of the analysis process appears in Table 2. At first the table may appear to record a completely failed study, but the exact opposite is true. These errors were detected semiautomatically by the elements of the process; some were quite unexpected.

Not surprisingly for a specification that involves significant looping structure, some of the student versions included recursion;[4] the magnitude of the problem was unexpected. In this phase, the parser clearly identified recursion in 13 programs, either directly with a message or by running out of stack space from repetitively substituting the called code in-line. Additionally, the parser crashed in different ways for four other programs, declaring the absence of some minimum syntax construct requirement.

Seven of these recursive programs were chosen to be partially reconstructed for further analysis, five from the first set and two from the second. This

reconstruction involved removing the recursion and inserting additional needed periods while leaving other features intact. The discarded ten fell into two categories: too convoluted for easy modification or too similar to one of the programs already chosen to be carried forward.

The remaining ten were carried forward into the second phase, producing a number of different results. Two of the programs produced an initial CFD that was homomorphic to the standard program, but thread analysis found only one thread (instead of two threads); these programs are labeled "Failed Thread Analysis" in Table 2. This indicated a missing behavior, later discovered to be the 'quit' option. Two others each produced two threads, but the CFDs exhibited different missing backward arcs when compared to the standard. Again this indicated a missing behavior; in fact, neither of these two programs will produce any results when run.

One program produced two threads and a CFD which contained a section homomorphic to the standard; however, arc condition analysis found a different arc condition which pointed out that the student had omitted one option – only thorough traditional testing could have found this. The extra nodes and arcs represented additional tasks that were being needlessly performed (and were not specified).

The arc conditions of three programs could not be rectified with the standard, yet tested perfectly: the conditions were used differently producing an alternate structure.

Finally, only one program was found to be fully code equivalent, correlating both in the analysis and run-time behavior.

Follow-up analysis of the ten discarded programs indicated that all were missing one of the backward

---

[4] The COBOL standard does not support recursion, but most implementations are stack-based and therefore allow it.

arcs, i.e., missing a part of the required behavior that would have been identified by analysis of the CFD.

## 5.2 First Insights and Limitations

Caveats should probably come first. It is clear that this problem is undecidable in general. Just having four sets of programs working with different data, which can be shown to be equivalent to each other, points out the difficulty in crossing from the syntax/structure view to the semantics/behavior realm. Then, thread determination involves generating computational paths, and each control structure will add a power of two to the number of possible paths. Our familiarity with the problem domain and the programs pose a potential threat in generalizing this process or in running good experiments (a good discussion of personal bias in an experimental study can be found in Rothermel [14]). However, understanding the desired behavior, essential for this analysis, should be a prerequisite for design and coding of the program. It is in this familiarity that success is possible [15]

Given the previous discussion, there seem to be some problems that can be identified quickly. Recursion is easily distinguished. Missing behaviors are often identifiable from the final CFD as are extraneous ones. However, use of extra variables can hide actual meaning and obscure the analysis. Also, nonequivalence of a program and the specification does not mean that the program is not correct; here we are emphasizing equivalence, but remember that this is only a sufficient condition for correctness, but not necessary.

## 5.3 Larger Program

In an attempt to extend our learning with this process, a larger working program was analyzed (about 280 LOC), which generated a report from sorted, user-selected data. This was compared to a CFD written by the author to reflect the specifications given to the programmer. The process did not take much longer, except for the thread determination, and there were no real surprises: the program has been tested extensively. However, arc condition analysis at the end revealed that one initial condition was not set and one was set twice! Traditional testing methods may have discovered this, but COBOL compilers handle an undefined variable in a number of fashions. If a default value were to be given based on the variable type (as with MicroFocus COBOL), the program would test and execute correctly; if some unknown value at the assigned memory location were to be used (as per HP 3000 COBOL), the program would succeed in all cases except for the special value(s) for that

variable (the one or ones for which the variable is to be checked) - traditional testing would find this error only in these latter cases; it also possible that a true 'undefined' value could be assigned – then testing would always find the error. The analysis algorithm of this paper would recognize both the undefined variable and the possibility that the program could be equivalent at the specification level. It also should be noted that several new features were present in this program which had to be modified for the parser.

## 5.4 Comments on Scalability

The F(p) representation language and tool of Cimitile [10] has succeeded on far larger programs than the ones with which this study has begun. The successful use of our Prolog parser, however, seems tenuous for programs of the magnitude referred to by that group: the nesting levels reached in our somewhat larger program seem to form the bottleneck for our entire process. This agrees with some preliminary complexity analysis we have done. Originally we thought that the number of paths we would have to analyze might grow as $O(n^m)$, where $n$ is the number of initial program points, and $m$ is the number of sections of the program into which the $n$ initial program points are partitioned. However, because of this partitioning, the growth appears to be just exponential at $O(2^m)$, fortunately not a strong function of $n$.

The remaining aspects of the processing is also related to $n$, but seem to grow at no more than $O(n^2)$ or $O(n^3)$, and are not exponential in $n$. For example, the overall checking of path validity seems to grow as $O(n^3)$. Note that the total number of nodes in the CFD is not a factor here, as the growth is just linear with the number of nodes in terms of processing the CFD. However, as the size of the CFD increases, the essential complexity parameter is $n$, the number of initial program points.

The parser will have to be rewritten to handle larger programs, or at least reorganized. Yet eventually this approach will be limited by the exponential number of paths to be considered, even with pruning which is done. We have also determined that partitioning of programs cannot help in this regard.

## 6. Related Work

A number of attempts to garner information from existing programs, to apply software reengineering, have occurred over the short life span of the field, as summarized by Chikofsky [9] and Arnold [1], for example. The many investigations have produced localized success, but it is clear that the greatest success will come from automation, as Bennett argued in 1991 [3].

From Chandra [8] working with program schemas, to Sneed [16] recreating specifications from the code, to Wong's work with redocumentation from the code [17], to the chunks of Burnstein [4], researchers have both realized success in using the target of their study and the inability to truly generalize the work. Sayyad-Shirabad [15] would probably agree that this is an expected result; it is in our familiarity with our testing environment and examples that we are able to move forward. Sayyad-Shirabad encourages this mirroring of a programming shop condition by research efforts; it should be the case that the programs are somewhat known beyond that they exist, rather than representing a fault in the research.

Bush [5] and others also found value in automatically manipulating COBOL code for better understanding, but their focus remained on enhancing the code view. The F(p) notation of the Cimitile group [6], [7], [10] gives a method for much clearer visualization and manipulation of the represented code and its underlying structure; the ability to extract information of such high clarity aids understanding, lends itself well to automatic and semiautomatic processing and analysis. This type of graphical representation has been tried and argued against over the years (for example, Horwitz, [12]), but every aid to understanding should be pursued.

Our seemingly unique combination of code and CFDs, with the addition of the identified feature called a thread, is found to be helpful and warrants further study.

## 7. Summary and Future Work

Although we would like software testing to be completely science, it clearly includes an element of art. Every testing tool has the potential to enhance our ability to be successful in the testing process. We have attempted to add to this repertoire a semi-automatic method in which the processes themselves point out problems in COBOL code.

Our method involves using a parser to massage the code to a set of conventions and then creates an extended F(p) translation which can be permuted to a canonical form. From this a CFD is created and thread analysis is done. A CFD alone does not provide sufficient information to determine homomorphism and equivalence of two computational models. One approach is to utilize threads, the simplest complete behaviors represented by shortest correct computational paths. These threads also provide additional insight for trimming incorrect paths.

Another approach is that of using backward arcs. The corrected CFD, including threads and backward arcs, can then be compared to the CFD of the specification to identify the level of equivalence between the two CFDs.

Each step of the process is capable of automatically establishing that an error exists, and usually the error itself. The parser can automatically identify both recursion and minor syntax errors that the compiler will ignore. Thread analysis is capable of flagging missing basic functionality and paring the corresponding CFD of its impossible paths. By comparing the CFDs, missing backward arcs point out additional missing functionality. Subsequent analysis of the arc conditions on the corrected CFDs marks logical mistakes in the control structure. The CFDs can be too different for analysis and still perform the desired tasks; equivalence is therefore a sufficient, but not necessary, condition. We can be certain that a program that evaluates to the specification equivalence level will perform all of the desired functions, and possibly more. A code equivalent result gives the highest confidence in correctness of the implementation. The final proof that a program is working on the correct task and using the correct files, etc. is certainly undecidable, but quickly established outside this process through local knowledge of the environment and details of the code and more traditional testing methods.

Much is left to do. The parser was designed around the smaller set of test programs and extended for the larger program. A more general approach would involve reorganization and addition of COBOL features not found in the test set. The ease in the first extension suggests that this modification is doable.

The success of these tests in automatically identifying errors urges us to investigate specific examples of programs known to be: below behavior equivalence, behavior equivalent, specification equivalent, and code equivalent. Further examples designed to include permutations of independent program control features will help to extend the understanding of our proposed canonical form. Finally, larger programs will push the limits for us to discover the magnitude of scalability possible.

We would like to acknowledge the assistance of Cimitile, Canfora, et. al. in sharing their tools for manipulating the F(p) notation and its corresponding database representation.

# References

[1] Arnold, Robert S. "A Road Map Guide to Software Reengineering Technology", in SRE, Arnold, Robert S. (ed.). *IEEE* Computer Press, Los Alamitos, CA (1993).

[2] Arnold, R. S. "Intro to Software Restructuring," in Tutorial on Software Restructuring, Arnold, R. (ed.). *IEEE* Press (1986)

[3] Bennett, K. H. "Automated support of software maintenance," Information and Software Technology, Vol. 33, No. 1, Jan./Feb. 1991, pp. 74-85.

[4] Burnstein, I. and Roberson, K. "Automated Chunking to Support Program Comprehension," Proc. Fifth International Workshop on Program Comprehension (1997).

[5] Bush, E. "The automatic restructuring of COBOL," Proceedings of the International Conference on Software Maintenance (1985).

[6] Canfora, G., Cimitile, A., and De Carlini, U. "A logic based approach to reverse engineering tools production," Proceedings of the International Conference on Software Maintenance, Sorento, Italy, 1991.

[7] Canfora, G., Cimitile, A., and De Carlini, U., and De Lucia, A. "An Extensible System for Source Code Analysis," *IEEE* Transactions on Software Engineering, 24(9):721-740 (1998)

[8] Chandra, A., and Manna, Z. "Program Schemas with Equality," Conf. Record, Fourth Annual ACM Symposium on Theory of Computing, 52-64 (1972).

[9] Chikofsky, Elliot J. and Cross, James H, II. "Reverse Engineering and Design Recovery: A Taxonomy", *IEEE* Software, Vol. 7, No. 1, Jan. 1990, pp. 13-17.

[10] Cimitile, A. and De Carlini, U. "Reverse engineering: Algorithms for program graph production," Software Practice and Experience, 21(12):519-537 (1991).

[11] IntelliCorp. "What are Control-Flow Diagrams?," from www.intellicorp.com/ ooieonline/qprocessdiagram.html

[12] Horwitz, S., Prins, J. and Reps, T. W. "On the Adequacy of Program Dependence Graphs for Representing Programs," Conf. Record of the Fifteenth Annual Symposium on Principles of Programming Languages, 146-157 (1988).

[13] Jorgensen, Paul C. Software Testing: A Craftman's Approach. CRC Press (1995)

[14] Rothermel, G., Untch, R. H., Chu, C. and Harrold, M. J. "Test Case Prioritization: An Empirical Study," Proc. of ICSM-99, 179-188 (1999).

[15] Sayyad-Shirabad, J., Lethbridge, T. and Lyon, S., "A Little Knowledge Can Go a Long Way Towards Program Understanding," International Workshop on Program Understanding (1997)

[16] Sneed., H. and Jandrasics, G. "Inverse Transformation of Software from Code to Specification, Proceedings of the International Conference on Software Maintenance. (1988)

[17] Sommerville, I. Software Engineering(4th ed.). International Computer Science Series, Addison-Wesley Publishing Company. (1992)

[18] Stern, Nancy and Stern, Robert A. Structured COBOL Programming (9th ed.). John Wiley & Sons, Inc. (2000)

[19] Wong, K., Tilley, S. R., Muller, H. A. and Storey, M. D. "Structural Redocumentation: A Case Study", *IEEE* Software, Vol. 12, No. 1, Jan. 1995

**Appendix: Analysis example**
**Simple program**

```
IDENTIFICATION DIVISION.
PROGRAM ID. JEK.
DATA DIVISION.
WORKING-STORAGE SECTION.
01  USER-ENTRY   PIC X(01)
                 VALUE SPACE.
    88  QUIT     VALUE "q".
PROCEDURE DIVISION.
MAIN-ROUTINE.
    DISPLAY "GO.".
    PERFORM GET-ONE UNTIL QUIT.
    DISPLAY "Final: ", USER-ENTRY.
    STOP RUN.
GET-ONE.
    DISPLAY "Enter a number: ".
    ACCEPT USER-ENTRY.
    DISPLAY "You said ",USER-ENTRY.
```

**Transformed program**

```
1 MOVE SPACE TO USER-ENTRY.
2 DISPLAY "GO.".
3 PERFORM UNTIL USER-ENTRY = q"
4     DISPLAY "Enter a number: "
5     ACCEPT USER-ENTRY
6     DISPLAY "You said ",USER-ENTRY
  END-PERFORM.
7 DISPLAY "Final: ", USER-ENTRY.
```

**Program modified F(p) –> Total DU distance = 11**

```
b(1,1,USER-ENTRY)   def-use dist =  5
out(2,1)
w(3,1,USER-ENTRY).
   (out(4,3)
    in(5,3,USER-ENTRY)
    out(6,3,USER-ENTRY))
b(7,1,USER-ENTRY)
```

**Canonical Program F(p) –> Total DU distance = 9**

```
out(2,1)
b(1,1,USER-ENTRY)      def-use dist =  3
w(3,1,USER-ENTRY).
   (out(4,3)
    in(5,3,USER-ENTRY)
    out(6,3,USER-ENTRY))
b(7,1,USER-ENTRY)
```

**Threads: only one possible**

```
2->1->3->4->5->6->7
```

**Initial Control Flow Diagram**

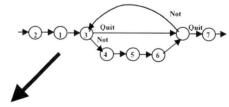

**Final Control Flow Diagram**
**(after analysis and coalescing)**

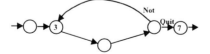

# Web Site Analysis: Structure and Evolution

Filippo Ricca and Paolo Tonella
ITC-irst
Centro per la Ricerca Scientifica e Tecnologica
38050 Povo (Trento), Italy
{ricca, tonella}@itc.it

## Abstract

*Web sites are becoming important assets for several companies, which need to incorporate sophisticated technologies into complex and large web based systems. As a consequence methodologies and tools are required for their design, implementation and maintenance. In particular the possibility for a site to evolve so as to provide updated and accessible information is a fundamental need.*

*In this paper web sites are considered the object of several analyses, focused on their structure and their history, with the purpose of supporting maintenance activities. Structural information may help understanding the organization of the pages in the site, while history analysis provides indications on modifications that do not correspond to the original design or that produce undesirable effects.*

*A tool was developed to implement the analysis of web site structure and evolution. Its application to some examples downloaded from the Web highlights several areas where the extracted information can improve the control on the maintenance phase and provide valuable support.*

## 1 Introduction

Maintenance of web sites is becoming a crucial issue for several companies, whose business strongly depend on their presence on the net. While tools and techniques for the development of web sites with increasingly more advanced features and appealing interfaces obtained a great attention, the problem of the evolution and modification of sites was somewhat neglected.

Similarly to the development of software systems, the production of high quality and reliable web sites can be achieved only if proper methodologies and techniques are adopted. Moving from the development of small, personal pages to big and complex industrial sites cannot be approached without considering that a phased, incremental process with well defined activities could help. Moreover,

the maintenance phase should be anticipated, designing the site for change and evolution, and then faced with the support of all available technologies. In fact, it is likely that maintenance is going to absorb a very relevant effort, as it occurs with software.

In this paper a set of analyses is presented which can be employed when the web site enters maintenance and needs to evolve while retaining and possibly improving its quality. Some of the proposed analyses were derived from those used with traditional software systems. They are divided into two main categories: analysis of the structure and analysis of the evolution.

The structure of a web site can be modelled with a graph, and several known analyses, working on graphs, can be applied. They include flow analyses, traversal algorithms and pattern matching. The evolution of a web site can be represented by using colors as time indicators. In this way the history of individual pages and links can be shown to the user in a compact and expressive form, highlighting updates that may degrade the original structure.

To implement the ideas mentioned above, the tool **ReWeb** was developed. It can download and analyze web sites and its graphical interface provides search and navigation facilities. It employs colors for the display of the history and popup windows for the outcome of structural analyses. The results obtained by using the tool with some real world web sites are presented to illustrate its potentialities.

The software engineering community is manifesting a growing interest in the study of web sites and of the underlying technologies, and recently an initiative focused on such themes was started: the *International Workshop on Web Site Evolution*. The existence of problems, in web site development, similar to those encountered in software before the advent of software engineering was recognized in [13], where the evolution of web sites is characterized by means of metrics, with the purpose of discovering troublesome maintenance patterns. The need to adopt a proper architectural organization, in which a site is decomposed into *virtual hosts*, and in turn hosts can be decomposed into units, physically associated to first level directories, is considered in [4]. Traffic and load analyses are proposed for the individual components. Other works [12, 14] deal with the problem of migrating or wrapping a legacy system so that it can be accessed through the web. Reverse engineering and restructuring issues are considered in such a context. The challenge represented by web sites for software maintenance and program understanding is discussed in [2].

Visualization techniques aimed at a compact and meaningful representation of the history of a system were mainly investigated in the framework of traditional software systems [3, 8, 9, 10]. Using different colors to display different versions of a software artifact allows high level and fine grain views of the evolution of the system. The extension of this approach to web sites is straightforward.

The paper is organized as follows: Section 2 describes the analyses that are performed on the structure of web sites, while Section 3 deals with the historical analysis of their evolution. The tool developed to implement such ideas, **ReWeb**, is presented in Section 4, and its usage for the analysis of real web sites is discussed in Section 5. Finally, conclusions are drawn and future research directions are given in Section 6.

## 2 Structure

Before considering the analysis of the structure of a web site, a conceptual model for its representation is proposed. Then several structural analyses are presented, relying on such model.

In the following a web site is identified as all the information that can be accessed from a given web server. Documents accessed through different servers are considered external to the given site. The web site structure is its organization into pages and links between pages.

### 2.1 Modelling the structure

The structure of a web site without frames can be represented as a directed graph $G = (N, E)$, where each node $n \in N$ represents a single HTML page, and an edge $e = (n_1, n_2) \in E$ connects two nodes $n_1, n_2$ if there is an HTML link from the page associated to $n_1$ to the page associated to $n_2$. In the following the terms *node* and *page* are used interchangeably, as well as *edge* and *link*.

The basic model for the structure of a web site has to be extended to account for the peculiarities of pages containing frames. A *frame* is a rectangular area in the current page where navigation can take place independently. Moreover the different frames into which a page is decomposed can interact with each other, since a link in a page loaded into a frame can force the loading of another page into a different

frame. This can be achieved by adding a `target` to the hyperlink. The representation of the structure of a web site has therefore to account for the composite structure of pages with frames. Edges assume different meaning as well, according to the entities they connect. A special link for the loading of a page into a different frame is also required.

The basic web site model is transformed by splitting $N$ and $E$ into different subsets of nodes and edges. Nodes are of three kinds: $N = N_1 \cup N_2 \cup F$. $N_1$ is the set of the nodes representing normal HTML pages, while nodes from $N_2$ are compound entities, containing the set of frames into which a page is decomposed. A node $n \in N_2$ is defined as a set of frames, rather than an atomic object: $n = \{f_1, f_2, ...\}$, where $f_1 \in F, f_2 \in F, ...$ and $F$ is the set of all frames. Nodes from $F$ can only be contained in a node from $N_2$. They are never found out of a container page.

Edges are also split into three subsets: $E = E_1 \cup E_2 \cup E_3$. $E_1$ is a subset of $N_1 \times (N_1 \cup N_2)$, and edges assume different meaning according to the kind of target node. An edge $e = (n_1, n_2) \in E_1$ represents the presence of a normal link from page $n_1$ to page $n_2$ if $n_1 \in N_1$ and $n_2 \in N_1$. It represents the decomposition of page $n_1$ into the frames in $n_2$ when $n_1 \in N_1$ and $n_2 \in N_2$. $E_2$ is the set of edges representing the loading of an initial page into a frame. Since frame nesting is allowed, the page loaded into a frame can in turn be a frame. Therefore $E_2$ is a subset of $F \times (N_1 \cup N_2)$, and the target of an edge $e \in E_2$ is a node from $N_1$ when a normal page is loaded into the frame, while it is a node from $N_2$ when it is itself a container of frames. Finally, $E_3$ represents the loading of a page into a given frame, which is specified as the label of the edge. $E_3$ is a subset of $N_1 \times N_1$, and an edge $e = (n_1, n_2)_f \in E_3$ connects $n_1 \in N_1$ to $n_2 \in N_1$ when a link exists in the page $n_1$ which forces the loading of $n_2$ into the frame $f \in F$, labelling the edge. Edges from each compound node $n = \{f_1, f_2, ...\} \in N_2$ to its constituents $f_1 \in F, f_2 \in F, ...$ are assumed implicitly, their explicit representation being redundant.

Figure 1 depicts an example of web site structure. The links between p3 and p5, and between p4 and p5 are normal navigation connections between HTML pages ($E_1$). The link between p1 and $\{$f1, f2$\}$ represents the internal organization of page p1 into the two frames f1 and f2 ($E_1$). The links between f1 and p2 and between f2 and p3 indicate that the pages initially loaded into f1 and f2 are respectively p2 and p3 ($E_2$). Finally, the dashed edge connecting p2 to p4 and labelled with f2 ($E_3$) is used to show that a link in p2 does not result in the navigation within f1 toward a different page, but rather produces the loading of page p4 into frame f2, with no regard to the page currently loaded into f2.

Complex web sites are usually organized by distributing the HTML pages associated to conceptually distinct portions of the site into different subdirectories. A typical ex-

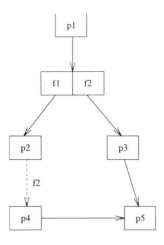

**Figure 1.** *Example of web site organization including the decomposition of a page into frames. Dashed edges represent page loading into the specified frame.*

ample is the web site organization usually employed by Internet providers. In order to give their clients the possibility to have their own space (a sort of *virtual* site), a natural choice is to assign a subdirectory to each virtual site. The graph representation of a web site, described above, can be abstracted by grouping pages according to the directory containing them. If no organization into directories is present, the abstract view, in the following called *system view*, contains a single node representing the root directory. Otherwise a node for each directory will be added. An edge connects two nodes $d_1$ and $d_2$ of the system view if, in the initial graph $G$ for the site, there is a page in the directory associated to $d_1$ connected to a page in the directory of $d_2$.

Flow analyses [1] have traditionally been applied to solve problems related to the static analysis of computer programs, as, e.g., dominators, reaching definitions, reachable uses, available expressions, copy-constant propagation. Given the graph representation of a web site proposed in this paper, it is simple to extend the range of applicability of flow analyses to the web sites.

## 2.2 Reaching frames

The computation of the reaching frames aims at determining the set of frames in which a page may appear. A page can be loaded into a frame as the initial page appearing in it, or it may be reachable from the initial page. Moreover there is the possibility that a page is loaded into a frame because a link in another page forces such loading. Pages reachable from it will also appear in the same frame.

To compute the reaching frames of the pages in a web site a specialization of the flow analysis framework [1] can be employed. The propagation of flow information is the

basic idea behind flow analysis. In the case of the reaching frames, the information to be propagated is the identifier (name) of the frame, and the generators of such information are the nodes of type frame ($F$) and the edges forcing page loading into a specified frame ($E_3$).

More specifically, the flow equations required for the computation of the reaching frames are the following:

$$
\begin{align}
GEN_n &= \{n\} \ if \ n \in F, & (1) \\
GEN_n &= \{f\} \ if \ \exists (m,n)_f \in E_3, & (2) \\
GEN_n &= \emptyset \ otherwise & (3) \\
KILL_n &= F \ if \ n \in F, & (4) \\
KILL_n &= \emptyset \ otherwise & (5) \\
IN_n &= \bigcup_{p \in pred(n)} OUT_p & (6) \\
OUT_n &= GEN_n \cup (IN_n \setminus KILL_n) & (7)
\end{align}
$$

A node $n$ generates itself as flow information if it is a frame ($n \in F$). In such a case it replaces any incoming flow information ($KILL_n = F$), since it overrides any previous frame. If a node $n$ is preceded by an edge from $E_3$ forcing its loading into frame $f$, the flow information representing $f$ is generated, but the incoming flow information is not killed ($KILL_n = \emptyset$). In fact alternative enclosing frames remain valid. The set $IN_n$ of each node $n$ collects the information about all possible enclosing frames as the union of the $OUT$ sets of the predecessors of $n$ ($pred(n)$), while its $OUT$ set is obtained by subtracting the $KILL$ set and adding the $GEN$ set. The root of the graph, associated to the first page provided by the site server, has empty $IN$ set, having no predecessor. Its $GEN$ set may contain a label (e.g., $g$) to be associated to the *global* frame, i.e., to the possibility to load pages at the top level, outside any enclosing frame.

Flow information is repeatedly propagated in the graph until a fixpoint is reached. It should be noted that flow propagation occurs along edges from $E_1$ and $E_2$, as well as from each node $n = \{f_1, f_2, ...\}$ from $N_2$ to the enclosed frames $f_1 \in F, f_2 \in F, ...$, while no propagation occurs along the edges from $E_3$, which do not represent navigation links, but rather page loading into an alternative frame. The result of the analysis, contained in the $OUT$ set of each node, is the collection of all frames into which the page associated to the node may appear, i.e., its reaching frames.

Figure 2 shows the result of computing the reaching frames for the example in Figure 1. The initial page of this site, p1, has a label $g$ in its $GEN$ set to denote the top frame. Frames f1 and f2 generate themselves as flow information, overriding any incoming data. The dashed edge from p2 to p4 is the reason for the $GEN$ of p4, containing f2, and for the empty $KILL$ set.

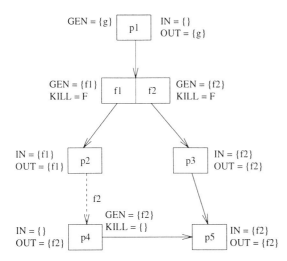

**Figure 2.** *Example of reaching frame computation.*

After propagating the flow information until the fixpoint is reached, the $IN$ and $OUT$ sets in Figure 2 are determined. It can be noted that the only page visible at the top level is p1. All other pages are displayed inside a frame. This is a consequence of the $KILL$ sets of f1 and f2. Page p5 can only appear in frame f2, for a twofold reason: it is reachable from p4, which is forced into f2 by p2, and it is reachable from p3, which is the initial page loaded into f2. If an edge is added from p1 to p5, its $IN$ and $OUT$ sets become $IN = OUT = \{g, f_2\}$, thus indicating that p5 can either be loaded at the top level or inside frame f2.

The outcome of the reaching frames analysis is useful to understand the assignment of pages to frames. The presence of undesirable reaching frames is made clear by this analysis. Examples are the possibility to load a page at the top level, while it was designed to always be loaded into a given frame, or the possibility to load a page into a frame where it should not be.

## 2.3 Dominators

When the pages of a web site are traversed to reach a document of interest, several alternative paths can be chosen. Nevertheless, it is impossible to reach a given page without traversing a set of other pages, called the *dominators* of the page of interest. The page initially provided by the site server, say index.html, is a dominator of any other page in the site. It will be considered the *root* of the graph representation of the web site.

More formally, given a graph rooted at node $r$, a node $m$ is a *dominator* of node $n$ if every path from $r$ to $n$ traverses $m$. The computation of the dominator set for each node of a rooted graph can be achieved by exploiting a well known specialization of the flow analysis framework, described, for example, in [1].

When applied to the example in Figure 1, the dominator analysis gives three dominators for p3: the root of the graph, p1, the frame container, {f1, f2}, and the frame f2. Any path leading to p3 traverses all its dominators. If page p5 is considered, its dominator set consists of the first two dominators of p3. In fact it is possible to reach p5 without traversing f2 and p3, by choosing the link in p2, loaded into f1, forcing page p4 into f2, and then navigating from p4 to p5. Since frame loading is automatic, users of this analysis may be interested in filtering out nodes of type frame and frame container from the set of dominators of a given node. In fact, only nodes belonging to $N_1$ have to be *actively* traversed to reach the page of interest.

The knowledge about the dominators of a page is useful to understand the navigation constraints of a web site. A web site designed to provide several alternative navigation paths is expected to have only the root in the dominator set of its nodes, while sites in which traversing a given page is considered mandatory, e.g., because it contains advertising material, will have it in the dominator set of every node.

## 2.4 Shortest path

Reaching a page of interest in a web site may require traversing several pages. A useful information about a web site is the minimum number of pages that must be visited before reaching the target document.

Given a graph rooted at node $r$, the *shortest path* from $r$ to each graph node $n$ is the path from $r$ to $n$ with the minimum total weight associated to the edges. In the present application of the shortest path, edges are weighted 1 when they represent real user selections (*mouse clicks*), while they are weighted 0 when page loading is automatic. In particular, edges going from a node $n_1 \in N_1$ to a node $n_2 \in N_2$ have weight 0, as well as implicit edges from a frame container node to its constituent frames. Moreover, the links connecting a frame $f \in F$ to its initial page (from $N_1$ or $N_2$) must be weighted 0, being the loading automatic. One of the most widely used algorithms for shortest path computation is the one proposed by Dijkstra, and described, e.g., in [6].

With reference to the example in Figure 1, the shortest path from p1 to p3 has weight 0 and consists of the sequence: p1, {f1, f2}, f2, p3. In fact, page p3 is automatically loaded into frame f2, which is built inside p1 at the beginning of the interaction. The link selection number to go from p1 to p5 is 1, since navigation from p3 to p5 is required. If the link from p3 to p5 is removed, the link selections from p1 to p5 become 2, and consist of the link in page p2, forcing the loading of p4 into f2, and the navigation link from p4 to p5.

Information about the shortest path to each page in the site is an indicator of potential troubles for the user searching a given document, when such path is long. A well designed web site should provide very short paths to the most relevant documents.

## 2.5 Strongly connected components

During navigation in a web site, some pages may become no longer reachable from the current page, unless restarting from the beginning or from a previously visited page. Often regions with fully circular navigation facilities are present in web sites, and in several cases the site is itself one such region as a whole.

Given a directed graph, its *strongly connected components* are the equivalence classes of nodes that are mutually reachable from each other. In other words, if nodes $n_1$ and $n_2$ belong to the same strongly connected component, a path is assured to exist from $n_1$ to $n_2$ and another path exists from $n_2$ to $n_1$. An algorithm for the computation of the strongly connected components is provided, e.g., in [6].

In the web site depicted in Figure 1 each node corresponds to a strongly connected component containing just that node, since no loop is present in the graph. If a link from p5 to p2 is added, nodes p2, p4 and p5 become the elements of a common strongly connected component. In fact, when one of these three pages is loaded into the browser, it is always possible to reach the other two pages, and to circularly navigate across them.

In a web site, the presence of strongly connected components containing several nodes suggests that the organization of the pages is aimed at promoting a navigation style that never gets stuck. Circular paths leading to previously visited pages allow the user to explore alternative pages.

## 2.6 Pattern matching

Recurrent patterns are expected to be used in the design of web sites. Matching a library of known patterns against a given web site results in the identification of portions of the site that are compliant with a predefined structure from the pattern library. Since patterns are in general represented by graphs themselves, the algorithms employed for their matching are those used to detect the isomorphism of a subgraph with respect to a set of model graphs, although ad hoc solutions may be conceived for specific patterns. A general approach to this problem can be found in [11].

Examples of reference patterns to be matched against a given web site are the *tree*, the *hierarchy*, the *diamond*, the *full connectivity* and the *indexed-sequence*. A portion of a web site is organized according to a *tree* pattern if its nodes and edges form a tree, i.e., its graph representation is acyclic and each node has exactly one parent, except for the tree root, having no parent. It matches the *hierarchy* pattern if it is acyclic, but more than one parent is allowed.

The *diamond* is a particular kind of hierarchy, characterized by a single entry point, a *top* node (root) with no parents, and a single exit point, a *bottom* node with no children. A *full connectivity* pattern is matched by a subgraph if each node in the subgraph is connected to all other nodes in the subgraph. A full connectivity subgraph is also a strongly connected component, but the inverse is not true. Pages are structured according to an *indexed sequence* if they are arranged into a singly or doubly linked list, so that from each page the next one is available, and optionally the previous one, and in addition an index page exists from which all other pages are directly accessible.

Different navigation styles are enforced by the different patterns implemented within a web site. Tree and hierarchy patterns are associated to a search strategy based on the refinement of general notions into more detailed ones. At each step the user makes some choice, thus successively restricting the area of interest. The diamond organization enforces a single exit point, associated, for example, to a final operation, to be performed after selecting the items of interest, or to a final document, to be displayed before the user leaves the site portion. Fully connected regions are conceived to provide full access to every document from each page, without any need of query refinement. All information is available at every time from everywhere. Pages are made available sequentially, according to the indexed-sequence pattern, when there is a natural order in which pages are expected to be traversed, as for the chapters of a book. The index allows jumping in the middle.

## 3 Evolution

Knowledge about the history of a web site is useful to document the events leading to its current organization and to identify the reasons for potential structural problems. The analysis of a web site evolution requires the ability to compare successive versions of its pages and to graphically display the differences. Works on history visualization for software systems [8, 9] greatly influenced the chosen approach.

### 3.1 Difference computation

Given two versions of a web site, downloaded at different dates, their comparison aims at determining which pages were added, modified, deleted or left unchanged. Tracing the evolution of an entity over time requires that a notion of identity be defined, so that the same object can be recognized at different times. In our case the problem is highly simplified if the assumption is made that the page name is preserved, when moving from a version to the next one. In this way a map exists between nodes in the graph representation of the previous site and nodes in the graph for the current site. It simply pairs nodes with the same name.

All nodes in the old graph without corresponding node in the new graph represent pages that were deleted from the site, while all nodes in the new graph without counterpart in the old graph are added nodes. When a corresponding node can be found in the old graph for a node in the new graph, it is classified either as a modified node or a node left unchanged according to the output of a character-by-character comparison of the associated HTML pages.

The choice to compare pages with preserved name through successive versions simplifies history traceability, since the mapping between old and new pages is given, and has not to be reconstructed. The drawback is that an unchanged page, whose name is modified, is considered as a deleted page, in the old graph, and an added page, in the new graph. Since the name of a page is its unique identifier, used by the other pages to access it and possibly referenced by external pages from other sites, it is likely to be preserved among successive site versions. In fact, changing the name of a page has an impact on all referencing pages, which must update their links, with the risk of missing some update. Therefore the assumption of name preservation seems a reasonable one, and few exceptions are expected to be found.

## 3.2 Visualization

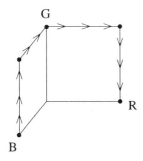

**Figure 3.** *Path in the RGB color cube, associated to the page introduction/modification date, going from the past to the present time.*

The graph representation of a web site can be enriched with information about its history by coloring the nodes and associating different colors to different time points. In particular, a scale of colors ranging from the blue (B), going through the green (G) and reaching the red (R) can be employed to represent nodes added/modified in the far past, in the medium past or more recently.

Figure 3 gives a path, in the RGB representation of the colors, that can be uniformly divided into segments to be associated to different time intervals. If, for example, 5 points are needed to represent 5 different versions of a site, the associated RGB color codes will be: `"0 0 1"`, `"0 1 1"`, `"0 1 0"`, `"1 1 0"`, `"1 0 0"`. The far past is thus represented with pure blue (`"0 0 1"`), then some green is added (`"0 1 1"`). The pure green is traversed before moving towards the red (`"1 0 0"`).

Several alternative paths have been evaluated, going from B to R in the RGB cube. Our choice was made by selecting a path providing a high number of intermediate colors, that can be visually distinguished, and at the same time ensuring a continuous scale from B to R, so that the distance in the past and the time proximity can be easily assessed by visual inspection. The path that was judged to be the best is the one depicted in Figure 3.

History visualization can also be applied to the links of a web site. When a link from a page to another page is first introduced, the edge in the graph representation of the site assumes the color of the source node, i.e., of the enclosing page. Then such a color is maintained even when the page evolves, changing its color, if modifications do not affect the link.

## 4    ReWeb

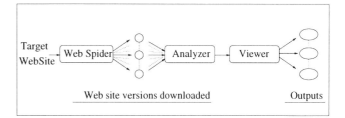

**Figure 4.** *Architecture of the tool **ReWeb**.*

The **ReWeb** tool was developed to download and to analyze web sites. Problems encountered in the construction of the tool are due to irregularities and ambiguities present in HTML code, also noted in [13], and to current state of Web technology, offering a large spectrum of alternatives to implement a web site. Similarly to [7] we classify sites according to a taxonomy characterized by content:

- Level 0: only HTML pages without frames.

- Level 1: HTML pages with frames.

- Level 2: HTML pages plus scripting languages and applets that do not communicate with their server.

- Level 3: dynamic contents such as CGI programs, servlets, applets that can communicate with servers.

The current version of **ReWeb** downloads and analyzes sites at level 0 or 1 while it is not able to fully handle those belonging to the other levels, although it can recognize the

81

| Web sites | Pages | Links | LOC | Frames | HTML+ | Last download date | Total versions | Significant versions |
|---|---|---|---|---|---|---|---|---|
| www.sta.co.uk | 17 | 68 | 1081 | no | no | 14-1-2000 | 96 | 1 |
| www.anasi.it | 22 | 64 | 6110 | no | yes | 15-1-2000 | 89 | 3 |
| www.storea.com | 44 | 81 | 2340 | yes | no | 12-1-2000 | 28 | 2 |
| www.ubicum.it | 57 | 232 | 3132 | yes | no | 12-1-2000 | 27 | 2 |
| www.alsi.it | 68 | 140 | 9512 | yes | no | 15-1-2000 | 29 | 3 |
| www.cartercopters.com | 76 | 243 | 9123 | no | no | 14-1-2000 | 95 | 4 |
| www.itc.it | 79 | 616 | 6543 | yes | no | 23-12-1999 | 89 | 8 |
| www.automatica-casali.com | 95 | 130 | 5118 | yes | yes | 12-1-2000 | 11 | 1 |
| www.psy.it | 128 | 216 | 24972 | no | no | 14-1-2000 | 82 | 8 |
| www.dei.unipd.it | 238 | 583 | 7486 | no | yes | 14-1-2000 | 91 | 6 |
| www.iqa.org | 245 | 1290 | 28690 | yes | no | 11-1-2000 | 10 | 1 |
| www.sund.ac.uk | 291 | 3121 | 19095 | no | no | 14-1-2000 | 91 | 6 |
| www.psy.unipd.it | 317 | 433 | 14685 | yes | no | 14-1-2000 | 87 | 4 |
| www.artifer.com | 358 | 2741 | 13758 | yes | no | 11-1-2000 | 11 | 1 |
| www.accademiadibrera.milano.it | 400 | 291 | 26073 | yes | no | 14-1-2000 | 9 | 1 |

**Table 1.** *Analyzed web sites. Frames is "yes" if the corresponding site uses frames. HTML+ is 'yes' if the site uses advanced presentation techniques, like Java, Java-script, dynamic objects, etc.*

level. The **ReWeb** tool consists of three modules: a Web Spider, an Analyzer and a Viewer (see Figure 4).

The Web Spider downloads all pages of a target web site starting from a given URL. Each page found within the site host is downloaded and added to a directory, named with the same name of the web site, but differentiated by date of downloading. The HTML documents outside the web site host are not considered.

The Analyzer uses different versions of the downloaded web site, the Web Spider's output, to calculate the difference between each two successive versions of the site, as explained in Section 3. The other analyses presented in Section 2 are computed in this phase. The results produced by the Analyzer are stored in files.

The Viewer provides a Graphical User Interface (GUI) to display the output of history analysis. The selection of a site version is done through a colored button menu on the left of the interface (see Figure 5). When a button is selected, a colored graph showing the *history view* appears in the right part of the GUI. The graphical interface supports a rich set of navigation and query facilities including zoom, search, focus and HTML code display. The facilities for focusing on and searching a node are useful when the visualized graphs are very large. With the focusing facility it is possible to focus the view on a selected node, and to specify the number of upward and downward levels to be displayed, i.e., the depth of the focus. The searching facility is used when a specific node has to be found within the graph. To display the result of structural analyses or to view HTML source code it is sufficient to select the related entry in a menu associated to each node in the history view. The

result is a pop-up window that contains the searched information. If the analyzed web site is organized into subdirectories, it is possible to visualize the system view of the site, introduced in Section 2, where every subdirectory is represented with a box. Figures 7 shows an example of **ReWeb** system view. **ReWeb** also permits exploding the elements of the system view. The result is the set of connected nodes in the subdirectory. Another interesting opportunity is the display of a report containing simple metrics at site level, like number of HTML pages, number of links, Lines Of Code (LOC) and *error links*, i.e., links leading to "ghost", non existing pages in the same host.

Web Spider and Analyzer are written in Java, while the Viewer is based on Dotty[1]. **ReWeb** is not complete yet. Future work will be devoted to improving the robustness of the tool, widening the spectrum of analyzable sites and enriching the set of facilities. In the next future, "adventurous" presentation mechanisms present at levels 2 and 3 such as scripting languages, applets and dynamic objects, will be handled.

## 5 Experimental results

Several web sites of different type – educational, commercial, institutional – were chosen for analysis. To study their history, the sites have been downloaded every day by **ReWeb** for over three months. Among all versions, only those *significant* were preserved, i.e., those that ex-

---

[1] Dotty is a customizable graph Editor developed at AT&T Bell Laboratories by Eleftherios Koutsofios and Stephen C. North.

hibit some change. A summary of their features is shown in Table 1. This table gives some metrics at site level, like number of HTML pages, number of links, Lines Of Code (LOC), and information on the technology used in the implementation of the site. The column *Frames* indicate if the pages of the corresponding site contain frames while column *HTML+* shows the usage of advanced presentation mechanisms, such as Java, Java-script, dynamic object, etc. For these latter sites it is possible that the collected information is a subset of the complete set of pages, since some links could have been missed. The size of the sites is between 17 and 400 HTML pages, the LOC number is between 1081 and 26073, and the maximum number of significant versions is 8. 9 sites use frames, while 3 use features beyond pure HTML (HTML+). In the following subsections we analyze some representative web sites in detail.

## 5.1 Example of evolution

| www.cartercopters.com |
| --- |
| compare: 21-10-1999 − > 24-11-1999 |
| **new nodes** = [pressrel14.html] |
| **deleted nodes** = [] |
| **new edges** = [pressrel14.html − > pressrel13.html, pressrel14.html − > index.html, contents.html − > pressrel14.html, pressrel14.html − > contents.html, pressrel.html − > pressrel14.html] |
| **deleted edges** = [contents.html − > NASA10TechGoals.html, contents.html − > pressrel13.html] |
| **changed nodes** = [pressrel.html, contents.html, index.html] |

**Table 2.** *Example of* **ReWeb** *textual comparison between two versions of the site www.cartercopters.com*

The site `www.cartercopters.com` (an aircraft manufacturer), used also in [13], is an interesting example because it had a high number of changed pages during the three months of monitoring. New pages and links were added, while others were removed. The significant versions of this site are four, at the dates: 21-10-1999, 24-11-1999, 23-12-1999, 25-12-1999. The tool **ReWeb** associates these dates to colors blue, light blue, yellow and red, thus permitting an immediate comparison between different versions. Colors are obtained by uniform sampling of the path in Figure 3. At the initial date the graph representation of the web site is all blue. When visualizing the second version, it is possible to note that there are nodes and edges light blue, i.e., the web site evolved. Specifically, the pages `pressrel14.html`, `pressrel.html`, `contents.html`, `index.html` are light blue. In fact, the first one was added to the site, while the others changed,

with respect to the previous versions. It can be noted that all new edges are links to the new page and that two edges were deleted. The tool **ReWeb** also provides a textual comparison between two versions. An example, summarizing the explanation given above, is proposed in Table 2. The third version introduces eight yellow nodes plus several yellow edges. There are five new nodes, while three changed with respect to the version dated 24-11-1999. In the last graph it is possible to see five red nodes and several red edges. It is not practical to display the entire site in a window, because it is too large, but it is possible to see a portion of it by exploiting the **ReWeb** focus. If `pressrel13.html` is chosen as focus, with upward and downward depth equal to 1, and date 25-12-1999, the graph in Figure 5 is obtained. Node `pressrel14.html` and its links were introduced on 24-11-1999. In fact their color is light blue. Page `pressrel.html` changed on 23-12-1999 and is consequently yellow. Pages `contents.html` and `index.html` changed on 25-12-1999, and are red, while the other nodes never changed and are blue, the color associated with the first date. In the structural design of this web site the pattern indexed-sequence, introduced in Section 2, is often used. The history study of this web site could not reveal phenomena of structural degradation. Even the largest insertion, occurred at date 23-12-1999, of the tree rooted at `pressrel15.html` preserved the previous structure of such portion: an indexed-sequence where each node can be in turn the root of another indexed-sequence.

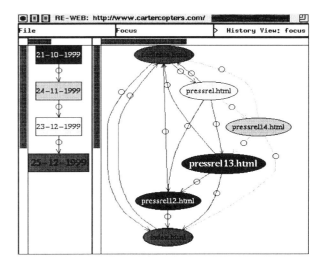

**Figure 5.** *Example of* **ReWeb** *history view depicting the site* `www.cartercopters.com` *at date 25-12-1999, focused on node* `pressrel13.html`.

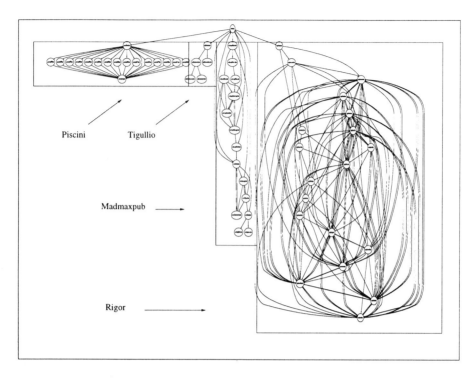

**Figure 6.** *Example of view depicting the entire site* `www.ubicum.it`.

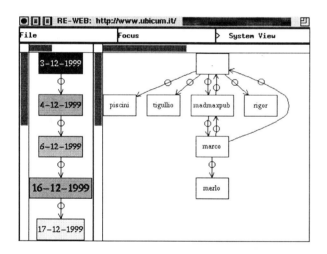

**Figure 7.** *Example of* **ReWeb** *system view depicting the site* `www.ubicum.it` *at date 16-12-2000.*

## 5.2 Example of pattern recognition

The web site `www.ubicum.it` (an Internet provider) shows an interesting structure, usually employed by Internet providers, but also some potential problems. This site is decomposed into four virtual sites (see Figure 7), physically associated with directories, that serve different clients (`piscini`, `tigullio`, `madmaxpub`, `rigor`). A potential problem can be noted in the system view of

the site by looking at the directories `marco` and `merlo`. The pages contained in `marco`, a personal site, cannot be reached from the root without passing through the virtual site `madmaxpub`. A better structure of the site would have put `marco`'s directory at the same level of the others. An analogous argument can be make for the directory `merlo`. The system view can be useful, during the maintenance phase, to control that changes do not produce undesirable effects like, for example, connecting pages that belong to different virtual sites. By exploding these virtual sites it is possible to recognize some patterns introduced in Section 2. In Figure 6, showing the entire site `www.ubicum.com`, it can be observed that the virtual site `piscini` matches the pattern diamond, `tigullio` matches a tree, `rigor` contains a large full connectivity region while `madmaxpub` has a form that does not agree with any well-known pattern. The virtual web site `rigor` does not match perfectly the full connectivity pattern. In fact, according to the **ReWeb** facility that calculates the strongly connected components, the site is composed of 19 nodes, of which 15 are strongly connected. Each of such 15 pages contains a menu at the bottom providing full access to all other pages. In sites that have a well-defined structure it can be verified that changes preserve the initial structure. The history views of these sites may reveal, during the maintenance phase, changes not corresponding to the original design.

## 5.3 Example of structure with frames

The web site www.storea.com (a carpet vendor) is a good example to illustrate frame visualization. The structure of this site is often used by medium size sites, offering a wide spectrum of products or services (other examples are www.coab.it, www.distillati.it, www.pierantonisrl.com). Typically, in these web sites the main page is composed of two frames: a frame is used as a menu to force the loading of pages in the other frame. The initial page of the site index.html, is decomposed into two frames, with identifiers LEFT and RIGHT. When a hyper-link is selected in the LEFT frame, the corresponding page is loaded in the RIGHT frame. A simplified view of this site is reproduced in Figure 8. The dashed edges labelled RIGHT indicate that pages associated to links in indice.htm are loaded in the RIGHT frame, i.e., the page that function as a menu is indice.htm. In this figure there is also an edge labelled with identifier _parent permitting the return to the home page of the site. In the page indice.htm a link forces the loading of the page index.html at the parent level of this frame, the top level, i.e., in the entire window of the browser. Another way to obtain the same effect, is to replace the edge labelled _parent with a dashed edge labelled RIGHT between the pages indice.htm and home.htm. By executing the **ReWeb** facility that calculates the reaching frames, the results mentioned above are confirmed: page index.htm is loaded in the entire window, indice.htm in the frame LEFT and all other pages are loaded only in the frame RIGHT.

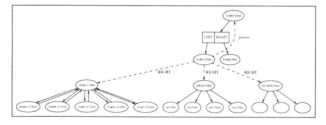

**Figure 8.** *Example of view depicting site* www.storea.com *that uses frames.*

## 5.4 Example of replacement

A phenomenon of complete restructuring, or better replacement, happened for the site www.itc.it (our cultural Institute). This fact could be observed, with the help of **ReWeb**, at the date 17-12-1999, when all nodes in the history graph changed color. It agrees with the considerations on web site evolution in [5], where replacement is conjectured to often substitute incremental update. A view

of **ReWeb**, particularly convenient in these cases, is the history representation with percentage bars [9] describing, in compact way, the percentages of nodes with the same color, i.e., the pages that were added or modified at the same time point. This view is interesting because main changes in the evolution of a site can be easily detected, being represented by "large" changes in color. An example of this view is provided in Figure 9.

By running, at the date 17-12-1999, the **ReWeb** facility that calculates the shortest path for each node it can be noted that the longest shortest path of the site is associated to page enMapITC.htm and has length equal to 4, a measure still acceptable but quite high. Before reaching the page enMapITC.htm, 4 other pages must be visited. The longest shortest path of a site can be an indicator of good structure. A high value of this measure can be associated to a possible structural problem. During maintenance, if this measure grows too much, then maybe it is better to start thinking about restructuring the site.

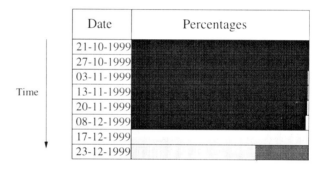

**Figure 9.** *Example of history representation with percentage bars, depicting the site* www.itc.it.

## 6 Conclusion

Several web site analyses, ranging from flow analyses to graph traversal algorithms and pattern matching, as well as the study of the site evolution, were implemented by the tool **ReWeb**. Such a tool can periodically download the entire set of pages in a site. Results of the analyses are then provided to the user, by exploiting different visualization techniques. Colors are employed in the history view, while structural and system views are enriched with powerful navigation facilities. Pop-up windows associated to nodes are used to show the textual results of the structural analyses.

The application of **ReWeb** analyses to 15 sites, that were periodically monitored, revealed interesting information on them. History traceability was combined with pattern recognition to verify whether the original design of the site was preserved or not during evolution. The system view provided indications on the high level organization of a site into subparts virtually independent. Pattern matching was useful to identify the enforcement of different navigation styles within regions of the site, while history analysis confirmed the existence of a phenomenon of very smooth evolution followed by a complete substitution of the site.

Future work will be devoted to extending the conceptual model of web sites so as to include advanced mechanisms associated to dynamically created pages. The tool **ReWeb** will correspondingly need several extensions, improving its ability to capture, analyze and display web sites exploiting sophisticated presentation techniques.

# References

[1] A. V. Aho, R. Sethi, and J. D. Ullman. *Compilers. Principles, Techniques, and Tools.* Addison-Wesley Publishing Company, Reading, MA, 1985.

[2] G. Antoniol, G. Canfora, A. Cimitile, and A. D. Lucia. Web sites: Files, programs or databases? In *Proc. of the International Workshop on Web Site Evolution*, Atlanta, GA, USA, October 1999.

[3] M. J. Baker and S. G. Eick. Visualizing software systems. In *Proceedings of the International Conference on Software Engineering*, pages 59–67, Sorrento, Italy, May 1994. IEEE Computer Society Press.

[4] L. Cherkasova and M. DeSouza. What: Web hosting analysis tool. In *Proc. of the International Workshop on Web Site Evolution*, Atlanta, GA, USA, October 1999.

[5] E. J. Chikofsky. Aspects to consider for understanding web site evolution. In *Proc. of the International Workshop on Web Site Evolution*, Atlanta, GA, USA, October 1999.

[6] T. H. Cormen, C. E. Leiserson, and R. L. Rivest. *Introductions to Algorithms.* MIT Press, 1990.

[7] D. Eichmann. Evolving an engineered web. In *Proc. of the International Workshop on Web Site Evolution*, Atlanta, GA, USA, October 1999.

[8] S. G. Eick, J. L. Steffen, and E. E. Sumner. Seesoft – a tool for visualizing line oriented software statistics. *IEEE Transactions on Software Engineering*, 18(11):957–968, November 1992.

[9] H. Gall, M. Jazayeri, and C. Riva. Visualizing software release histories: the use of color and third dimension. In *Proceedings of the International Conference on Software Maintenance*, pages 99–108, Oxford, England, August-September 1999. IEEE Computer Society press.

[10] R. Holt and J. Y. Pak. Gase: Visualizing software evolution-in-the-large. In *Proceedings of the Working Conference on Reverse Engineering*, pages 163–166, Monterey, 1996.

[11] B. T. Messmer and H. Bunke. A new algorithm for error-tolerant subgraph isomorphism detection. *IEEE Transactions on Pattern Analysis and Machine Intelligence*, 20(5):493–503, May 1998.

[12] J. Verner and H. Muller. Management of web site evolution. In *Proc. of the International Workshop on Web Site Evolution*, Atlanta, GA, USA, October 1999.

[13] P. Warren, C. Boldyreff, and M. Munro. The evolution of websites. In *Proc. of the International Workshop on Program Comprehension*, pages 178–185, Pittsburgh, PA, USA, May 1999.

[14] Y. Zou and K. Kontogiannis. Enabling technologies for web-based legacy system integration. In *Proc. of the International Workshop on Web Site Evolution*, Atlanta, GA, USA, October 1999.

# Re-Engineering

# Software Architecture Transformations

Hoda Fahmy
*Dep't. of Computer Science*
*University of Toronto*
*fahmyh@cs.toronto.edu*

Richard C. Holt
*Dep't. of Computer Science*
*University of Waterloo*
*holt@plg.math.uwaterloo.ca*

## Abstract

*In order to understand and improve software, we commonly examine and manipulate its architecture. For example, we may want to examine the architecture at different levels of abstraction or zoom-in on one portion of the system. We may discover that the extracted architecture has deviated from our mental model of the software and hence we may want to repair it. This paper identifies the commonality between these architectural transformation actions – that is, by manipulating the architecture in order to understand, analyze, and modify the software structure, we are in fact performing graph transformations. We categorize useful architectural transformations and describe them within the framework of graph transformations. By describing them in a unified way, we gain a better understanding of the transformations and thus, can work towards modeling, specifying and automating them.*

*Keywords: software architecture, graph transformation, reverse engineering, program understanding*

## 1. Introduction

Often, software developers are expected to maintain poorly understood legacy systems. Unfortunately, due to the lack of proper understanding of the system, any extensions or modifications often lead to spaghetti-like code. Specifically, each modification moves the structure of the system away from its original design. Maintenance becomes increasingly difficult and if such systems are to survive, they need to be repaired or reengineered. To make maintenance easier, we need to understand the system's components and how they interact [22]. In other words, we need to extract the system's *architecture* [3,25]. Depending on what we are interested in learning about the system, we may want to create different views of the architecture (see e.g., [28]). If we determine that the *concrete* architecture of the system, which defines the way the components in the code interact, is not consistent

with our mental or *conceptual* architecture of the system, then we need to investigate the possibility of repairing the system's structure[1]. We may also need to restructure the architecture to fit new operational requirements or computing platforms. In short, architectural understanding, analysis and modification are often necessary during the maintenance phase of the software-life cycle. This paper identifies *architectural transformations* that occur during maintenance (specifically during architectural understanding, analysis, and modification) and identifies the commonality between them.

Architecture extraction is subject to considerable software reengineering research; this has resulted in extraction tools such as Acacia [5], Rigi [18], PBS [20] and ManSART [28]. Given the source code, these tools determine how low-level components interact. Just as important, we need to determine the *system hierarchy* of the system: how are the modules grouped into subsystems and how are the subsystems grouped into higher level subsystems? This hierarchy or decomposition can be determined from file naming conventions, directory information, program structure information, interviewing persons familiar with the software, etc. It is our position that the component interactions (including program level dependencies such as calls from procedure to procedure), together with the system hierarchy, define the software's structure or architecture.

It is common to use a directed typed graph G to represent the system's architecture (see Figure 1): (Note that we will use Figure 1 to illustrate a number of architectural transformations.)

- Each *node* in G represents a component in the system. We can have several types of nodes. In Figure 1, we have only two types of nodes: modules and subsystems. Modules are drawn using boxes with thin lines, while subsystems are drawn using boxes with thick lines. Each node is labeled by the software component's name.

---

[1] We have adopted the terms concrete and conceptual architectures from Tran [26].

- Each *edge* in G represents a relation between components. We can have several types of relations. In Figure 1, we show only two types of relations: *contain* and *use*. The *contain* relation defines the system hierarchy of the software, which is a tree. There are two common ways to draw the *contain* relation; we can use nested boxes as shown in Figure 1(a), or we can use directed edges as shown in Figure 1(b). If *x* is contained in *y*, we say that *y* is *x*'s parent. We refer to nodes as *siblings* if they have the same parent and are distinct. We say that *x* is a *descendant* of *y* if *x* is nested directly or indirectly in *y* or equivalently, there is a non-empty path of *contain* edges from *y* to *x*. Besides the *contain* relation, there are dependency relations between components such as the *use* relation. In Figure 1, the *use* relation is represented as dotted edges.

- Graph nodes and/or edges may have associated *attributes*, which store information that is not conveniently expressed within the graph structure itself. Attributes may be of any type, including integer, real, text, list and table. For example, we may want to associate with each subsystem node the names of programmers who have worked on that subsystem using the *programmers_names* attribute.

In this paper we observe that once the extraction phase is complete, graph G is commonly transformed in a number of ways in order to better understand and analyze the system and to update its structure. For example, the ManSART tool recovers primitive architecture views of a software system yet these views are often too fragmented or too complex for performing software engineering work [28]. Thus, in [28], the authors proposed that such views are combined and/or simplified to produce hierarchies, hybrids, and abstractions. In general, the transformations that occur range from those simply extracting or "mining" information from G in order to gain a better understanding of the system's structure, to those actually altering G (perhaps as a part of preventive software maintenance [16]). Each of these manipulations can be thought of as applying a graph transformation function T to G to create graph G', i.e., G'=T(G). If we can collect a useful set of these transformations, this can help us understand the process of large-scale software maintenance. Furthermore, collecting, analyzing, and describing these transformations within a common framework can lead to modeling and formally specifying these transformations, which in turn can lead to their automation.

This paper takes a step towards categorizing and describing commonly used architectural transformations in the framework of graph transformations. We are concentrating on the architectural level, and so we do not

include source-code transformations. In this paper, we will discuss three classes of the transformations, which are applied to the graph models of software architectures:

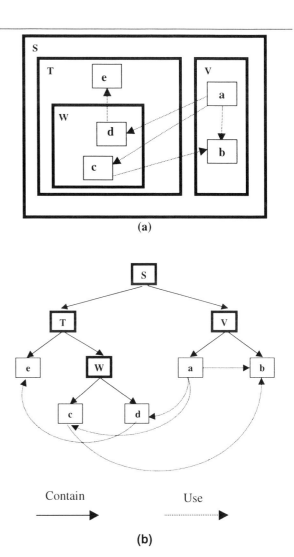

(a)

(b)

**Figure 1. Two graphical representations of a software architecture. Part (a) uses nested boxes to model containment. Part (b) uses directed edges to model containment. Nodes representing subsystems have thick lines; nodes representing modules have thin lines. In this example, S contains subsystems T and V; T contains module *e* and subsystem W; subsystem W contains modules *c* and *d*; and subsystem V contains two modules *a* and *b*; module *a* uses *b*, *c* and *d*; *c* uses *b*; and *d* uses *e*.**

1. *Transformations for understanding.* We use these transformations when we are building a graph model

89

of the system, and when we wish to explore this model to help us understand its structure. In doing this, we determine the system's hierarchical structure and we create views based on this structure.

2. *Transformations for analysis.* We use these transformations to discover various kinds of information about the software system. For example, we may want to know what modules interact in a cyclic pattern. This kind of information is commonly used to determine how we will go about modifying the system.

3. *Transformations for modification.* We use these transformations to change the system structure. For example, from our analysis we may find unexpected interactions between subsystem V and W and by moving certain modules we may eliminate these interactions.

Sections 2, 3 and 4, respectively, discuss these three classes of transformations.

## 2. Architecture Understanding

Tools such as RIGI and PBS extract facts from source code and use these to visualize how components such as files/modules[2] interact. For large software systems, the graph G will be huge (often containing hundreds of thousands of edges); hence directly viewing such a graph is of no help. During *architecture understanding*, we need to describe the module interactions at higher-levels of abstraction (e.g., at the top subsystem level) and also, we need to be able to simplify this information to produce various architectural views.

In the rest of this section, we will introduce the *lift* and the *hide* transformations, which help us understand a software architecture. Section 2.1 describes the lift transformation, which raises low-level relations to higher levels in the system hierarchy in order to view dependencies at various levels of abstraction. Section 2.2 discusses the hide transformation, which is used to hide the interiors/exteriors of subsystems in order to produce various views of the architecture.

### 2.1. Lift Transformations

It is often necessary to *lift* dependency relations to a higher level in order to study the structure at various levels of abstraction [8,12,14,19]. For example, if a function in module *a* in subsystem V calls a function in module *d* of subsystem W, then we can view that subsystem V calls subsystem W (see Figure 2). We can

consider lifting[3] to be a graph transformation: applying a lifting function to a graph G adds edges to G (see Figure 2). In the rest of this section, we describe three kinds of lifting functions in terms of graph manipulations.

We begin by giving a more formal description of the lifting function applied to the architecture shown in Figure 1 with the result shown in Figure 2. If module *x* uses module *y*, and *x* is a descendant of PX and *y* is a descendant of PY, then we lift the edge (*x*,*y*) to (PX,PY) only if PX and PY are distinct nodes and PX is not a descendant or ancestor of PY. The resultant edges are formed between subsystem nodes. In other words, we have abstracted the module-module relations to subsystem-subsystem relations.

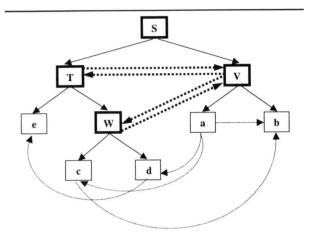

**Figure 2. Lifting Transformation. Edges resulting from lifting the low-level use relations are shown as thick dashed edges. For example, since *c* uses *b*, subsystem W uses subsystem V.**

Secondly, Feijs [8] defines a lifting function in terms of relation partition algebra. Here, we describe their lifting function in terms of graph transformations: for each *use* edge (*x*,*y*), create a new *use* edge between Parent(*x*) and Parent(*y*), only if Parent(*x*) and Parent(*y*) are distinct nodes. The new *use* edge is in turn lifted upwards in the system hierarchy one level at a time until it has reached the top level of the hierarchy. This algorithm implicitly assumes that the modules in the system are all at the same depth in the system hierarchy. This is not the case for the system shown in Figure 1 and most large industrial systems.

Lastly, Holt [12] defines a lifting function using Tarski's algebra. Holt defines a *family path* for each edge (*x*,*y*). If *x* is neither a descendant nor an ancestor of *y* and

---

[2] In this paper, we will use the terms *module* and *file* interchangeably.

---

[3] We will use the term *lifting* from Feijs [8]. Holt [12] refers to a *lifted* edge as an *induced dependancy*.

*x* and *y* are distinct nodes (as is the case for module-module *use* edges), the family path is the shortest path from *x* to *y* consisting of parents then exactly one sibling, and then children. The edges resulting from lifting (*x,y*) are all those edges that go from one node in (*x,y*)'s family path to a later node in the path. For example, when lifting the edge (*c,b*) of Figure 1, the edges created are {(*c*,W), (W,T), (T,V), (V,*b*), (*c*,T), (W,V), (T,*b*), (*c*,V), and (W,*b*)}. Despite the mathematical appeal of Holt's lifting function, it produces more edges than are commonly expected for a lifting function. In fact, it produces a superset of the edges produced by the first two lifting functions discussed in this section.

## 2.2. Hide Transformations

Similar to the lift transformation, the hide transformation is useful when trying to understand the structure of a software system. When a system contains several hundred files, with thousands of inter-dependencies, we need to hide parts of this information, which is not important to a particular perspective. In this section, we describe two hide transformations, hide exterior and hide interior, in terms of graph transformations.

During architecture understanding, we may want to focus our attention on one subsystem. We may want to answer questions like, which files in the subsystem are used by other subsystems? Or, which files in the subsystem use files belonging to other subsystems. When these are the questions we want to answer, we can apply the *Hide Exterior* transformation [12]. This transformation accepts the graph representing the architecture and the name of a particular subsystem we are interested in, and hides all the nodes and edges outside of the subsystem. In Figure 3a, we have applied this transformation to the graph shown in Figure 1 to hide the exterior of subsystem V. For each node *x* in V, if it is being used by something outside of V, then we added a *sell* (or *export*) edge between V and *x* since V "sells" *x* to components outside of it. If node *x* in V uses something outside of V, then we added a *buy* edge between the *x* and V since it "buys" a service outside of V. For example, in Figure 3a, V sells *b* and lets *a* buy exterior services. Finally, we deleted all edges outside of V. It would also be useful to generalize the *Hide Exterior* transformation to take as input a set of subsystems, *I*, so that only the contents of those subsystems belonging to *I*, the interactions between them, as well as the buy/sell edges to and from components that interact with anything outside of *I*, are contained in the resultant graph.

When we are not interested in the details of a particular subsystem, but rather how it interacts with the rest of the system, we can hide the interior of that subsystem using the *Hide Interior* transformation. In Figure 3b, we have hidden the interior of subsystem T as follows. For each

component *x* in T that uses a component *y* outside of T, we added an edge from T to *y*. For each component *x* in T that is used by another component *y* outside of T, we added an edge from *y* to T. Finally, we deleted all components in T (i.e., nodes that are descendants of T). Like the *Hide Exterior* transformation, this transformation can also be generalized to take a set of subsystems as input.

Since hiding certain details within G has proven useful, it is also beneficial to collect relevant information from the hidden parts. For example, assume we have an attribute, num_of_programmers, associated with each of the nodes in G storing the number of programmers who have worked on that component. As we hide the interior of a subsystem *T* by collapsing the subtree rooted at *T* into one node, we can calculate the number of programmers who have worked on *T* given the information contained in the (hidden) descendant nodes. This is referred to as *attribute aggregation* [13].

It should be noted here that the edges formed as a result of the hide interior and hide exterior transformations can be formed using Holt's lifting transformation [12]. For example, any edge (*x,y*) produced from lifting, where *x* is a descendant of *y*, is a *buy* edge, and any edge (*x,y*), where *y* is a descendant of *x*, is a *sell* edge.

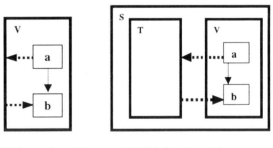

(a) Hide exterior of V          (b) Hide interior of T

**Figure 3. Hide Transformation shown using nested box representation. In part (a), the exterior of subsystem V of Figure 1 is hidden. Thick dashed edges are the use edges added as a result of this transformation: edge (a, V) indicates that *a* uses or "buys" some service outside of V; edge (V, b) indicates that V exports or "sells" *b* to something outside of V. In part (b), the interior of subsystem T is hidden. The thick dashed edge from T to *b* indicates that something in T uses *b*; similarly, the thick dashed edge from *a* to T means that *a* uses something in T.**

In summary, we use lifting and hiding to help us understand a software system. Lifting abstracts low-level interactions into higher-level interactions. Hiding allows us to zoom in and out to concentrate on views of interest. These transformations are used in the PBS Toolkit to allow the user to navigate the structure of the software; they are specified using Tarski's algebra and calculated using Grok [12].

## 3. Architecture Analysis

In this section we focus on *architecture analysis*, during which we discover various kinds of information about the system that can help us restructure or modify the architecture. Questions like, "How are the concrete and conceptual architectures different and what has caused the inconsistencies?"[19] or "Which modules should be made local to other modules?"[8] or "Which modules exhibit poor information-hiding?"[15] need to be answered so that we can decide what should be changed. In this section, we describe two types of transformations that support architecture analysis: diagnostic transformations (Section 3.1) and sifting transformations (Section 3.2).

### 3.1. Diagnostic Transformations

Once we have extracted the concrete model of the software architecture, it often becomes evident that as the software evolved, it deviated from the intended structure or conceptual architecture [22,26]. The conceptual model may be provided by the software's architects who have determined which subsystems should interact. After lifting the low-level edges, we may determine that certain subsystems interact though they should not. For example, as shown in Figure 2, after lifting the low-level edges given in Figure 1, we determine that subsystem T uses Subsystem V and vice versa. In our conceptual model of the architecture, we may have expected that subsystem V uses T and not the other way around. In this example, we need to see what module-module edges cause the unexpected subsystem-subsystem edge (T,V). We can isolate these unexpected interactions by performing *diagnostic transformations*. We identify a high-level *use* edge between subsystems that is not expected and convert it to an *unexpected* edge. Then we *lower* [8] it (the reverse of the lifting), by identifying lower-level edges which cause the higher-level unexpected edges until we reach the bottom level (see Figure 4). Given the lifting shown in Figure 2, we determine the unexpected lower-level edges as follows. If there is an *unexpected* edge (*x,y*), then any *use* edge from *x,* or any of *x*'s descendants, to *y,* or any of *y*'s descendants, is changed to an *unexpected* edge.

The identification of inconsistencies between the concrete and conceptual model is common in reengineering software [8,19,26]. For example, Murphy [19] has developed a tool to isolate these inconsistencies, and used it to reengineer NetBSD, an implementation of Unix comprised of 250,000 lines of C code. It has also been applied to aid in the understanding and experimental reengineering of the Microsoft Excel spreadsheet product.

### 3.2. Sifting Transformations

During architecture analysis, we are often determining how to change the software system. This requires that we identify what parts need to be changed. In this section, we describe *sifting* transformations, which sift the software components looking for components which will play a role in the change. These transformations identify such components by examining their interrelationships with other components and update the graph by marking such components using corresponding node attributes. For example, we may wish to find and eliminate cycles in the software structure. To do so, we need to identify the components which are involved in a cycle. We can define a boolean attribute called *cycle* which is true if the component uses itself via a cycle, and false otherwise. The sifting transformation when applied to G will update G such that all components involved in a cycle will have the *cycle* attribute set to true. A more detailed example is discussed in the remaining of this section.

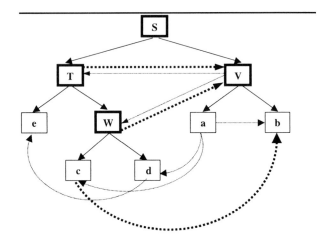

**Figure 4. Diagnostic Transformations. Applying diagnostic transformations to the graph shown in Figure 2. The problematic or "Unexpected" relations are shown as thick dashed edges. Once we assert that T should not use V, then this information is *lowered* down the system hierarchy. We find out that W should not use V and *c* should not use *b*.**

We may want to modify the software architecture to restructure it to fit the layering paradigm [8]. The components of the system are to be organized in layers so that each component use only components belonging to the same layer or the layer beneath it. In order to restructure the architecture in this way, we first need to identify components that are candidates for the top and bottom layers. Components which are not used but use others potentially belong to the top layer, and components which are used but do not use others potentially belong to the bottom layer. Let us define boolean attributes *top*, which is true if and only if the software component satisfies the requirements of belonging to the top layer of a layering architecture, and *bottom*, which is true if and only if the component satisfies the requirements of belonging to the bottom layer. We apply sifting transformations which inspect G and set the *top* and *bottom* values for each node. We can then use these attributes to help us restructure the architecture as a layering architecture.

In summary, we use diagnostic and sifting transformations to help us plan changes in the system structure. These create or modify edges and update nodes' attribute values, which identify problems or indicate components that may be changed or moved.

## 4. Architecture Modification

During the software life cycle, the need to keep the architecture up to date increases. For example, we may want the architecture to meet new requirements [4] or fit a new architectural style. Or, we may want to improve the modularity of the code by performing reclustering [23,24]. These *architecture modifications* are a part of the maintenance phase of the software life cycle. In this section, we focus on a type of modification called *repair*, which minimizes the inconsistencies between concrete and conceptual architectures. Section 4.1 describes repair transformations applied to the concrete architecture, while Section 4.2 describes those applied to the conceptual architecture.

### 4.1. Forward Repair Transformations

*Forward repair* transformations are used to minimize inconsistencies between the concrete and conceptual architectures by modifying the concrete architecture[4]. Once we have identified the unexpected relations in the concrete architecture, we apply forward repair transformations that move software components or even split components in order to help eliminate the inconsistencies. Tran [26,27] identifies two basic

---

[4] The terms forward repair and reverse repair (see Section 4.2) are taken from Tran[26].

manipulations that he used to help minimize unexpected dependencies in the Linux and VIM architecture:

(1) **Kidnapping** moves a program entity, module or subsystem from one parent (e.g. subsystem) to a new one. For example, let us consider kidnapping component *c* from Subsystem W to Subsystem V (see Figure 1), since it doesn't use any component in subsystem W nor is it used by anything in W. If we do that, Subsystems T and W no longer use Subsystem V, and hence, we have to eliminate the unexpected edges (T,V) and (W,V) (see Figure 5). Tran [26] performs kidnapping to repair Linux's concrete architecture. For example Linux has 7 top-level subsystems, two of which are the Network Interface subsystem and the Process Scheduler subsystem [3]. The Process Scheduler subsystem unexpectedly depended on the Network Interface, and it was determined that the inet.h module, which is only used by modules in the Network Interface subsystem, was the cause of this dependency. By having the Network Interface subsystem kidnap inet.h, the unexpected dependency was eliminated.

(2) **Splitting** breaks a module or subsystem into parts. Usually, one part remains where it is, and the others are moved to other subsystems.

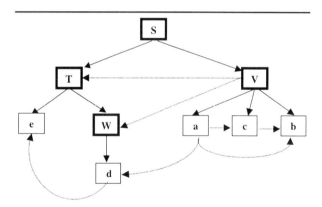

**Figure 5. An example of a forward repair transformation. We have applied a kidnapping transformation to the graph shown in Figure 1. When we kidnap *c* from subsystem W to subsystem V then W and T no longer use V. Note that component *c* has all its original use edges.**

For all these repair actions, we need to determine the appropriate conditions for application. In other words, when should we apply them? For example, we can say, if a component is involved in an unexpected dependency and it is not used by and does not use anything in its subsystem (like module *c* in Figure 1), then it becomes a

93

candidate for kidnapping. We can use a sifting transformation (Section 3.2) to determine such candidates.

When we perform a repair action on G, we need to assess whether the resultant graph G', is better or worse than the original graph G. To assess G', we can apply lifting and diagnostic transformations again to determine whether new *unexpected* edges have been created as a result of the repair. If the modified graph G' is worse, we should revert to the original graph G.

## 4.2. Reverse Repair Transformations

When we want to modify the conceptual architecture so that it is more consistent with the concrete architecture, we can apply *reverse repair* transformations. The main reason for wanting to modify the conceptual architecture of a system is to minimize any misunderstanding of the system so as to make maintenance easier. We will now give two examples of reverse repair.

Tran [26] performed forward repair to Linux's concrete architecture, but found that discrepancies remained between it and the conceptual architecture. Hence, he performed reverse repair on the conceptual architecture to further minimize the discrepancies. Reverse repair actions, like forward repair actions, include kidnapping and splitting as described in Section 4.1.

Another example of reverse repair transformations is discussed in Fahmy [7]. (Related work is described in Mancoridis [17].) In this case, we assume that the software architects have imposed *scoping constraints* to control how software components are allowed to interact. During software evolution, the software may no longer conform to these constraints. If this is the case, the system contains *illegal relations*. In order to eliminate illegal relations without altering the source code, we can add new allowable interactions in the conceptual model, in such a way that the illegal relations become legal. For example, Holt [11] identifies four scoping styles, one of which is the Import/Export Style. In this style, a component may export, import and use another component. X can export Y only if Y is X's child. X can import Y only if they are siblings or if X's parent imports Y's parent and Y's parent exports Y. X can use Y if they are siblings or if Y is an exported item (any number of levels of export) of X's sibling or of X's parent's imports. (This style is much like that used in various module interconnection languages (MILs) [21], as well as languages such as Java [9] and Object-Oriented Turing[10].) Without any import or export edges in the architecture shown in Figure 1, the *use* edge $(a,b)$ is legal given the Import/Export scoping style; all others are not. To make the edge $(a,d)$ legal, we can add *import* edges (V, T) and (V,W) and *export* edges (T,W) and (W,d).

In summary, forward repair transformations modify the concrete architecture to match the conceptual architecture, while reverse repair transformations modify the conceptual architecture to match the concrete architecture. By reconciling the conceptual and concrete architectures, we are less apt to make erroneous maintenance decisions.

## 5. Conclusions

This paper categorizes a number of architectural transformations that are useful during program maintenance. These include lifting and hiding transformations (Section 2), diagnostic and sifting transformations (Section 3), and repair transformations (Section 4); see Table 1. Since it is common to represent a software architecture as a typed, directed graph, we can think of these architectural transformations as graph transformations. In this paper, we have presented these in a unified way, which we hope will help us (1) *model* them so that (2) we can develop *executable specifications* for them, which (3) can lead to *tools* which automate them.

### Table 1. Summary of Architectural Transformations Discussed in this Paper

| Class | Type | Description |
|---|---|---|
| Architecture Understanding | Lifting | Lift low-level use edges up the system hierarchy |
| | Hide Interior/ Exterior | Eliminate information to make the structure more understandable |
| Architecture Analysis | Diagnostic | Given high-level unexpected edges, lower them down the system hierarchy to identify low-level unexpected edges |
| | Sifting | Mark components, using node attributes, that play some role in the desired change of the software structure |
| Architecture Modification | Forward Repair | Alter the concrete architecture to be more consistent with the conceptual architecture |
| | Reverse Repair | Alter the conceptual architecture to be more consistent with the concrete architecture |

To model these in a common framework, we can use a graph or relation-based model. Krikhaar uses a relational approach to model some of the described transformations [8,14], and similarly, Holt uses Tarski's algebra. Holt has been successful in using the Grok tool to execute specifications for some of these transformations [12].

Another possibility is to use *graph grammars* or *graph rewriting* [1] to model these transformations, and the PROGRES [2] tool, to execute specifications for them. PROGRES, which is an acronym for PROgrammed Graph REwriting Systems, is a visual graph-transformation language which supports the manipulation of directed attributed graphs. It shows promise; for example, Cremer [6] has used it to develop a redesign tool to migrate existing software into distributed environments. Each architectural transformation can be specified using graph rewrite rules. The application of a graph rewrite rule (1) identifies a pattern in the graph, and then (2) transforms the graph in some way based on that pattern. In other words, graph inspection as well as graph transformation is performed. Given the way we have described each of the architectural transformations discussed in this paper in terms of graphs and graph transformations, it is straightforward to specify these transformations as graph rewriting rules.

Regardless of how these transformations are specified and implemented, we hope that our framework of architectural transformations or graph transformations provides a better understanding of the maintenance of large software systems.

## Acknowledgements

This work has been made possible by the first author's NSERC Postdoctoral Fellowship. The authors would like to thank Dorothea Blostein, Bob Schwanke, and the anonymous referees who provided a number of valuable suggestions, which helped improve this paper.

## References

[1] D. Blostein, H. Fahmy, A. Grbavec. "Issues in the Practical Use of Graph Rewriting," *Lecture Notes in Computer Science*, Vol. 1073, 1996, pp. 38-55.

[2] D. Blostein and A. Schürr. "Computing with Graphs and Graph Transformations," Software- Practice and Experience, Vol. 29(3), pp. 197-217, 1999.

[3] I.T. Bowman, R.C. Holt, and N.V. Brewster. "Linux as a Case Study: Its Extracted Software Architecture," *Proceedings in the 21st International Conference on Software Engineering*, Los Angeles, May 1999.

[4] S.J. Carriere, S. Woods, and R. Kazman. "Software Architectural Transformation," *Proc. 1999 Working Conference on Reverse Engineering*, Oct. 1999.

[5] Y.-F.Chen, M.Y. Nishimoto, and C.V. Ramamoorthy. "The C Information Abstraction System," *IEEE Transactions on Software Engineering*, Vol. 16, pp. 325-334, 1990.

[6] K. Cremer. "GraphBased Reverse Engineering and Reengineering Tools," *Proc. AGTIVE Workshop,* Aug. 1999.

[7] H. Fahmy, R.C. Holt, and S. Mancoridis. "Repairing Software Style using Graph Grammars," *Proceedings of the IBM Centre of Advanced Studies Conference*, Nov. 1997.

[8] L. Feijs, R. Krikhaar and R. Van Ommering. "A Relational Approach to Support Software Architecture Analysis," *Software-Practice and Experience*, Vol. 28(4), pp. 371-400, April 1998.

[9] J. Gosling, B. Joy, and G. Steele. The Java Language Specification, Addison-Wesley, 1997.

[10] R.C. Holt, T. West. Turing Reference Manual, 5th Edition, H.S.A. Inc., 1994.

[11] R. Holt. "Binary Relational Algebra Applied to Software Architecture," *CSRI Technical Report 345*, Computer Systems Research Institute, University of Toronto, June 1996.

[12] R.C. Holt. "Structural Manipulations of Software Architecture Using Tarski Relational Algebra," *Proceedings of the 5th Working Conference on Reverse Engineering 1998*, Honolulu, Hawaii, October 12-14, 1998.

[13] R.C. Holt. "Software Architecture Abstraction and Aggregation as Algebraic Manipulations," in *Proceedings of the IBM Centre of Advanced Studies Conference*, Nov. 1999.

[14] R. Krikhaar, A. Postma, A. Sellink, M. Stroucken, and C. Verhoef. "A Two-phase Process for Software Architecture Improvement". Available at http://adam.wins.uva.nl/~x/sai/sai.html.

[15] R. Lange and R.W. Schwanke. "Software Architecture Analysis: A Case Study," *Proceedings of the 3rd International Workshop on Software Configuration Management*, 1991, pp. 19 – 28.

[16] B. Leintz, E.B. Swanson, and G.E. Tompkins. "Characteristics of Applications Software Maintenance," *Communications in the ACM*, Vol. 21, 1978, pp. 466-471.

[17] S. Mancoridis and R.C. Holt. "Algorithms for Managing the Evolution of Software Designs," *Proceedings of the '98 International Conference on Software Engineering and Knowledge Engineering*, San Francisco, CA, June '98.

[18] H. Muller, O. Mehmet, S. Tilley, J. Uhl. "A Reverse Engineering Approach to Subsystem Identification," *Software Maintenance and Practice*, Vol. 5, pp. 181-204, 1993.

[19] G.C. Murphy, D. Notkin, and K. Sullivan. "Software Reflexion Models: Bridging the Gap Between Source and High-Level Models," *Proceedings of the Third ACM Symposium on the Foundations of Software Engineering*, Oct. 1995.

[20] Portable Bookshelf (PBS) tools. Available at http://www.turing.cs.toronto.edu/pbs

[21] R. Prieto-Diaz and J.M. Neighbors. "Module Interconnection Languages," *Journal of Systems and Software*, Vol. 6, 1986, pp. 307-334.

[22] R.W. Schwanke, R.Z. Altucher, and M.A. Platoff. "Discovering, Visualizing, and Controlling Software Structure," *Proceedings of the 5th International Workshop on Software Specification and Design*, 1989, pp. 147-154.

[23] R.W. Schwanke. "An Intelligent Tool for Re-engineering Software Modularity," *Proc. of the 13th International Conference on Software Engineering*, 1991, pp. 83-92.

[24] R.W. Schanke and S.J. Hanson. "Using Neural Networks to Modularize Software," *Machine Learning*, Vol. 15, 1994, pp. 137-168.

[25] M. Shaw and D. Garlan. Software Architecture: Perspectives on an Emerging Discipline, Prentice Hall, 1996.

[26] J.B. Tran and R.C. Holt. "Forward and Reverse Repair of Software Architecture," *Proceedings of the IBM Centre of Advanced Studies Conference*, Nov. 1999.

[27] J.B. Tran, M.W. Godfrey, E.H.S. Lee, and R.C. Holt. "Architecture Analysis and Repair of Open Source Software," to appear in *Proceedings of International Workshop on Program Comprehension*, 2000.

[28] A.S. Yeh, D.R. Harris, and M.P. Chase. "Manipulating Recovered Software Architecture Views," in *Proceedings of International Conference on Software Engineering*, 1997, pp. 184-194.

# Restructuring Program Identifier Names

Bruno Caprile and Paolo Tonella
ITC-irst
Centro per la Ricerca Scientifica e Tecnologica
38050 Povo (Trento), Italy
{caprile, tonella}@itc.it

## Abstract

*The identifiers chosen by programmers as entity names contain valuable information. They are often the starting point for the program understanding activities, especially when high level views, like the call graph, are available.*

*In this paper an approach for the restructuring of program identifier names is proposed, aimed at improving their meaningfulness. It considers two forms of standardization, associated respectively to the lexicon of the composing terms and to the syntax of their arrangement. Automatic and semiautomatic techniques are described which can help the restructuring intervention. Their application to a real world case study is also presented.*

## 1 Introduction

Software entities are born and live with their names. The destiny and fortune of a program in part depend on the documenting ability of the names used for its identifiers (*nomen est omen* [4]). Identifiers convey relevant information about the role and properties of the objects they are intended to label.

In this paper a semiautomatic technique for the restructuring of program identifier names is proposed. It is aimed at improving the meaningfulness of identifier names and to make identifiers self descriptive. The consequences of such an intervention on the maintainability and understandability of the program are extremely relevant. In fact, identifier names are one of the most important sources of information about program entities. They are exploited to obtain an initial idea on the role of each entity in the whole program architecture. They may also give an extremely concise description of behavior or functionality. Several program understanding support tools (e.g., call graph extractors) label program entities with their identifiers, so that the semantic information possibly carried by the names is made available

to facilitate program comprehension. An implicit assumption on the usefulness of identifier names is therefore made.

Restructuring of program identifiers involves two main steps. Firstly, the lexicon is standardized by using only standard terms as composing words within identifiers. Secondly, the arrangement of standard terms into a sequence has to respect a structure that conveys additional information in itself. For example, the syntax of an indirect action, where the verb is implicit, is different from the syntax of a direct action.

A tool was developed to support the restructuring process. It allows automatic extraction and replacement of identifiers. Their modification according to standard lexicon and syntax is achieved semi-automatically, with the aid of a graphical user interface, providing hints and suggestions to the human operator. A real public domain program, `gzip`, was used as a case study, to verify the applicability of the proposed approach. Details on how identifiers of `gzip` were restructured and a discussion of the results obtained will be given in this paper.

The most closely related work [1] deals with the analysis of file names, with the purpose of clustering those sharing common concepts. In particular, the problem of automatically building an abbreviation dictionary to segment file names into their component abbreviations is discussed. It is constructed by exploiting different alternative sources, among which an English dictionary, the set of substrings ($n$-grams) shared among file names, comments and function identifiers. A similar dictionary-based approach to word segmentation is adopted also in this paper, but with relaxed constraints on the level of automation to be reached. Manual interventions are considered unavoidable and supported by a tool which facilitates them.

In a previous work [4], we concentrated on a preliminary descriptive analysis of function identifiers. The hypothesis was investigated that function identifiers possess a structure, and that such a structure can be described as a particular kind of non formal language. The lexicon and syntax extracted for the language of function identifiers are

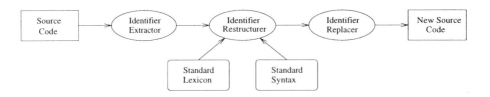

**Figure 1.** *Main steps of the restructuring process.*

presented in [4]. One of the future applications envisaged in the section about application areas is program identifier restructuring, i.e., the focus of the present paper.

Other related works deal with the analysis of informal information. In [9] sequences of words, taken from comments or identifiers, are classified against a concept tree, provided by a human expert, by means of an artificial neural network. The natural language description of a system is analyzed by a parser exploiting a link grammar in [10]. Parsed sentences are then filtered through a set of rules which extract candidate classes, attributes and relations to be inserted in the object diagram of the system.

Identifiers and comments are important sources of information. Choosing meaningful identifiers is considered a strong help to traceability in [6]. These are the basis for automatic traceability check and design evolution in [2]. Their role during the program understanding activities is investigated in [12], and compared with the role of the comments. Source code comments are analyzed in [11] to build a knowledge base in support to program understanding. The most common English words and names of data structures, routines and files make up the initial list of concepts. Terms are also extracted from the comments in [8] with a different purpose: indexing a reuse library accessed through a case based reasoning system.

Non code sources are the object of the analyses in [3, 5, 7]. System documentation is (partially) parsed to extract boundary conditions and constraints, used in test case generation in [7], while data flow diagrams are examined to extract business rules in [5] and to obtain a formal description of the system in terms of agents and events in [3].

The paper is organized as follows: Section 2 provides an overview of the restructuring process and highlights the role of each module required. Section 3 describes a procedure to define a standard form for program idenifiers at the lexical level. The extraction of a descriptive grammar from a corpus is the basis for the definition of the standard syntax, presented in Section 4. Section 5 is devoted to the restructuring tool that was developed to support the process in Section 2, while its application to the `gzip` case study is discussed in Section 6. Finally, conclusions are drawn and future research directions are given in Section 7.

## 2 The restructuring process

The main steps involved in the process of restructuring program identifier names are those depicted in Figure 1. The initial program source code is transformed into a restructured code by three sequential steps. First of all, a module, called **Identifier Extractor** in Figure 1, retrieves a list of identifiers from the code the names of which are to be restructured. Such module is a modification of a parser for the programming language under analysis, able to recognize the identifiers of interest and to report them. No hypothesis is made here on the kind of programming language to be analyzed. According to the language, different identifier categories are available for a potential restructuring intervention. Class, field and method identifiers are examples valid for object oriented programming languages, like C++ and Java, while global variables and functions are commonly used by several procedural languages, like C and Fortran. The **Identifier Extractor** parses the input code and reports all identifiers belonging to the category of interest.

The second step, performed by the **Identifier Restructurer** module, generates a map associating each old identifier with its standard form. The standard form of an identifier can be obtained by enforcing the compliance with a standard lexicon and a standard grammar. The input identifier is first segmented into its composing words. Each word is then required to belong to a dictionary of standard words (lexical standardization). In addition, the sequence of words in the identifier is required to be compliant with a grammar, prescribing the rules for the construction of legal identifiers from individual words. To avoid name clashes, the map produced by the **Identifier Restructurer** should be injective. Such property can be easily verified as a final operation performed by this module, which can prompt the user to give univoque names to conflicting functions. Elimination of such superpositions is not only a technical requirement for the executability of the program, but forces programmers to find more meaningful names, which explicitly highlight the main differences with other similar functions. The issues related to standardizing lexicon and syntax are discussed in Sections 3 and 4.

The last step in Figure 1 consists of the transformation of the original code into the new one, with all identifiers mapped according to the output of the **Restructurer**. The

**Identifier Replacer** module cannot treat its input as a sequence of characters, to avoid the substitution of a name with the restructured counterpart when such name is, for example, a substring of a longer name, or is within a comment or a constant string. In general, the **Identifier Replacer** module consists of a parser, building the Abstract Syntax Tree (AST) for the program, a transformation engine, operating the substitution of the identifiers of interest in the AST, and a pretty printer, generating a well formatted textual representation of the AST. For languages with macro substitution, like C and C++, the pretty print of the AST produces a code remarkably different from the original one, since all macro definitions and include directives have to be expanded before building the AST. The pretty printed code may consequently become unrecognizable and unreadable for the programmer. A solution in such cases is to perform the replacement operation at a level intermediate between the plain character sequence view of the program and the AST: the lexical level. A lexical analyzer generates a sequence of tokens, instead of characters, for the input code. When the token under analysis is of type *identifier*, it is substituted with its restructured version. The advantage of such an approach, apart from simplicity, is that macro expansion is no longer required for the transformation to take place, and therefore the output code is easily recognizable to the programmer. All original formatting is maintained together with the macros and the include directives. The obvious disadvantage is that there is no control on the syntactic role of the identifier being replaced. Consequently it is not possible to restrict the substitution to a syntactic category of interest (e.g., global variables but not functions). A mixed approach, yet to be implemented, in which syntactic information collected by the parser is used as additional input by the lexical level identifier replacer may solve such problem.

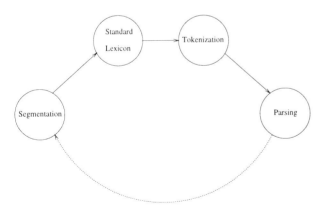

**Figure 2.** *States traversed by the* **Identifier Restructurer**.

While the operations performed by the **Extractor** and the **Replacer** modules can be fully automated, by adapting a parser for the programming language of interest, the **Identifier Restructurer** needs human intervention, when choosing the lexical terms and the grammatical structure that best summarize the semantics of the entity whose name is being restructured. Yet, some automatic support can still be provided.

The main states traversed during restructuring are shown in Figure 2. In the **Segmentation** state the identifier is split into its composing words. Automatic support can exploit a dictionary of known words and a set of word separation strategies (e.g., using the underscore or the capitalization of the first letter) to suggest a candidate segmentation, to be manually revised. Then each word has to become a standard term. If a synonym dictionary is available, candidate terms can be automatically suggested. Then words are associated to their lexical type (e.g., verb vs. noun). A manual intervention is required only when more than a lexical type can be associated to the standard form of a word. Finally the token sequence is parsed. If a parse error results, words have to be rearranged into a sequence compliant with the standard syntax, and all four states have to be traversed again.

## 3 Lexical standardization

After segmenting an input identifier, each composing word has to be mapped into its standard form. For this purpose a dictionary of allowed terms has to be available to the restructurer. It will be called, in the following, the *standard lexicon dictionary*. A company may define its own standard lexicon dictionary and the internal procedures for its update. A second, more empirical approach is to build the standard lexicon dictionary by looking at existing code and extracting the terms to be considered standard. An advantage of this approach is that its outcome is not limited to the standard lexicon dictionary. In fact, when a non standard term (e.g., a contraction) is encountered, the correspondence with the associated standard form can be recorded in a *synonym dictionary*, which becomes a second output of the process. It contains pairs of words, the first of which is a non standard term, while the second one is the corresponding standard form.

Given the standard lexicon dictionary and optionally the synonym dictionary, it is possible to check the words composing an identifier for compliance with the standard lexicon and, when some word is non standard, to suggest a possible standard term, if an entry can be found for the non standard term in the synonym dictionary. In practice it may be convenient to double both dictionaries (standard lexicon and synonyms) and have a general version of the dictionaries, adopted as a company standard, and an application specific version of the dictionaries, containing standard forms and synonyms that are not expected to be of general usage outside the current application.

The construction of standard lexicon dictionary and synonym dictionary from existing code requires that each identifier be segmented into the words it is composed of. So, for example, identifier `isoptpending` is very plausibly composed of words 'is', 'opt' and 'pending'. The first and the third word can, for example, be considered standard terms, while the second one can be mapped to the standard term 'option'.

Starting from (possibly empty) standard lexicon dictionary and synonym dictionary, a segmentation support tool tries to split one identifier after the other. Whenever the task fails, the operator is presented with the incomplete results of the segmentation, and prompted to input a word contained in the unsegmented portion of the identifier. The word is then added to the standard lexicon dictionary or to the synonym dictionary according to the user indication.

Once a standard lexicon dictionary is available, we can proceed to the definition of the *standard lexicon typed dictionary*, i.e., the association of dictionary words to the actual grammatical functions they play in the identifiers. The operation is carried out manually, with the support of a tool able to show the use being made, of a given string, in the identifiers of a given program. Instead of considering all the possible grammatical functions that a term may play, we account only for those actually occurring in the program. For example, the term "free" may be an adjective, a verb, as well as an adverb. In all programs in our database, it shows up only as a verb: in the typed dictionary, word 'free' will therefore appear associated only to the function <verb>.

| Program | LOC | Function IDs |
|---------|------|-------------|
| mandel | 2671 | 46 |
| cache | 4081 | 100 |
| h261 | 4890 | 49 |
| gdbm | 5936 | 54 |
| bc | 10279 | 85 |
| grep | 11480 | 127 |
| less | 17350 | 300 |
| gawk | 19435 | 205 |
| bash | 54776 | 990 |
| mosaic | 99668 | 1348 |

**Table 1.** *Lines Of Code (LOC), header files excluded, and number of function identifiers in the analyzed programs.*

With reference to the C programming language and the names of function identifiers, the production of a standard dictionary and of a synonym dictionary was performed by extracting it from existing code. The database of analyzed programs includes 9 public domain and 1 industrial (`cache`) C programs (see Table 1). Their size in Lines Of Code (LOC), header files excluded, ranges from 2 KLOC (`mandel`) to about 100 KLOC (`mosaic`). The number of functions is between 46 and 1348.

The programs in the database are representative of different application domains and different programming styles. Some of them are system utilities (`grep`, `less`, `gawk`), while some deal with database management (`gdbm`, `cache`). Two programs are in the field of image processing (`mandel`, `h261`), and one performs mathematical function computation (`bc`). Finally, a Unix shell (`bash`), and the popular Internet browser `mosaic` were also examined.

| Standard dictionary | |
|---------------------|------|
| Words | 974 |
| Synonym dictionary | |
| Word pairs | 233 |

**Table 2.** *Features of standard and synonym dictionaries extracted from available programs.*

Among the standard terms and synonym pairs encountered during the analysis of the programs in Table 1, those considered representative of general notions of the whole domain of programming, were added to the respective general dictionaries. As shown in Table 2, the standard lexicon dictionary contains 974 words, while the synonym dictionary contains 233 word-synonym pairs. All words are associated only to their observed grammatical functions. So, for example, the word 'free' is associated only to the grammatical function <verb>, since this is the only use of it made in the identifiers of the database. Moreover, not all the inflections of all words are contemplated, but only those actually encountered in the database. For example, the word 'bit' appears in the standard lexicon dictionary, while 'bits' does not.

Standard and synonym dictionaries extracted from the 10 analyzed programs have to be considered *general* dictionaries, which were constructed independently from any specific domain or application. They are a good starting point, since they contain several terms of wide use in programming, but they need to be extended in the future with additional general terms. Furthermore, their practical use requires that they be complemented by application specific dictionaries, containing terms that are required by the given program. In fact, such terms represent important notions, which are not enough general to be inserted into the general purpose dictionary, intended to cover the full spectrum of programming.

100

| | | | |
|---|---|---|---|
| FunctionId | ::= | [Context] (Action \| PropertyCheck \| Transformation) | |
| Context | ::= | Qualifier <noun> | |
| Qualifier | ::= | (<adjective> \| <noun>)* | |
| Action | ::= | SimpleAction \| ComplexAction | |
| SimpleAction | ::= | DirectAction \| IndirectAction | |
| ComplexAction | ::= | ActionOnObject \| DoubleAction | |
| **IndirectAction** | ::= | Qualifier <noun> ActionSpecifier | {Head word = <noun>} |
| **DirectAction** | ::= | <verb> ActionSpecifier | {Head word = <verb>} |
| **ActionOnObject** | ::= | <verb> Qualifier <noun> | |
| | | ActionSpecifier | {Head words = <verb>, <noun>} |
| **DoubleAction** | ::= | (DirectAction \| ActionOnObject)$^2$ | |
| | | {Head words from DirectAction and/or ActionOnObject} | |
| ActionSpecifier | ::= | (<adjective> \| <adverb> \| <preposition> Qualifier <noun>)* | |
| **PropertyCheck** | ::= | "is" Qualifier (<adjective> \| <noun>) | |
| | | ActionSpecifier | {Head word = <adjective> \| <noun>} |
| **Transformation** | ::= | Source TransformOp Target | {Head words from Source and Target } |
| Source | ::= | Qualifier (<adjective> \| <noun>) | {Head word = <adjective> \| <noun>} |
| Target | ::= | Qualifier (<adjective> \| <noun>) | {Head word = <adjective> \| <noun>} |
| TransformOp | ::= | "to" \| "2" | |

**Figure 3.** *Grammar for the language of the function identifiers. The main classes of identifiers are in bold face, and head words are specified for them.*

## 4 Syntactical standardization

The structure of program identifiers, i.e., the organization of the words in each identifier according to their grammatical function, can also be standardized. A grammar can exploit the classification of identifiers according to the kind of properties they are intended to express, and for each identifier category (*main class* in the following), a grammatical structure is defined, which specifies the ordering of different words (verbs, nouns, etc.) and the places where optional terms can be inserted (qualifiers, context specifiers, etc).

A grammar for program identifiers can be introduced as a company standard. A second approach is to derive it from existing code, by selecting "good" examples and using them as the basis for the grammar, and then to enforce its usage within the company. We experimented the latter approach, trying to derive a grammar for the identifiers of functions from the 10 C programs in Table 1. We concentrated on the C language and on the identifiers of *function* names, but the same approach can be easily applied in the context of a different programming language and/or different kinds of identifiers.

An initial grammar was first produced by simply reading several examples of function identifiers and trying to model the features that seemed to recur more frequently. The grammar was then refined through successive iterations. On each iteration the performances of the grammar were evaluated in terms of coverage and ambiguity, and proper corrective actions were taken to keep their improvement balanced. The *coverage* of a grammar for a non formal language is the ratio of strings of the language for which at least one syntactic derivation can be obtained from the grammar. The grammar *ambiguity* is the possibility to produce a given string of the language with more than one syntactic derivation. Increasing coverage and decreasing ambiguity are contrasting objectives, to be carefully balanced: although a grammar which does not impose many constraints on the identifier structure may in principle cover a high number of cases, it is likely to be ambiguous and of little usage in the improvement of the identifier structure.

After two major iterations on the initial grammar (and several micro-iterations), the productions in Figure 3 resulted. The meta-symbols used in Figure 3 have a straightforward interpretation: [ ] are used for optional symbols, | for the alternatives, an exponent gives the number of repetitions, while * indicates an arbitrary number of repetitions. Terminal symbols (*tokens* in the following) are represented through a lexical type inside angular brackets or directly as strings inside double quotes. *Head words*, shown within curly brackets, are the terminal symbols of the production holding relevant semantic information.

According to the grammar in Figure 3, a function identifier may be prefixed with an optional, possibly qualified, context, representing information on the general operating

101

conditions. For example, functions for opening, updating or closing a database may be named `db_open`, `db_update` and `db_close`, thus sharing the context information `db`. Three categories of functions are then distinguished: actions, characterized by the specification of an operation, property checks, used to verify boolean conditions, and transformations, converting data in a format into data in another format. Actions may be simple and complex. Simple actions express the intended operation through a single central (head) word, which is a verb for the direct actions and a noun for the indirect ones. Indirect actions do not explicitly express the operation through a verb, since it can be implicitly determined, and is typically *get* or *compute*. Examples of direct and indirect actions are `open` and `length` (the implicit verb for the latter may be *get*). The verb and the noun which respectively characterize the two kinds of simple actions are considered head words of the production.

Complex actions specify both the action and the object on which the action is performed, or are built as a sequence of two simple actions. In the former case the head words are the verb expressing the action and the noun representing the object of the action, while in the latter case the head words are collected from the component simple actions. A property check contains the "is" token and an indication of the property to be checked, which is recorded as head word. A transformation is qualified by the token "to" or "2". The words occupying the place of source and target of the operation are collected as head words.

The six *main classes* of non terminals corresponding to the different categories of identifiers are in bold face in Figure 3. For each of them the respective head words are specified.

The grammar in Figure 3 enjoys several properties, coming from the attention paid to its improvement during each refinement iteration. It is straightforward to show that the language recognized by the grammar is a regular language. The grammar is ambiguous, in general, but ambiguity is kept under control. For example `array_length` may be interpreted as an indirect action either with the head word preceded by a context or with a qualified head word. However, there is never ambiguity in the association of a string with its main class, nor in the determination of the head words to be associated to the main class. In fact, each main class is characterized by a feature that always allows to distinguish it from the other classes. The classes **PropertyCheck** and **Transformation** are the easiest to recognize, since the associated strings must contain respectively the special token "is" and one of the special tokens "to" or "2". The **IndirectAction** is the only remaining class with no verb. The **DirectAction** contains a verb, and can be distinguished from the **ActionOnObject** because in the latter the verb is followed by a (possibly qualified) noun, while in the former nouns after the verb can only be present as action

specifiers, preceded by a preposition. Finally the **Double-Action** class is characterized by the presence of two verbs. Similar arguments can be used to show that even the identification of the head words gives never origin to ambiguity.

The grammar in Figure 3 has not to be considered a final and immutable reference scheme. It actually can be adopted as a standard for the development of new identifiers, but further revisions may be necessary to cover all cases of interest and to make it an effective means for the improvement of the identifier names within a particular industrial context.

## 5 The restructuring tool

A tool was developed for the restructuring of function identifiers of C programs. It exploits the standard and synonym dictionaries described in Section 3 and the grammar presented in Section 4. Its **Identifier Extractor** was built on top of Refine/C[1], and produces the list of function names for an input C program. The graphical user interface of the **Identifier Restructurer** is shown in Figure 4, while the **Identifier Replacer** is a modification of the C scanner that is part of the Unravel[2] public domain tool.

The list of function identifiers is semi-automatically processed by the **Identifier Restructurer**, when each identifier is in turn examined for standardization. The input identifier is shown on the top field of the user interface (`updstd_form` in Figure 4). The tool then tries to segment the identifier into composing words, according to simple heuristics as, e.g., the presence of the underscore character or the capitalization of the first letter. When the segmentation is not completely correct, the user can edit it through the text field in the second line of the user interface (labelled **Segmented Identifier**). In the example shown in Figure 4, the tool produced the two words `updstd` and `form`, being unable to split `updstd` into `upd` and `std`. For such purpose a manual intervention is necessary. The next step, shown in the third line of Figure 4 (**Standard Form**), is the lexical standardization. The tool proposes a candidate standard form for the words having an entry in the synonym dictionary or differing from a known standard form only for character capitalization. If a word cannot be associated to or recognized as a standard form, a question mark is displayed in brackets. The user can then edit the text field with the standard form, until all words in the sequence are recognized as belonging to the standard dictionary. In the example in Figure 4, the tool displayed the following string inside the **Standard Form** text field: `upd (?) std (Standard) form (Form)`. The first term, `upd`, has no entry in the synonym dictionary, and therefore it has to

---

[1] Refine and Refine/C are trademarks of Reasoning Systems Inc.

[2] Unravel is a CASE Tool to assist evaluation of high integrity software, developed at National Institute of Standards and Technology.

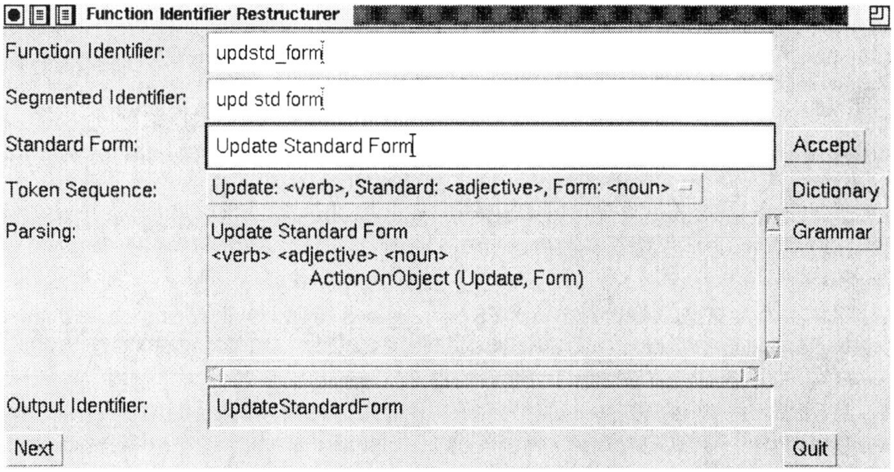

**Figure 4.** *User interface of the identifier restructuring tool. The word* upd *was manually separated from* std.

be manually adjusted into Update, which is in turn recognized as a standard lexicon. A synonym is instead available for std, and is proposed in brackets. Finally the standardization of the term form requires only the capitalization of the first letter, being one of the terms that can be directly found in the standard dictionary. To accept the tool suggestions to replace std with Standard and form with Form, a click on the **Accept** button is sufficient.

After producing a sequence of lexically standard terms on the **Standard Form** text field (no more question mark or suggestion in brackets is present), words are associated to their grammatical function, resulting in one or more token sequences. In fact, when a standard term may play more than a grammatical function, there is ambiguity in the token sequence to be considered. The tool interface presents all alternative token sequences as a menu of choices, and the user can select the proper one just by clicking on it. In the example presented in Figure 4 there is no ambiguity in the grammatical role of the terms, so that one single choice is displayed, needing no user selection.

The token sequence selected from the user interface is passed to a parser, which implements the grammar described in Section 4. If the token sequence can be successfully parsed, an output similar to that in Figure 4 is displayed, and the standard terms in the third line of the user interface are concatenated, resulting in the **Output Identifier**, shown in the bottom field of the interface. The main syntactical class associated to the identifier is displayed, with the head words in brackets, inside the text area labelled **Parsing**. In our example, the identifier was successfully parsed as an **Action On Object** main syntactical class, and the related head words are respectively the verb for the action, Update, and the object of the action, Form. When a parse error occurs, a user intervention is required, so that the token sequence associated to the identifier is arranged accord-

ing to a legal syntactical form. No **Output Identifier** is produced in case of parse error.

During lexical and syntactical standardization the user may need to browse respectively the standard dictionary and the identifier grammar to choose the appropriate terms and their arrangement. The two buttons **Dictionary** and **Grammar** on the right column of the user interface provide a popup window displaying respectively the standard dictionary and the standard syntax.

Once the input identifier is put in standard form, and the related output identifier has been produced, the association between original function name and restructured one is recorded in a file, which will be used by the **Identifier Replacer** for the automatic transformation of the given program into a standard one, with identifiers restructured.

## 6 Case study

| LOC | 7332 |
|---|---|
| Function identifiers | 97 |
| Capitalization only | 60 |
| Lexical standardization only | 36 |
| Syntactical standardization | 1 |

**Table 3.** *Lines Of Code (LOC) and identifiers of* gzip. *At the bottom, number of identifiers which required respectively capitalization of the initial word letters, replacement of non standard words, or rearrangement of words according to the grammar.*

The identifier restructuring process supported by the tool we developed was applied to the public domain program

103

gzip, a widely used utility for file compression. Table 3 gives some data on this program. It is made of 7332 Lines Of Code (LOC), header files excluded, and it contains 97 function identifiers.

With the help of the **Identifier Restructurer** user interface, all 97 function identifiers of gzip were updated. For 60 of them the modification was superficial, since only the capitalization of the first letter of each composing word was necessary. In fact, they contain only standard terms arranged into a sequence that respect the adopted grammar. 36 function identifiers required the translation of a non standard term into its standard equivalent. Such an operation exploited the entries of a general and a specific synonym dictionary, and typically involved the expansion of a contraction. The resulting token sequence was accepted by the parser, so that no syntactical standardization was performed. Revision of the syntactical structure was indeed necessary for just 1 identifier.

| General standard terms | 23 |
|---|---|
| General synonyms | 2 |
| Specific standard terms | 11 |
| Specific synonyms | 14 |
| Affected identifiers | 54 |

**Table 4.** *Terms added to general/specific standard/synonym dictionaries for the lexical standardization of* gzip.

The general standard lexicon and synonym dictionaries (see Table 2), extracted from the programs in Table 1, were exploited during the lexical standardization of gzip. They were complemented by gzip specific standard and synonym dictionaries. Each word encountered during restructuring for which no entry was available in the general dictionaries, was classified either as widely used in software development, or as specific to the given application. Consequently it was inserted in the general dictionaries of standard terms or synonyms, or in the gzip specific ones. It was necessary adding 23 terms to the general standard lexicon dictionary, and 2 synonym pairs to the general synonym dictionary (see Table 4). 8 of the 23 new general terms are only inflections of terms already present in the general dictionary. Typically the plural is missing, as for words *Bits* and *Codes*. 11 terms that could not be retrieved from the general dictionary were considered standard terms that are specific to the gzip application, and thus to be inserted into a specific standard dictionary. Examples are *Huffman*, *CRC*, *zip* and *unzip*. Finally, there are 14 contractions that were judged application specific and therefore were inserted into a specific synonym dictionary. An example is *lm*, to be

expanded into *LongestMatch*.

About a half (precisely, 43/97) of function identifiers of gzip could be mapped to their standard form by exploiting *only* information retrieved from the available general dictionaries (Table 2). The usefulness of a general dictionary is thus confirmed by this case study: the effort required for restructuring is about halved, if the general dictionary is adopted. Many of the terms not in the general dictionary were judged to represent general notions, deserving an entry in it. This suggests that the general dictionary extracted from the programs in Table 1 is not complete, although already useful and usable, and that its extension could lead to even better performances during restructuring of a new program. While only 2 additional general synonym pairs were encountered, when processing gzip, 14 synonyms were added to the gzip specific synonym dictionary. This may indicate that while expanded terms not handled by the available general dictionary can often contribute to the general set of standard forms, contractions are typically application or domain specific, and consequently need a special entry in a specific synonym dictionary. The relatively high number of standard terms added to the gzip specific dictionary, 11, with respect to the 15 terms (inflections excluded) added to the general dictionary, may be interpreted as an indication of richness of the general dictionary, since many of the new terms are not in it, being specific to the particular application.

Table 5 shows some cases of lexical standardization. For example, the function name lm_init was mapped to LongestMatchInitialize. Expansions of the composing words, lm into LongestMatch and init into Initialize, could be obtained by accessing respectively the specific and the general synonym dictionary entries. The advantage of the new function name with respect to the old one is fairly apparent in this case. In fact, it is not straightforward to imagine that the two characters l and m are extreme contractions of the words Longest and Match. A maintainer of this program is expected to benefit from the new more meaningful and self explanatory name.

Table 6 contains the only case of function identifier that required a restructuring at the syntactical level. The composing words of pqdownheap are pq, down and heap. The first word, pq, has no entry in the synonym dictionary. Actually, it was not possible to find a proper expansion for it by reading the comments and the code for this function. Therefore the decision was taken to remove it from the identifier and to replace it with the term propagate, that seemed to express the behavior of the function in a meaningful and concise way. The token sequence associated to Propagate Down Heap is: <verb>, <adverb>, <noun>. No grammar production can recognize it. It is possible to respect the syntactical prescriptions of the grammar by modifying the token sequence into: <noun>,

| | |
|---|---|
| bi_init | BitStringInitialize |
| lm_init | LongestMatchInitialize |
| copy_stat | CopyStatus |
| check_ofname | CheckOutputFileName |
| make_ofname | MakeOutputFileName |
| get_istat | GetInputStatus |
| huft_free | HuffmanTableFree |
| huft_build | HuffmanTableBuild |
| ct_tally | CodeTreeTally |
| build_bl_tree | BuildBitLengthTree |
| gen_codes | GenerateCodes |
| gen_bitlen | GenerateBitLength |
| ct_init | CodeTreeInitialize |
| decode_p | DecodePointers |
| decode_c | DecodeCodes |
| read_c_len | ReadCodesLength |
| read_pt_len | ReadPointersLength |
| write_buf | WriteBuffer |
| flush_outbuf | FlushOutputBuffer |
| fill_inbuf | FillInputBuffer |
| clear_bufs | ClearBuffers |

**Table 5.** *Examples of identifier restructuring involving lexical standardization.*

<verb>, <adverb>. The new token sequence is associated to the main class **Direct Action**, and the verb playing the role of head word is Propagate. The term Heap provides some *context* information, while the adverb Down is an *action specifier*.

| | |
|---|---|
| pqdownheap | HeapPropagateDown |

**Table 6.** *Identifier restructuring involving syntactical standardization.*

Table 7 provides the list of most frequently used terms within function identifiers of gzip, after restructuring. As one could expect, the term Tree has several occurrences. In fact, the compression algorithm implemented by gzip is based on Huffman trees. Next terms, Bit and File, refer to the basic unit of compression, the bit, and to the input and output entities, files.

Then, identifier substitution took place for the gzip case study, and the resulting restructured program could be compiled and executed without any problem. The whole restructuring process took about 4 hours, including all manual interventions required for the lexical and syntactical standard-

| | | | |
|---|---|---|---|
| Tree | 9 | Block | 5 |
| Bit | 8 | Buffer | 5 |
| File | 8 | Decode | 5 |
| Get | 7 | Initialize | 5 |
| Code | 6 | Length | 5 |
| Inflate | 6 | Read | 5 |
| Name | 6 | String | 5 |

**Table 7.** *Occurrences of words within restructured identifiers in decreasing frequency order.*

ization, and for all ancillary operations.

Programs sharing with gzip library functions whose names were restructured have to be updated by running the **Identifier Replacer** on them, to replace the old names with the new ones. Alternatively, the old function names can be made available for compatibility through an automatically generated interface module, the functions of which have the old names and just invoke the corresponding ones with new name.

A linear increase in the number of functions to examine is expected to occur when scaling to programs larger than gzip, but it should be noted that the size of a program is not the main factor affecting the effort spent in the time consuming manual interventions. Actually, the greatest difficulty encountered in the restructuring process is associated with the presence of extreme and cryptic contractions in the words composing the identifiers. Mapping them to meaningful terms may require reading comments, documentation and possibly the code itself, and is even more complex if a person different from the programmer who wrote the code performs such a task. Their presence in a small program may result in a restructuring process highly expensive, while a fast process can be achieved for large programs, if the composing words are easy to map, at least for the person involved in the restructuring, to their standard form.

### 6.1 Tool self-restructuring

The graphical user interface of the identifier restructuring tool was developed in Java. Although full operability of all tool modules is at the moment granted only for the C language, a preliminary version handling C++ and Java is under construction. It was employed for the restructuring of the tool user interface itself. In fact, the identifiers chosen for the graphical user interface objects were given a name constructed according to the following conventions: the first letter identifies the kind of object (e.g., l for Label, b for Button), while the successive number provides the line, in the window interface, where the object is displayed. Thus,

| Label | l1 | functionIdentifierLabel |
|---|---|---|
| Label | l2 | segmentedIdentifierLabel |
| Label | l3 | standardFormLabel |
| Label | l4 | tokenSequenceLabel |
| Label | l5 | parsingLabel |
| Label | l6 | outputIdentifierLabel |
| Label | l7 | emptyLabel |
| Button | b3 | acceptButton |
| Button | b4 | dictionaryButton |
| Button | b5 | grammarButton |
| Button | b7_1 | nextButton |
| Button | b7_2 | quitButton |
| TextField | t1 | functionIdentifierText |
| TextField | t2 | segmentedIdentifierText |
| TextField | t3 | standardFormText |
| TextField | t6 | outputIdentifierText |
| Choice | c4 | tokenSequenceChoice |
| TextArea | a5 | parsingTextArea |

**Table 8.** *Names of the tool user interface objects before and after restructuring. The left column gives the class of each object.*

e.g., b5 is the identifier of a Button appearing on the fifth line of the interface window. After a period of evolution of this program, the initial choice for the graphical object names revealed unhappy, because the function of the object is not explicitly represented in its name, and only its type and layout can be inferred from it. In other words, initially layout was privileged over functionality, but later functionality was recognized to be the information really needed, together with type. The restructuring shown in Table 8 was therefore manually defined, and it could be automatically enforced by means of the **Identifier Replacer** for Java. The new version of the program was still compilable and working, and it is now the official version. Its restructuring took less than half of an hour, including all necessary operations.

## 7  Conclusion

Restructuring of program identifiers was achieved by exploiting a standard lexicon for the composing words and a standard syntax for their arrangement. The lexicon was described by a dictionary of standard terms, complemented by a synonym dictionary for the mapping of non standard words. The syntax was inferred from examples representative of the different forms that can be associated to the main grammatical functions.

A tool was developed to support the standardization process. It was successfully applied to the public domain gzip

program. Moreover, it was applied to the Java program implementing the graphical user interface of the tool itself. In both cases, names could be migrated to a more meaningful standard form, thus increasing their self documenting ability. The resulting code could be compiled and executed without problems, with the names of its entities replaced with more meaningful ones. The reference lexicon and grammar exploited for the standardization of C function names were derived from a set of 10 real world applications, 9 of which are public domain, and one is industrial.

The whole restructuring process for gzip could be achieved with a very limited effort, even though it is not a fully automated process. In part this is due to the support tools that were exploited. Identifier extraction and replacement was totally automatic. Identifier standardization required the intervention of humans, but there is still room for tools to help them. For example, entries in the synonym dictionary provided a lexically standard alternative, that could be selected through a simple mouse click, while non compliances with the grammar were only seldom encountered and could be easily fixed. Exploiting the available general dictionaries of standard forms and synonyms allowed a very fast restructuring of gzip function identifiers. For about half of them, the standardization only required that the forms, automatically suggested by the restructuring tool, were confirmed by the user.

Future work will be devoted to improving the general standard and synonym dictionaries. Additional case studies will be conducted to obtain a better evaluation of costs and effects of restructuring. The extension of the available tool to other programming languages and paradigms will give the opportunity to perform a comparative study, both in terms of lexicon and syntax, on the different *dialects* that are used to construct program identifiers.

## References

[1] N. Anquetil and T. Lethbridge. Extracting concepts from file names; a new file clustering criterion. In *Proc. of the International Conference on Software Engineering*, pages 84–93. IEEE Computer Society, April 1998.

[2] G. Antoniol, A. Potrich, P. Tonella, and R. Fiutem. Evolving object oriented design to improve code traceability. In *Proc. of the International Workshop on Program Comprehension*, pages 151–160, Pittsburgh, PA, USA, May 1999.

[3] G. Butler, P. Grogono, R. Shinghal, and I. Tjandra. Retrieving information from data flow diagrams. In *Proc. of the Working Conference on Reverse Engineering*, pages 22–29. IEEE Computer Society, July 1995.

[4] B. Caprile and P. Tonella. Nomen est omen: Analyzing the language of function identifiers. In *Proc. of the Working Conference on Reverse Engineering, WCRE'99*, pages 112–122, Atlanta, Georgia, USA, October 1999.

[5] J. C. S. do Prado Leite and P. M. Cerqueira. Recovering business rules from structured analysis specifications. In *Proc.*

*of the Working Conference on Reverse Engineering*, pages 13–21. IEEE Computer Society, July 1995.

[6] M. Lindvall and K. Sandahl. Practical implications of traceability. *Software: Practice and Experience*, 26(10):1161–1180, October 1996.

[7] P. Lutsky. Automating testing by reverse engineering of software documentation. In *Proc. of the Working Conference on Reverse Engineering*, pages 8–12. IEEE Computer Society, July 1995.

[8] S. Matwin and A. Ahmad. Reuse of modular software with automated comment analysis. In *Proc. of the International Conference on Software Maintenance*, pages 222–231. IEEE Computer Society, September 1994.

[9] E. Merlo, I. McAdam, and R. D. Mori. Source code informal information analysis using connectionist models. In *Proc. of the International Joint Conference on Artificial Intelligence*, pages 1339–1344, 1993.

[10] S. Nanduri and S. Rugaber. Requirements validation via automated natural language parsing. *Journal of Management Information Systems*, 12(3):9–19, January 1995.

[11] J. Sayyad-Shirabad, T. C. Lethbridge, and S. Lyon. A little knowledge can go a long way towards program understanding. In *Proc. of the International Workshop on Program Comprehension*, pages 111–117. IEEE Computer Society, May 1997.

[12] A. Takang, P. Grubb, and R. Macredie. The effects of comments and identifier names on program comprehensibility: An experimental study. *Journal of Programming Languages*, 4(3):143–167, 1996.

# The Application Of Correctness Preserving Transformations To Software Maintenance

J. Paul Gibson, Thomas F. Dowling
Department of Computer Science
National University of Ireland, Maynooth
Kildare, Ireland
{pgibson,tdowling}@cs.may.ie

Brian A. Malloy
Department of Computer Science
Clemson University
Clemson, SC 29634
malloy@cs.clemson.edu

*Abstract*— The size and complexity of hardware and software systems continues to grow, making the introduction of subtle errors a more likely possibility. A major goal of software engineering is to enable developers to construct systems that operate reliably despite increased size and complexity. One approach to achieving this goal is through formal methods: mathematically based languages, techniques and tools for specifying and verifying complex software systems. In this paper, we apply a theoretical tool that is supported by many formal methods, the *correctness preserving transformation* (CPT), to a real software engineering problem: the need for optimization during the maintenance of code. We present four program transformations and a model that forms a framework for proof of correctness. We prove the transformations correct and then apply them to a cryptography application implemented in $C++$. Our experience shows that CPTs can facilitate generation of more efficient code while guaranteeing the preservation of original behavior.

*Keywords*— Reverse engineering, formal methods, public key cryptography, correctness preserving transformation, code optimization.

## I. INTRODUCTION

The size and complexity of hardware and software systems continues to grow, making the introduction of subtle errors a more likely possibility. Some of these errors may cause inconvenience or loss of money, while some errors may even cause loss of life. A major goal of software engineering is to enable developers to construct systems that operate reliably despite increased size and complexity. One approach to achieving this goal is through formal methods: mathematically based languages, techniques and tools for specifying and verifying complex software systems[8]

Although formal methods have increasingly been applied to the specification and verification of software models and systems, they have rarely been applied to software maintenance[24]. Perhaps the rare application of formal methods to maintenance is due to the difficulties involved: the program developer has complete control over the structure and organization of the development process, whereas the reverse engineer must maintain a completed system, possibly poorly documented and poorly constructed. Due to this difficulty, many attempts at applying formal methods to software maintenance have targeted toy programs rather than real applications[24].

In this paper, we apply a theoretical tool that is supported by many formal methods, the *correctness preserving transformation* (CPT), to a real software engineering problem: the need for optimization during the maintenance of code. We present four program transformations and a model that forms a framework for proof of correctness. We prove the transformations correct and then apply them to a cryptography application[11] implemented in the $C++$ programming language[1]. Our experience shows that CPTs can facilitate generation of more efficient code while guaranteeing the preservation of original behavior. Our ongoing work includes the application of the CPTs to other sections of the cryptography application, and reusing the CPTs in other applications[21], [22].

The remainder of this paper is organized as follows. In the next section we provide background about cryptography, the cryptography application that we use as a case study, and the formal techniques that we employ in this paper. In Section III we present our methodology for proving correctness. Section IV contains the four CPTs and the proofs of correctness. In Section V we present the results of our case study where we apply the CPTs to a cryptography application[22], showing a dramatic increase in efficiency with only a single application of the CPTs. Finally, in Section VI, we draw conclusions.

## II. BACKGROUND

In the next section we provide background about a cryptography application that we use to demonstrate the ef-

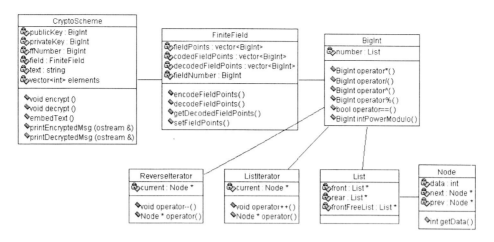

Fig. 1. *Class diagram for cryptography application.* This figure illustrates the important classes in our application for encryption and decryption. All four of our CPTs were applied to the BigInt and List classes. However, the other classes contain opportunity to apply some of the CPTs that we present.

ficiency of our CPTs. Section II-B contains background about the formal techniques that we use in this paper.

### A. The Cryptography Application

Our cryptography application uses *public key* encryption where the encryption and decryption keys are distinct. It's possible to determine the decryption key from the encryption key but, by using sufficiently large keys, this determination is computationally infeasible. This protection is achieved by the use of a *trapdoor process*. A trapdoor process is computationally trivial in one direction but computationally infeasible in the opposite direction without some additional information. There are many examples of trapdoor processes in mathematics but our application uses finite fields. To make decryption computationally infeasible we will use sufficiently large Finite Fields. By sufficiently large we mean the number of elements in the field to be of the order of one hundred digits.

The implementation that we use is based on the El Gamal encryption scheme[12]. The finite field version works as follows: Let the integer equivalent of the message to be transmitted be denoted by $P$. Users A and B start by deciding upon a very large finite field $\mathbf{F}_p$ and a generator $g$ of that field. User A randomly chooses an integer $a$ in the range $0 < a < p - 1$. This is the secret deciphering key. A then computes and publishes $g^a$. This is the public key. User B does the same thing. To send a message to user A, an integer $k$ is chosen at random and A is sent the following pair of elements of $\mathbf{F}_p$,

$$(g^k, Pg^{ak})$$

Recall that $g^a$ is publicly known but $a$ is known only to the user A. With this knowledge the user A can strip off the $g^{ak}$ and retrieve $P$, but without the knowledge of $a$ no one else can retrieve $P$.

Figure 1 illustrates the important classes for implementing our cryptography application. Users of the system need only instantiate CryptoScheme, the class shown in the upper left corner of Figure 1, with the text to be encrypted or decrypted. CryptoScheme contains methods to encrypt or decrypt the text, and uses a finite field to afford public key protection. The FiniteField class uses extended precision numbers; thus the association with BigInt, shown in the upper right corner of the figure. To implement extended precision numbers, the digits of the number are stored in a list, with iterators to traverse the number in either direction. The List class and corresponding iterator classes are shown at the bottom of Figure 1. All of our CPTs were applied to the BigInt and List classes.

### B. Formal Methods and CPTs

Software development has reached the point where the complexity of the systems being modeled cannot be handled without a thorough understanding of underlying fundamental principles. Such understanding forms the basis of scientific theory as a rationale for software development techniques that are successful in practice. This scientific theory, as expressed in rigorous mathematical formalisms, must be transferred to the software development environment. In this way, we can more accurately refer to the development of software systems as *software engineering*: the application of techniques, based on mathematical theory, towards the construction of abstract machines as a means of solving well defined problems. This paper reports on such a *technology transfer*.

## B.1 Introducing Formal Methods

Formal methods are techniques whose principle goal is the construction of theories (and tools based on these theoretical models) for the development of *correct* software[10], [2]. A theoretical tool that is supported by many formal methods is the *correctness preserving transformation* (CPT). In this paper we are concerned with the practical application of this theory in a real software engineering problem: the need for optimization during the evolution and maintenance of code, without compromising an already *well behaved* system.

## B.2 Targeting Formal Methods

Formal methods are not widely used in real software development (the best-known exceptions are in telecommunications, safety-critical systems and embedded systems). In many cases, this is because they are not suitably supported with development tools. Furthermore, engineers are justifiably wary of some of the over-inflated claims coming from the formal methods community. This, in turn, has led to a certain mythology about the use and abuse of formal methods [16], [3]. Finally, these methods, for a variety of reasons, are viewed as being *costly*. A partial solution to this problem, supported by this paper, is the application of a very specific formal technique, in a specific problem domain, in order to provide much needed focus, so that software engineers can make up their own minds about the utility of formality.

We acknowledge that it is impossible for a software system to be *perfect*. When developing software we must decide upon the primary characteristics that will drive the process. Correctness is only one such characteristic among many others such as: time-to-market, user-friendliness, completeness, performance, fault tolerance, scale-ability, extensibility, portability, re-usability and cost. In this paper we report on our choice to employ formal techniques in the verification of our code optimizations. Our experience shows that *correctness preserving transformations* can facilitate the generation of more efficient code while guaranteeing the preservation of original behavior.

## B.3 Transformational Design in formal development

Design is the process that transforms an initially abstract (implementation independent) specification of system requirements into a final, more constructive (implementation oriented) specification. A fundamental notion in this work is design trajectory: a sequence of steps, where each step changes the previous specification in some way. The important thing is that something must also be preserved along this trajectory: the *correctness of the design*[23].

At each step, a transformation can be applied that reflects some architectural choice, without altering the external (observable) behavior of the system. In theory, it is possible to verify the correctness of any given design (or programming) step by mathematical means[10], [26]. In practice, the complete formal verification of most design steps is not possible because of combinatorial problems. In these cases, specifications are partly verified by simulation and testing.

In this paper we take the view that a code optimization corresponds precisely to the formal methods notion of a design transformation. We treat the non-optimum code as if it were a functional specification of the required behavior, and we consider the optimized code to be the result of applying some sort of design modification to the original code. A formal framework provides the means of proving that the transformation (optimization) is *correct*, by proving that the functional behavior is maintained. Of course, such proofs can be long and tedious and prone to error. However, if we can re-use the formal analysis or proof every time we perform the same transformation, then this re-use would go a long way toward overcoming the expense of the proof. This re-use is one of the contributions of this paper.

## B.4 Re-usable Proofs — CPTs

In CPT-driven design, we get verification *for free* because we apply only transformations (design changes) whose correctness has already been proven. For a classic CPT-driven approach to verification we recommend the paper by Brown[5]. We proceed by introducing formal terminology about CPTs.

A specification can be said to be *correct* if it fulfills some property. Assume a specification $S$, a transformation $T$ and define $S' = T(S)$, i.e. $S'$ is the result of applying $T$ to $S$. $T$ can be said to be correctness preserving with respect to the property $P$ if $P(S) \Rightarrow P(S')$. In other words, the property $P$ is preserved across the transformation $T$.

We chose to distinguish between external and internal

properties. *External* properties are those that can be observed through interaction with a system at its external interface. They are said to be purely functional as they are concerned with *what* the system does rather than *how* (well) it does it. *Internal* properties are those that can be derived through examination of the text that specifies the system in question. They cannot be 'extracted' through interaction with the system interface alone. Formulation of these properties requires the definition of a non-standard interpretation of the specification. This interpretation is said to provide a *view* on the system. In this paper we are concerned with CPTs that maintain external properties. Such CPTs are said to be *structural*.

By differentiating between what should stay the same and what should be different, as the result of a design change, an elegant and formal statement of the requirements of a design step can be given as follows. Given:

A specification $S_1$
An implementation relation $R$
A view function $V$, which has $S_1$ in its domain
A view property $P$ that is fulfilled by $V(S_1)$, i.e. $P(V(S_1))$ is true.
A view property $P'$ and a second view $V'$ such that not($P'(V'(S_1))$)

A *structural* design change corresponds to the specification of $S_2$, the next design, such that:
$R(S_1, S_2)$, and $R$ is a strong bisimulation equivalence[1].
$P(V(S_2))$ and $P'(V'(S_2))$

In other words, $S_2$ maintains the external behavior of $S_1$, maintains the view property $P$ and adheres to a new view property $P'$, which was not fulfilled by $S_1$. One could say that the reason for defining $S_2$ was the fulfillment of this new property.

### B.5 Code Optimizations as CPTs

The formulation of a code optimization as a CPT is straightforward:

$S_1$ corresponds to the original piece of code to be optimized
$S_2$ corresponds to the new code
$V$ is some view formalized by the algorithmic complexity
$P$ is some (complexity) property exhibited by $S_1$
$P'$ is some (complexity) property exhibited by $S_2$ but not $S_1$
$V'$ is usually taken to be the same as $V$, but it could be formulated, for example, as a more precise statement of complexity that could address such issues as best/worst-case scenarios and/or memory usage.

### III. METHODOLOGY: REVERSE ENGINEERING FOR CORRECTNESS

In our formulation of a code optimization as a CPT, we have hidden the crux of the problem, namely: proving that the final behavior of our 2 pieces of code are functionally

---

[1] Strong bisimulation equivalence states that the behavior trees offered by $S_1$ and $S_2$ are the same (even if the way in which they are specified is different). In programming languages, this would correspond to being functionally equivalent.

equivalent. The semantics of our chosen programming language ($C++$) make such a proof practically impossible to construct, given the current state-of-the-art, in all but the most trivial cases. However, this does not imply that we should completely abandon our theoretical goal of proving the optimization to be correct. In fact, we can, using expert knowledge of $C++$ and the implementation of its semantics (as specified by the compiler), argue for equivalence in a semi-formal (rigorous) manner. Our first goal should be to verify the soundness of such rigorous arguments. This can best be achieved by expressing the argument in a formal framework. There are two possibilities:

• The $C++$ code was developed from a formal specification and we can re-use this specification framework in order to formulate and verify our reasoning. (In the current context of software engineering, this is very unlikely.)

• No formal specification of the code exists and we have to reverse engineer the functional requirements through a process of abstract interpretation, in order to verify our reasoning.

In this paper, we report on our experiences with the second case. The advantage over the first case is that we can choose to formulate our reasoning in whatever framework best suits our needs. The disadvantage is that we have more work to do in order to build an abstract model.

### A. The problem of multi-semantic models

We must acknowledge that a weakness inherent in our approach arises from our use of at least two potentially very different semantic frameworks. The proof of consistency between models in different semantic domains is a very important area of on-going research (see [13], [15] for some of our previous work in this area). Without consistency, our reasoning in one domain may not be valid in the other. It is beyond the scope of this paper to directly address this issue: we do return to it in later sections and argue that our experiments provide further motivation for continuing the research into constructing unified mixed-semantic models.

### B. Abstract interpretation for reverse engineering

When we reverse engineer the code to a more formal mathematical model, it is important that we abstract away from irrelevant implementation details[20]. The goal is to develop an abstract interpretation that captures precisely the functional requirements, the internal view and the nonfunctional properties (and no more). In many cases, this

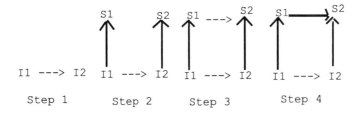

Step 1   Step 2   Step 3   Step 4

Fig. 2. Implementation Oriented Optimization

will require a close structural mapping between implementation code and the reverse engineered specification. This could prove problematic if the structures supported in the implementation language are not directly supported in the formal framework. However, as we shall see later in this section, the use of object oriented structuring mechanisms makes it easier for us to find correspondences between structures at all levels of abstraction (see [14] for a more comprehensive treatment of this argument).

### C. Implementation oriented optimization

Consider the diagram in Figure 2.

The four steps, of the implementation oriented optimization, are as follows:

**Step 1 —**
Transform the initial code, $I_1$, to optimize it as $I_2$. Sketch an argument that the transformation is correct.
**Step 2 —**
Reverse engineer $I_1$ and $I_2$ to $S_1$ and $S_2$, respectively.
**Step 3 —**
Formulate a proof, in the formal framework, that $S_2$ is correct with respect to the functional requirements of $S_1$. This proof must follow the argument sketched in step 1.
**Step 4 —**
Attempt to verify the proof (using tools available in the formal domain). If the proof is correct then we have verified our informal reasoning of the correctness of the optimization. Otherwise, we can change $I_2$, in order to *fill in the holes in the proof*, or we can change our reasoning process, in order to re-formulate the proof.

In this approach we say that the optimization is implementation-oriented because the transformation is first formulated at the code level. This is the approach followed in this paper.

### D. Specification oriented optimization: re-usable correctness

Consider the diagram in Figure 3.

The three steps, of the specification oriented optimization, are as follows:

**Step 1 —**
Reverse engineer the code, mapping $I_1$ to $S_1$.

**Step 2 —**
Apply an already proven CPT to transform $S_1$ into $S_2$, where $S_2$ fulfills the additional properties required in our optimization.
**Step 3 —**
Use $S_2$ to develop $I_2$. This development could possibly be supported by some sort of automated code generator.
**Ideal step —**
If the reverse engineer mapping and the code generation mapping can be proven to be correct then we have a fully formalized proof that $I_2$ is correct with respect to the external functionality of $I_1$.

### E. Correctness of the mappings

Proving the correctness of the mappings across semantic frameworks is a difficult task. However, progress has been made and this is continuing research[19]. It is clear that it is much easier to analyze the mappings when the semantic domain is small. Consequently, proving the correctness of our reverse engineering of the $C++$ code is a much more difficult task than proving the correctness of our code generation from the formal specification. In fact, the mapping from specification to implementation can be relatively straightforward to formulate: in the next section we see how the $C++$ class can be mapped onto an abstract data type (ADT[2]) specification of a type. (It is well accepted that an ADT can be conceptualized as an abstract class specification[4], [9].) This is the basis upon which we build the mappings (in both directions).

## IV. Proof of Correctness

In this section, we apply our methodology for reverse engineering the functional requirements through a process of abstract interpretation, in order to verify our transformations. Each transformation represents an ad-hoc, expert-driven optimization; currently, application of the transformations is not automated. We begin each section by describing the transformation under consideration, and then we proceed with a proof of correctness.

---

[2]The text by Cardelli[6] provides a good introduction to such algebraic specification languages.

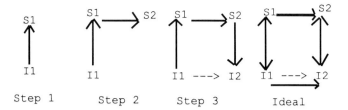

Fig. 3. Specification Oriented Optimization

```
BigInt BigInt::power(const BigInt & exponent) const {

    if (exponent == 0) return 1;
    else if (exponent == 1) return number;
    else {
        BigInt temp = power(exponent/2);
        if (exponent % 2 == 0) {
            return temp * temp;
        }
        else {
            return ((*this) * temp * temp);
        }
    }
}
```

Fig. 4. Tree Pruning (TP). This figure illustrates the C++ version of
our optimization to improve the efficiency of raising an extended
precision number to a power.

### A. The TP transformation

The goal of the tree pruning transformation, tree pruning
(TP), is to reduce the computation, from O(n) to O(log n),
through the use of a symmetrical argument whereby both
branches of a tree can be shown to evaluate to the same
value. As an example of this transformation, consider raising an extended precision number (BigInt) to an exponent.
Half of the computation can be obviated by computing the
result of raising the number to half of the exponent and
then using multiplication to square the result. Then, in
the evaluation of one branch of the tree, the same argument can be re-applied recursively. The C++ version of
our code for TP is illustrated in Figure 4.

We formalize this transformation by modeling the two
functions as ADT operations, on a BigInt type, and proving equivalence (through consistency analysis) of the two
operations. Consider, below, the specification, written in
ACT ONE (an ADT used in an LOTOS[18], an interna-
tionally recognized formal method).

**TYPE** BigInt **SORTS** BigInt
**OPNS** 0,1:-> BigInt
+,*: BigInt, BigInt -> BigInt
equals: BigInt, BigInt -> Bool
power1: BigInt, BigInt -> BigInt
power1local: BigInt, BigInt, BigInt, BigInt -> BigInt
**EQNS FORALL** this,exponent,answer,count: BigInt

power1(this, exponent) = power1local(this,exponent,1,0);
[equals(count,exponent)] =>
power1local(this,exponent,answer,count) = answer;
[not(equals(count,exponent))] =>
power1local(this,exponent,answer,count) =
power1local(this,exponent,answer*this,count+1);
**ENDTYPE** (*BigInt*)

This is the formal specification that arises when we reverse engineer the original **power** method of the BigInt
C++ class. There are a number of things to note, in general, about this reverse engineering process:

• The methods of the class correspond to operations of
the ADT type. This maps the purely syntactic notion of
interface.

• The method bodies of the class correspond to the equations of the type. This maps the semantics (meaning) of
the code to be reverse engineered.

• We explicitly represent the C++ **this** operator as the
first parameter in each of the ADT operation definitions.

• We have abstracted away from the operation overloading
of the C++ power operator. It is not relevant to our proof.

• We have not given the semantics for the operators +,-,*
and **equals**: for the moment we assume that they work as
required ... we re-examine this assumption when we return
to our proof of correctness.

• We explicitly provide the literal constructors (for the values 0 and 1) of **BigInt**.

Now let us consider the mapping of the C++ **while** loop.
There is a standard technique for this type of reverse engineering, which we summarize below:

• The **while** condition is mapped directly onto an expression precondition (in the square brackets).

• The use of temporary variables in the **while** loop (the
**count** and the **answer**) requires us to define a local function, called **power1local**, in which these values are stored
as additional parameters.

• The initialization of the local parameters, before the
**while** loop, corresponds to our call to the local function

113

where the parameters are given the required values.

- The body of the loop maps to the re-initialization of the parameter values, in the recursive calls, as required.

The next step is to reverse engineer the optimized code, as specified by `power2` in $C++$. The resulting ADT specification is:

**TYPE** BigInt **SORTS** BigInt
**OPNS** 0,1:-> BigInt
+,*,mod,/: BigInt, BigInt -> BigInt
equals: BigInt, BigInt -> Bool
power2: BigInt, BigInt -> BigInt
**EQNS FORALL** this,exponent,temp: BigInt
square(temp) = temp*temp;
[equals(exponent,0)] => power2(this,exponent) = 1;
[equals(exponent,1)] => power2(this,exponent) = this;
[(exponent>= 1) and equals((exponent mod 2),0)] =>
power2(this,exponent) = square(power2(this, exponent/2);
[(exponent>= 1) and not(equals((exponent mod 2),0))] =>
power2(this,exponent) = this* square(power2(this, exponent/2);
**ENDTYPE** (*BigInt*)

The mapping procedure is similar to the first function, but we make the additional notes:

- We have additional assumptions to make about the operators `mod` and `/`.

- The recursive structure of the second $C++$ function maps directly onto the same recursive structure in the ADT specification

- We introduce a `square` operation in order to store the the value of our temporary variable `temp`, defined as `power2(this, exponent/2)`.

- The sequence of $C++$ `if-else` statements *requires a bit more work* in the ADT specification because there is no syntactic sugar for representing the `else` case. (However, the generation of the equivalent sequence of preconditions is easy to automate.)

To prove that power1 and power2 are equivalent in our formal framework, we follow the following strategy:

- Formulate the assumptions that we make about the operators of the BigInt class as preconditions of correctness. It is straightforward to prove these preconditions, in our formal ADT framework, but we do not report on this as part of this paper.

- State the equivalence property as: `power1(x,y) = power2(x,y)`, forall x and y of type BigInt.

- Prove the property by using the ADT tools to prove consistency of the BigInt specification containing `power1`, `power2` and the equivalence property; or prove the property directly using a proof by structural induction on the y variable.

It is beyond the scope of the paper to report on the use of the ADT tool to prove consistency of specifications.

However, we do *sketch* the proof by structural induction, below:
The **base case (when y =0)** —
By definition of `power1` and `power2`,
`power1(x,0) = power1local(x,0,1,0) = 1` and `power2(x,0) = 1`
Thus, `power1(x,y) = power2(x,y)` when y = 0.

The **inductive case** —
We assume that:
`power1(x,y) = power2(x,y)` for some y, and we are required to prove that:
`power1(x,y+1) = power2(x, y+1)`

By definition of `power1` and `power1local`,
`power1(x,y+1)=power1local(x,y+1,1,0)=power1local(x,y+1,x,1)`.
Now, for any two BigInts (a and b, say) then `a equals b` iff `a+1 equals b+1`, thus:
`power1local(x,y+1,x,1) equals power1local(x,y,x,0)`
By definition of `*`, `power1` and `power1local`,
`power1local(x,y,x,0) equals (x*power1local(x,y,1,0)) equals (x * power1(x,y))`
Now, by the induction hypothesis, this equals `x*power2(x,y)`.

It remains only to show that: `power2(x, y+1) equals x*power2(x,y)`. This is done by considering the case where y is odd and the case where y is even. Each follows from the definition of `power2(x,y)` and the assumption that the `*` operator is *correctly defined*.

(A complete copy of the proof can be obtained from the authors, on request.)

*B. The AR transformation*

The goal of the array reference transformation (AR), is to obviate an O(n) array lookup. To do this, data values, that are to be searched in the array, are mapped to an integer that will be used as an index into the array. Then, rather than searching the array for the value and returning the corresponding index in O(n) time, the value can be found with a direct lookup in O(1) time.

The proof of the correctness of this transformation is based upon proving that the alphabet array corresponds to the identity function. In the reverse engineering of the original non-optimized code, we map the notion of an array into a function whose domain is the set of valid array indices. For this, we chose a pure functional language (like SML[25]) as our formal framework (whose semantics corresponds to the lambda-calculus of Alonzo Church [7]). We *sketch* the proof, below:
Define: `alphabet = [ (0,0); (1,1); (2,2); ...(255,255)`
`arrayindex((x,y)::z, i)= if i=x then y else arrayindex(z,i)`
Now, we prove that:
`arrayindex(alphabet, x) = x`, provided 0<= x <= 255
Thus, the non-optimum access function defined as:
`access1 (alphabet, i) = arrayindex(alphabet, expression(i))`
Can be re-written as an equivalent function `access2`, defined as:
`access2 (alphabet, expression(i)) = expression(i)`

Although this proof is straightforward, we have gained some insight into why it is superior to reasoning directly in the $C++$ framework: the formulation of the abstract interpretation improves our understanding of the reasoning process and identifies assumptions that need to be verified for the transformation to be correct. In this example, there is an important aspect of this abstract interpretation that needs explanation: the `expression(i)` in our formal model is evaluated twice without any side-effects. In fact, our reasoning would break down if there were any side-effects in the expression when used in the $C++$ code. Through simple inspection, we argue that instantiating the expression as `(int)text[i]` is valid (since its evaluation is side-effect free in $C++$).

## C. The MM transformation

The goal of the memory management transformation (MM), is to minimize calls to new and delete to manage dynamic memory. In MM, the delete operator is overloaded to place the deleted object into a free list. Also, the new operator is overloaded and the actions of new are to first check the free list: if the free list is not empty, then the requested storage is allocated from the free list; otherwise, the system new is used to allocate memory from the heap.

The proof of correctness of this transformation cannot be treated satisfactorily in this paper. It is more complex than the other three: we are preparing a separate paper on the approach taken to prove this complicated transformation to be correct. (For those interested, the crux of the problem is in finding a suitable abstract interpretation for the memory in the system and choosing the best formal representation. Unlike the other transformation, these choices are not straightforward.)

## D. The BA transformation

The goal of the boundary analysis transformation (BA), is to avoid a computation by exploiting the shortcut provided by a boundary computation. For example, when computing the modulus two of a number, the result is determined by the digit in the unit position: if this digit is even, then the result is zero, if this digit is odd, then the result is one.

The modeling of this transformation is trivial, in almost any formal framework. The proof of correctness is also trivial: all we need is an abstraction (defined as a function, `AI`, say) of the data values that specifies an equivalence between different numbers provided they return the same result with respect to the specified modulus computation. Then, in the optimized function, the computation can be defined directly on the abstraction rather than on the number itself. The proof can then be formulated as:

`Modulus (number) = Modulus2 (AI(number))`, for all valid numbers

## V. Applying the CPTs to an Application: A Case Study

In this section, we report on the efficiency improvement that we achieved by applying the four correctness preserving transformations (CPTs) to a cryptography application[22]. All executions that we report were executed on a 500 MHz Dell Optiplex, running the Linux Red Hat 6.1 operating system. We implemented the cryptography application with the egcs $C++$ compiler, release 1.1.2. Each of the executions that we report represent the results of twelve executions, the lowest and highest value was discarded and the reported result is the average of the ten remaining values.

In the next section we report our results after applying each of the four CPTs in turn, so that we can compare the effect of each optimization. We used profile information, acquired from the gprof profiling tool, to guide placement of each of the CPTs.

In Section V-B, we report our results after applying all four CPTs to the application; we only applied each CPT a single time to facilitate clarity of analysis. We applied the CPT at the same point in the application that it was applied for the executions described in Section V-A.

## A. Results for each individual CPT

Figure 5 illustrates the results of applying each of the CPTs, in turn, to the cryptography application. The table at the top of the figure shows the execution times after applying each of the CPTs, the bar graph at the bottom of the figure further illustrates these timings. For the table, the first column illustrates the applied optimization; the remaining columns illustrate reported results. For example, the second column illustrates the number of seconds required to both encrypt and decrypt a file containing 1000 randomly generated characters. The first row of data illustrates timings for the original program, without any optimizations applied, the second row illustrates timings for the array reference optimization (AR), the third row for the memory management optimization (MM), the fourth row for the boundary analysis optimization (BA) and the last row illustrates timings for the tree pruning optimization (TP). For example, in the original program using none

| Program Optimization | seconds for 1000 bytes | seconds for 2000 bytes | seconds for 3000 bytes | seconds for 4000 bytes | seconds for 5000 bytes |
|---|---|---|---|---|---|
| original | 9.13 | 16.98 | 25.18 | 34.70 | 43.14 |
| AR | 8.96 | 16.39 | 24.60 | 33.78 | 42.09 |
| MM | 5.67 | 10.50 | 15.75 | 21.58 | 26.74 |
| BA | 6.21 | 11.52 | 17.28 | 23.66 | 29.54 |
| TP | 6.35 | 11.95 | 17.97 | 24.69 | 30.64 |

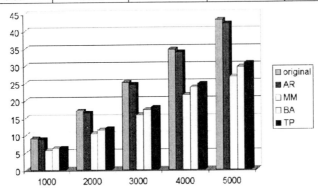

Fig. 5. *The effect of each optimization.* The results depicted in this table show the outcome of applying each of the optimizations once in the program.

of the transformations, the average time to encrypt and decrypt a file of 1000 characters was 9.13 seconds, as shown in the first row, second column of the table.

The bar graph in Figure 5 better illustrates our results. Time, in seconds, is plotted on the y-axis of the graph and file size, in 1000 byte increments, is plotted on the x-axis of the graph. The first set of five bars represents timings for the original program and each of the four optimizations. For each set of experiments, the highest bar is always the original program and the lowest bar is always the program containing the MM optimization. The array reference transformation provided the smallest improvement in execution time, but consistently provided improvement. This transformation was not placed in an area of code that was frequently executed.

### B. Results for all four CPTs

Figure 6 illustrates the results of applying all four of the CPTs, a single time, to the cryptography application. The table at the top of the figure illustrates timings for both the original program and for the program containing all four transformations. The columns are similar to those in Figure 5. The bar graph at the bottom of the figure further illustrates our timings, where the four transformations consistently provided sixty percent increase in efficiency. We found many more opportunity for exploiting some of the transformations; for example, we found seven places in the cryptography application where we could apply the BA transformation but only two places where we could apply

the AR transformation. By applying each transformation only once, we can better see the cumulative effect of the four transformations.

## VI. CONCLUDING REMARKS

In this paper, we applied *correctness preserving transformations*, CPTs, to a real software engineering problem: the need for optimization during the maintenance of code. We have presented a framework for proving CPTs correct and four CPTs together with proofs of their correctness. We have applied the CPTs to an existing cryptography application, implemented in $C++$, and have shown dramatic improvement in efficiency with only a single use of each CPT. Our ongoing work on this project includes efforts to apply the CPTs to other sections of the cryptography application as well as the development of additional CPTs. We are also applying the CPTs to other applications to further demonstrate their re-use. Our future work includes an examination of the effects of the transformations on test set adequacy[17].

## VII. ACKNOWLEDGEMENT

We would like to thank Paul Redkoles for his help acquiring profile information and for his tireless experiments with gprof.

## REFERENCES

[1] ISO/IEC JTC 1. *International Standard: Programming Languages - C++.* Number 14882:1998(E) in ASC X3. American National Standards Institute, first edition, September 1998.

| Program Optimization | seconds for 1000 bytes | seconds for 2000 bytes | seconds for 3000 bytes | seconds for 4000 bytes | seconds for 5000 bytes |
|---|---|---|---|---|---|
| original | 9.13 | 16.98 | 25.18 | 34.70 | 43.14 |
| All four | 3.75 | 7.01 | 10.50 | 14.49 | 17.83 |

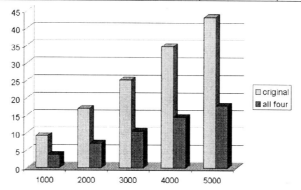

Fig. 6. *The effect of applying all four optimizations.* The results depicted in this table show the outcome of applying all four of the optimizations once in the program.

[2] R.L. Baber. *The Spine of Software — Designing Provably Correct Software: Theory and Practice, or: A Mathematical Introduction To The Semantics Of Computer Programs.* John Wiley and Sons, 1987.

[3] J. Bowen and M. Hinchley. Seven more myths of formal methods. *IEEE Software,* 12(4):34–41, 1995.

[4] R. Breu. *Algebraic Specification Techniques in Object Oriented Programming Environments.* Springer-Verlag, 1991. Lecture Notes in Computing Science, number 562.

[5] N. Brown. Correctness-preserving transformations for the design of parallel programs. In *ECOOP '94 Workshops : Models and Languages for Coordination and Parallelism and Distribution.* Springer Verlag, 1995.

[6] L. Cardelli and P. Wegner. On understanding types, data abstraction, and polymorphism. *ACM Computing Surveys,* 17(4):471–523, December 1985.

[7] Alonzo Church. The calculi of lambda conversion. *Annals of Mathematics Studies,* 6, 1941.

[8] E. M. Clarke, J. M. Wing, and et al. Formal methods: State of the art and future directions. *ACM Computing Surveys,* 28(4):626–643, December 1996.

[9] S. Danforth and C. Tomlinson. Type theories and object-oriented programming. *ACM Computing Surveys,* 20(1):29–72, March 1988.

[10] J.W. de Bakker. *Mathematical Theory of Programming Correctness.* Prentice-Hall, 1980.

[11] T. Dowling and B. A. Malloy. The design of a component-based encryption scheme. *Proceedings of the Fifth International Conference on Computer Science and Informatics,* February 2000. (to appear).

[12] T. El Gamal. A public key cryptosystem and a signature scheme based on discrete logarithms. *IEEE Transactions on information Theory IT-31,* pages 469–472, 1985.

[13] J.-P. Gibson and D. Méry. A Unifying Model for Multi-Semantic Software Development. Rapport Interne CRIN-96-R-110, CRIN, Linz (Austria), July 1996.

[14] J.Paul Gibson. *Formal Object Oriented Development of Software Systems Using LOTOS.* Tech. report csm-114, Stirling University, August 1993.

[15] Mermet Gibson and Méry. Feature interactions: A mixed semantic model approach. In *Irish Workshop on Formal Methods,* Dublin, Ireland, July 1997.

[16] Anthony Hall. Seven myths of formal methods. *IEEE Software,* 7(5):11–19, 1990.

[17] M. J. Harrold. The effects of optimizing transformations on dataflow-adequate test sets. *Proceedings of the Symposium on Testing, Analysis and Verification,* pages 130–138, 1991.

[18] ISO. LOTOS — a formal description technique based on the temporal ordering of observed behaviour. Technical report, International Organisation for Standardisation IS 8807, 1988.

[19] Andy Galloway Keijiro Araki and Kenji Taguchi (editors). *Integrated Formal Methods conference (IFM99).* Springer, 1999.

[20] B. Liskov and J. Guttag. *Abstraction and Specification in Program Development.* MIT Press, 1986.

[21] B. A. Malloy, D E. Bushey, and S. Yang. Using jet routes to model path re-routing in the national airspace system. *Proceedings of the 13th European Simulation Multiconference (ESM99),* pages 543–550, June 1994.

[22] B. A. Malloy, J. D. McGregor, and S. Hughes. Integrating a gui into a command driven application. *International Journal of Computer and Applications,* 2000. (to appear).

[23] Helmut A. Partsch. *Specification and Transformation of Programs: A Formal Approach To Software Development.* Springer-Verlag, 1990.

[24] M. P. Ward. Reverse engineering through formal transformation. *Technical Report for Computer Science Labs,* pages 1–19, August 1994. http://www.dur.ac.uk/ dcs0mpw/martin/papers/.

[25] A. Wikstrom. *Functional Programming Using Standard ML.* Prentice-Hall, 1987.

[26] N. Wirth. Program development by step-wise refinement. *Comm. ACM,* 14:221–227, 1971.

# Notes

# Empirical Studies I

# Identifying Reasons for Software Changes Using Historic Databases

Audris Mockus
Bell Laboratories
Software Production Research Department
263 Shuman Blv. Rm. 2F-319
Naperville, IL 60566
audris@research.bell-labs.com

Lawrence G. Votta
Senior Member of Technical Staff
High Availability Platform Development
Motorola, Inc.
Arlington Heights, IL 60004 USA
lvotta1@email.mot.com

## Abstract

*Large scale software products must constantly change in order to adapt to a changing environment. Studies of historic data from legacy software systems have identified three specific causes of this change: adding new features; correcting faults; and restructuring code to accommodate future changes.*

*Our hypothesis is that a textual description field of a change is essential to understanding why that change was performed. Also, we expect that difficulty, size, and interval would vary strongly across different types of changes.*

*To test these hypotheses we have designed a program which automatically classifies maintenance activity based on a textual description of changes. Developer surveys showed that the automatic classification was in agreement with developer opinions. Tests of the classifier on a different product found that size and interval for different types of changes did not vary across two products.*

*We have found strong relationships between the type and size of a change and the time required to carry it out. We also discovered a relatively large amount of perfective changes in the system we examined.*

*From this study we have arrived at several suggestions on how to make version control data useful in diagnosing the state of a software project, without significantly increasing the overhead for the developer using the change management system.*

## 1  Introduction

The traditional approaches to understanding the software development process define specific questions, experiments to answer those questions, and instrumentation needed to collect data (see, e.g., the GQM model [2]). While such an approach has advantages (i.e., in some cases defines a controlled experiment), we believe that a less intrusive and more widely applicable approach would be to obtain the fundamental characteristics of a process from the extensive data available in every software development project. To ensure that our methods could be easily applied to any such project, we used data from a version control system. Besides being widely available, the version control system provides a data source that is consistent over the duration of the project (unlike many other parts of the software development process). Our model of a minimal version control system (VCS) associates date, time, size, developer, and textual description with each change.

Implicit in our approach is the assumption that we consider only software process properties observable or derivable from the common source — VCS. Because VCSs are not designed to answer questions about process properties (they are designed to support versions and group development), there is a risk that they may contain minimal amounts of useful process information despite their large size. There may be important process properties that can not be observed or derived from VCSs and require more specialized data sources.

The quantitative side of our approach focuses on finding main factors that contribute to the variability of observable quantities: size, interval, quality, and effort. Since those quantities are interdependent, we also derive relationships among them. We use developer surveys and apply our methods on different products to validate the findings.

This work exemplifies the approach by testing the hypothesis that a textual description field of a change is essential to understand why that change was performed. Also, we hypothesize that difficulty, size, and interval would vary across different types of changes.

To test our hypotheses, we analyzed a version control database of a large telecommunications software system (System A). We designed an algorithm to classify automatically changes according to maintenance activities based on the textual description field. We identified three primary reasons for change: adding new features (adaptive), fixing faults (corrective), and restructuring the code to accommodate future changes (perfective), consistent with previous studies, such as, [22]. It should be noted that our characterizations of adaptive and perfective maintenance are not entirely consistent with the literature (see, e.g., [9]), where new features requested by a user are considered to be perfective maintenance, while new features required by new hardware or new software interfaces are considered to be adaptive maintenance.

We discovered a high level of perfective activity in the system, which might indicate why it has been so long on the market and remains the most reliable among comparable products. We also discovered that a number of changes could not be classified into one of the primary types. In particular, changes to implement the recommendations of code inspections were numerous and had both perfective and corrective aspects. The three primary types of changes (adaptive, corrective, perfective), as well as inspection rework, are easily identifiable from textual description and have strikingly different size and interval. The types of changes and frequency of changes have been found to be related to the age and size of a software module in [14].

To verify the classification we did a survey where we asked developers of System A to classify their own recent changes. The automatic classification was in line with developer opinions. We describe methods and results used to obtain relationships between the type of change and its size or interval.

We then applied the classifier to a different product (System B) and found that the change size and interval varies much less between products than between types of changes. This indicates that size and interval might be used to identify the reason for a change. It also indicates that this classification method is applicable to other software products (i.e., it has external validity). We conclude by suggesting new ways to improve the data collection in the configuration management systems.

Sections 2 describes the System A software product. Section 3 introduces the automatic classification algorithm and Section 4.1 describes the developer validation study. We illustrate some of the uses of the classification by investigating size, interval, and difficulty for different types of changes in Section 5. In Subsection 5.2 the classifier is applied to System B. Finally, we conclude with recommendations for new features of change control systems to allow analysis of the changes and hence the evolution of a software product.

## 2 Software product data

Our database was version control and maintenance records from a multi-million line real-time software system

that was developed over more than a decade. The source code is organized into subsystems with each subsystem further subdivided into a set of modules. Each module contains a number of source code files. The change history of the files is maintained using the Extended Change Management System (ECMS) [16], for initiating and tracking changes, and the Source Code Control System (SCCS) [19], for managing different versions of the files. Our data contained the complete change history, including every modification made during the project, as well as many related statistics.

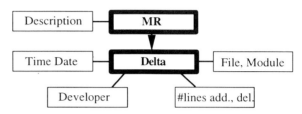

**Figure 1. Changes to the code (bold boxes) and associated attributes. Each modification request contains a number of deltas.**

Each logically distinct change request is recorded as a Modification Request (MR) by the ECMS (see Figure 1). Each MR is owned by a developer, who makes changes to the necessary files to implement the MR. The lines in each file that were added, deleted and changed are recorded as one or more "deltas" in SCCS. While it is possible to implement all MR changes restricted to one file by a single delta, but in practice developers often perform multiple delta on a singe file, especially for larger changes. For each delta, the time of change, the login of the developer who made the change, the number of lines added and deleted, the associated MR, and several other pieces of information are all recorded in the ECMS database. This delta information is then aggregated for each MR. Each MR has associated English text describing reasons for the change and the change itself. There is no protocol on how and what information is entered, but the text is sufficient for other developers to understand what changes were made and why. A detailed description of how to construct change measures is provided in [17].

In the analysis that follows we use the following measures of size: the number of deltas, numbers of lines of code added, deleted, and unmodified by the change. To obtain these measures we simply count all deltas in a change and add the last three measures over all deltas in a change (each SCCS delta records numbers of lines of code added, deleted, and unmodified). We measure interval of a change by the time lag between the first and the last delta in a change.

We selected a subsystem (System A) for our analysis.

121

The subsystem contains approximately $2M$ source lines, 3000 files, and 100 modules. Over the last decade it had 33171 MRs, each having an average of 4 deltas. Although it is a part of a larger system, the subsystem functionality is sold as a separate product to customers.

## 3 Classification of Maintenance Activities

Although the three primary maintenance activities (adaptive, corrective, and perfective) are well known, it is not clear what portion of the total number of changes resulted from each type of activity, or whether additional types of maintenance activities exist. Since the version control data generally does not keep an attribute that would identify the purpose of a change, we looked for this information by analyzing the textual abstract of the change. Information retrieval literature (see [20, 18, 13]) deals with text categorization problems focusing on information retrieval, i.e., obtaining a set of documents relevant to user query, large text documents (change abstracts have only 4 to 20 words), and extensive training collections. Since we are not interested in retrieving abstracts that match a particular user query, but instead in discovering purposes, amounts, and locations (in time and within the source code) of different maintenance activities, we had to design an algorithm that is fine-tuned for this kind of classification of change abstracts.

The classification proceeds in five steps:

1. cleanup and normalization;

2. word frequency analysis;

3. keyword clustering and classification and simple classification rules;

4. MR abstract classification;

5. repetition of the analysis starting from step two on unclassified MR abstracts.

### 3.1 Normalization Step

In the normalization step, the abstracts were cleaned by removing non-alphanumeric symbols, converting all words to lower case, and obtaining the stem of each word using publicly available WordNet [3] software. This step was done to reduce the number of keywords; for example, *fix*, *fixing*, and *fixes* are all mapped to a single term *fix*. We did not use the synonym capability of WordNet since the relationship between concepts used in software maintenance might differ from the relationships found in the natural language.

### 3.2 Word Frequency Analysis

The next step consists of word frequency and semantic analysis. We obtained frequencies of all the words in the textual description of maintenance requests and manually classified the most frequent terms as being neutral (e.g., the, for, to, code, etc.), or reflecting a particular type of maintenance activity. We envisioned three primary types of maintenance: fault fixes for keywords such as *fix, problem, incorrect, correct;* new code development for keywords *add, new, modify, update;* and code improvement for keywords *cleanup, unneeded, remove, rework.*

### 3.3 Keyword Clustering

Since some of the words (especially frequent words) might be used in abstracts describing types of changes not associated with the primary meaning of the keyword, we ensured that keywords have enough discriminating power by using the following procedure:

1. For each selected term we read the description of 20 randomly selected changes that contained the term to see if the abstract describes the change of the same type as that assigned to the keyword.

2. If a term matched less than three fourths of the randomly selected abstracts, the term was deemed to be neutral.

The described decision rule is designed to reject the null hypothesis at 0.05 level that half or less of the MR abstracts containing the term belong to the type assigned to the keyword.

As a result of this activity, we discovered that the term *rework* is frequently used in conjunction with code inspection. The development process in this environment requires formal code inspections for any changes in excess of 50 lines of source code. Code inspection is performed by a team of experts who review the code and recommend changes [7, 8]. Typically, those changes are then implemented by a developer in a separate MR. The purpose of such changes is both corrective and perfecting, reflecting errors found and minor code improvements recommended in a typical code inspection. Since code inspection changes are an essential part of the new code development and contain a mixture of purposes, we chose to place code inspection changes in a separate class to be able better to discern the patterns of changes that have a single purpose. As it turned out, the developer perception of change difficulty and the size of code inspection changes were distinct from other types of changes.

After keyword classification, we looked at keywords and designed simple rules to resolve some of the conflicts when keywords of several types are present in one abstract. For example, the presence of code inspection terms would assign an abstract to the inspection category, independent of the presence of other terms like *new*, or *fix*. The rules were obtained based on our knowledge of the change process (to interpret the meaning of the keyword) and the knowledge obtained from classifying the keywords.

## 3.4 MR Classification Rules

MR classification rules are applied in sequence and each rule is applied only if no class has already been assigned by a previous rule.

1. Any inspection keyword implies code inspection class. Since the inspection change usually has both perfective and corrective aspects, that is often reflected by appropriate keywords in the abstract. The rule, in effect, ignores such keywords to identify the inspection change.

2. If *fix, bug, error, fixup, fail* are present, the change is classified as corrective. In the keyword classification step, all changes with such keywords in their abstracts had been corrective, indicating that the presence of such keyword strongly increases the probability that the change is corrective. This rule reflects that knowledge.

3. Presence of a keyword determines the type, but if more than one type of keyword is present, the type with most keywords in the abstract prevails, with ties resolved in favor of perfective and then corrective types.

Following examples illustrate the three rules (the actual module, function, and process names have been replaced by three letters). The abstract "Code inspection fixes for module XXX" will be classified as an inspection because of keyword *inspection*. The abstract "Fix multiple YYY problem for new ZZZ process" will be classified as corrective because of keyword *fix*. The abstract "Adding new function to cleanup LLL" will be classified as adaptive because there are two adaptive keywords *add* and *new* and only one perfective keyword *cleanup*.

The MRs abstracts where none of the rules applied, were subjected to classification step 2 (word frequency analysis) and then step 3. There were 33171 MRs of which 56 percent were classified (one of the rules did apply) in the first round and another 32 percent in the second round leaving 12 percent unclassified after the second round. As we later found from developer survey, the unclassified MRs were mostly corrective. One of the possible reasons is that adaptive, perfective, and inspection changes need more explanation, while corrective activity is mostly implied and the use of corrective keywords is not considered necessary to identify

the change as a fault fix. The resulting classification is presented in Table 1. It is worth noting that the unclassified MRs represent fewer delta than the classified MRs (12% of MRs were unclassified but less than 10% of delta, added, deleted, or unmodified lines).

A number of change properties are apparent or can be derived from this table.

1. Adaptive changes accounted for 45% of all MRs, followed by corrective changes that account for 34% (46% if we consider the fact that most unclassified changes are corrective).

2. Corrective changes add and delete few lines (they account for 34% to 46% of all changes and only for 18% to 27% of all added and deleted lines).

3. Inspection changes are largest in delta, deleted lines, and unchanged lines.

4. Perfective changes delete most lines per delta (we can see that by looking at the ratio of percentages in the deleted lines row divided by percentages in the delta row).

5. Adaptive changes changed smallest files (ratio of percentages in the unchanged lines row divided by percentages in the MR row). This is not too surprising, since new files are often created to implement new functionality and problems are fixed in larger, mature files.

A more detailed analysis of size and interval relationships is presented in Section 5.1.

## 4 Validation

The automatic algorithm described above performs classification based solely on textual abstract. To validate the results we collected additional data via the developer survey described in the next section. We also used change size and interval (Section 5.1) to validate the algorithm on a different product (Section 5.2).

### 4.1 Developer Survey

To calibrate our automatic classification with the developer opinions, we asked a sample of developers to classify their recent MRs. To minimize respondent time and to maximize respondent recall, the survey was done in two stages. In the preliminary stage, a questionnaire containing 10 MRs was given to two developers who were asked to "debug" the survey process and to fine-tune the questions. In the second stage, five other developers were asked to classify 30 of their MRs. The sampling of MRs and the number of

## Table 1. Result of the MR Classification Algorithm.

|  | Corrective | Adaptive | Perfective | Inspection | Unclassified | Total |
|---|---|---|---|---|---|---|
| MR | 33.8% | 45.0% | 3.7% | 5.3% | 12.0% | 33171 |
| delta | 22.6% | 55.2% | 4.3% | 8.5% | 9.4% | 129653 |
| lines added | 18.0% | 63.2% | 3.5% | 5.4% | 9.8% | 2707830 |
| lines deleted | 18.0% | 55.7% | 5.8% | 10.8% | 9.6% | 940321 |
| lines unchanged | 27.2% | 48.3% | 4.5% | 10.3% | 9.6% | 328368903 |

NOTE: Percentages and totals are presented for MRs, delta, and for lines added, deleted, or unmodified by an MR. In the totals column the number of unmodified lines are added over all changes and is much higher than the total number of lines in any version of the source code.

classes was changed in accordance with the results from the preliminary survey.

### 4.1.1 Survey Protocol

First we have randomly selected 20 candidate developers who had been working in the organization for more than 5 years and completed most 50 MRs over the last two years. The developer population at the time was stable for the last six years so most developers were not novices.

The subsystem management then selected 8 developers from the list of candidates. The management chose them because they were not on tight deadline projects at the time of the survey. We called the developers to introduce the goals, format, and estimated amount of developer time (less than 30 minutes) required for the survey and asked for their commitment. Only one developer could not participate.

After obtaining developer commitment we sent the description of the survey and the respondents' "bill of rights":

> The researchers guarantee that all data collected will be only reported in statistical summaries or in a blind format where no individual can be identified. If any participants at any time feel that their participation in this study might have negative effects on their performance, they may withdraw with a full guarantee of anonymity.

None of the developers withdrew from the survey. The survey forms are described in Appendix.

### 4.2 Survey design and results

All of the developers surveyed have completed many more than 30 MRs in the past two years, so we had to sample a subset of the MRs to limit their number to 10 in the preliminary phase and 30 in the secondary phase.

In the first stage we sampled uniformly from each type of MR. The results of the survey (see tables below) indicated almost perfect correspondence between developer and automatic classification. The MRs classified as *other* by the

developer were typical perfective MRs, as was indicated in the response comment field and in the subsequent interview. We discovered that perfective changes might be classified both as corrective or adaptive, while all four inspection changes were classified as adaptive.

### Table 2. Classification Correspondence Table.

| Dev. Clsfn. | Automatic Classification | | | | |
|---|---|---|---|---|---|
|  | Corr. | Adapt. | Perf. | Insp. | Uncl. |
| Corrective | 6 | 0 | 1 | 0 | 0 |
| Adaptive | 0 | 5 | 2 | 4 | 1 |
| Other | 0 | 0 | 1 | 0 | 0 |

NOTE: This table compares labels for 20 MRs between the program doing automatic classification (columns) and developer classification in the preliminary study. Consider the cell with the row labeled "Adaptive" and the column labeled "Perfective". There are 2 MRs in this cell indicating that the developer classified the MRs as "Adaptive" and the program classified them as "Perfective".

To get a full picture in the second stage we also sampled from unclassified MRs and from the perfective and inspection classes. To obtain better discrimination of the perfective and inspection activity we sample with higher probability from from the perfective and inspection classes than from other classes. Otherwise we might have ended with one or no MRs per developer in these two classes.

The survey indicates that automatic classification is much more likely to leave corrective changes unclassified. Hence we assigned all unclassified changes to the type corrective. In the results that follow we assume that all unclassified changes are corrective. This can be considered as the last rule of the automatic classification in Section 3.4.

The overall comparison of developer and automatic classification is in Table 4.

We discussed the two MRs in the row "Other" with the developers. Developers indicated that both represented a perfective activity, however we excluded the two MRs from the further analysis.

**Table 3. Comparison Between Automatic and Developer Classification in Follow-up Study of 150 MRs.**

| Dev. Clsfn. | Automatic Classification | | | | |
|---|---|---|---|---|---|
| | Corr. | Adapt. | Perf. | Insp. | Uncl. |
| Corr. | 16 | 10 | 4 | 1 | 13 |
| Adapt. | 7 | 18 | 1 | 0 | 3 |
| Perf. | 6 | 8 | 27 | 9 | 4 |
| Insp. | 1 | 0 | 0 | 21 | 0 |
| Other | 0 | 0 | 1 | 0 | 0 |

**Table 4. Comparison Between Automatic (columns) and Developer Classification in Both Studies**

| Dev. Clsfn. | Automatic Classification | | | |
|---|---|---|---|---|
| | Corr. | Adapt. | Perf. | Insp. |
| Corr. | 35 | 10 | 5 | 1 |
| Adapt. | 11 | 23 | 3 | 4 |
| Perf. | 10 | 8 | 27 | 9 |
| Insp. | 1 | 0 | 0 | 21 |
| Other | 0 | 0 | 2 | 0 |

More than 61% of the time, both the developer and the program doing the automatic classification put changes in the same class. A widely accepted way to evaluate the agreement of two classifications is Cohen's Kappa ($\kappa$) [4] which can be calculated using a statistics package such as SPSS. The Kappa coefficient for Table 4 is above 0.5 indicating moderate agreement [6].

To investigate the structure of the agreement between the automatic and developer classifications we fitted a log-linear model (see [15]) to the counts of the two-way comparison table. The factors included margins of the table as well as coincidence of both categories.

Let $m_{ij}$ be counts in the comparison table, i.e., $m_{ij}$ is the number of MRs placed in category $i$ by automatic classification and category $j$ by developer classification. We modeled $m_{i,j}$ to have Poisson distribution with mean $C + \alpha_i + \beta_j + \sum_{i,j=\mathbf{a},\mathbf{c},\mathbf{p},\mathbf{i}} I(i = j)\gamma_{ij}$, where $C$ is the adjustment for the total number of observations; $\alpha_i$ adjusts for automatic classification margins ($\sum_j m_{ij}$); $\beta_j$ adjusts for developer classification margins ($\sum_i m_{ij}$); $I(i = j)$ is the indicator function; $\gamma_{ij}$ represents interactions between the classifications; and indexes $\mathbf{a},\mathbf{c},\mathbf{p},\mathbf{i}$ denote adaptive, corrective, perfective, and inspection classes.

In Table 5 we compare the full model to simpler models. The low residual deviance (RD) of the second model indi-

cates that the model explains the data well. The difference between the deviances of the second and the third models indicates that the extra factor $\gamma_{\mathbf{ii}}$ (that increases the degrees of freedom (DF) by 1) is needed to explain the observed data.

**Table 5. Model Comparison**

| Model formula | DF | RD |
|---|---|---|
| $c + \alpha_i + \beta_j + \sum_{i,j=\mathbf{a},\mathbf{c},\mathbf{p},\mathbf{i}} I(i = j)\gamma_{ij}$ | 5 | 8.7 |
| $c + \alpha_i + \beta_j + \sum_{i,j=\mathbf{a},\mathbf{c},\mathbf{p},\mathbf{i}} I(i = j)\gamma + \gamma_{\mathbf{ii}}$ | 7 | 9.2 |
| $c + \alpha_i + \beta_j + \sum_{i,j=\mathbf{a},\mathbf{c},\mathbf{p},\mathbf{i}} I(i = j)\gamma$ | 8 | 26.5 |

NOTE: Model comparison shows that inspection changes are much more likely to have automatic and developer classifications match than are the other types of changes (estimates in the second model are $\gamma_{\mathbf{ii}} = 1.7, \gamma = 0.65$).

ANOVA table for the second model (Table 6) illustrates the relative importance of different factors.

**Table 6. ANOVA Table for the Second Model**

| Factor | DF | Deviance | Resid. DF | RD |
|---|---|---|---|---|
| $C$ | | | 15 | 157 |
| $\alpha_i$ | 3 | 9.4 | 12 | 147 |
| $\beta_j$ | 3 | 16.5 | 9 | 131 |
| $\gamma$ | 1 | 104.4 | 8 | 26.5 |
| $\gamma_{\mathbf{ii}}$ | 1 | 17.4 | 7 | 9.16 |

NOTE: This table shows that the similarity between two classifications is the most important factor in explaining count distribution, followed by even stronger similarity for the inspection class.

The fact that the coefficient $\gamma$ is significantly larger than zero shows that there is a significant agreement between the automatic and developer classifications. The fact that the coefficient $\gamma_{\mathbf{ii}}$ is significantly larger than zero shows that inspection changes are easier to identify than other changes. This is not surprising, since for the less frequent types of changes, developers feel the need to identify the purpose, while for the more frequent types of changes the purpose might be implied and only a more detailed technical description of the change is provided.

## 5 Profiles of Maintenance Types

This section exemplifies some of the possibilities provided by the classification. After validating the classification using the survey, we proceeded to study the size and interval properties of different types of changes. Then we validated the classification properties by applying them to a different software product.

The change interval is important to track the time it takes to resolve problems (especially since we determined which changes are corrective), while change size is strongly related to effort, see, e.g. [1].

## 5.1 How purpose influences size and interval

Figure 2 compares empirical distribution functions of change size (numbers of added and deleted lines) with change interval for different types of changes. Skewed distribution, large variances, and integer values make more traditional summaries, such as boxplots and probability density plots, less effective. Because of a large sample size, the empirical distribution functions had small variance and could be reliably used to compare different types of maintenance activities.

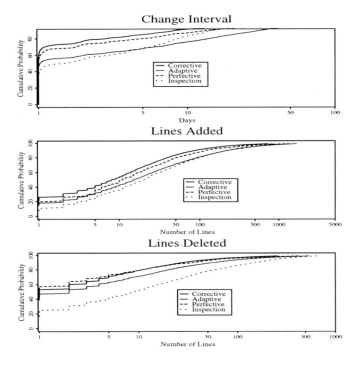

**Figure 2. The three plots compare empirical distribution functions of change interval, added lines, and deleted lines for corrective (solid line), adaptive (dotted line), perfective (dashed line), and inspection (long-dashed line) types of changes. Adaptive changes add the most code and take the most time to complete. Inspection changes delete the most code, and corrective changes take the least time to complete.**

The empirical distribution functions in Figure 2 are interpreted as follows: the vertical scale defines the observed probability that the value of a quantity is less than the value of the corresponding point on the curve as indicated on the horizontal axis. In particular, the curves to the right or below other curves indicate larger quantities, while curves above or to the left indicate smaller quantities.

The interval comparison shows that corrective changes have the shortest intervals, followed by perfective changes. The distribution functions for inspection and adaptive changes intersect at the 5 day interval and 65th percentile. This shows that the most time consuming 35 percent of adaptive changes took much longer to complete than the the most time consuming 35 percent of inspection changes. On the other hand, the least time consuming 60 percent of inspection changes took longer to complete than corresponding portion of adaptive changes. This is not surprising, since formal inspection is usually done only for changes that add more than 50 lines of code. Even the smallest inspections deal with relatively large and complex changes so implementing the inspection recommendations is rarely a trivial task.

As expected, new code development and inspection changes add most lines, followed by perfective, and then corrective activities. The inspection activities delete much more code than does new code development, which in turn deletes somewhat more than corrective and perfective activities.

All of those conclusions are intuitive and indicate that the classification algorithm did a good job of assigning each change to the correct type of maintenance activity.

All the differences between the distribution functions are significant at the 0.01 level using either the Kruskal-Wallis test or the Smirnov test (see [12]). Traditional ANOVA also showed significant differences, but we believe it is inappropriate because of the undue influence of extreme outliers in highly skewed distributions that we observed. Figure 3 shows that even the logarithm of the number of deleted lines has a highly skewed distribution.

## 5.2 Variation across products

This section compares the size and interval profiles between changes in different products to validated the classification algorithm on a different software product. We applied the automatic classification algorithm described in Section 3 to a different software product (System B) developed in the same company.

Although System B was developed by different people and in a different organization, both systems have the same type of version control databases and both systems may be packaged as parts of a much larger telecommunications product. We used the keywords obtained in the classification of System A, so there was no manual input to the automatic classification algorithm. System B is slightly bigger

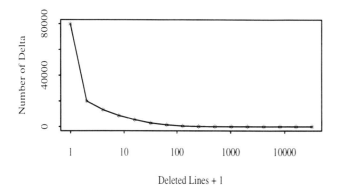

**Figure 3. The histogram for the numbers of lines deleted by a delta. Even the logarithm has a highly skewed distribution.**

and slightly older than System A and implements different functionality.

Figure 4 checks whether the types of changes are different between the two products in terms of the empirical distribution functions of change size (numbers of added and deleted lines), and change interval.

The plots indicate that the differences between products are much smaller than the differences between types of changes. This suggests that the size and interval characteristics can be used as a signature of change purpose across different software products. However, there are certain differences between the two systems:

1. all types of changes took slightly less time to complete in System B;

2. all types of changes added more lines in System B;

3. corrective changes deleted slightly more lines in System B.

We can not explain the nature of these small differences except that they might be due to the different functionality and developer population in System B.

## 5.3 Change difficulty

This section illustrates a different application of the change classification by a model relating difficulty of a change to its type. In the survey (see Section 4.1) developers matched purpose with perceived difficulty for 170 changes. To check the relationship between type and difficulty we fitted a log-linear model to the count data in a two-way table: type of changes (corrective, adaptive, perfective, or inspection) versus difficulty of the change (easy, medium, and hard). Table 7 shows that corrective changes are most likely to be rated hard, followed by perfective changes. Most inspection changes are rated as easy.

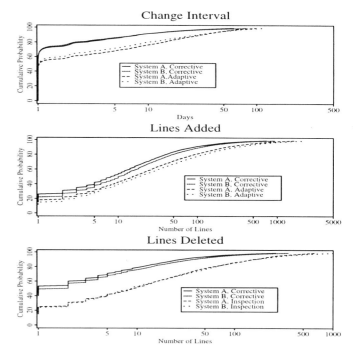

**Figure 4. Comparison of two products in terms of empirical distribution functions of change interval and numbers of added or deleted lines for corrective, adaptive, perfective, and inspection changes.**

**Table 7. Difficulty versus Type of Change.**

|            | Easy | Medium | Hard |
|------------|------|--------|------|
| corrective | 18   | 21     | 12   |
| perfective | 35   | 18     | 1    |
| adaptive   | 30   | 8      | 3    |
| inspection | 18   | 3      | 1    |

NOTE: Corrective changes tend to be the hardest while inspection changes are almost always easy.

127

In the next step we fitted a linear model to find the relationship between difficulty and other properties of the change. Since the difficulty might have been perceived differently by different developers, we included a developer factor among the predictors. To deal with two outliers in the interval (the longest three MRs took 112, 91, and 38 days to complete); we used a logarithmic transformation on the intervals.

We started with the full model:

$$Difficulty = Size + log(Interval + 1) +$$
$$isAdaptive + isCorrective + isPerfective +$$
$$isInspection + Developer + Error.$$

Using stepwise regression we arrived at a smaller model:

$$Difficulty = Size + log(Interval + 1) +$$
$$isCorrective + isPerfective + Developer + Error.$$

Because numbers of delta, numbers of added or deleted lines, and numbers of files touched were strongly correlated with each other, any of those change measures could be used as a change size predictor in the model. We chose to use the number of delta because it is related to the number of files touched (you need at least one delta for each file touched) and to the number of lines (many lines are usually added over several days often resulting in multiple check-ins). As expected, the difficulty increased with the numbers of deltas, except for the corrective or perfective changes, which may be small but are still very hard. Not surprisingly, developers had different subjective scales of difficulty. Table 8 gives an analysis of variance (ANOVA) for the full model and Table 9 gives ANOVA for the model selected by stepwise regression. Since $R$ values are so similar, the second model is preferable because it is simpler, having three fewer parameters. We see that the three obvious explanatory variables are size, corrective maintenance, and developer identity. The other two explanatory variables (interval and perfective type), although present in the final model, are not as strong because their effect is not clearly different from zero. This may appear surprising, because interval seems like an obvious indicator of difficulty. However, this is in line with other studies where the change interval (in addition to size) does not appear to help predict change effort [1, 11, 21]. One possible explanation is that the size might account for the difficult adaptive changes, while corrective changes have to be completed in a short time, no matter how difficult they might be.

## 6 Summary

We studied a large legacy system to test the hypothesis that historic version control data can be used to determine

**Table 8. The Full Model with $R = 0.642$**

| Factor | DF | Sum of Sq. | direction |
|---|---|---|---|
| $Size$ | 1 | 7 | + |
| $log(Interval + 1)$ | 1 | 0.4 | + |
| isCorrective | 1 | 11.8 | + |
| isAdaptive | 1 | 1e-2 | − |
| isPerfective | 1 | .5 | + |
| isInspection | 1 | .3 | − |
| Developer | 6 | 10.3 | |
| Residuals | 156 | 43.6 | |

**Table 9. The Full Model with $R = 0.633$**

| factor | DF | Sum of Sq. | p-val. | dir. |
|---|---|---|---|---|
| $Size$ | 1 | 7 | 0 | + |
| $log(Interval + 1)$ | 1 | 1.4 | 0.027 | + |
| isCorrective | 1 | 11.5 | 0 | + |
| isPerfective | 1 | 0.6 | 0.12 | + |
| Developer | 6 | 10 | 0 | |
| Residuals | 159 | 45.8 | | |

the purpose of software changes. The study focused on the changes, rather than the source code. To make results applicable to any software product, we assume a model of a minimal VCS so that any real VCS would contain a superset of considered data.

Since the change purpose is not always recorded, and when it is recorded the value is often not reliable, we designed a tool to extract automatically the purpose of a change from the textual description. (The same algorithm can also extract other features). To verify the validity of the classification, we used the developer surveys and we also applied the classification to a different product.

We discovered four identifiable types of changes: adding new functionality, repairing faults, restructuring the code to accommodate future changes, and code inspection rework changes that represent a mixture of corrective and perfective changes. Each has a distinct size and interval profile. The interval for adaptive changes is the longest, followed by inspection changes, with corrective changes being the smallest.

We discovered a strong relationship between the difficulty of a change and its type: corrective changes tend to be the most difficult, while adaptive changes are difficult only if they are large. Inspection changes are perceived as the easiest. Since we were working with large non-Gaussian samples, we used non-parametric statistical methods. The best way to understand size profiles was to compare empirical distribution functions.

In summary, we were able to use data available in a version control system to discover significant quantitative and qualitative information about various aspects of the software development process. To do that we introduced an automatic method of classifying software changes based on their textual descriptions. The resulting classification showed a number of strong relationships between size and type of maintenance activity and the time required to make the change.

## 7 Conclusions

Our summaries of the version control database can be easily replicated on other software development projects since we use only the basic information available from any version control database: time of change, numbers of added, deleted, and unchanged lines, and textual description of the change.

We believe that software change measurement tools should be built directly into the version control system to summarize fundamental patterns of changes in the database.

We see this work as an infrastructure to answer a number of questions related to effort, interval, and quality of the software. It has been used in work on code fault potential [10] and decay [5]. However, we see a number of other important applications. One of the questions we intend to answer is how perfective maintenance reduces future effort in adaptive and corrective activity.

The textual description field proved to be essential to identify the reason for a change, and we suspect that other properties of the change could be identified using the same field. We therefore recommend that a high quality textual abstract should always be provided, especially since we cannot anticipate what questions may be asked in the future.

Although the purpose of a change could be recorded as an additional field there are at least three important reasons why using textual description is preferable:

1. to reduce developer effort. The description of the change is essential for other purposes, such as informing other developers about the content of the change;

2. to reduce process influences. The development process often specifies deadlines after which no new functionality may be contributed, but in practice there are exceptions that result in relabeling of the true purpose of the change according to process guidelines;

3. to minimize developer bias. Developers opinions may vary and thus influence the labeling of MRs. Using textual description avoids this problem (however it may introduce a different bias due to differences in vocabulary different developers use to describe their MRs.

## Acknowledgments

We thank the interview subjects and their management for their support. We also thank Dave Weiss and IEEE TSE reviewers for their extensive comments.

## References

[1] D. Atkins, T. Ball, T. Graves, and A. Mockus. Using version control data to evaluate the effectiveness of software tools. In *1999 International Conference on Software Engineering*, Los Angeles, CA, May 1999. ACM Press.

[2] V. R. Basili and D. M. Weiss. A methodology for collecting valid software engineering data. *IEEE Transactions on Software Engineering*, 10(6):728–737, 1984.

[3] R. Beckwith and G. A. Miller. Implementing a lexical network. *International Journal of Lexicography*, 3(4):302–312, 1990.

[4] J. Cohen. A coefficient of aggreement for nominal scales. *Educational and Psychological Measurement*, 20:37–46, 1960.

[5] S. G. Eick, T. L. Graves, A. F. Karr, J. S. Marron, and A. Mockus. Does code decay? Assessing the evidence from change management data. *IEEE Transactions on Software Engineering*, 2000. To appear.

[6] K. El Emam. Benchmarking kappa for software process assessment reliability studies. Technical Report ISERN-98-02, International Software Engineering Network, 1998.

[7] M. E. Fagan. Design and code inspections to reduce errors in program development. *IBM Systems Journal*, 15(3):182–211, 1976.

[8] M. E. Fagan. Advances in software inspections. *IEEE Trans. on Software Engineering*, SE-12(7):744–751, July 1986.

[9] C. Ghezzi, M. Jazayeri, and D. Mandrioli. *Software Engineering*. Prentice Hall, Englewood Cliffs, New Jersey, 1991.

[10] T. L. Graves, A. F. Karr, J. S. Marron, and H. P. Siy. Predicting fault incidence using software change history. *IEEE Transactions on Software Engineering*, 2000. to appear.

**Table 10. MR Information Requested from the Developer for the Calibration Survey.**

| MR | Type (N/B/I/C/O) | Effort (E/M/H) | Project | MR Opened | Last Delta |
|---|---|---|---|---|---|
| wx486218aF | | | Foo5_2f | 1/9/95 | 1/17/95 |
| Description: | Define a new feature bit mask for LUHN check | | | | |
| Modules: | uhdr/wx | Files: | WXgl5ac2.G | | |
| Comment: | | | | | |

[11] T. L. Graves and A. Mockus. Inferring change effort from configuration management databases. *Metrics 98: Fifth International Symposium on Software Metrics*, November 1998.

[12] M. Hollander and D. A. Wolfe. *Nonparametric Statistical Methods*. John Willey, New York, 1973.

[13] P. S. Jacobs. *Text-Based Intelligent Systems*. Lawrence Erlbaum, 1992.

[14] C. F. Kemerer and S. A. Slaughter. Determinants of software maintenance profiles: An empirical investigation. *Software Maintenance: Research and Practice*, 9(4):235–251, 1997.

[15] P. McCullagh and J. A. Nelder. *Generalized Linear Models, 2nd ed.* Chapman and Hall, New York, 1989.

[16] A. K. Midha. Software configuration management for the 21st century. *Bell Labs Technical Journal*, 2(1), Winter 1997.

[17] A. Mockus, S. G. Eick, T. L. Graves, and A. F. Karr. On measurement and analysis of software changes. Technical Report BL0113590-990401-06TM, Lucent Technologies, 1999.

[18] C. J. Van Rijsbergen. *Information Retrieval*. Butterworths, London, 1979.

[19] M. J. Rochkind. The source code control system. *IEEE Trans. on Software Engineering*, 1(4):364–370, 1975.

[20] G. Salton. *Automatic text processing: the transformation, analysis, and retrieval of information by computer*. Addison-Wesley, Reading, Mass., 1989.

[21] H. P. Siy and A. Mockus. Measuring domain engineering effects on software coding cost. In *Metrics 99: Sixth International Symposium on Software Metrics*, pages 304–311, Boca Raton, Florida, November 1999.

[22] E. B. Swanson. The dimensions of maintenance. In *Proc. 2nd Conf. on Software Engineering*, pages 492–497, San Francisco, 1976.

# Appendix

### 7.0.1 Survey Form

The preliminary survey form asked the developers to limit their time to 20 minutes and presented a list of MRs to be classified. (Table 10 shows the classification information for one MR requested from the developer.) The list was preceded by the following introduction.

> Listed below are 10 MRs that you have worked on during the last two years. We ask you to please classify them according to whether they were (1) new feature development, (2) software fault or "bug" fix, (3) other. You will also be asked to rate the difficulty of carrying out the MR in terms of effort and time relative to your experience and to record a reason for your answer if one occurs to you.
>
> For each MR, please mark one of the types (N = new, B = bug, O = other), and one of the levels of difficulty (E = easy, M = medium, H = hard). You may add a comment at the end if the type is O or if you feel it is necessary.

The second stage survey form began with the following introduction.

> Listed below are 30 MRs that you have worked on during the last two years. We ask you to please classify them according to whether they were (1) new feature development, (2) software fault or "bug" fix, (3) the result of the code inspection, (4) code improvement, restructuring, or cleanup, (5) other. You will also be asked to rate the difficulty of carrying out the MR in terms of effort and time relative to your experience, and to record a reason for your answer if one occurs to you.
>
> For each MR, please mark one of the type options (N = new, B = bug, I = inspection, C = cleanup, O = other), and one of the levels of difficulty (E = easy, M = medium, H = hard), You may add a comment at the end if the type is O or if you feel it is necessary.

# Evolution in Open Source Software:
# A Case Study

Michael W. Godfrey and Qiang Tu
Software Architecture Group (SWAG)
Department of Computer Science, University of Waterloo
email: {migod,qtu}@swag.uwaterloo.ca

## Abstract

*Most studies of software evolution have been performed on systems developed within a single company using traditional management techniques. With the widespread availability of several large software systems that have been developed using an "open source" development approach, we now have a chance to examine these systems in detail, and see if their evolutionary narratives are significantly different from commercially developed systems. This paper summarizes our preliminary investigations into the evolution of the best known open source system: the Linux operating system kernel. Because Linux is large (over two million lines of code in the most recent version) and because its development model is not as tightly planned and managed as most industrial software processes, we had expected to find that Linux was growing more slowly as it got bigger and more complex. Instead, we have found that Linux has been growing at a super-linear rate for several years. In this paper, we explore the evolution of the Linux kernel both at the system level and within the major subsystems, and we discuss why we think Linux continues to exhibit such strong growth.*

## 1 Introduction

Large software systems must evolve, or they risk losing market share to competitors [15]. However, maintaining such a system is extraordinarily difficult, complicated, and time consuming. The tasks of adding new features, adding support for new hardware devices and platforms, system tuning, and defect fixing all become more difficult as a system ages and grows.

Most published studies of software evolution have been performed on systems developed "in house" within a single company using traditional development and management techniques [3, 4, 12, 15, 23]. In this paper, we present a case study of the evolution of the Linux operating system

[9, 8, 7]. This system has been developed using an "open source development" approach that is quite different from the way most industrial software is created [18].

## 2 Related Work

Lehman *et al.* have built the largest and best known body of research on the evolution of large, long-lived software systems [13, 15, 14, 23]. Lehman's laws of software evolution [15], which are based on his case studies of several large software systems, suggest that as systems grow in size, it becomes increasingly difficult to add new code unless explicit steps are taken to reorganize the overall design. Turski's statistical analysis of these case studies suggests that system growth (measured in terms of numbers of source modules and number of modules changed) is usually sub-linear, slowing down as the system gets larger and more complex [14, 23].

Gall *et al.* examined the evolution of a large telecom switching system both at the system level and within the top-level subsystems [4], much as we have done with Linux. They noted that while the system-level evolution of the system seems to conform to the traditionally observed trend of reduced change rates over time, they noted that the major subsystems may behave quite differently from the system as a whole. In their case study they found that some of the major subsystems exhibited "interesting" evolutionary behaviours, but that these behaviours cancelled each other out when the full system was viewed at the top level. They argue that it is not enough, therefore, to consider evolution from the topmost level; one must also be concerned about the individual parts as well. Our own investigations strongly support this view.

Kemerer and Slaughter have presented an excellent survey of research on software evolution [12]. They also note that there has been relatively little research on empirical studies of software evolution.

Parnas has used the metaphor of decay to describe how

and why software becomes increasingly brittle over time [16]. Eick *et al.* extend the ideas suggested by Parnas by characterizing software "decay" in ways that can be detected and measured [3]. They used a large telephone switching system as a case study. They suggest, for example, that if it is common for defect fixes to require changes to large numbers of source files, then the software system is probably poorly designed. Their metrics are predicated on the availability of detailed defect tracking logs that allow, for example, a user to determine how many defects have resulted in modifications to a particular module. We note that no such detailed change logs were available for our study of Linux.

Perry presented evidence that the evolution of a software system depends not only on its size and age but also on factors such as the nature of the system itself (*i.e.,* its application domain), previous experience with the system, and the processes, technologies, and organizational frameworks employed by the company that developed the software [17].

# 3  Open Source Software Development

Although the term "open source" is relatively recent, the fundamental ideas behind it are not [10, 18]. The single most important requirement of an open source software system is that its source code must be freely available to anyone who wishes to examine it or change it for their own purposes. That is, a user must always be able to "look under the hood" and be allowed to tune, adapt, or evolve a system for his/her personal needs.

While the development of open source software (OSS) is often highly collaborative and geographically distributed, this is not a strict requirement. Many corporations and individuals have developed source code in-house as a proprietary project only to release later it as "open source" or with a license that allows great freedom for personal use of the system. Examples of this include the Netscape web browser (*i.e.,* the Mozilla project), the `Jikes` Java compiler from IBM, and Sun's Java Development Kit.

The "other" kind of open source system is one that is developed from very early days as a highly collaborative project done "out in the open"; that is, these systems follow an open source development (OSD) model.[1] Usually, such a project begins with a single developer who has a personal goal or vision. Typically, that person will begin work on their system either from scratch or by cannibalizing an extant older system. For example, Linux's creator, Linus Torvalds, started with a version of the Minix operating system, while VIM's creator, Bram Moolenar, began with a older clone of the `vi` text editor called `stevie` [11].

---

[1] Eric Raymond has written an informative book on open source development called *The Cathedral and the Bazaar* [18].

## 3.1  Open Source Development vs. Traditional Processes

Once the originator is ready to invite others into the project (s)he makes the code base available to others and development proceeds. Typically, anyone may contribute towards the development of the system, but the originator/owner is free to decide which contributions may or may not become part of the official release.[2]

The open source development (OSD) model is different from traditional in-house commercial development processes in several fundamental ways. First, the usual goal of an open source project is to create a system that is useful or interesting to those who are working on it, not to fill a commercial void. Developers are often unpaid volunteers who contribute towards the project as a hobby; in return, they receive peer recognition and whatever personal satisfaction their efforts bring to them. Sometimes this means that much of the effort on an OSD project concentrates on what part-time programmers find interesting, rather than on what might be more essential. It can be difficult to direct development toward particular goals, since the project owner holds little power over the contributing developers. This freedom also means that it can be difficult to convince developers to perform essential tasks, such as systematic testing or code restructuring, that are not as exciting as writing new code.

Other notable features of open source development include:

- *Scheduling:* There is usually little commercial pressure to keep to any hard schedule, and most OSD developers have "day jobs" that take up most of their time. While this may entail longer development cycles, this is also an advantage since OSD projects are largely immune from "time-to-market" pressures; a system need not be released until the project owners are satisfied that the system is mature and stable.

- *Code quality* and standards can vary widely. Since code is contributed, it is hard to insist on particular standards, although many projects do have official guidelines.

- *Unstable code* is common, as developers are eager to submit their "bleeding edge" contributions to the project. Some OSD projects, including Linux, address this issue by maintaining two concurrent development paths: a "development" release path contains new or experimental features, and a "stable" release contains

---

[2] Some open source projects have forked into distinct development streams when developers were unhappy with the route taken by the "official" branch. Under most open source license agreements, this splitting is explicitly permitted. The FreeBSD/NetBSD/OpenBSD systems are an example of this phenomenon.

mostly updates and bug fixes relative to the previous stable release. (In addition, when new "development" features are considered to be stable, they are sometimes migrated into the current stable release without waiting for the next major baseline to be established.)

- *Planned evolution, testing, and preventive maintenance* may suffer, since OSD encourages active participation but not necessarily careful reflection and reorganization. Code quality is maintained largely by "massively parallel debugging" (*i.e.,* many developers each using each other's code) rather than by systematic testing or other planned, prescriptive approaches.[3]

## 3.2   Evolution of OSD Systems

We have been examining the growth and evolution patterns of OSD projects to see how they compare to previous studies on the evolution of large proprietary software systems developed using more traditional in-house processes. There are now many large OSD systems that have been in existence for a number of years and have achieved widespread use, including two that we have investigated in some detail: the Linux operating system kernel (2,200,000 lines of code) [9], and the VIM text editor (150,000 lines of code) [11].[4]

Naively, we had expected that since evolution of OSD software is usually much less structured and less carefully planned than traditional in-house development that "Lehman's laws" would apply [15]; that is, as the system grew, the rate of growth would slow, with the system growth approximating an inverse square curve [14]. Indeed, recently the maintainers of the Perl project have undertaken a massive redesign and restructuring of the core system [20], since the project owners felt that the current system has become almost unmaintainable.[5] However, as we explain below, this is not at all what we found with Linux.

---

[3]The development model of the FreeBSD operating system [6], a rival to Linux, is a cross between traditional closely managed development and the relatively unstructured approach used by many OSD projects. The FreeBSD system accepts contributions from outsiders, but such contributions are more carefully scrutinized before being accepted into the main source tree. The FreeBSD development team also performs much more stringent testing of code than Linux. As a result, FreeBSD tends to support fewer devices and development proceeds more slowly than Linux.

[4]Our preliminary analysis of VIM shows that it has also been growing at a super-linear rate for a number of years.

[5]One of the core developers, Chip Salzenberg, has said of the current version of Perl: "You really need indoctrination in all the mysteries and magic structures and so on before you can really hope to make significant changes to the Perl core without breaking more things than you're adding." [20]

## 4   The Linux Operating System Kernel

Linux is a Unix-like operating system originally written by Linus Torvalds, but subsequently worked on by hundreds of other developers [1].[6] It was originally written to run on an Intel 386 architecture, but has since been ported to numerous other platforms, including the PowerPC, the DEC Alpha, the Sun SPARC and SPARC64, and even mainframes and PDAs.

The first official release of the kernel, version 1.0, occurred in March 1994. This release contained 487 source code files comprising over 165,000 lines of code (including comment and blanks lines). Since then, the Linux kernel has been maintained along two parallel paths: a *development* release containing experimental and relatively untested code, and a *stable* release containing mostly updates and bug fixes relative to the previous stable release. By convention, the middle number in a kernel version identifies to which path it belongs: an odd number (*e.g.,* 1.3.49) denotes a development kernel, and an even number (*e.g.,* 2.0.7) denotes a stable kernel.

At the time of writing (January 2000), the most recent stable kernel is version 2.2.14, and the most recent development kernel version is 2.3.39. There have been 369 development kernel releases along four main threads (1.1.X, 1.3.X, 2.1.X, and 2.3.X) and 67 stable kernel releases along four main threads (1.0, 1.2.X, 2.0.X, and 2.2.X).

## 5   Methodology

We have measured various aspects of the growth of Linux using a variety of tools and assumptions, which we now describe.

We examined 96 kernel versions in total, including 34 stable kernel releases and 62 development kernel releases. We decided to measure relatively more of the stable kernels as they were released less frequently.

The size of the full distribution was measured as a `tar` file compressed using `gzip`; this file included all source artifacts of the kernel, including documentation, scripts, and other utilities (but no binary files). That is, the `tar` files were the versions available from the Linux Kernel Archives website [8].

We use the term "source file" to mean any file whose name ends with ".c" or ".h" that appeared in the original `tar` file.[7] We ignored other source artifacts such as configuration files and Makefiles. We also explicitly ignored

---

[6]Kernel version 2.3.39 released in January 2000 lists over 300 names in the credits file as having made significant contributions to the development of the Linux kernel.

[7]Performing a system build creates additional source files, depending on the options chosen. We ignored these additional files in the interest of uniformity and simplicity.

source files that appeared under the `Documentation` directory, as we felt these were not part of the kernel code *per se*.

We counted lines of code (LOC) using two approaches: first, we used the Unix command "`wc -l`" which gave a raw count that included blanks lines and comments in the totals; second, we used an `awk` script that causes blank lines and comments to be ignored.[8] Finally, we used the program "exuberant ctags" to count the number of global functions, variables, and macros [5].

In considering the major subsystems of Linux, we have used the directory structure of each source release as our definition of the subsystem hierarchy. Others have created customized subsystem hierarchies (*i.e.,* source-based software architectures) based on detailed analyses of particular versions of Linux [2, 22, 21]. We chose not to follow this route for two reasons: first, creating customized subsystem hierarchies for 96 versions of the Linux kernel, each of which contains between 500 and 5000 source files was a daunting task without clear benefit; second, our analyses of the subsystems' evolution would have been peculiar to our own ideas of what the software architecture ought to look like, and would not conform to the mental model of most Linux developers.

Lehman suggests using the number of "modules" as the best way to measure the size of a large software system [15]. However, we decided to use the number of uncommented lines of code ("uncommented LOC") for most of our measurements for several reasons. First, as discussed below, we found that total system uncommented LOC seemed to grow at roughly the same rate as the number of source files; however, as shown by the difference between average and median file size below, there was great variation in file size in some parts of the system. We decided, therefore, that using number of source files would mean losing some of the full story of the evolution of Linux, especially at the subsystem level.

## 6    Observations on the Evolution of Linux

We examined the evolution of the Linux kernel both at the system level as well as within each of the major subsystems; we found that the system as a whole exhibited such a strong rate of growth that an investigation of the major subsystems was appropriate. We now discuss our observations.

### 6.1    System Level Growth

We first examined how the system has grown using several common metrics. For example, Fig. 1 shows the growth in size of the compressed `tar` files for the full kernel release, and Fig. 2 shows the growth of the number of lines of code (LOC). We also measured the growth of the number of source files and the growth of the number of global functions, variables, and macros; however, we have omitted the graphs for these measurements for the sake of brevity as the growth patterns they show are very similar to those of Fig. 1 and Fig. 2.

It is interesting that these measurements all seem to tell the same story. They clearly show that the development releases are growing at a super-linear rate over time, which contradicts Lehman and Turski's inverse square growth rate hypothesis [14, 23].[9] The early stable kernel paths (versions 1.2.X, and 2.0.X, which can be seen on the graphs as starting in March 1995 and July 1996 respectively) are growing at a much slower rate than the corresponding development release paths, as one would expect. However, the most recent stable release path, version 2.2.X (which started in January 1999), has shown remarkable growth for a "stable" path. Subsequent investigation has determined that most of this growth has been in the addition of new features and support for new architectures rather than defect fixing [7]. The recent rapid rise in the popularity of Linux has resulted in a large amount of contributed stable code from third parties, such as IBM for their S/390 mainframe [24], together with external pressure to "fast track" integration of this code into the stable release path.

We plotted all growth against time rather than version number (Lehman *et al.* suggest the latter approach [14]). It made no sense to us to plot stable and development paths that were parallel in real time as being sequential; to do so would have led to apparent "dips" where one kind of release path finished and another began. Also, the behaviour of the two kinds of paths were understandably different: development kernels were released with great frequency and varied greatly in size, while early stable kernel releases varied in frequency but (until version 2.2.X) were relatively small in size. We also note that Linux emphatically does not appear to obey Lehman's third law of software evolution, which states that the incremental effort spent on each release remains constant throughout a system's lifetime [15]; for example, the update "patch" files within the 2.3.X release path

---

[8]We also plotted the difference between the two counts and we found that the percentage of source file lines that were comments or blank stayed almost constant at between 28 and 30 percent. We consider this constancy to be a healthy sign. A decrease in the amount of commenting often indicates poorly maintained code, and a significant increase in commenting often indicates that a system has become difficult to understand and requires extra explanation.

[9]Our statistical analysis shows that the growth rate of uncommented LOC along the development release paths fits well into a quadratic model. If $X$ is the number of days since version 1.0 was released and $Y$ is the size of the Linux kernel in uncommented LOC, then the following function is a good model of the growth, as calculated using a "least squares" approximation:
$$Y = 0.21 * X^2 + 252 * X + 90,055$$
The co-efficient of determination for this model is 0.997.

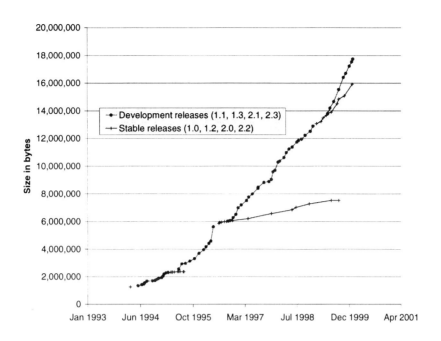

**Figure 1. Growth of the compressed `tar` file for the full Linux kernel source release.**

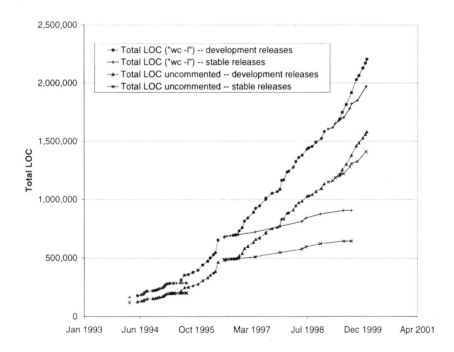

**Figure 2. Growth in the number of lines of code measured using two methods: the Unix command "`wc -l`", and an `awk` script that removes comments and blanks lines.**

varied in size from a few hundred bytes to a few megabytes. We hypothesize that this is a direct consequence of the OSD process model, for reasons stated above.

Since the growth patterns seem to be similar for each of the metrics we used, we tried dividing one measure by another to see if the resulting curve was a straight line. We therefore plotted the average file sizes (total uncommented LOC divided by number of source files) as well as the median sizes of both "dot-c" (implementation) and "dot-h" (header) source files. Figure 3 and Fig. 4 show that median file sizes were fairly stable, with slight growth in the size of dot-c files, while average file sizes showed definite growth over time. This indicates that while some dot-c files are becoming quite large, most are not. Our subsequent investigation showed that almost all of the largest files were drivers for complicated hardware devices.[10] We consider the flatness of the median dot-h file size curve to be a good sign, as it suggests that new features were not being added indiscriminately to the dot-h files. Investigation into the rise in average size of dot-h files revealed that there were a small number of very large dot-h files for device drivers that contained mostly data; these very large dot-h files tended to skew the overall average file size.

An interesting trend arises beginning in mid-1996 with the stable release 2.0.X and its parallel development release 2.1.X as shown in Fig. 3 and Fig. 4. Along release path 2.0.X, we can see that the average dot-c file size increased, while along release path 2.1.X this value decreased before eventually beginning to increase again. At the same time, the average dot-h file size along release path 2.0.X increased slowly but steadily, while along 2.1.X the average dot-h file size increased more significantly and dominated the stable release path. By cross referencing this graph with the growth in the number of files, we note that the number of source files grew slowly along stable release 2.0.X, while there was a larger steady increase in the number of source files along 2.1.X, with a significant jump at the same point where its average dot-c file size dipped.[11] This suggests that along the stable release path, its increase in average file size is likely due to bug fixes and simple enhancements that added code to existing files, as one would expect from a stable release path. Along the development release path, it is likely that many new small files were created due to new features being added, causing the average dot-c file size to decrease.[12] We consider it a healthy sign that new develop-

ment seemed to result in additional infrastructure (*i.e.,* new small files) that were then "filled out" over time.

## 6.2 Growth of Major Subsystems

After investigating the growth of Linux at a system-wide level, we then decided to investigate the growth of the major subsystems (as defined by the source directory hierarchy). There are ten major source subsystems [19]:

- `drivers` contains a large collection drivers for various hardware devices;

- `arch` contains the kernel code that is specific to particular hardware architectures/CPUs, including support for memory management and libraries;

- `include` contains most of the system's include (dot-h) files;

- `net` contains the main networking code such as support for sockets and TCP/IP (code for particular networking cards is contained in the `drivers/net` subsystem);

- `fs` contains support for various kinds of file systems;

- `init` contains the initialization code for the kernel;

- `ipc` contains the code for inter-process communications;

- `kernel` contains the main kernel code that is architecture independent;

- `lib` contains the (architecture independent) library code; and

- `mm` contains the (architecture independent) memory management code.

Figure 5 shows the growth of the major kernel subsystem. We can see immediately that the `drivers` subsystem is not only the largest subsystem it is also the fastest growing, with almost one million (uncommented) lines of code in the latest release. Figure 6 shows that this subsystem has grown steadily relative to the rest of the system to the point where it now comprises more than 60 percent of the total system.

The size and growth rate of the `drivers` subsystem actually makes it difficult to see what has happened to the rest of the system in Fig. 5. Fig.7, therefore, shows the relative size of these subsystems as a percentage of the total system. We can see that the `arch`, `include`, `net`, and `fs` subsystems are significantly larger than the remaining five,

---

[10]For example, in the most recent development kernel (v2.3.39) while six of the largest eight dot-c files were drivers for SCSI cards, four of the six largest dot-h files were for network card drivers. This led us to the initial conjectures that SCSI cards have complicated logic, and network cards have complicated interfaces. It turned out that while SCSI cards *do* have complicated logic, most of the content of the network card dot-h files was simply data.

[11]At the same time, the ratio of the number of dot-c files to dot-h files remained almost constant along both paths.

[12]The large jump in average dot-h file size that occurred at release 2.1.20

in January 1997 was mostly due to the addition of one very large device driver dot-h file for a network card.

**Figure 3. Median and average size of implementation files ("\*.c").**

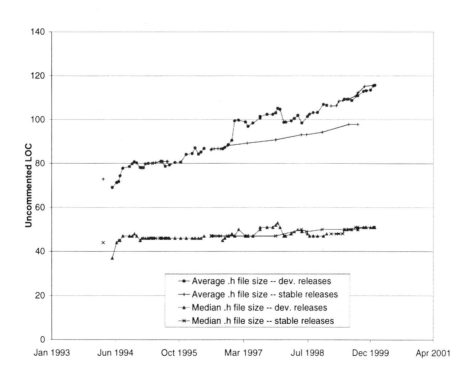

**Figure 4. Median and average size of header files ("\*.h").**

137

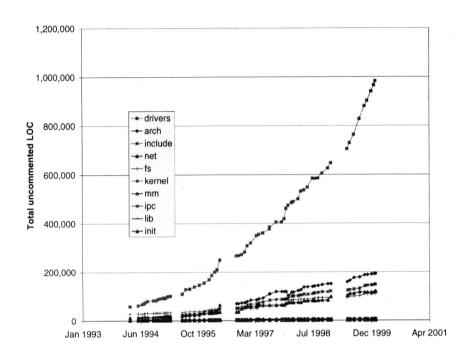

**Figure 5. Growth of the major subsystems (development releases only).**

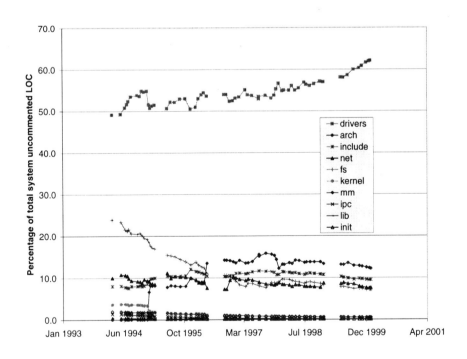

**Figure 6. Percentage of total system LOC for each major subsystem (development releases only).**

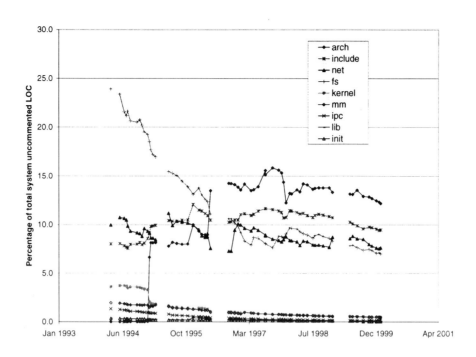

**Figure 7. Percentage of total system LOC for each major subsystems, ignoring the** `drivers` **subsystem (development releases only).**

and that these four have continued to grow at a rate that appears to be linear or better. Figure 7 also shows that the `fs` subsystem has grown more slowly than the others, and its relative size as a percentage of the total kernel size has significantly decreased over time.

Figure 8 shows the growth rate of the five smallest subsystems. We can see that while `kernel` and `mm` are growing steadily, these subsystems actually comprise a very small amount of code. However, these five subsystems are part of the core of the kernel; almost all of the code in these subsystems in included in kernel compilations regardless of the target hardware. Additionally, since operating system kernels are usually designed to be as small and compact as possible, undue growth in these core subsystems would probably be regarded as an unhealthy sign.

Figure 9 shows the growth of development releases of the sub-subsystems of `drivers`. The largest and fastest growing is `drivers/net` which contains driver code for network devices such as ethernet cards. The growth in this subsystem is a reflection of the number of network devices supported by Linux, the relative complexity of creating drivers for them, and the fact that sometimes a lot of device-specific data must be stored in the source files. We note that the average size of a source file in the `drivers` subsystem for the most recent development kernel (2.3.39) was over 600

lines of code, which was the highest average among the major subsystems. Most of the sub-subsystems of `drivers` showed significant growth, a sign of the growing acceptance of Linux as more users desire to run it with many different makes of devices.

However, we note the growth and size of the `drivers` subsystem distorts the idea of how large and complicated the Linux system is. First, the nature of a device driver is that it translates a common and well understood request into a task that a particular hardware device can execute efficiently. Device drivers are often quite large and complicated, but also relatively self-contained and independent of each other and of the rest of the system. Second, we note that while old hardware may die out, old drivers tend to live long lives, just in case some users still need them. Consequently, there is a large number of relatively unused (and relatively unmaintained) "legacy" drivers distributed with each kernel version. Finally, we note that even for current device drivers, most users tend to require only a few of the range of possible drivers. For example, the two largest `drivers` sub-subsystems are `net` and `scsi`, yet the vast majority of PCs are sold today without network or SCSI cards.

Figure 10 shows the shows the growth of development releases of the sub-subsystems of `arch`, each of which rep-

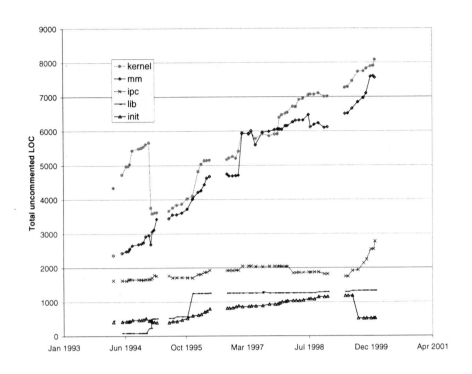

**Figure 8. Growth of the smaller, core subsystems (development releases only).**

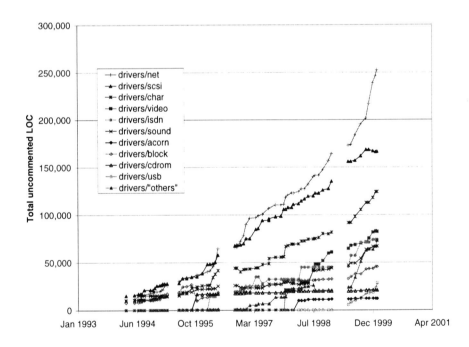

**Figure 9. Growth of the** `drivers` **subsystem (development releases only).**

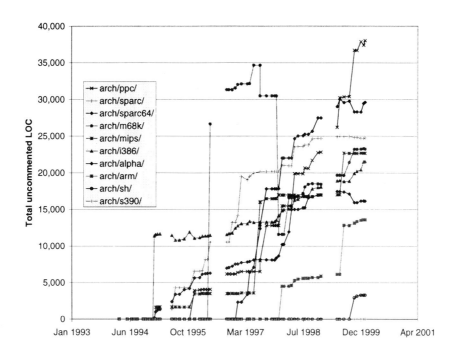

**Figure 10. Growth of the `arch` subsystem (development releases only).**

resents a major CPU/hardware architecture supported by Linux. What is most interesting here is the sudden upward leaps made by many of these subsystems. The first such leap occurred in early 1995, when it was decided to incorporate support for the Alpha, Sparc, and Mips architectures into Linux, and which also led to code that was specific to the Intel 386 architecture being moved from the main `kernel` subsystem into `arch/i386`. Subsequent leaps in other `arch` sub-subsystems have resulted from externally developed code being added in one large lump. In many cases, this architecture support is developed and maintained separately from the main Linux development kernel release by relatively independent teams of developers (and sometimes by corporations). A common growth pattern for such a subsystem is for large jumps as major new revisions are added, followed by periods of relative stability involving only minor revisions and bug fixes.

## 7    Conclusions

The Linux operating system kernel is a very successful example of a large software system in widespread use that has been developed using an "open source" development (OSD) model. We have examined the growth of Linux over its six year lifespan using several metrics, and we have found that at the system level its growth has been superlinear. This strong growth rate seems surprising given (a)

its large size (over two million lines of code including comments and blank lines), (b) its development model (a highly collaborative and geographically distributed set of developers, many of whom contributing their time and effort for free), and (c) previously published research that suggests that the growth of large software systems tends to slow down as the systems become larger [14, 4, 23].

We found that, as previously suggested by Gall *et al.* [4], it is useful to examine the growth patterns of the subsystems to gain a better understanding of how and why the system seems to have been able to evolve so successfully. We suggest further that a "black box" examination is not enough; one must investigate the *nature* of the subsystems and explore their *evolutionary patterns* to gain an understanding of how and why the system as a whole has evolved. We found that while the entire source tree for Linux is quite large, more than half of the code consists of device drivers, which are relatively independent of each other; we found that a large part of the remaining system consists of parallel features that are specific to particular CPUs; and we found that the small, core kernel subsystems comprise only a small part of the full source tree. That is to say, the Linux operating system kernel is not as large at it might seem since (based on our own experiments) any compiled version is likely to include only fifteen to fifty percent of the source files in the full source tree.

Finally, we consider this case study to be an important

data point in the study of large software system evolution. We hope that this will encourage further investigation into the evolution of OSD software systems, as well as comparisons with systems developed using more traditional approaches.

## 8  Acknowledgments

We thank David Toman for providing several useful comments on the FreeBSD operating system, and we thank Hugh Chipman and Dale Schuurmans for help on statistical modelling.

## References

[1] I. T. Bowman and R. C. Holt. Reconstructing ownership architectures to help understand software systems. In *Proc. of the 1999 IEEE Workshop on Program Comprehension (IWPC'99)*, Pittsburgh, PA, May 1999.

[2] I. T. Bowman, R. C. Holt, and N. V. Brewster. Linux as a case study: Its extracted software architecture. In *Proc. of the $21^{st}$ Intl. Conf. on Software Engineering (ICSE-21)*, Los Angeles, CA, May 1999.

[3] S. G. Eick, T. L. Graves, A. F. Karr, J. S. Marron, and A. Mocku. Does code decay? Assessing the evidence from change management data. to appear in *IEEE Trans. on Software Engineering*.

[4] H. Gall, M. Jazayeri, R. Kloesch, and G. Trausmuth. Software evolution observations based on product release history. In *Proc. of the 1997 Intl. Conf. on Software Maintenance (ICSM'97)*, Bari, Italy, Oct 1997.

[5] D. Hiebert. The Exuberant CTAGS homepage. Website. http://home.HiWAAY.net/~darren/ctags/.

[6] http://www.freebsd.org. The FreeBSD homepage. Website.

[7] http://www.kernelnotes.org. kernelnotes.org: The official website of Linux kernel information. Website.

[8] http://www.kernel.org. The Linux kernel archives. Website.

[9] http://www.linux.org. The Linux homepage. Website.

[10] http://www.opensource.org. The open source homepage. Website.

[11] http://www.vim.org. The VIM homepage. Website.

[12] C. F. Kemerer and S. Slaughter. An empirical approach to studying software evolution. *IEEE Trans. on Software Engineering*, 25(4), July/August 1999.

[13] M. M. Lehman and L. A. Belady. *Program Evolution: Processes of Software Change*. Academic Press, 1985.

[14] M. M. Lehman, D. E. Perry, and J. F. Ramil. Implications of evolution metrics on software maintenance. In *Proc. of the 1998 Intl. Conf. on Software Maintenance (ICSM'98)*, Bethesda, Maryland, Nov 1998.

[15] M. M. Lehman, J. F. Ramil, P. D. Wernick, D. E. Perry, and W. M. Turski. Metrics and laws of software evolution — the nineties view. In *Proc. of the Fourth Intl. Software Metrics Symposium (Metrics'97)*, Albuquerque, NM, 1997.

[16] D. L. Parnas. Software aging. In *Proc. of the $16^{th}$ Intl. Conf. on Software Engineering (ICSE-16)*, Sorrento, Italy, May 1994.

[17] D. E. Perry. Dimensions of software evolution. In *Proc. of the 1994 Intl. Conf. on Software Maintenance (ICSM'94)*, 1994.

[18] E. S. Raymond. *The Cathedral and the Bazaar: Musings on Linux and Open Source by an Accidental Revolutionary*. O'Reilly and Associates, Oct 1999.

[19] D. A. Rusling. The Linux Kernel. Website. http://www.linuxhq.com/guides/TLK/tlk.html.

[20] C. Salzenberg. Topaz: Perl for the 22nd century. http://www.perl.com/pub/1999/09/topaz.html.

[21] J. B. Tran, M. W. Godfrey, E. H. S. Lee, and R. C. Holt. Architecture analysis and repair of open source software. In *Proc. of 2000 Intl. Workshop on Program Comprehension (IWPC'00)*, Limerick, Ireland, June 2000.

[22] J. B. Tran and R. C. Holt. Forward and reverse repair of software architecture. In *Proc. of CASCON 1999*, Toronto, Nov 1999.

[23] W. M. Turski. Reference model for smooth growth of software systems. *IEEE Trans. on Software Engineering*, 22(8), Aug 1996.

[24] L. Vepstas. Linux on the IBM ESA/390 mainframe architecture. Website. http://linas.org/linux/i370/i370.html.

# Studying the Evolution and Enhancement of Software Features

Idris Hsi[1], Colin Potts[2]

College of Computing

Atlanta, Georgia 30332-0280, USA

[1] +1 404 385 1101, [2] +1 404 894 5551

idris@cc.gatech.edu, potts@cc.gatech.edu

## Abstract

*The evolution and enhancement of features during system evolution can have significant effects on its coherence as well as its internal architecture. Studying the evolution of system features and concepts across a product line from an external or problem domain perspective can inform the process of identifying and designing future features. We show how we derive three primary views, morphological, functional, and an object view, from the user-level structures and operations of a system, using a case study of Microsoft Word's evolution. We show how these views illustrate feature evolution over three versions of Word. Lastly we discuss the lessons learned from our study of feature evolution.*

## 1. Introduction

"Feature creep" is a phenomenon of system evolution where successive releases of a product not only grow in size and complexity, but also show a reduction in the conceptual homogeneity or intellectual coherence of the product as experienced by the user. Thus a text editor may become a page layout program, a document management system, a knowledge-based authoring tool. Just as modules or lines of code are size units for software architecture or implementation, respectively, features are the units of software function or usefulness.

Up to a point, more features are better than fewer, and it is a matter for design judgment and human-factors evaluation to decide when a product has grown too big to be useful or usable. But when this point is reached, engineering questions arise such as whether it will be possible to separate a given feature cluster (e.g. spell-checking) into a separate module so that users can plug in new versions or select among "lite", "professional" or "enterprise" editions.

More significantly, given that a major goal of modern software engineering is the assembly and directed evolution of systems from pluggable components [5], we would like to be able to anticipate these questions far in advance so that we may predict where significant feature growth is likely to occur or prove problematic in the future. Or, alternatively, if an organization is planning a new product line, it is only sensible to analyze the feature space that the product line will occupy, so that component-based assembly can be planned from the outset.

In this paper, we present a view of feature evolution that is defined exclusively in terms of *user-accessible features* and concepts. This is not to argue that software architecture is unimportant to evolution. Obviously it is. Rather, we are claiming that the terms used in questions such as "can we replace X?" should ultimately be couched in the vocabulary of the problem domain and not that of software architecture. "Checking spelling" is what it is whether it is done with a dictionary and blue pencil or an online spell-checker. It is the coherence and integrity of the activity of checking spelling, not the fact that there is a module in the design documentation or a recovered design abstraction re-engineered from the code called the "SpellChecker Module" that makes spell-checking a plausible substitution for "X" in the question above.

Given that features make sense in problem-domain or user-activity terms, we would like to be able to depict the *feature architecture* of a product independently (at least initially) of the underlying software architecture. If we want to find which modules in the architecture are implicated in spell-checking, then the very question presupposes that spell-checking is a sensible feature-oriented abstraction in the first place.

Our term "feature architecture" may sound like a "domain model." In domain analysis, application domain knowledge is modeled independently of systems to support the forward engineering (including maintenance and evolution) of product families [4,5,7]. However, the source of this application knowledge is generally domain experts or the intuitions of the designer. When existing systems or product families are the starting point for an integration or evolution project, as is more after the case, it is necessary to use the current system as a source of the 'theory' of its domain. Previous research into reverse engineering has adopted this approach [4,7] mainly from a starting point of code and code-level documentation. The forward- and reverse-engineering approaches to domain modeling differ not only in their practical aims but also in what the resulting domain model represents. In forward-engineering, a domain model is a normative, expert-generated model of what the problem domain is like. It thus constrains the software architecture by *prescribing* a view of the problem domain but does not reflect it. The reverse-engineering approach takes a domain model to be a *description* of the problem domain exhibited by the current product, not a prescription imposed from outside.

Our approach to feature architecture takes the reverse engineering approach, but differs in one crucial respect from the previous approaches: We reconstruct externally relevant feature objects and operations from the morphology (externally visible interfaces) of an application, and developed a reverse-engineering version of domain analysis. There is no single domain model, but rather a tripartite view of the domain/product features as follows:

- The *morphological* view is the user-visible analog for feature architecture of the source code content of a software architecture. It consists of the user-interface composition and navigation structure.

- The *functional view* is the description of what the features do. A thorough analysis of functionality would require a detailed model of interactions based on data flow or control abstractions. In this paper, we restrict ourselves to enumerating the *operations*, the activities that the system performs.

- The *object view* is a description of the subject-matter of the feature. Like an object model produced during software design or an information model for database design, the object view consists of static relationships between objects in the problem domain. In the case of the feature architecture, however, the objects are derived from user-visible phenomena, especially the user interface components from the morphological view. The objects in the feature architecture may be correlated with the objects underlying the implementation if it is object-oriented or the data structures and files if it is not, but they need not be. Again, it is the problem domain that makes the products' objects appropriate or inappropriate, not the fact that they are to be recovered from the code.

Thus these three views of feature architecture are

derived without knowledge of the source code and without recourse to specialist domain expertise. Rather, the feature architecture encompasses the *working domain model* and functional repertoire of the existing product. "Spell checking" can therefore be thought of, if rather fancifully, as what a word-processing product tells us about spell-checking.

Studies of system growth or evolution from the software-maintenance perspective (e.g. [10]) address evolution as changes in the size and relational complexity of the code base of the product. To our knowledge, there have been no comparable implementation-independent studies of feature evolution, where feature architectures have been objectively defined and measured.

In addition to its potential practical value in helping us to understand the dynamics of feature evolution, we think such studies have an intrinsic interest. Significant software products affect society in numerous obvious and subtle ways, and it is appropriate for software engineering to undertake precedence studies [8] similar to those of architecture and urban planning, two professional disciplines whose products have similarly wide-ranging effects. Tracking the evolution of features in office products, for example, could tells us much about how technology drives social processes, how technology infrastructure and social phenomena affect what features grow at what epoch in a product's life history, and how the two actors in this interaction—technology and its contexts of use—co-evolve.

To this end, we are studying office productivity packages, time-management and scheduling packages, computer games, camera controls, and telephony features [2]. In this paper, we present a case study examining three versions of Microsoft Word for Windows.

This paper is a prospectus and example of this approach to studying feature architectures and their evolution and its possible value in planning future feature evolution through component assembly. Section 2 builds on this approach and describes a specific methodology for deriving the three views of feature architectures: System Morphology, System Operations, and the System Object Model. The results of applying this methodology are discussed in Section 3, in which feature evolution is documented for three versions of Microsoft Word. In Section 4, we discuss the findings of the case study. Lastly, we conclude with some benefits of the approach for forward-engineering of software in practice.

## 2. Three Views of Feature Architecture

### 2.1 System morphology

Morphology is the study of the form and structure of an organism without consideration of function. An application's morphology is the structure that organizes its features, consisting of user interface elements including menu items, user input device commands, and information displays. These provide *portals* through the external to the domain features.

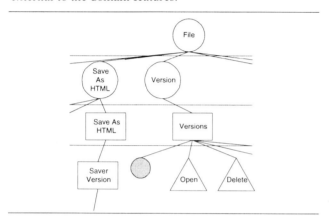

**Figure 1. An example of system morphology – a portion of the Word 97 File Menu**

We construct the representation without analysis of functionality or design intent by tracing paths through the interface elements and developing them into a graph representation.

Figure 1 shows a portion of the Word 97 File menu morphology. We generated the graph by traversing the File menu, identifying all the menu items listed. The menu's main items are represented as large circles. Rectangles represent dialog boxes. Small circles are simply generic terminators like OK/Cancel. They also become leaf nodes in the graph because they cause the activity to return to the top level morphology. Small triangles are actions specific to that dialog box that also act as leaf nodes. The horizontal dotted lines show how "deep" that particular path reaches. Every time an action invokes another interface structure, the path gets deeper. Other items represented by the morphological view, but not shown in the example, include mode changes, parallel dialog structures, toolbars, mouse actions, displays, and menu bars. Items not represented by this view include dialog box details such as radio buttons, selectors, dials, and so on. We chose not to represent the smaller structures within the dialog boxes to simplify the representation.

### 2.2 System functional view

The functional view consists of an enumeration of all the operations that the user can call through the normal operation of the system. In the absence of documentation or program specifications, we uncover these by traversing the morphological views, observing, sometimes inferring, the operations that the program performs. Fortunately, for this case study, we were able to use the lists of operations that MS Word provides to program macros and set button and keyboard shortcuts.

After we obtain the list of operations, we categorize them by whether they are old, new, or have been removed since the last release, which interface structures are used to call them, what object they affect, and a description (if needed) of the function's action. At this point, we define an object to be something that can be accessed by a user through the system's morphology or a system operation. Most of the objects can be taken directly from the operation's name and behavior. Occasionally, they have to be inferred from the morphology and action they perform. An operation called "Exit" for example, infers an Application object that you exit from.

Table 1 shows all the operations associated with the bulleted list in Word 95. From Word 2.0 to Word 95, there have been three new operations added and none removed. The fact that the older operations have no interfaces connected to them implies that they are unused in the later version and may be present for backwards compatibility or to support user-level macros created in Word 2.0.

**Table 1. Functional view of Bulleted List Operations in Word 95. (Not shown are the descriptions of the operations.)**

| Name | Status | Menu Access | Toolbar Access | Input Device | Object |
|------|--------|-------------|----------------|--------------|--------|
| ApplyListBullet | New | None | none | Ctrl+Shift+L | Bulleted List |
| FormatBulletDefault | New | None | Formatting | None | Bulleted List |
| FormatBulletsAndNumbering | New | Format | None | Right Mouse Button | Bulleted List |
| ToolsBulletListDefault | Old | None | None | None | Bulleted List |
| RemoveBulletsNumbers | Old | None | None | None | Bulleted List |

### 2.3 System object model

Using the objects derived from the system operations and morphology, we can build a modified entity-relationship diagram that describes how those objects interact to form the underlying domain model. There are three types of relationships that we examine because of their relevance to the work product domain.

- *has* – Object A *has* Object B if, very simply, A can physically contains B or can possess B as a subproperty or concept. This is an optional, not a mandatory relationship. The *has* relationship is also directed. Object A must be located higher than B in the morphological hierarchy for Object A to *have* Object B. The relationship is derived from a morphological connection between A and B but only the closest connection is considered in the hierarchy. For example, a page can have words and a paragraph can have words. But pages must first have paragraphs before they can have words. So in an object representation, we represent a *has* relationship between page and paragraph, and one between paragraph and word but not page and word.

- *strictly contains* – Object A *strictly contains* Object B if Object A must have Object B to exist. The *strictly contains* relationship is a subset of the *has* relationship. Fonts can optionally have a Font Underline but must have a Color. Therefore, Fonts *strictly contain* Font Color. *Strictly contains* relationships are important because they help to define tight relationships between objects. A change to this kind of relation can imply a fundamental conceptual change to the parent object.

- *type of* – Object B is a *type of* Object A if A, as the morphological parent references B from a set of equivalent objects. Fonts can have a Font Underline but in the morphology, there are 11 different *types of* Font Underlining.

Based on these relationships, we can isolate system concepts which we call *teleons*, from the Greek word *teleos* meaning goal, using the following definition.

- *teleon* – A *teleon* parent is any node that has at least one child resulting from a *has* or *type of* relationship. The teleon is then formed by tracing the graph until a node with a shared ancestor or subtypes is reached. That last node is included in the graph and the trace ends. The resulting subgraph is the complete *teleon*.

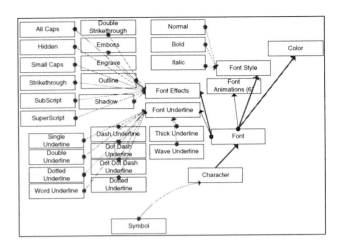

**Figure 2. Object view of the character teleon in Word 97.**

Figure 2, shows the Character teleon. The dashed lines represent *Type Of* relationships, the thin lines represent *has* relationships, and the thick lines represent *strictly contains* relationships. The Character teleon consists of the Symbol, Character, and Font nodes. It also contains subteleons such as Font, which consists of Font Effects, Font Underline, Font Animations, Font Style, and Color. Color, in this representation, is not a teleon because it does not have a child.

## 3. The evolution of MS Word

We use these system descriptions to study how an application evolves in structure and functionality over the lifetime of the product line. In addition, this approach has revealed a relationship between these three views of the system that suggests some feedback mechanisms that impact this evolution. Here we examine the evolutionary trends that we have observed in MS Word.

### 3.1 Morphological evolution

Evolution of system morphology has two implications. First, that there is more underlying functionality to be accessed and second, that more portals are being opened to frequently used operations. We observed two basic trends in the morphological evolution of Word: changes in the size and complexity of the overall morphological structure and to the types of primary interfaces used in the morphology.

146

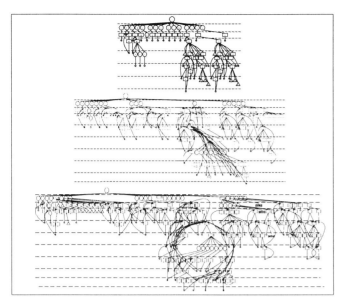

**Figure 3. An overview of the graphs representing the Insert Menu morphology for Word 2.0, Word 95, and Word 97, respectively.**

Figure 3 shows the evolution of the Insert menu over the three versions of MS Word. The menus (with the exception of the File menu) visibly grow in depth and breadth reflecting an increase in the types of objects that can be contained in a document. The curved lines from the bottom most nodes back to a middle layer node represent a return to a previous dialog box in the trace. So in addition to growing in overall size, there are now more loops in the graph. While the Insert menu is the most pronounced example of growth that we encountered, similar behavior can be seen across most of the other morphologies.

The other basic trend that we observed was the changes to the types of primary interfaces. For example, Word 95 and 97 employ more mode shifts and toolbars to accomplish tasks. Also, Word 97 departs from redundant accessibility, where a function could be reached from menu and toolbar. Instead, it employs unique accessibility, or specialized portals, where a function can only be reached from a particular toolbar that can be accessed during a particular mode.

### 3.2 Functional evolution

The number of operations provided by each word processor significantly increased over versions. This seems to be a reasonable result given the changes to the morphology: more portals implies more operations on average.

## Table 2. Function Growth in MS Word

| Version | # New Operations | # Kept from last version | # Removed from Last | % Growth | Total # of Operations |
|---------|------------------|--------------------------|---------------------|----------|----------------------|
| 2.0 | 311 | | | | 311 |
| 95 | 362 | 253 | 58 | 97% | 614 |
| 97 | 383 | 572 | 42 | 56% | 955 |

Table 2 shows a brief quantitative analysis of how the numbers of operations evolved. The removed operations were actually renamed, consolidated, or relocated to other parts of the operating environment. For example, Word 2.0 used to have file management capabilities and Word 97 uses Visual Basic to manage its macros.

The numbers imply that Word experiences a steady, calculable growth in functionality. However, further examination reveals that almost half of the new operations in Word 97 are related to graphics teleons, specifically 3D drawing objects, 125 new drawing objects, and Word Art. Some of these operations also support the management of these drawing objects. Other objects, such as Tables or Bulleted lists, see a few new operations that extend their capabilities but not significantly. Our general finding is that functional evolution in the MS Word product line is not evenly distributed, as one might see in an application that experiences monotonic, conservative growth.

### 3.3 Object evolution

To help constrain our analysis for this study, we chose to limit our object model to the electronic and paper document that Word produces. We did not look at the window and application mechanisms or the supporting operations, such as spelling and grammar checking.

After deriving the object representations, we noticed some general tendencies in the object model. With the exception of the character/font teleons from Word 2.0 to Word 95, older teleons rarely changed their existing subgraph. Teleons changed by either increasing their potential space or by increasing the number of different types associated with it.

For example, Paragraph is a very important teleon. Word 2.0 has 9 nodes in the Paragraph teleon. Word 95 has 18. Word 97 has 21. In general, Word changed significantly from Word 2.0 to Word 95 but the extensions to the Paragraph teleon in Word 95 were almost all new teleons that could now be contained in a paragraph, such as a Cross Reference. Word 97 simply adds three more items, such as Hyperlink, to this list. What this implies is that Paragraph is becoming a more stable teleon in definition and is growing in capability.

The other behavior, increasing the number of types,

can be seen in Word 97's Drawing Objects (added 115 objects). The functional growth described earlier is partly the result of adding over a hundred drawing objects. Each object needs a minimum of one function to be used in a document. Other things that developed more types included Field, Font Effects, Document, and Links.

We also examined the conceptual evolution of the Word document. Table 3 shows that the growth of new teleons over the versions. If we removed "sub-teleons", such as 3D Lighting (a sub-teleon of 3D object), we're left with an evolutionary model that indicates conservative growth – adding a small number of teleons to the document per release.

**Table 3. Conceptual Evolution of the Document in MS Word**

| Word 2.0 Teleons | Word 95 – New Teleons | Word 97 - New Teleons |
|---|---|---|
| Annotation | Caption | 3D Direction |
| Border | Cross-Reference | 3D Lighting |
| Character | Database | 3D Object |
| Column | Drawing | 3D Surface |
| Document | Drawing Object | Comment |
| Envelope | Font | Font Animation |
| Field | Font Effects | HTML Document |
| Font Style | Font Underline | OCX Object |
| Footer | Form Field | |
| Footnote | Heading | |
| Frame | List | |
| Header | Note | |
| Index | Numbering | |
| Line Numbering | Revisions | |
| Object | Table of Authorities | |
| Page | Table of Figures | |
| Paragraph | | |
| Picture | | |
| Section | | |
| Shading | | |
| Style | | |
| Summary Info | | |
| Tab Alignment | | |
| Table | | |
| Table Cell | | |
| Table of Contents | | |
| Tabs | | |
| Word | | |

## 4. What changed and why?

From the data, we know that none of the teleons vanish from the new domain model. In fact, they become more entrenched, growing more connections to different objects and morphologies over time. Intuitively, one can say with some confidence that the teleons outlined in the Word 2.0 represent a set of teleons that are core to a document produced in the MS Word family. In fact, the objects introduced in Word 97, with the exception of HTML Document, seem to have only peripheral relevance to what you might expect to find in a typical document.

In order to analyze this evolution, it is important to be able to separate the changes that are a result of technological advances in hardware or implementation from those that represent fundamental changes to the concepts embodied in the software. The former type of change tends to be primarily morphological in nature: better graphics, new widgets, and new interactive devices. We consider these changes to be superficial in nature. They alter the outward appearance of the application and sometimes give the illusion of significant enhancement. We are more concerned with the evolution of the software's concepts.

### 4.1 "True" conceptual evolution

Concepts that evolved through the different versions of Word did so almost exclusively by the addition of new subtypes of the object or the addition of new contained objects. However, these new objects were almost never strictly contained and the concept structure grew monotonically without restructuring. This suggests an operational method to deliver stable and core features: they grow but do not have to be restructured; and they accrete new parts, but not in a way that necessarily affects what already exists.

Studies of conceptual evolution in other areas reveal a similar phenomenon. For example, Thagard [11] shows that the conceptual schemas of science, before and after major paradigm shifts are structured differently, with different classification and containment relations holding between concepts. However, normal science proceeds more routinely by the addition of specialized and component concepts.

This suggests, by analogy, that occasional changes to core feature concepts are likely to have radical effects, either immediately or in subsequent releases. An example of this may be present in the inclusion in Word 97 of the 'HTML document' – which is not merely a new kind of document but is likely to affect the concepts of document sections, pages, etc. It is, of course, more common for changes to be made for functional reasons than because the domain concepts have changed [1,6,14]. Such shifts do, however, occur occasionally, and it is vital to identify the objects most vulnerable to radical change.

Older features, representing the "core" of the application experience less change and evolution over the lifetime of the product line, stabilizing with each version. Newer features tend to be added to the periphery, either as small extensions of existing concepts or as large "clumps" of functionality that expand the overall domain.

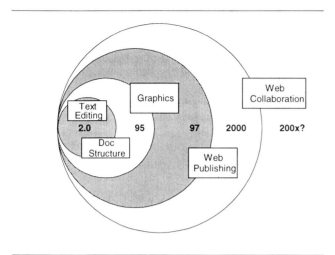

**Figure 4. Feature "clumps" in successive versions of MS Word**

Figure 4 shows how Word 2.0's text editing capabilities were extended by changes to document structure management in Word 95. Then Word 97 added graphics capabilities. Our initial work with Word 2000 shows additional Web publishing features as its large clump. In each case, the clumps grew from existing concepts in previous versions. Using this heuristic, we can hypothesize that the next version of Word will have more Internet collaboration capabilities, extending the existing email and web publishing capabilities.

## 4.2 Morphological and conceptual changes

While morphological changes have important implications for the efficiency and usability of these applications, they do not tend to alter what we consider to be the core teleology of a product. Changes to teleons naturally affect the morphology, reflecting the intuition that the "deep structure" of the application affects the "surface structure." We would therefore expect changes in the morphological scale and complexity of the product to reflect the underlying functional and object-oriented complexity. However, the MS Word evolutionary record shows that its morphological changes far outstripped any underlying changes.

It would be an exaggeration to say that the user interface of Word has become extremely rich, whereas the product has not evolved substantively; our analysis of MS Word does show a large growth in morphology and only a small growth in the number of teleons. Some changes may therefore be imposed by interface efficiencies. In the case of user interfaces, this could lead to user opinions that a product had become complex and "bloated" far beyond its actual functional and conceptual

growth.

Features are composed of these teleons and objects. In order to understand the differences between the small changes to the teleons and the dramatic changes to the morphology, we need to examine how introducing objects to create features or enhance existing ones can affect operations and morphology. Consider the simple example of a single object, with one function, accessed by a single morphological port shown in Figure 5.

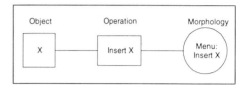

**Figure 5. 1:1:1 correspondence**

Many objects in an application tend to have attributes, options, and capabilities, each of which requires a function to use it properly. If the user wants to be able to change a Font Style from Normal to Bold, an extra function is needed. This situation is better portrayed by Figure 6 than the simple correspondences of Figure 5.

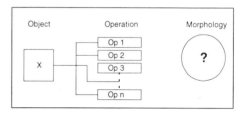

**Figure 6. 1:n correspondence between object and operations.**

But in order for these operations to be useful, they require some form of accessibility from the system morphology. Important or frequently used operations may also require multiple portals to increase accessibility. Figure 7 shows how the final morphology grows from adding a new object.

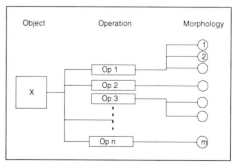

**Figure 7. 1:n:m correspondences with object in system**

This illustration shows how introducing or extending a features can have tremendous impacts on the overall morphological complexity of the system. The rapid structural changes in the morphology of Word compared with the relative stability of its core features reinforces the standard architecture guideline to decouple user interface code from application features.

## 5. What is in a feature?

In proposing a feature architecture independent of implementation architecture, we have assumed a traditional function/data split in describing the deep structure of the application. Our description of features consists of two representations: a modified object model showing the structure of a teleon as a network of related or contained objects, and a list of operations that create, access, update, or delete such objects.

Object structuring, particularly ownership and containment, is an appropriate organizing principle for a word processor's feature architecture, because word processing is a "work piece" problem frame [9]. That is, the software features are responsible for creating an artifact that can subsequently be inspected and manipulated but which does not exist independently in the world outside the software or change independently of it. A different set of basic categories would probably be more appropriate for control, information management or transform applications (which correspond broadly to Jackson's control, information system and JSP problem frames).

For example, control features, such as setting reminders in real time or controlling the operation of a device like a camera, have the achievement of goals as a primary category for these application features. These have to be modeled as the achievement of event-recognizing and phenomenon-affecting goals [2,12].

## 6. Feature Coherence

The application itself is a source not only of the teleons and operations represented in its features but also their relative centrality and connectivity. Earlier we argued that 'core' and peripheral' teleons evolve differently, but did not define these terms independently of their age ("core" teleons being the earliest).

We are investigating graph-theoretic and statistical clustering techniques for quantifying and presenting teleon structure independently of their evolution, an approach complementary to Waters's use of lattice-theoretic techniques ("concept analysis") for reverse engineering architectural concepts [13].

Extending existing features or adding new ones requires developing new associations with the current features. Older features tend to be more entangled with associations and will therefore require more effort to modify in later releases. New features with effective conceptual relationships to existing features may also require many associations with them. This difficulty may account for the tendency to supply new features that only loosely associate with old features and are thus peripheral to the core teleology of the application.

A major practical consideration for developers is how to manage the design and architecture of a version to allow for the coherent evolution of its features. Developers planning to evolve systems need to design and structure architectures to support such coherent growth. We have argued that a more principled definition of feature architecture as a combination of morphology, functional model, and object model is a viable way to describe a product's feature set independently of its code architecture and that such planning of feature evolution could be framed in these terms.

## 7. Acknowledgements

We thank the reviewers for their helpful comments.

## 8. References

[1] Abowd, G., Ertmann-Christiansen, C., Goel, A., et al., "MORALE: Mission Oriented Architectural Legacy Evolution", *Proc. International Conference on Software Maintenance'97* (Bari Italy, 1997), IEEE Computer Society Press, 1997, pp. 150-159.

[2] Antón, A. I. and C. Potts, "The Use of Goals to Surface Requirements for Evolving Systems", *Proc. 20th International Conference on Software Engineering (ICSE '98)*, (Kyoto Japan, 1998), IEEE Computer Society Press, 1998, pp. 157-166.

[3] Anton, A. I and C. Potts, "Requirements Engineering in the Long Term: Fifty Years of Telephony Evolution", Accepted to *International Workshop on Feedback and Evolution in Software and Business Processes (FEAST 2000)*, (London UK, 2000).

[4] Arango, G., "Domain Analysis: From Art Form to Engineering Discipline", *Proc. International Workshop on Software Specification and Design*, (Pittsburgh PA, 1989), IEEE Computer Society Press, 1989, pp. 152-159.

[5] DeBaud, J.-M. and K. Schmid., "A Systematic Approach to Derive the Scope of Software Product Lines", *Proc. International Conference on Software Engineering*, (Los Angeles CA, 1999), IEEE Computer Society Press, 1999, pp. 34-43.

[6] Easterbrook, S. and B. Nuseibeh. "Managing Inconsistencies in an Evolving Specification", *Proc. RE'95: Second IEEE International Symposium on*

*Requirements Engineering*, (York UK, March 1995) IEEE Computer Society Press, 1995, pp. 48-55.

[7] Fischer, G., "Seeding, Evolutionary Growth and Reseeding: Constructing, Capturing and Evolving Knowledge in Domain-Oriented Design Environments", *Automated Software Engineering*, Boston, MA, Kluwer Academic Publishers, **5**(4), 1998, pp. 447-464.

[8] Hillier, B., Space is the Machine: A configurational theory of architecture. Cambridge, UK, Cambridge University Press, 1996.

[9] Jackson, M.A., Software Requirements and Specification, Reading, MA, Addison-Wesley, 1995.

[10] Lehman, M. and L. Belady, Program Evolution, New York, NY, Academic Press, 1985.

[11] Thagard, P. Conceptual Revolutions. Princeton, New Jersey, Princeton University Press, 1992.

[12] van Lamsweerde, A. and E. Letier, "Integrating Obstacles in Goal-Driven Requirements Engineering", *Proc. 20th International Conference on Software Engineering* (Kyoto Japan, 1995) IEEE Computer Society Press, 1995, pp. 53-63.

[13] Waters, R. and G. Abowd, "Architectural Synthesis: Integrating Multiple Architectural Perspectives", *Proc. Sixth Working Conference on Reverse Engineering* (Atlanta GA, 1999). IEEE Computer Society Press, 1999, pp. 10-15.

[14] Zowghi, D. and R. Offen, "A Logical Framework for Modeling and Reasoning about the Evolution of Requirements", *RE'97: Third IEEE International Symposium on Requirements Engineering*, Annapolis, Maryland, January 6-10, IEEE Computer Society Press, 1997, pp. 247-2.

# Notes

# Empirical Studies II

# Can Metrics Help to Bridge the Gap Between the Improvement of OO Design Quality and Its Automation?[*]

Houari A. Sahraoui
DIRO, Université de
Montréal
C.P. 6128, succ. CV,
Montreal (QC)
Canada H3C 3J7
sahraouh@iro.umontreal.ca

Robert Godin
Université du Québec à
Montréal
C.P.8888, Succ.CV,
Montreal (QC), Canada
H3C 3P8
godin.robert@uqam.ca

Thierry Miceli
Pixel Systems Inc.
4750 Henri-Julien,
Montréal (Québec) Canada
H2T 2C8
tmiceli@sympatico.ca

## Abstract

*During the evolution of object-oriented systems, the preservation of correct design should be a permanent quest. However, for systems involving a large number of classes and subject to frequent modifications, detection and correction of design flaws may be a complex and resource-consuming task. The use of automatic detection and correction tools can be helpful for this task. Various works propose transformations that improve the quality of an object-oriented system while preserving its behavior. In this paper we propose to investigate whether some object-oriented metrics can be used as indicators for automatically detecting situations where a particular transformation can be applied to improve the quality of a system. The detection process is based on analyzing the impact of various transformations on these object-oriented metrics using quality estimation models.*

## 1. Introduction

Design flaws, introduced in early stages of the development or during system evolution, are a frequent cause of low maintainability, low reuse, high complexity and faulty behavior of the programs [19]. The preservation of correct design should be a permanent quest. However, for large systems subject to frequent modifications, detection and correction of design flaws may be a complex and resource-consuming task. Automated tools for assisting this process can help alleviate this task.

Previous work on improving the quality of object systems includes using metrics for quality estimation and automated transformations to improve quality. However both aspects have been treated mostly independently of each other. A natural extension to these efforts is to

analyze the interaction of particular transformations and metrics in a systematic manner in order to suggest the use of transformations that may be helpful in improving quality as estimated by metrics.

At first, we formally analyzed the impact of several common transformations on several metrics. This knowledge is incorporated in our OO1 prototype corrector tool. The tool is used to help improving the quality of C++ programs. The function of the tool is analogous to a linguistic assistant for a text processor. The tool computes several quality metrics on the source code. The metrics are used to detect potential design flaws. Based on these estimations, the tool suggests particular transformations that can be automatically applied in order to improve the quality as estimated by the metrics. Evidently, this should be seen as a heuristic process and, as for linguistic aids, the process may include some form of human intervention and acknowledgement before applying the suggested transformations. Although our initial investigation has addressed OO program code, the same idea could be applied to earlier software design artifacts or to non-OO software.

The remainder of this paper is organized as follows. Section 2 surveys the related work in the area of software metrics and transformations. Section 3 gives an overview of the proposed technique. Section 4 describes the prototype tool and a case study. Section 5 presents our conclusion for this work.

## 2. Related work

Related work cuts across several research areas and particularly object-oriented software reengineering and OO quality estimation. For the case of OO software, Basili & al. show in [1] that most of the metrics proposed by Chidamber and Kemerer in [3] are useful to predict fault-

---

[*] This work was partly funded by CRIM Montreal.

proneness of classes during the design phase of OO systems. In the same context, Li and Henry showed that maintenance effort could be predicted from combinations of metrics collected from source code of OO components [9]. In [4], Demeyer and Ducasse show for the particular domain of OO frameworks, that size and inheritance metrics are not reliable to detect problems, but are good indicators for the stability of a framework. More recently our team proposed a set of models for different quality characteristics in [8], [11], [12] and [13]. In this work, machine-learning techniques are used to build the estimation models. These techniques generate interesting results even with small-size learning sets.

Reengineering of OO software using transformations to improve its quality has been addressed by several researchers. Some techniques involving decomposition of class hierarchy transformations in smaller modifications are proposed by Casais and more recently by Opdyke. In [2], Casais enumerates a set of primitive update operations that can be used to decompose class modifications. The completeness and correctness issues are presented but not formally addressed. Similar work has been conducted by Opdyke (see [15] and [16]). He introduces the notion of behavior-preserving transformations named *refactorings*. A set of low-level refactorings is used to decompose high-level refactorings without introducing new errors in the system or modifying the program behavior. Preservation of the program behavior for each low-level refactoring is guaranteed when some preconditions are verified. A tool called *The Refactoring Browser* [18] was created using these transformations in the Smalltalk environment. Recently, Tokuda and Batory show that programs can be automatically reengineered using design patterns [21]. In this work, the authors propose transformations that implement most of the design patterns. Most of the efforts in this research direction concentrate on the definition of transformations and their implementation. To our knowledge, there is no effort on the automatic detection of the situations where these transformations can apply.

Several authors have addressed the particular problem of class hierarchy design and maintenance. In these works, transformations are used typically to abstract common behavior into new classes. Work in the context of the Demeter System has addressed the design of class hierarchies using an optimization process [10]. The objective function used in the optimization process is a global class hierarchy metric that measures the overall complexity of the class hierarchy. This work is therefore a first step in using metrics to guide the choice of useful transformations. Casais (1991) proposed a local reorganization algorithm for a class hierarchy that relies on the user to specify the immediate superclasses of a new class. Godin and Mili in [6] propose the use of concept (Galois) lattices and derived structures as of formal framework for dealing with class hierarchy design or

reengineering that guarantees maximal factorization of common properties including polymorphism. The ARES algorithm builds the Galois subhierarchy while preserving initial *relevant* classes and also deals with the automatic detection of specialization relationships between properties [5]. The GURU tool proposed by Moore (in [14]) deals with refactoring of methods and the class hierarchy in an integrated manner. In [7], reengineered hierarchies are compared using global class hierarchy metrics.

## 3. Diagnosis of design flaws

Experienced designers/programmers have a relative precise idea on what should be a good application/program relatively to a quality perspective (maintainability, reliability, reusability, etc.) This knowledge is built from their experiences and from the common knowledge related to the design/programming paradigm. Books like [19] for example, give a set of rules that help developing good and understandable programs. Most of the time, these rules cannot be implemented to detect automatically symptomatic situations in a design/code. The main reason is that these rules are fuzzy by definition. If we consider the rule that states that we have to avoid long methods or methods that contain a lot of variables, it is hard to derive a threshold for the size of a method or for the number of variables from which we consider that we have a symptomatic situation.

To solve this problem, two directions seem promising. The first one is to use fuzzy logic to implement the quality rules/models. The second direction consists of using these rules as starting hypotheses, and deriving precise rules by the way of empirical studies (i.e. building quality estimation models). Due to lack of space, we focus in this paper on the second direction.

| Symbol | Name |
|--------|------|
| CLD | Class-to-Leaf Depth |
| NOC | Number Of Children |
| NMO | Number of Methods Overridden |
| NMI | Number of Methods Inherited |
| NMA | Number of Methods Added |
| SIX | Specialization Index |
| CBO | Coupling Between Object classes |
| DAC' | Data Abstraction Coupling |
| IH-ICP | Information-flow-based inheritance coupling |
| OCAIC | Others Class-Attribute Import Coupling |
| DMMEC | Descendants Method-Method Export Coupling |
| OMMEC | Others Method-Method Export Coupling |

Table 1. Inheritance and coupling metrics

Roughly speaking, building a quality estimation model consists of establishing a relation of cause and effect between two types of software characteristics: 1) internal attributes which are directly measurable such as size, inheritance and coupling, and 2) quality characteristics which are measurable after a certain time of use such as maintainability, reliability and reusability. The process we follow to build such models is based on classical machine learning algorithms, particularly C4.5 [17]. More details on the different steps can be found in [13].

Before giving an example on the obtained rules, we present in Table 1, the sets of metrics, which will be used in this paper. Readers who are interested in the formal definitions of these metrics can find more details in [8].

The two following rules are examples of quality estimation rules:

**Rule INH7**: $NMI(c) > 22 \Rightarrow class(c) = 1$    *[75.8%]*
**Rule CPL1**: $CBO(c) > 14 \Rightarrow class(c) = 1$    *[88.2%]*

Rule INH7 (for inheritance rule number 7), for example, states that a class c, which inherits more than 22 methods, is hard to maintain (level 1 of maintainability). This rule is valid for 75.8% of the learning examples (classes). Rule CPL1 (for coupling rule number 1) states that a class that uses or is used by more than 14 classes is hard to maintain. This rule is valid for 88.2% of the learning examples.

Beyond the fact that the magic numbers 22 and 14 depend on the sample used in the learning process, these rules show that big values for CBO (Coupling Between Objects) and NMI (Number of Methods Inherited) are bad for design. They have also the merit to propose thresholds values that enable detecting design flaws.

## 4. Prescription

Once a symptomatic situation is detected using a quality model, the next step is to propose possible transformations that improve the quality of a program while preserving its behavior. Using the quality models, we can establish a cause-to-effect relationship between some combinations of metric values and a poor design quality. The principle of prescription is to define another relationship between transformations and the improvement of the quality. To derive such a relationship, we us the intuitive hypothesis which states that if a good design corresponds to a good combination of metric values, then there are strong chances that a good combination of metric values corresponds to a good design. For example, if NMI of a class c is less than 22 we can presume that c is not hard to maintain, with the hypothesis that no other negative rule applies.

This type of reasoning is close to what some researchers call the abductive inference. Usually, this type of reasoning is not highly reliable. However, in our case, it can give good results for two reasons:

- Our goal is to help the programmer/maintainer to concentrate on certain parts of the system, which are possibly problematic, and not to decide which transformations must be applied.
- The estimation models use metrics that measure user meaningful artifacts rather that derived metrics. This helps the programmer/maintainer to decide which prescription makes sense.

Up to now, we showed that by changing the values of certain metrics, we presume that we can improve the quality of an application/program. The problem to solve now is then, how to change the value of a metric? An intuitive solution is to find out which transformation (or set of transformations) allows changing the value of a particular metric (or set of metrics). For example, if the rule INH7 applies to a class d (NMI(d) = 24), which transformations allow decreasing the number of inherited methods while preserving the behavior of d?

To respond to such a kind of question, we need to study the impact of a predefined set of transformations on a predefined set of metrics. The example of Figure 1 shows how we study the impact of the creation of an abstract class $C_b$ to factorize a set of classes $C_1$, $C_2$, ..., $C_n$ on the inheritance metrics (see section 5.1 for the details). The creation process is composed of three steps (1) creating an empty class $C_b$ in the same level as the classes $C_1$, $C_2$, ..., $C_n$, (2) changing the superclass of these latest classes to $C_b$, and (3) abstracting the common methods and moving common code segments to $C_b$. We can notice that these three elementary transformations do not change the behavior of the involved classes.

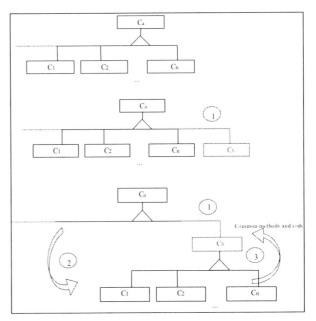

Figure 1. The three steps for the creation of an abstract class

To study the impact of the global transformations on

transformation and then derive the global impact. Table shows the impact of the elementary and global transformations on the inheritance metrics (defined in 1) of the different classes involved in the

positive or negative change in the value of a metric. N is the number of factorized classes, M the number of abstracted methods, and M the number of methods created from the common code abstracting the common

| | $C_a$ | Anc. of $C_a$ | $C_i$ |
|---|---|---|---|
| (1) Creating $C_b$ | NOC +1 | | |
| (2) Changing super-class of $C_i$s | NOC -N CLD +{0, 1} | CLD +{0, 1} | |
| (3) Moving common methods and code from $C_i$s to $C_b$ | | | NMA - [0, \|$M_A$\|] NMO +[0, \|$M_A$\|] NMI +\|$M_C$\| |
| Global variations | NOC +1-N CLD +{0, 1} | CLD +{0, 1} | NMA - [0, \|$M_A$\|] NMO +[0, \|$M_A$\|] NMI +\|$M_C$\| |

Table 2. Impact of the transformation of Figure 1 on the inheritance metrics

If we go back to the example of the class d, we can say that at least the transformation of Figure 1 cannot decrease the value of NMI and therefore it is not useful for this case.

# 5. A case study (Coupling/inheritance vs. maintainability)

In this section, we study the particular case of the diagnosis of bad maintainability by using the values of metrics for coupling and inheritance as symptoms. We particularly focus on the quality models used (and their corresponding metrics), on how to build a diagnosis and prescription tool, and on how to use this tool. We end this section by presenting and discussing some examples.

## 5.1    Quality models and derived metrics

The two models used in our study allow detecting the fault-prone classes (an important factor for the maintainability) using the values of respectively inheritance and coupling metrics. These models are trees in the beginning which are then transformed into rule sets using tree pruning. They were obtained by application of C4.5, a machine learning algorithm on a set of

approximately 100 classes for which the number of faults is known. A classification 1 means that the class generated at least one fault. For a simplification purpose, we present here only the negative rules of each model (i.e. rules that give classification 1):

- Predicting the fault-proneness using inheritance metrics

  o   *Rule INH5:*
  $CLD(c) = 0 \wedge NMA(c) > 7 \wedge SIX(c) > 0.222222$
  $\Rightarrow class(c) = 1 [91.2\%]$

  o   *Rule INH6:*
  $NOC(c) \leq 1 \wedge NMO(c) = 0 \wedge NMI(c) \leq 6$
  $\Rightarrow class(c) = 1 [79.9\%]$

  o   *Rule INH7:*
  $NMI(c) > 22$
  $\Rightarrow class(c) = 1 [75.8\%]$

- Predicting the fault-proneness using coupling metrics

  o   *Rule CPL1:*
  $CBO(c) > 14$
  $\Rightarrow class(c) = 1 [88.2\%]$

  o   *Rule CPL2:*
  $IH\text{-}ICP(c) > 16$
  $\Rightarrow class(c) = 1 [87.1\%]$

  o   *Rule CPL3:*
  $DAC'(c) \leq 2 \wedge OCAIC(c) > 0 \wedge OMMEC(c) > 9$
  $\Rightarrow class(c) = 1 [83.3\%]$

  o   *Rule CPL4:*
  $OCAIC(c) = 0 \wedge DMMEC(c) = 0$
  $\Rightarrow class(c) = 1 [81.9\%]$

The metrics used in these models are given in Table 1 (only those that appear in the negative rules).

## 5.2    Building a diagnosis and prescription tool

The diagnosis part of the tool consists of an engine that applies the rules of the quality estimation models to the classes of a given system. We suppose that the values of the metrics were extracted beforehand. In our case, we use a separate tool for the extraction. We developed a generic tool called OO1 that can be extended automatically to support any quality model expressed in term of classification rules.

The prescription part of the tool is based on the analysis of the impact of the transformations on the metrics as presented in section 4. In this study we used three different transformations: (1) creating an abstract class (c.f. section 4), (2) creating specialized subclasses, and (3) creating an aggregated class.

**Creating an abstract class**. This transformation is presented in section 4. To be complete, we show its impact on the coupling metrics in Table 3. Note that N.D. means that there is an impact but we cannot determine whether it is positive or negative. $P_A$ is the number of parameters added when creating the new methods from the common code.

| Classes | Global variations |
|---|---|
| Classes that reference the abstracted methods | IH-ICP +i (I >= 0) |
| Classes referenced in the common code | CBO $-[0, N-1]$<br>DMMEC -i (i >= 0)<br>OMMEC -i (i >= 0) |
| $C_i$ | CBO N.D.<br>IH-ICP N.D |

Table 3. Impact of the transformation of Figure 1 on the coupling metrics.

**Creating specialized subclasses**. The aim of this transformation is to create new subclasses for a class that is initially a leaf of the inheritance tree. The candidate subclasses are determined from the detection of conditions that suggest new specialized abstractions. The class $C_a$ is the initial class, the $C_1$, $C_2$,..., $C_N$ classes are the created subclasses. $C_a$ is assumed to initially have no descendant. The low-level transformations (steps) involved are:

- *Step 1*: Find conditional expressions for which conditions suggest subclasses.
- *Step 2*: For each condition create a subclass.
- *Step 3*: For each condition expression, create a method in each subclass. Simplify and specialize the method's body for each subclass according to the conditions represented by the subclass.
- *Step 4*: Specialize some or all of the expressions that create instances of the initial class.

| Classes | Global variations |
|---|---|
| $C_a$ | NOC +N<br>CLD +1<br>NMA $+|ExpCond|$ |
| Classes referenced in the code of conditional expressions | CBO $+[0, |N|]$<br>DMMEC +i (i >= 0)<br>OMMEC +i (i >= 0) |
| Ancestors of $C_a$ | NOD +N<br>CLD +{0,1} |

Table 4. Impact of creating specialized subclasses on the inheritance and coupling metrics

Using the same impact analysis technique as for the first transformation, the global metric variations for the classes impacted by this high-level transformation are summarized in Table 4. *ExpCond* is the set of conditional expressions, and N the number of created subclasses.

**Creating an aggregated class**. This transformation consists of grouping a subset of a class $C_a$ members into a new class $C_b$. An instance of $C_b$ will be part of an instance of $C_a$. We assume that other classes do not inherit the grouped members. The elementary transformations involved are:

- *Step1:* Create $C_b$ and move the considered members.
- *Step2:* Insert a new attribute in $C_a$ that will contain the instance of $C_b$.
- *Step3:* Modify the references to the transferred methods
- *Step4:* Delete the transferred members from $C_a$.

Table 5 summarizes the changes in the values of coupling and inheritance metrics. ATR is the set of transferred attributes. Note that no inheritance metric is affected by the transformation.

| Classes | Global variations |
|---|---|
| $C_a$ | CBO +1-i (i >= 0)<br>DAC' $+1-[0, |A\,TR|]$<br>OCAIC $+1-[0, |A\,TR|]$<br>IH-ICP -i (i >= 0) |
| Classes referenced by the transferred methods | CBO +{0,1} |

Table 5. Impact of creating an aggregated class on the inheritance and coupling metrics

### 5.3 Applying the corrector

As presented in the above section, the three transformations can vary the ranges of values for the metrics of the involved classes. This is what we precisely need to improve the quality of an application (see section 4). From the corresponding tables (Table 3 to Table 5), we can detect what are the transformations that can make the metrics values of a class fit into the desired range (good combination of metric values). Each column of a table is dedicated to one class or one category of classes involved in a transformation, thus choosing a particular column of a particular table determines both the transformation to apply and the role played by the class within the transformation context.

Once the transformation and the role of the class are determined, it is necessary to verify that the transformation makes sense in the particular context of the application. OO1 proposes all the possible transformations that can be applied when it detects a symptomatic situation. The user can then select the appropriate transformation.

The following algorithm summarizes the diagnosis and prescription as implemented by OO1

```
AC is the set of the classes of the
application
  For each class c of AC do
    - Calculate the metric values
    - Apply quality rules
    If a negative rule applies then
        - Choose the metrics and the desired
changes to their values
        - Select transformations that allow
these changes
            - Propose the transformations that correspond to the
            context of c
    EndIf
  EndFor
```

## 5.4    Examples and discussion

To illustrate the approach proposed in this paper, we present two examples of the application of OO1 in this section. These examples are classes of a multiagent system coded in C++ called LALO.

**Example 1: The case of XrulesKB classes**. Three classes were detected by OO1 as a bad design from the maintainability point of view according to rules INH6 and CPL4. These three classes are called respectively ExecRulesKB, OrdRulesKB and MsgRulesKB. The values for the inheritance and coupling metrics are given in Table 6.

| Metrics | ExecRulesKB | MsgRulesKB | OrdRulesKB |
|---------|-------------|------------|------------|
| CLD | 0 | 0 | 0 |
| NOC | 0 | 0 | 0 |
| NMO | 0 | 0 | 0 |
| NMI | 0 | 0 | 0 |
| NMA | 9 | 9 | 9 |
| SIX | 0 | 0 | 0 |
| CBO | 3 | 3 | 3 |
| IH-ICP | 0 | 0 | 0 |
| DAC' | 0 | 0 | 0 |
| ACAIC | 0 | 0 | 0 |
| DMMEC | 0 | 0 | 0 |
| OMMEC | 2 | 2 | 2 |

Table 6. Inheritance and coupling metrics for the XRulesKB classes

To avoid that rule INH6 applies for each of the three classes, we have to increase the value of *NOC* or increase the value of *NMO* or increase the value of *NMI*. From Table 2, column $C_i$, we can suggest to create an abstract class for the three classes. As the three classes have 5 common methods (*add, remove, export_engine_data, registration* and the = operator), the NMO values for the three classes increase to 5, which is sufficient to avoid the application of rule INH6.

This prescription is appropriate according to the context of the application. We were not surprised to find in the same system, three other classes named respectively ExecRule, OrdRule and MsgRule with an abstract class Rule (see Figure 2).

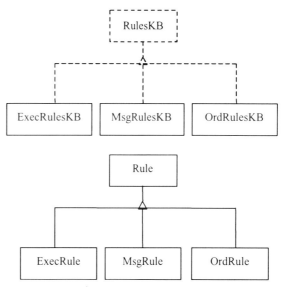

Figure 2. A partial view of the system LALO and the prescription of OO1 (dotted lines)

Another prescription is given by Table 4, column $C_a$. OO1 proposes to create a set of specialized subclasses for each class. The three classes are small and are already pretty much specialized. A user can then reject this suggestion. Figure 3 shows the suggestions of OO1 for this particular case.

From the coupling point of view, if we want to avoid the application of rule CPL4, we have to increase OCAIC or DMMEC at least by 1 (see rule CPL4 in section 5.1 and Table 1).

Increasing the value of OCAIC by 1 can be possible if the following conditions are true:
1. We can create an aggregated class from an XrulesKB class as stated by Table 5, column $C_a$ (OCAIC $+1-[0,|A\,\text{TR}|]$).
2. No attribute is transferred to the created class attributes ($/A\text{TR}/=0$).

After examining the content of the three classes, such a transformation is not concretely feasible. Therefore, a user can reject this prescription.

Another possible prescription is to create specialized subclasses to increase the value of *DMMEC* (see Table 4, column "Classes referenced in the code of conditional expressions"). Even if this transformation is theoretically possible, the particular context of the application does not allow it.

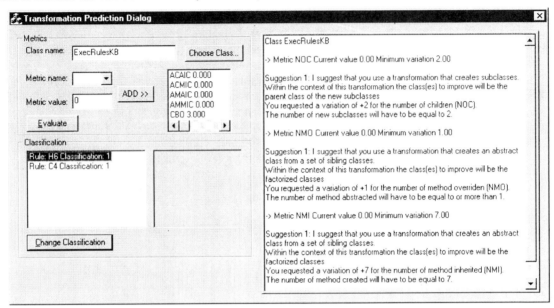

Figure 3. Some prescription alternatives given by OO1 for the case of XRulesKB classes

**Example 2: The case of KQMLObject class.** A class named KQMLObject was detected by OO1 as having bad maintainability according to rules INH5, CPL3 and CPL4 (see Table 7 for the values of metrics).

| Metrics | KQMLObject |
|---------|------------|
| CLD | 0 |
| NOC | 0 |
| NMO | 10 |
| NMI | 0 |
| NMA | 14 |
| SIX | 0.41 |
| CBO | 3 |
| IH-ICP | 0 |
| DAC' | 0 |
| ACAIC | 0 |
| DMMEC | 0 |
| OMMEC | 76 |

Table 7. Inheritance and coupling metrics for KQMLObject class

To prevent the application of rule INH5, we have to increase the value of CLD or decrease the value of NMA. Four possible transformations to increase CLD appear in the impact tables:

1. Create an abstract class as a direct subclass of KQMLObject (Table 2, column $C_a$).
2. Create an abstract class as descendant but non-direct subclass of KQMLObject (Table 2, column "Ancestors of $C_a$").
3. Create specialized subclasses of KQMLObject (Table 4, column $C_a$)
4. Create specialized subclasses of one of the subclasses of KQMLObject (Table 4, column "Ancestors of $C_a$").

As KQMLObject is a leaf class, only transformation 3 is proposed. All the others suppose that KQMLObject has subclasses. When we examined the code to verify if transformation 3 is concretely possible, we found that some condition expressions concern the possible values of a particular attribute (*performative_number*). This is an indicator of a bad design. Creating subclasses that corresponds to the different values of this attribute will simplify the code of KQMLObject.

Another possible suggestion was to propose to factorize KQMLObject with other possible classes to decrease the value of NMA according to Table 2 and column $C_i$.

However, KQMLObject is already factorized with the only sister it has (see Figure 4).

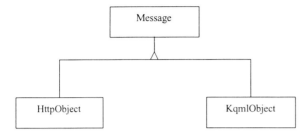

Figure 4. Hierarchy of KQMLObject

From the coupling point of view, the only interesting prescription is to create an aggregated class. This avoids the application of rules CPL3 and CPL4 by varying the value of OCAIC (Table 5, column $C_a$). The class KQMLObject is too large and too complex to make such a transformation possible. The only condition is to find a subset of methods to transfer without transferring any attribute ($+1-[0, |A\,TR|] > 0$).

## 6. Conclusion

In this work, we have investigated the use of metrics for detecting potential design flaws and for suggesting potentially useful transformations for correcting them. Initial experiments with the OO1 prototype have demonstrated the feasibility of the approach and its usefulness. Indeed, our approach can help a designer/programmer by suggesting transformations. It can also help her or him to focus on a particular part of a large system.

From the perspective of automation, the response to the paper title question (Can metrics help to bridge the gap between the improvement of OO Design Quality and its automation?) can be yes and no. Yes, using metrics is a step towards the automation of quality improvement. If we look to the whole process of detecting flaws and correcting them, metrics can help to automate a large part of it. The response can be no. Indeed, the results of our experiments show that a prescription cannot be executed without a validation of a designer/programmer. Our approach cannot capture all the context of an application to allow such a type of automation.

A direction that we will explore in our future work is to better capture the context of an application. This will enable us to refine the suggestions by eliminating those that are not relevant. Another direction is to incorporate into our tool transformations implementing design patterns as proposed by the work of Tokuda and Batory mentioned in section 2. They show that it is possible to automate the implementation of a design pattern into an existing code. However, they do not address the automatic detection of

the situations where these transformations should be applied.

**Acknowledgment**

The authors would like to thank Pr. Hafedh Mili for his comments on this work.

## References

[1] Basili V., Briand L. & Melo W., How Reuse Influences Productivity in Object-Oriented Systems. *Communications of the ACM*, Vol. 30, N. 10, pp104-114, 1996.

[2] Casais E., *Managing Evolution in Objet Oriented Environments: An Algorithmic Approach*, thèse de Doctorat, université de Genève, 1989.

[3] Chidamber S. & Kemerer C. A Metrics Suite for Object-Oriented Design, *IEEE Transactions on Software Engineering*, June, 1994, p. 476-492.

[4] Demeyer S., Ducasse S., Metrics, *Do they really help ?*, In Proc. of LMO, 1999.

[5] Dicky, H., Dony, C., Huchard, M. & Libourel, T. On Automatic Class Insertion with Overloading. In *Proceedings of the ACM Conference on Object-Oriented Programming Systems, Languages, and Applications (OOPSLA'96)*, CA, USA: ACM SIGPLAN Notices, pp. 251-267, 1996

[6] Godin, R. & Mili, H. Building and Maintaining Analysis-Level Class Hierarchies Using Galois Lattices. In *Proceedings of the ACM Conference on Object-Oriented Programming Systems, Languages, and Applications (OOPSLA'93)*, A. Paepcke (Ed.), Washington, DC: ACM Press, pp. 394-410, 1993.

[7] Godin, R., Mili, H., Mineau, G. W., Missaoui, R., Arfi, A. & Chau, T.-T. Design of Class Hierarchies based on Concept (Galois) Lattices. *Theory and Application of Object Systems*, **4**(2), 117-134, 1998

[8] Ikonomovski, S., *Detection of Faulty Components in Object-Oriented Systems using Design Metrics and a Machine Learning Algorithm*, Master Thesis, Mc Gill University, Montréal, 1998.

[9] Li W. & Henry S., Object Oriented Metrics that Predict Maintainability. *Journal of Systems and Software*. Vol.23, No.2., 1993.

[10] Lieberherr, K. J., Bergstein, P. & Silva-Lepe, I. From Objects to Classes: Algorithms for Optimal Object-Oriented Design. *Journal of Software Engineering*, **6**(4), 205-228, 1991.

[11] Lounis H., Melo W., Sahraoui H. A*., Identifying and Measuring Coupling in OO systems*, technical report CRIM-97/11-82, 1997.

[12] Lounis H., Sahraoui H. A., Melo H. A., Towards a Quality Predictive Model for Object -Oriented Software, *L'Objet*, Volume 4 (4), Ed. Hermes. 1998 (in french).

[13] Mao Y., Sahraoui H. A. and Lounis H., Reusability Hypothesis Verification Using Machine Learning Techniques: A Case Study, *Proc. of IEEE Automated Software Engineering Conference*, 1998.

[14] Moore, I. Automatic Inheritance Hierarchy Restructuring and Method Refactoring. In *Proceedings of the ACM Conference on Object-Oriented Programming Systems, Languages, and Applications (OOPSLA'96)*, CA, USA: ACM SIGPLAN Notices, pp. 235-250, 1996

[15] Opdyke F. W., *Refactoring Object-Oriented Frameworks*, PhD thesis, University of Illinois, 1992.

[16] Opdyke F. W. & Johnson E. R., Creating Abstract Superclasses by Refactoring, in *Proceeding of CSC'93: The ACM 1993 Computer Science Conference*, February 1993.

[17] Quinlan J. R., *C4.5: Programs for Machine Learning*, Morgan Kaufmann Publishers, 1993.

[18] Roberts D., Brant J., Johnson E. J.: A Refactoring Tool for Smalltalk*, Theory And Practice of Object Systems*, Volume 3 (4): 253-263, (1997).

[19] S. Skublics, E. J. Klimas, D. A. Thomas, *Smalltalk with Style*, Prentice Hall, 1996.

[20] Sommerville I., *Software Engineering*, Addison Wesley, fourth edition, 1992.

[21] L. Tokuda and D. Batory, Evolving Object-Oriented Designs with Refactorings, *Proc. of IEEE Automated Software Engineering Conference*, 1999.

# Metrics of Software Evolution as Effort Predictors - A Case Study

Juan F. Ramil     Meir M. Lehman
Department of Computing
Imperial College of Science, Technology and Medicine
180 Queen's Gate
London SW7 2BZ, UK
tel. + 44 20 7594 8214;   fax  + 44 20 7594 8215
{ramil,mml}@doc.ic.ac.uk

## Abstract

*Despite its importance, cost estimation in the context of continuing software evolution has been relatively unexplored. This paper addresses this omission by describing some models that predict effort as a function of a suite of metrics of software evolution. It presents a case study relating to the evolution of the kernel of a mainframe operating system. Six models based on eight different indicators of evolution activity are proposed, their predictive power is examined and compared to that of two baseline models. Predictions with errors of the order of 20 percent of the actual values have been obtained from the models, when fitted and tested to historical data over a segment of 10 years of kernel's continuing evolution. Appropriateness of the proposed models as predictors appears to be restricted to homogeneous evolution segments, that is, periods with relatively small variations in the level of effort applied. It was found that models based on coarse granularity measures, such as "subsystem counts", provided a Mean Magnitude of Relative Error similar to those based on finer alternatives, such as "module counts".*

## 1. Introduction

*E*-type software [21] is defined as software embedded in and actively used in a real-world domain. The ultimate criterion of satisfaction with an *E*-type system is acceptability to stakeholders. This will depend on the current needs and desires of stakeholders and the current state of the operational domain. But needs, desires, and opportunities are changing and *E*-type operational domains are unbounded and dynamic, that is, also changing. Hence, while being actively used, continuing adaptation and enhancement is required if stakeholder satisfaction is to be maintained [21]. The vast majority of the systems upon which organisations and businesses increasingly rely for their operations are of type *E*, hence its relevance.

In this paper software *evolution* tasks relate to the work, programming and other activities, performed to produce new versions or releases of an existing operational software. In this sense evolution encompasses both, post-first release development and maintenance. So defined, system evolution may include early lifecycle stages, as for example when very complex software is constructed as a sequence of operational releases with increasing functionality [15,18].

Since the mid-sixties [27] numerous approaches have been proposed for estimation of the cost of *ab initio* software development. The effectiveness of these approaches varies, with predictive accuracy of 30 percent or so of the actual being reported [11]. Techniques for estimation in the software maintenance context have also been reported (see section 6), though the topic has received less attention than the *ab initio* case. Boehm indicates that "...the majority of the software costs are incurred during the period after the developed software has been accepted..." [6, p. 533]. In spite of its importance, estimation in the context of software evolution, as defined here, appears not to be thoroughly treated in the literature.

It would be useful for managers to be able to estimate the amount of effort and related schedule required for accomplishing software evolution tasks. The problem is encountered, for example, in bidding, planning, staffing, and in cost/benefit studies. Effort models may help in assessment of programming productivity, its trends, and to establish whether it declines as a system ages and gets more complex [30] or increases due, for instance, to experience gains by developers and/or to effective process improvements. Estimation models may also play a role in deciding when it is appropriate to replace an aging system.

In seeking for good predictors of effort, this paper examines the predictive power of a suite of software evolution metrics that can be derived from *unplanned* historical records, such as the change logs that generally are included in source code files. The work presented here is part of the on-going FEAST/2 project [14].

The effort required for understanding, changing, adding, deleting and replacing source code is, in general, a significant fraction of the total software evolution effort. Our current focus is on this aspect and any reference to effort must be so interpreted unless otherwise indicated.

The structure of the paper is a follows: section 2 defines the problem, section 3 discusses the approach adopted, section 4 presents the results of a case study recently conducted, section 5 discusses the results and section 6 provides pointers to some of the related work.

## 2. The Problem

In *ab initio* software development the cost and schedule estimation problem consists primarily of estimating the effort and interval required for the development of a software system of a given functionality size and quality. Effort estimation is seen as part of software project planning, management and control. In contrast, software evolution generally occurs on a *continuing* basis. In this context the effort estimation problem may take a variety of forms. Since many software organisations structure their work around sequences of software releases, the effort and schedule estimation problem could be stated as follows:

*"Given an amount of work required to evolve an operational system from release n to release n+1, estimate the required effort in person-hours, ΔE, and/or the schedule in days or months, ΔT".*

This statement of the problem is illustrated in Fig. 1. An alternative statement of the problem would refer to equally spaced time intervals, that is evolution activity from time *t* to time *t+1*. In this latter formulation, the schedule is considered fixed and *ΔT=1*, expressed in the relevant units (months, quarters, years). Which formulation is more effective or of more practical interest will depend on circumstances. Similarly, whether the emphasis should be placed either on effort or schedule estimation may depend on particular circumstances. This paper focuses on the cased of a fixed schedule intervals.

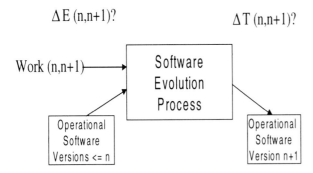

**Figure 1 - A view of the problem**

## 3. Solution approach

It has been found that, in general, *E*-type software evolution attributes tend to display regularities, patterns and invariances [10,14,21,22,23]. The latter have been attributed to the presence of systemic influences in the software process that result in a degree of regularity in behavioural attributes of such process. Some of these appear to be feedback driven [10,14,23]. In the context of effort prediction, such regularities do not appear to have been thoroughly investigated. One may start the investigation of such regularities by obtaining empirical data and by estimating from such data a productivity function *f()*. The empirical data that one would expect to be involved in the estimation of *f()* are represented by the variable classes in Eq. 1:

$$\Delta Effort(t,t+1) = f( Activity(t,t+1), Control(t,t+1)$$
$$, Environment(t,t+1)$$
$$, \textbf{History}(t-k-1,...,t-2,t-1,t) )$$
$$+ error(t,t+1) \qquad \text{Eq. 1}$$

where *ΔEffort(t,t+1)* represents the estimated effort, that is, the effort required to evolve the system from interval *t* to *t+1*. *ΔEffort(t,t+1)* may be scalar or vector. The latter arises if different classes of effort, such as, planning, analysis, implementation, rework, integration and validation must be considered. In this paper consideration is restricted to the scalar case. *Activity(t,t+1)*, represents the amount of work (e.g., number of changes to existing functionality, new functionality) accomplished (either a scalar or a vector) over the interval. *Control (t,t+1)* are the values of the cost drivers under direct management control (probably a vector). *Environment(t,t+1)* are the cost drivers outside direct management control (probably a vector), and *error(t,t+1)* is the modelling error. The above variable classes are defined over the interval *t* to *t+1*. **History***(t-k-1,...,t-2,t-1,t)* would be a matrix (*k* x *j*), hence the bold type, which represents the *k* most recent values of *j* attributes of the software process and product, accounting for dynamic effects [35]. *t* may represent a time interval or a release interval, as appropriate. In this paper *t,* representing fixed time intervals (rather than release intervals or release sequence numbers), is used. Effort estimation based on releases is left for a future study. Problems may, however, arise due to the small size of the release-based data sets. In general, the number of observations (releases) is less than, say, thirty or so [14].

Ideally one would wish to determine *f()* using a sound modelling procedure from historical data representing the different variable classes in Eq. 1. Once *f()* is so determined, the resultant model may be used to predict future effort requirements.

In practice only variables for which data are available are useful, but the availability of more complete theoretical models, as, for example, the one proposed in [37], is to guide planned data collection. Following a top-down model building process, a guideline that is part of the FEAST approach to quantitative modelling of the software process [10,14], one first seeks to study what are suggested to be the most influential factors. One may expect *Activity(t,t+1)* to be a major cost driver. Therefore, it provides a reasonable starting point for model building. The other variable classes suggested in Eq. 1 may be incorporated into the models at a later stage as understanding grows. Thus, the modelling effort presented in this paper has focused on the role of *Activity(t,t+1)* as effort predictor, that is, in models of the form presented in Eq. 2.

$$\Delta Effort(t,t+1) = f(Activity(t,t+1)) + error(t,t+1) \quad \text{Eq. 2}$$

Further refinement of the model is possible if one considers the fact, that programming activity consists, essentially, of additions of new elements, changes to existing elements and deletions. Initially it is assumed that the effort required to perform deletions is negligible. Given this particular refinement, Eq. 2 is expressed as:

$$\Delta Effort(t,t+1) = f( New(t,t+1), Changes(t,t+1)) + error(t,t+1) \quad \text{Eq. 3}$$

How does one measure *Activity(t,t+1)* in the continuing evolution context? Estimation approaches discussed in the literature generally involve *lines of source code* (LOC) [6] or *function points* (FP) [1] as indicators of work or activity. Contrary to popular belief, extended sequences over long term evolution periods of such data may be less widely available than might be thought from literature references to LOC and FP. However, other metrics can often be extracted from, for example, configuration management databases or change-log records, which tend to be longer lived.

The granularity [24] at which measurements are taken represents yet another degree of freedom in variable selection. One may obtain indicators of *Activity(t,t+1)* at different levels of granularity [24] such as subsystems, modules, procedures, classes and objects, for example. The present authors' experience suggests that the empirical data most readily available from industrial change log records is the one that reflects activity at the module and subsystem levels. The dependence between such levels is illustrated in Fig. 2 for a software system consisting of *j* functional subsystems and showing that subsystem number one contains *k* modules.

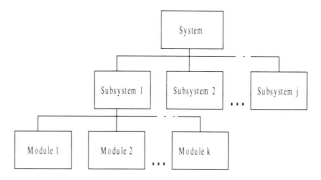

**Figure 2 - Subsystems and modules**

One metric set, that evolved from 70s and 80s studies [21,22], includes the indicators presented in Table 1. Note that for the sake of simplicity in Table 1 the argument '*(t)*' is used instead of '*(t,t+1)*' but with the same meaning. The shorter notation is followed in the rest of this paper.

Whichever metric suite is adopted, the determination of *f()* will benefit from an iterative approach, to enable variable pruning and model refinement.

| Indicator Based on | Abbreviation (Full name) | Description Symbol '#' to be read as 'count over interval *t* to *t+1*' |
|---|---|---|
| Modules | *ModifHandlings(t)* (Number of Modification Handlings) | # of changes to modules as reflected by number of change log modification entries, referred to as *handlings* |
| Modules | *ModulesChanged(t)* (Number of Modules Changed) | # of modules modified |
| Modules | *ModulesCreated(t)* (Number of Modules Created) | # of modules added to the system |
| Modules | *TotalHandlings(t)* (Total Number of Handlings) | # of total change log entries, that is, including both creation entries and modification entries |
| Modules | *ModulesHandled(t)* (Number of Modules Handled) | # of modules which were either added to the system or modified, or both (if both, module is counted once) |
| Subsystems and Modules | *SubsysChanged(t)* (Number of Subsystems Changed) | # of subsystems that underwent modifications to their modules |
| Subsystems and Modules | *SubsysHandled(t)* (Number of Subsystems with Modules Handled) | # of subsystems that underwent either additions or changes to their modules, or both (if both, subsyst. is counted once) |
| Subsystems and Modules | *SubsysInclCreations(t)* (Number of Subsystems that include Modules Created) | # of subsystems which underwent module additions |

**Table 1 - A suite of indicators of software evolution activity**

A possible procedure is one inspired by *system identification* [28] techniques and also by statistical regression guidelines [32,35]. These, together with the authors' experience in studying software evolution, suggest the following set of steps for the investigation:

1. Locate historical data reflecting the classes of variables in Eq.1, from which, at least, $\Delta Effort(t)$ and $Activity(t)$ may be derived

2. Extract from these data sets indicators that reflect the models and types of variables of interest, as suggested in Eq. 1.

3. Plot the indicators, search for trends, detect outliers and break points in trends, examine correlation [32]

4. Split the data set into a model training subset, for model calibration, and a subset for model testing

5. Determine model parameters using training set

6. Assess models based, *inter alia*, on their predictive power over the test data set

7. If more accuracy is needed or desired, refine model structure and variable list and repeat the procedure from either step 1 or step 2 as appropriate.

Validation of this procedure, and of the hypothesis that reasonably accurate effort models can be built from the suite of indicators suggested in Table 1, requires access to data, reflecting relevant variables. The availability of a large data set of source code change records, relating to an operating system kernel made possible the initial application of the procedure as outlined in the next section.

## 4. A case study - ICL VME Kernel

The empirical data used in this case study relates to the evolution of the ICL VME mainframe operating system. The system was initially released during the seventies to run on ICL mainframe computers. Since then it has been continuously evolved. Its functionality has been progressively adapted over a period exceeding 20 years to support several generations of hardware technology. Its most recent versions run on a wider hardware variety (OpenVME). VME is implemented using SDL - System Description Language. The underlying language is called S3, which is, in many respects, similar to Algol68.

VME evolution has been studied in the past. System growth trends and other attributes were examined by Kitchenham [20] for the system in its two parts: the *kernel* and the *director*. The kernel is the VME's part that accounts for most of the low-level and hardware dependent functionality. The director deals primarily with the interface to and service for user applications. More recently FEAST/1 studied the evolution of the kernel [10,22,23]. Both studies found that VME displayed regularities previously observed in other systems and encapsulated Lehman's Laws of Software Evolution as formulated at the time of each study [21,23]. The VME data available to FEAST/1 supported six of the eight laws. The remaining two (law IV and law VII) were neither supported nor negated by the available data and require further investigation [23]. FEAST/1 limited the analysis to the kernel, the only part from which data was made available. So does the present study.

In VME terminology the source code elements referred to in this study as *modules* are termed *holons*. The VME kernel raw data that has been made available for this further study consists of some 60,000 source code change-log entries. In the interest of generality we use the former term. This data originates from the continuing use, by VME developers, of an integrated design, support and configuration management environment, named CADES [29], which include change data recording facilities. Such entries include both additions and modifications (no deletions or data on deleted modules is included) and were captured between the years 1981 to 1998. However, recording of changes was not made compulsory until 1986. This indicates that records before that date do not necessarily reflect the totality of effort and activity applied to kernel's evolution. It is assumed that data on the period 1981-1986 is a representative sample for the study of the relationship between effort applied and activity. In other words, it is assumed that the developers that actually generated change logs recorded over the 1981-1986 period worked, on average, at approximately the same productivity of those developers that did not generate change logs over the period.

The authors performed data extraction and cleansing using a script written in the *Perl* programming language [36]. Such language has proven to be useful due to its pattern matching and string processing features. The text of the script used can be made available if requested to one of the authors (JFR).

The extracted data set consists of 211 multivariate observations, covering a period that exceeds 17 years of software evolution, that is, from February 1981 to August 1998. Figure 3 presents $\Delta Effort(t)$ applied to VME evolution as estimated from the data. At request of the data owners the values have been normalised. Monthly effort applied to programming was calculated as follows. The number of person-months applied to development was assumed to be equal to the number of different developer's name initials present in the records during each month. This procedure was followed under the assumption that the developers worked for kernel evolution on a full time basis.

The relatively small level of effort applied over the period 1981-1983 may not be correct, with the error mainly due to activity not captured in the data before 1986, as explained above. Taking that into account, Figure 3 suggests that there were at least two distinct periods of evolution activity. The first of these displays higher work intensity than does the second. They appear as two different segments with the breakpoint around 1990 or so, to be more precisely determined by an appropriate procedure [3].

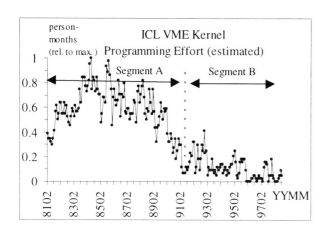

**Figure 3 - Effort (ΔEffort) applied to VME kernel's evolution in approx. number of person-months dedicated per month (rel. to maximum)**

The underlying causes of the behaviour in Fig. 3 are not explored in this study (see [10] for an investigation into the drivers of kernel's evolution). One may, however, consider the following implication. For large changes of the effort variable its relationship to the predictor variables must be expected to be nonlinear. Consider, for example, that the non productive effort consumed by interpersonal communication and task co-ordination is likely to be increasing at about the square of the size of the programming group [9]. Small variations, however, of the effort variable may be considered as linearly related to the predictors. Since the effort applied differs significantly between the two segments, one would expect deteriorating model performance when using the linear models from the first to predict the second. Hence, we start by exploring linear models, leaving the nonlinear refinements for what would be further model refinements. This interpretation suggests that, initially, different linear models would be required for the two identified segments in ICL kernel.

The remaining of this section concentrates on the prediction of ΔEffort over the 1981 - 1990 segment. Following the overall modelling procedure stated in the previous section, a data set based on intervals of one month was extracted from the raw data. This yielded the suite of metrics of software evolution defined in the previous section (see Table 1). For the purposes of this study the data set corresponding to the first segment, 1981 - 1990, was split into two sets: a *training* set (1981-86) with 61 observations (months) and a *test* set (1986-90) with 60 observations (months).

Table 2 displays the linear correlation with ΔEffort of the predictors as obtained from the training set, that is the first 61 data points (months). An unexpected, though with hindsight reasonable (see discussion in section 5), result is that those variables based on subsystem counts, that is, the coarsest measure in terms of granularity, display the highest correlation.

| Indicator | ΔEffort |
|---|---|
| *SubsysInclCreations* | 0.7406 |
| *SubsysChanged* | 0.7030 |
| *SubsysHandled* | 0.6906 |
| *ModulesCreated* | 0.4833 |
| *ModulesHandled* | 0.4743 |
| *ModulesChanged* | 0.4403 |
| *TotalHandlings* | 0.3431 |
| *ModifHandlings* | 0.3011 |

**Table 2 - Correlation of independent variables with ΔEffort, over training set (N=61)**

As justified, *f()* is assumed to be a linear function:

$$f(x_1, x_2, ..., x_{n-1}, x_n) = \\ = A_1 x_1 + A_2 x_2 + ... + A_{n-1} x_{n-1} + A_n x_n + B \quad \text{Eq. 4}$$

where *n* represents the number of predictor variables included in the model, $A_i$ the coefficient for the *i*th variable and *B* the intercept. When combining the possible models suggested by Eq. 3 with the variables available from the extracted data set (see Table 1), six models are obtained. Two measures are also included as baseline values. The two baseline measures (M1-M2) and six models (M3-M8) considered are presented in Table 3.

A module is most likely to undergo modification during the first month of its creation. Hence, the variables *ModulesCreated,* and the variables that represent 'modification' such as *ModulesChanged* and *ModifHandlings* tend to be strongly correlated. This may affect regression results, by yielding, for example, a negative coefficient $A_1$, in models such as M6 and M7 unless *ModulesCreated* is substracted from the other two variables as shown in these models (see Table 3).

One outlier observation was detected (Sept. 1981) and substituted by the interpolation of the values of the previous and subsequent months.

The coefficients of the models M3 - M9 were estimated using the Microsoft Excel regression function. Model assessment was based on the performance measures used by Jorgensen [17], evaluated over the test data set.

The model assessment criteria were:

MMRE – Mean Magnitude of Relative Error, defined as *average* over test set of
(|*Predicted Effort – Actual Effort*| /*Actual Effort*)

MdMRE – Median Magnitude of Relative Error, defined as *median* over test set of
(|*Predicted Effort – Actual Effort*| /*Actual Effort*)

PRED(10) – Number of observations in test data set for which MMRE is equal or lower than 10 %

PRED(25) – Number of observations in test data set for which MMRE was equal or lower than 25 %

The results of the application of these measures are shown in Table 4.

| Model | Expression |
|---|---|
| M1 Baseline 1 | $\Delta Effort(t)$ = Average effort over training set of $N$ observations = $\Sigma\Delta Effort(t)/N$ |
| M2 Baseline 2 | $\Delta Effort(t) = ModulesHandled(t) \times$ [Avg. monthly productivity over training set of $N$ observ.] $= ModulesHandled(t) \times [(1/N)\ \Sigma\Delta Effort(t)/ModulesHandled(t)]$ |
| M3 | $\Delta Effort(t) = A.ModulesHandled(t) + B$ |
| M4 | $\Delta Effort(t) = A.SubsysHandled(t) + B$ |
| M5 | $\Delta Effort(t) = A.TotalHandlings(t) + B$ |
| M6 | $\Delta Effort(t) = A_1.ModulesCreated(t) + A_2.(ModulesChanged(t) - ModulesCreated(t)) + B$ |
| M7 | $\Delta Effort(t) = A_1.ModulesCreated(t) + A_2.(ModifHandlings(t) - ModulesCreated(t)) + B$ |
| M8 | $\Delta Effort(t) = A_1.SubsysInclCreations(t) + A_2.SubsysChanged(t) + B$ |

**Table 3 - Effort prediction models**

| | Model | MMRE In percent. | MdMRE In percent. | PRED(10) | PRED(25) |
|---|---|---|---|---|---|
| Baseline 1 | M1 | 39.7 | 17.9 | 18 | 39 |
| Baseline 2 | M2 | 35.5 | 36.7 | 5 | 14 |
| Univ. Reg. | M3 | 19.6 | 14.9 | 18 | **47** |
| " | M4 | 32.8 | 18.8 | 10 | 39 |
| " | M5 | 21.6 | 18.7 | 17 | 42 |
| Multiv.Reg | M6 | 19.6 | 16.3 | 12 | **47** |
| " | M7 | 20.0 | 15.8 | 21 | 45 |
| " | M8 | **19.3** | **14.0** | **22** | 44 |

**Table 4 – Predictive power assessed over test set (N=60) (Univ.Reg = Univariate Regression, Multiv.Reg = Multivariate Regression)**

## 5. Discussion

The MMRE's of all of the models in Table 4 appear to be lower than that of the lines of code (LOC)-based models as in for example, [17], in which the lowest reported MMRE was 60 percent. Values of MMRE presented in Table 4 which are close to 20 percent are encouraging. Unexpectedly, the best model (M8) in terms of MMRE and MdMRE is based on coarse granularity variables (subsystems), which at first sight appears to be counterintuitive, since one tends to associate less resolution (and larger error) with coarse granularity measures. If this result is confirmed for other data sets may have wider implication in the variable selection for estimation purposes. This finding appears to be related with that of Lindvall [24], who found that prediction of changes based on a coarse metric, such as classes, yielded better accuracy in the prediction of the impact of changes for an industrial software process than alternatives of finer granularity. One possible explanation is that at coarser levels of granularity indicators are likely to reflect a higher level of functional integrity. This has been argued, for example, when suggesting that modules provide a more meaningful indicator than, for example, LOC [14,22]. On the other hand, coarser indicators imply measuring scales of less resolution than finer indicators. Moreover, modules and subsystems are subject to restrictions when one wishes to compare productivity between different software systems and processes. In summary, the granularity issue, in particular, in the context of effort modelling, and, in general, of software metrics, appears to deserve closer examination.

Fig. 3 suggest that a significantly smaller effort was applied to the evolution of VME Kernel during the later period, the 1991-1998 segment, the system displaying a significant slower evolution rate. As anticipated, application of the six models (M3-M8) estimated over the earlier segment (results not shown in the present paper), yield poorer predictive results over the second segment.

The immediate conclusion is that one must recalibrate the models once a significant change [3] in the mean effort applied has taken place. This suggests that, as in control systems applications, linear models may reasonably represent non-linear system behaviour only for small changes about a given operating point. If validity over a wider range is required, either a set of linear models, one for each operating point of interest, or a non-linear model would be required [12]. In fact, the use of linear models may be generalised as follows. Models are expected to be most useful (display highest predictive power) over *homogenous* segments in the applied effort trend, that is, over segments during which, in principle,

- only relatively small changes in the level of effort applied have taken place.

- no major changes in the nature of the application, the software itself and/or the evolution process are apparent.

After detection of a break point in the level of effort applied (by a suitable method e.g., [3]) or any other change that is expected to impact the productivity function (e.g., process change or the introduction of new programming languages, new development tools) one may proceed to accumulate new data. Once sufficient data is available, proceed to re-calculate model parameters.

It is likely that improved models of behaviour will, to a certain extent, have to capture time-varying behaviour [16,35]. Models may increase in their predictive power by incorporating lagged values of the variables, to reflect dynamic effects. Recursive estimation of the time-varying parameters to track changes in effort model coefficients, is an alternative to deal with time varying behaviour. This and related issues may be explored in future work.

Modelling over the low activity segments, such as the most frequent ICL Kernel segment, with zero values in some of the observations (e.g., months with no module creations reported) may require techniques to deal with missing values described elsewhere [25,26].

The inclusion of predictor variables reflecting quality and other factors (such as program maintainability or complexity) in the models will require further data extraction. However, as Boehm points out "...in most cases, the maintenance activity will settle into a fairly predictable equilibrium..." [6, p. 546]. Unless significant changes in the application or its evolution domain are experienced, only a small number of factors may have to be considered to attain reasonably accurate models [10]. A reduced number of variables also complies with the FEAST top-down modelling approach, which emphasises simple models, refined in successive steps as understanding is gained [14].

There are a number of limitations in the modelling which arise from the use of historical, unplanned data, that is "...data arising from continuous operations and not from a designed experiment..." [13]. These may apply not only to the present case study but, in general, to those studies which rely on observational (as opposed to experimental) data. Some of the dangers arise as follows [8,13]:

- Errors in the model may not be random but a result of the joint effect of several variables not included in the model (possibly, not even measured)

- An observed false effect of a visible variable may be caused by an unmeasured latent variable. If the latter changes, the model may yield misleading results

- Variables that would be effective predictors may, for operational reasons, be restricted to small ranges, which may, then, cause the regression coefficients to appear as 'non significant'

- Operating feedback loops, such as operating policies, that involve rules such as "if predictor $x_1$ goes high, reduce $x_2$ to compensate", may cause multicollinearity (large correlation between predictors); this would make it very difficult to determine whether the changes in $y$ are due to changes in $x_1$ or $x_2$

Some of the above limitations may become increasingly severe when investigators look at an increasing number of variables or factors. This makes it stronger the case in favour of simple models.

Other issues affecting data collection and analysis in the context of software evolution in general, and this study in particular, have been discussed elsewhere [31].

# 6. Related work

Work in cost estimation for *ab initio* software development has been reported since the mid-sixties [27]. Sommerville, for example, summarises the techniques that appear to be most widely used [34]. Less work has been done in seeking to extend the techniques or determine alternatives applying to software maintenance [33] and evolution. Some early work in this area was undertaken in the seventies [4]. Recent studies are exemplified by Jorgensen work [17]. Most of the work, apart from that of Lehman and co-workers appears to have LOC-based measures as a basis. Jorgensen discusses, as an alternative measure, function points (FP) [1], and suggests several disadvantages of this measure in the context of software maintenance. Exploration of the applicability of alternative measures, such as those based on subsystems and modules, to effort estimation in the context of software evolution as described in this paper, does not appear, to the knowledge of the present authors, to have been previously undertaken. Equally innovative appears to be the proposal of a top-down modelling approach, as described in the FEAST literature [14], for the effort estimation issue. The rest of this section provides pointers to and brief summaries of some examples of the related work.

## 6.1. The Woodside model

Woodside [37] proposed a model based on Lehman's Laws of Software Evolution [21] that enabled exploration of the consequences of different evolution strategies and the effects of growing complexity. The model explores how these may influence system growth trends, and, in particular, the role different management policies, such as, for example, the alternation of growth and clean-up releases. Given the number of variables involved in

Woodside's model, its full calibration based on typically obtainable unplanned historical data appears to be difficult. Nevertheless, the model offers a starting point from which variables may be identified for planned data collection efforts and subsequent models may be developed.

## 6.2. Extensions of *ab initio* cost estimation models

Several extensions to *ab initio* software cost estimation have been proposed in the literature. An example of this technique is the one included as part of Constructive Cost Model (COCOMO), proposed and implemented by Boehm [6]. A number of refinements have followed since early introduction of the model to account for more observations and for changes in the software process and its technology [eg 7,11]. COCOMO is an example of *algorithmic* cost modelling [6].

The *ab initio* effort model is given by

$$(PM)_{DEV} = A . Size^{B} \qquad \text{Eq. 5}$$

where $(PM)_{DEV}$ is the development effort in person-months, $A$ and $B$ are model parameters which represent the effect of various cost factors. The software maintenance extension is

$$(PM)_{M} = (EAF)(ACT)(PM)_{DEV} \qquad \text{Eq. 6}$$

where $ACT$ is the annual change traffic, defined as "...the fraction of the software product's source instructions which undergo change during a (typical) year, either through addition or modification..." [6]. $(PM)_{M}$ is the maintenance effort in person-months and $(EAF)$ is a maintenance effort adjustment factor that would reflect the difference in cost effort multipliers between the development and maintenance situation [6]. Later refinements of the original COCOMO model replaces the $ACT$ by an extension of the reuse model for *ab initio* projects to the maintenance case, with emphasis on the role of program understanding [7]. Model's parameters were determined using purposively collected data on a number of industrial software projects, with the models reflecting, the average behaviour of the projects in the data set.

It appears that the extensions of *ab initio* models are most useful for estimation during the early phases of system lifecycle, that is, when little or no historical data is available that reflects the actual evolution process.

## 6.3. Software maintenance task effort prediction

Jorgensen's work [17] compared the prediction accuracy of models based on regression, neural networks and optimised set reduction (a pattern recognition approach). He used a purpose-gathered (as opposed to unplanned)

data set, reflecting 109 randomly selected maintenance tasks within an organisation where 70 applications were being maintained by 110 people. Collected data was based on individual maintenance tasks whose size was measured in LOC. He discarded the use of FP. Some of the limitations of the latter identified by Jorgensen are the following:

- FP application require human expertise to obtain the counts
- FP do not tend to reflect the maintenance tasks that do not impact system functionality as perceived by its users
- FP did not seem to be appropriate for measurement of the size of small tasks such as those encountered in maintenance.

He followed Balda's proposal [2], and measured task size by the expression:

$$\begin{aligned} Maintenance\ Task\ Size\ =\ &Added + Updated \\ &+ Deleted \qquad \text{Eq. 7} \end{aligned}$$

where all variables were measured in LOC.

Jorgensen measured productivity in LOC handled per maintenance day and considered nine other variables as candidate predictors of effort. He only selected four of them for inclusion in his models as predictors. These were:

- Cause: if corrective maintenance then Cause = 0, otherwise = 1
- Change: if more than 50 percent of the effort is to be spent in inserting and deleting (as opposed to changing) code then Change =1, otherwise = 0
- Mode: if more than 50 percent of the effort is to be spent in the development of new modules for the system Mode = 0, otherwise = 1
- Confidence: if the confidence of the maintainer that he/she knows how to solve the task is high, then Confidence = 0, otherwise =1

The other variables considered in the study did not show a significant correlation with the maintenance productivity. They were:
- type of language
- maintainer experience
- task priority
- application age
- application size.

As Jorgensen points out, this does not imply that these variables did not impact productivity. There are other issues to be considered. For example, he explains that when one measures productivity in LOC/maintenance-day, one must expect that more experienced maintainers write more compact code. They are also likely to be assigned the more difficult tasks. Thus, they may appear to be less productive than their novice colleagues.

In some aspects Jorgensen's work is close to that reported in the present paper. There are, however, a number of important differences. For example, Jorgensen's study was based on purposively collected data from a number of different applications of different size and age reflecting maintenance activity over a relatively short period of time (not more than 2 years) in the same organisation. The focus of the work reported in this paper has been on simple effort estimation models reflecting the evolution of a single system over 10 years of its lifetime, and on the exploration of a suite of metrics of software evolution based on module and subsystem counts.

## 7. Final remarks

The work reported in this paper focuses on cost estimation in the context of evolving systems, one of the aspects of interest within a wider project (FEAST/2) [14]. The work is part of a larger study that, *inter alia*, considers the following questions:
- what variables are good effort predictors?
- what approaches to effort modelling are appropriate in some defined sense ?
- what are the implications of such models in the context of software evolution process management and improvement; in the context of a theory of that process?

The initial results reported here are encouraging. They seem to indicate that a suite of metrics of software evolution obtained from software change records provide a useful source of data for the building of reasonably accurate estimation models. The predictive power of such metric suite must be ratified in other systems before establishing the general validity of the approach. Work is currently being undertaken to extract appropriate data sets from other systems and to replicate the study. The long term goal of this investigation is the design and validation a comprehensive procedure to build effort prediction models from, unplanned software evolution data, such as change logs records that are, in general, available is many industrial organisations.

## Acknowledgements

Grateful thanks are due to Professors Berc Rustem and Vic Stenning for their comments. Also to Brian Chatters, ICL, for having facilitated our obtaining the industrial data set and the information needed to analyse it, as well as for his comments on an earlier version of the paper. Many thanks are also due to the anonymous referees for their detailed comments. Financial support from the UK EPSRC, grants GR/K86008 (FEAST/1) and GR/M44101 (FEAST/2), is gratefully acknowledged.

## References

[1] Albrecht AJ and Gaffney JE, Software Function, Source Lines of Code, and Development Effort Prediction: A Software Science Validation, IEEE Trans. on Softw. Eng., Vol. SE-9, No. 6, June 1983, pp 639 - 648

[2] Balda DM, Cost Estimation Models for the Reuse and Prototype Software Development Life-cycles, ACM Softw. Eng. Notes, vol. 15, July 1990, pp 42 - 50

[3] Basseville M and Nikiforov IV, Detection of Abrupt Changes: Theory and Application, PTR Prentice Hall, Englewood Cliffs, NJ, 1993

[4] Belady LA and Lehman MM, Programming System Dynamics or the Metadynamics of Systems in Maintenance and Growth, IBM Res Rep, T J Watson Res. Centre, Yorktown Heights, NY 10598, RC 3546, Sept. 71, p 30. Reprinted in [21]

[5] Belady LA and Lehman MM, An Introduction to Program Growth Dynamics, in Statistical Computer Performance Evaluation, W Freiburger (ed), Academic Press, New York, 1972, pp. 503 - 511. Reprinted in [21]

[6] Boehm B, Software Engineering Economics, Englewood Cliffs, N.J, Prentice-Hall, 1981

[7] Boehm B et al, Cost Models for Future Software Life Cycle Processes: Cocomo 2.0, Annals of Software Engineering Special Volume on Software Process and Product Measurement, J.D. Arthur and S.M. Henry, eds., J.C. Baltzer Ag, Science Publish., Amsterdam, 1995, pp. 57-94

[8] Box GEP, Hunter WG and Hunter JS, Statistics for Experimenters - An Introduction to Design - Data Analysis and Model Building, Wiley, New York, 1978

[9] Brooks FP, The Mythical Man-Month - Essays on Software Engineering, 1975, 25th Aniv. Edition, Addison Wesley, Reading, MA, 1995, 322 p.

[10] Chatters BW et al., Modelling a Software Evolution Process, ProSim'99, Softw. Process Modelling and Simulation Workshop, Silver Falls, Oregon, 28-30 June 99. Also as Modelling a Long Term Software Evolution Process in J. of Softw. Proc.: Improvement and Practice, 2000 v. 5, iss. 2/3, July 2000, pps. 95 - 102

[11] Clark B, Devnani-Chulani S and Boehm B, Calibrating the COCOMO II Post-Architecture Model, Proceedings of ICSE'20, April 19-25, Kyoto, Japan, 1998, pp. 477 - 480

[12] Cook PA, Nonlinear Dynamical Systems, 2nd. Ed. Prentice-Hall, New York, 1994

[13] Draper NR and Smith H, Applied Regression Analysis, 2nd. ed., Wiley, New York, 1981

[14] FEAST *Feedback, Evolution and Software Technology*, 1999. <http://www-dse.doc.ic.ac.uk/~mml/feast/>

[15] Gilb T., Evolutionary Development, ACM Software Eng. Notes, April 1981

[16] Humphrey WS and Singpurwalls ND, Predicting (Individual) Software Productivity, IEEE Transactions on Software Eng., Vol. 17, No. 2, Feb. 1991, pp. 196 - 207

[17] Jorgensen M, Experience With the Accuracy of Software Maintenance Task Effort Prediction Models, IEEE Trans. Softw. Eng., Vol. 21, No. 8, 1995, pp. 674 - 681

[18] Katayama, T, A Theoretical Framework of Software Evolution, IWPSE'98 Int. Workshop on Princip. of Softw. Evol., ICSE'20, April 20-21, 1998, Kyoto, Japan, pp. 1 – 5

[19] Kemmerer C and Slaugther S, Determinants of Software Maintenance Profiles: An Empirical Investigation, Software Maintenance Research & Practice, 9, 1997, pp. 235 - 251

[20] Kitchenham B, System Evolution Dynamics of VME/B, ICL Tech. J., May 1982, pp 42 - 57

[21] Lehman MM and Belady LA, Program Evolution – Processes of Software Change, Academic Press, 1985

[22] Lehman MM, Perry DE and Ramil JF, Implications of Evolution Metrics on Software Maintenance, Proc. of Int. Conf. on Softw. Maintenance, ICSM'98, Bethesda, Maryland, Nov. 16-20, 1998, pp. 208-217

[23] Lehman MM, Perry DE and Ramil JF, On Evidence Supporting the FEAST Hypothesis and the Laws of Software Evolution, Proc. Metrics'98, Bethesda, Maryland, Nov. 20-21, 1998, pp. 84-88

[24] Lindvall M, Monitoring and Measuring the Change-Prediction Process at Different Granularity Levels: An Empirical Study, Software Process. Improvement and Practice, 4, 1998, pp. 3-10

[25] Little R and Rubin D, Statistical Analysis with Missing Data, Wiley, NY, 1987

[26] Long J, Regression Models for Categorical and Limited Dependent Variables, Thousand Oaks, CA, Sage 1997

[27] Nelson EA, Management Handbook for the Estimation of Computer Programming Costs, AD-A648750, System Development Corp., Oct. 31, 1966

[28] Norton JP, An Introduction to Identification, Academic Press, London, 1986

[29] McGuffin RW, Elliston AE, Tranter BR and Westmacott PN, CADES - Software Engineering in Practice, Proc. ICSE'4, Munich, Sept 17-19, 1979, pp 136-144

[30] Parnas DL, Software Aging, Proc. ICSE 16, May 16-21, 1994, Sorrento, Italy, pp 279-287

[31] Ramil JF and Lehman MM, Challenges facing Data Collection for Support and Study of Software Evolution Processes, ICSE 99 Workshop on Empirical Studies of Softw. Dev. and Evol., Los Angeles, May 18, 1999, 5 p.

[32] Rosenberg J, A Methodology for Evaluating Predictive Metrics, submitted for publication, July 1999, 21 p.

[33] Sneed HM, Estimating the Costs of Software Maintenance Tasks, Proceedings of the Int. Conf. on Softw. Maint. ICSM, Nice, France, Oct. 17 - 20, 1995, pp. 168 - 181

[34] Sommerville I, Software Engineering, 5th Ed., Addison-Wesley, Wokingham, UK, 1996

[35] Thomas RS, Modern Econometrics - An Introduction, Addison-Wesley, Harlow, England, 1997

[36] Wall L, Christiansen T and Schwartz RL, Programming Perl, 2nd. Ed., O'Really Associates, Inc, Sebastopol, CA, 1996, 645 p

[37] Woodside CM, A Mathematical Model for the Evolution of Software, CCD, Imperial College, Res. Rep. 79/55, Apr. 1979, also in, J. Sys. and Softw., Vol. 1, No. 4, Oct. 1980, pp. 337- 345. Reprinted in [21].

# A Survey of Black-Box Modernization Approaches for Information Systems

**Santiago Comella-Dorda**
*Software Engineering Insitute*
*scd@sei.cmu.edu*

**Kurt Wallnau**
*Software Engineering Institute*
*kcw@sei.cmu.edu*

**Robert C. Seacord**
*Software Engineering Institute*
*rcw@sei.cmu.edu*

**John Robert**
*Software Engineering Institute*
*jer@sei.cmu.edu*

## Abstract

*Information systems are critical assets for modern enterprises and incorporate key knowledge acquired over the life of an organization. These systems must be updated continuously to reflect evolving business practices. Unfortunately, repeated modification has a cumulative effect on system complexity, and the rapid evolution of technology quickly renders existing technologies obsolete. Eventually, the existing information systems become too fragile to modify and too important to discard. For this reason, organizations must consider modernizing these legacy systems to remain viable. The commercial market provides a variety of solutions to this increasingly common problem of legacy system modernization. Understanding the strengths and weaknesses of each modernization technique is paramount to select the correct solution and the overall success of a modernization effort. This paper provides a survey of modernization techniques including screen scraping, database gateway, XML integration, CGI integration, object-oriented wrapping, and "componentization" of legacy systems. This general overview enables engineers performing legacy system modernization to preselect a subset of applicable modernization techniques for further evaluation.*

## Introduction

Information technology (IT) is revolutionizing commercial and government organizations by enabling efficiency improvements and creating opportunities for new business practices. Organizations depend on enterprise information systems (EISs) to codify these business practices and collect, process and analyze business data. No less an authority on the subject than

Federal Reserve Chairman Alan Greenspan testified before the Joint Economic Committee (U.S. Congress on June 14, 1999) that current U.S. and global economic growth is rooted in advances in IT. Chairman Greenspan specifically credited IT, saying:

> *An economy that twenty years ago seemed to have seen its better days, is displaying a remarkable run of economic growth that appears to have its roots in ongoing advances in technology. Innovations in information technology—so-called IT—have begun to alter the manner in which we do business and create value, often in ways that were not readily foreseeable even five years ago.*[1]

In many ways, these information systems are to an enterprise what a brain is to the higher species—a complex, poorly understood mass upon which the organism relies for its very existence. John Salasin characterized enterprise information systems as large, heterogeneous, distributed, evolving, dynamic, long-lived, mission critical, systems of systems. EISs are large because the organizations they support are large

---

[1]  Remarks by Chairman Alan Greenspan, *High-Tech Industry in the U.S. Economy,* testimony before the Joint Economic Committee, U.S. Congress. June 14, 1999.

and complex, and because EISs evolve through accretion. Much of the code in these systems is likely to be redundant, often providing the same or similar capabilities in different subsystems that make up the overall EIS. EISs are heterogeneous for much the same reason. As features are added to an EIS, new technologies and components are selected and integrated.

The importance of EISs requires organizations to manage system evolution as business practices change and new information technologies that can provide competitive advantage become available. EIS evolution becomes more difficult with time as systems are repeatedly modified and become increasingly outdated. Managing the evolution of outdated systems requires periodically modernizing these legacy systems to support evolving business practices and to incorporate modern information technologies.

This document enumerates, describes and, to some extent, evaluates popular legacy system modernization techniques. In addition, we define system modernization and the role it plays in managing system evolution.

## 2. System Evolution

System evolution is a broad term that covers a continuum from adding a field in a database to completely re-implementing a system. These system evolution activities can be divided into three categories [Weiderman 97]: maintenance, modernization, and replacement. Figure 1 illustrates how different evolution activities are applied at different phases of the system life cycle. The dotted line represents growing business needs while the solid line represents the functionality provided by the information system. Repeated system maintenance supports the business needs sufficiently for a time, but as the system becomes increasingly outdated, maintenance falls behind the business needs. A modernization effort is then required that represents a greater effort, both in time and functionality, than the maintenance activity. Finally, when the old system can no longer be evolved, it must be replaced.

Determining the category of evolutionary activity that is most appropriate at different points in the life cycle is a daunting challenge. Should we continue maintaining the system or modernizing it? Should we completely replace the system? To make the correct decision, we need to assess the legacy system and analyze the implications of each action. Ransom et al describe an assessment technique for determining if a legacy system should be replaced, modernized or maintained [Ransom 98]. This document focuses on one phase in the life of a system: modernization. In particular, we concentrate on black-box modernization techniques because they provide a good way to leverage the existing investment in the legacy systems with a limited effort. To better understand the extent of modernization, however, first we briefly describe the other two phases in the life of a deployed system: maintenance and replacement.

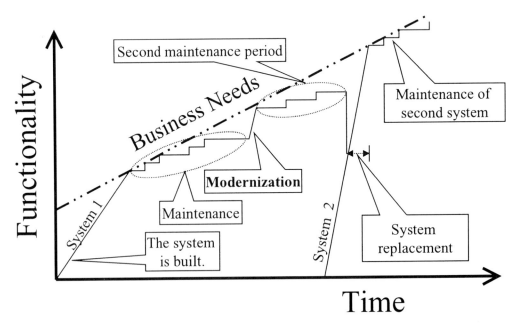

Figure 1:    Information System Life Cycle

## 2.1. Maintenance

Maintenance is an incremental and iterative process in which small changes are made to the system. These changes are often bug corrections or small functional enhancements and should never involve major structural changes. Maintenance is required to support the evolution of any system, but it does have limitations:

1. Competitive advantage derived from adopting newtechnologies is seriously constrained. Netcentric computing or graphical user interfaces, for example, are not typically considered as a maintenance operation.

2. Maintenance costs for legacy systems increase with time. Finding needed expertise in out-of-date technologies becomes increasingly difficult and expensive.

3. Often, the compound impact of many small changes is greater than the sum of the individual changes due to the erosion of the system's conceptual integrity. Information systems tend to expand with time as efforts to remove unused code are seldom funded. Modifying a legacy system to adapt it to new business needs becomes increasingly difficult.

## 2.2. Replacement

Replacement (aka big bang approach or cold turkey) [Bisdal 97] is appropriate for legacy systems that can not keep pace with business needs and for which modernization is not possible or cost effective. Replacement is normally used with systems that are undocumented, outdated, or not extensible. However, replacement has risks that should be evaluated before selecting this technique:

1. Replacement is basically building a system from scratch and is very resource intensive. In addition, IT resources are typically fully allocated performing maintenance tasks and may not be familiar with new technologies that can be utilized on the new system.

2. Replacement requires extensive testing of the new system. Legacy systems are well tested and tuned, and encapsulate considerable business expertise. There is no guarantee that the new system will be as robust or functional as the old one (and as shown in Figure 1, it may cause a period of degraded system functionality with respect to business needs).

Replacement is a broadly studied problem with plenty of supporting literature. For a description of different replacement techniques see [Brodie 95]. Seng and Tsai illustrate in [Seng 99] a complete replacement process.

## 2.3. Modernization

Modernization involves more extensive changes than maintenance, but conserves a significant portion of the existing system. These changes often include system restructuring, important functional enhancements, or new software attributes. Modernization is used when a legacy system requires more pervasive changes than those possible during maintenance, but it still has business value that must be preserved.

System modernization can be distinguished by the level of system understanding required to support the modernization effort [Weiderman 97]. Modernization that requires knowledge of the internals of a legacy system is called white-box modernization, and modernization that just requires knowledge of the external interfaces of a legacy system is called black-box modernization.

### 2.3.1. White-Box Modernization.
White-box modernization requires an initial reverse engineering process to gain an understanding of the internal system operation. Components of the system and their relationships are identified, and a representation of the system at a higher level of abstraction is produced [Chikofsky 90].

Program understanding is the principal form of reverse engineering used in white-box modernization. Program understanding involves modeling the domain, extracting information from the code using appropriate extraction mechanisms, and creating abstractions that help in the understanding of the underlying system structure.[2] Analyzing and understanding old code is a difficult task because with time, every system collapses under its own complexity [Phoenix Group]. Although some advances have been made in program understanding, it is still a risky and work-intensive task [von Mayrhauser 94, Haft 95].

After the code is analyzed and understood, white-box modernization often includes some system or code restructuring. Software restructuring can be defined as "the transformation from one representation form to another at the same relative abstraction level, while preserving the subject system's external behavior (functionality and semantics)." [Chikofsky 90] This transformation is typically used to augment some quality

---

[2] Tilley, Scott R. & Smith, Dennis B. *Perspectives on Legacy Systems Reengineering* (draft). Reengineering Center, Software Engineering Institute, Carnegie Mellon University. 1995.

attribute of the system like maintainability or performance. Program (or code) slicing is a particularly popular technique of software restructuring. A description of a semi-automatic restructuring technique to improve cohesion of legacy procedures can be found in [Lakhotia 98].

### 2.3.2. Black-Box Modernization.

Black-box modernization involves examining the inputs and outputs of a legacy system within an operating context to gain an understanding of the system interfaces. Although acquiring an understanding of a system interface is not an easy task, it does not reach the degree of difficulty associated with white-box modernization.

Black-box modernization is often based on wrapping. Wrapping consists of surrounding the legacy system with a software layer that hides the unwanted complexity of the old system and exports a modern interface. Wrapping is used to remove mismatches between the interface exported by a software artifact and the interfaces required by current integration practices [Wallnau 97, Shaw 95]. Ideally, wrapping is a "black-box" reengineering task in that only the legacy interface is analyzed and the legacy system internals are ignored. Unfortunately, this solution is not always practical, and often requires an understanding of the software modules' internals using white-box techniques [Plakosh 99].

# 3. Modernization Techniques

Legacy systems may be modernized at the functional (logic), data, or user interface level. In this section, we present a collection of techniques for each of these modernization levels and discuss typical applications.

## 3.1. User Interface Modernization

The user interface (UI) is the most visible part of a system. Modernizing the UI improves usability and is greatly appreciated by final users.

A common technique for UI modernization is screen scraping [Carr 98]. Screen scraping consists of wrapping old, text-based interfaces with new graphical interfaces. The old interface is often a set of text screens running in a terminal. In contrast, the new interface can be a PC-based, graphical user interface (GUI), or even a hypertext markup language (HTML) light client running in a Web browser. This technique can be extended easily, enabling one new UI to wrap a number of legacy systems. The new graphical interface communicates with the old one using a specialized commercial tool.[3] These tools often generate the new screens automatically by mapping the old ones.

From the perspective of the legacy system, the new graphical interface is indistinguishable from an end user entering text in a screen. From the end user's point of view, the modernization has been successful as the new system now provides a modern, usable graphical interface. However, from the IT department's perspective, the new system is as inflexible and difficult to maintain as the legacy system. Screen scraping is basically a "makeover" for legacy systems. Derogatorily, this approach has been called "whipped cream on road kill." It can, however, be effective for stable systems where the principle objective is to improve usability.

Another interesting application of screen scraping is to generate application program interfaces (APIs) from legacy user interfaces. This technique was applied in a large defense program integrating an enterprise resource planning (ERP) with other systems. Screen scraping was used to extract data from the ERP, reversing the normal use of this wrapping technique because the ERP did not provide a callable application programming interface.

## 3.2. Data Modernization

Data wrapping enables accessing legacy data using a different interface or protocol than those for which the data was designed initially. Data wrapping improves connectivity and allows the integration of legacy data into modern infrastructures.

### 3.2.1. Database Gateway.

A database gateway is a specific type of software gateway that translates between two or more data access protocols [Altman 99]. There are many vendor-specific protocols used to access databases, but fortunately there are a few that are de facto industry standards:

1.  Open Database Connectivity (ODBC) is Microsoft's interface for accessing data in a heterogeneous environment of relational and non-relational database management systems. Based on the Call Level Interface specification of the SQL Access Group, ODBC provides an open, vendor-neutral way of accessing data stored in a variety of proprietar personal computer, minicomputer, and mainframe databases [Microsoft 95].

---

[3] For example, OC://WebConnect Enterprise Integration Server™ from Open-Connect Systems or QuickApp™ from Attachmate.

2.  Java Database Connectivity (JDBC) is an industry standard defined by Sun for database-independent connectivity between Java applets/applications and a broad range of SQL databases. JDBC benefits from the "Write Once, Run Anywhere" characteristics of Java. The JDBC API defines Java classes that represent database connections, SQL statements, result sets, and database metadata [JDBC].

3.  ODMG is the standard of the Object Data Management Group for persistent object storage. It builds upon existing database, object, and programming language standards (including the Object Management Group [OMG]) to simplify object storage and ensure application portability [Barry98].

A database gateway normally translates a vendor-specific access protocol into one of these standard protocols. This translation is useful because modern applications and development platforms typically support one or more of these standard protocols. Using a database gateway to access legacy data improves connectivity, enables remote access, and supports the integration of legacy data with modern systems.

Given that there are multiple "standard" protocols for accessing databases, the database gateway available for a specific legacy system and the protocol supported by the new system may not match. Figure 2, for example, shows a legacy system for which an ODBC gateway is available while the modern system requires a JDBC interface. One solution is a special gateway called a bridge that translates one standard protocol into another—in this case a JDBC-ODBC bridge.

### 3.2.2. XML Integration

The Extensible Markup Language (XML™) is a broadly adopted format for structured documents and data on the Web. XML is a simple and flexible text format derived from standard generalized markup language (SGML) (ISO 8879) and developed by the World Wide Web Consortium® (W3C).

XML is expanding from its origin in document processing and becoming a solution for data integration [Karpinski 98]. XML excels in inter-application data exchange because of its flexible and extensible method for describing data and its capability to communicate over the Internet using the standard HTTP protocol [WebMethods 99].

This flexibility makes XML a powerful mechanism for business-to-business (B2B) application integration. B2B integration is the automated exchange of information between systems from different organizations. B2B, for example, improves external processes such as supply chain integration or shipping/logistics tracking [WebMethods 99]. XML-based B2B is gaining momentum as XML vocabularies emerge in specific business domains such as finance. In addition, a growing number of commercial enterprise application solutions are embracing XML.

The keystone in the XML-based B2B architecture is the XML server (Figure 3). The XML server acts as the contact point between the corporate infrastructure and the rest of the world. The XML server communicates by various means with the internal infrastructures including ERP systems, databases, EDIs, etc. On the other hand, the server interoperates with external organization by exchanging XML messages. There is an active market of solutions for non-intrusive integration of legacy infrastructures into XML servers. In addition, most of the commercial XML servers support a wealth of communication protocols and this enables cost-effective integration with the most usual legacy applications.

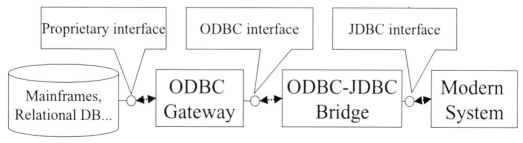

**Figure 2:      Gateways and Bridges**

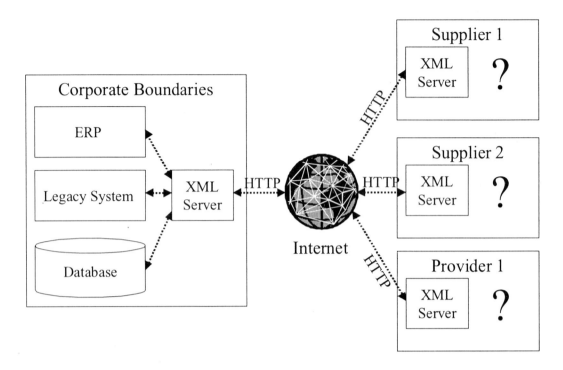

**Figure 3:     XML integration**

### 3.3. Functional (Logic) Modernization

In contrast with data wrapping, functional (or logic) wrapping encapsulates not only the legacy data, but also the business logic embedded in the legacy system. Logic wrapping can be used, for instance, to leverage existing COBOL code implanted in Transaction Monitor (TM) procedures. The logic wrapping techniques presented here can provide access to legacy data, if required, in addition to legacy logic.

**3.3.1. CGI Integration.** The Common Gateway Interface (CGI) is a standard for interfacing external applications with information servers, such as HTTP or Web servers. Legacy integration using the CGI [Shklar, Eichman 95] is often used to provide fast web access to existing assets including mainframes and transaction monitors. As in

screen scraping, a new graphical user interface (in this case always HTML pages) is created, but instead of wrapping the old user interface, the new GUI communicates directly with the core business logic or data of the legacy system. CGI integration is more flexible than screen scraping because the new interface does not need to match the old user interface. However, it shares the advantages and disadvantages of screen scraping in that it is relatively easy to implement but does not fully address maintenance issues.

A typical CGI access configuration is shown in Figure 4. A Web server, powered with a CGI extension to access legacy systems, invokes some function in the legacy system and generates HTML pages to be served to remote browsers. Although not depicted in the figure, CGI is used to access legacy data in addition to the logic.

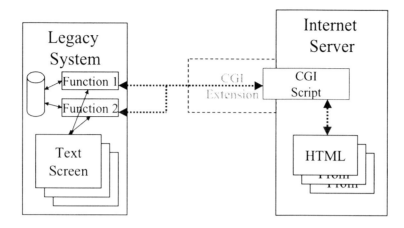

**Figure 4:**      **Legacy System Wrapping Using CGI Extensions**

An example of using CGI to integrate legacy systems occurred in the National Software Data and Information Repository (NSDIR) when Perl scripts were used to access legacy data contained within the repository [Card 96].

**3.3.2. Object-Oriented Wrapping.** Objects have been used to implement complex software systems successfully. Object-oriented systems can be designed and implemented in a way that closely resembles the business processes they model [Phoenix Group]. Additionally, the use of abstraction, encapsulation, inheritance, and other object orientation (OO) techniques make object-oriented systems easier to understand.

To support object distribution, we need a more powerful means of communication than that provided by normal inter-object communication mechanisms. Distributed object technology (DOT) is the combination of distributed technology with OO [Wallnau 97]. In effect, DOT extends object technology to the net-centric information systems of modern enterprises by using *object middleware*. The most prevalent object middleware is the Common Object Request Broker Architecture (CORBA) from OMG, with its platform-neutral object specification language, robust remote method calls, interoperable protocols, and rich set of services.

The conceptual model of object-oriented wrapping is deceptively simple: individual applications are represented as objects; common services are represented as objects; and business data is represented as objects. In reality, object-oriented wrapping is far from simple and involves several tasks including code analysis, decomposition, and abstraction of the OO model. The project ERCOLE (Encapsulation, Reengineering, and Coexistence of Object with Legacy) describes an exemplifying process to wrap legacy applications with OO systems [De Lucia 97]. Of the multiple technical

difficulties involved in wrapping a legacy system, two are of special relevance: the definition of appropriate object-level interfaces and the need for integrated infrastructure services.

Translating the monolithic and plain semantics of the often procedural legacy system to the richly hierarchic and structured semantics of an object-oriented system can be a difficult task. A good knowledge of the domain can greatly help in the translation. For example, Stets describes an experience in which the Win32 API is translated into objects [Stets 99]. To create meaningful objects, domain-specific knowledge of the structure of an operating system is used. Unfortunately, developers wrapping a system rarely possesses such deep domain knowledge. Some techniques have been developed to perform the legacy to OO mapping more automatically. For example, in one such method, every coarse-grained persistent item is mapped into an object, and services are assigned to objects with an algorithm that minimizes coupling [Cimitile 97]. Although these and other techniques are useful in extracting objects from legacy systems, the mapping problem is far from being solved.

The second challenge of translating an OO system using DOT is integrating infrastructure services in the OO system. Almost any DOT middleware provides some set of services such as security, transactions or persistence. However, it is often the case that to get the expected level of services the developer must integrate two or more of these middleware solutions. This integration is at least problematic due to unexpected interactions and incompatibilities between theoretically compatible products [Seacord 99]. To address this need for integrated services, the industry has developed what is commonly known as application servers (aka server-side component frameworks). An application server is a product that integrates a set of services and defines a component model. Components developed conforming to this model are able to leverage all the services provided by the application server.

The OMG is following this approach in the CORBA 3 specification, which defines a component framework (known in CORBA 3 jargon as component container) and addresses a range of infrastructure issues as well.

### 3.3.3. Component Wrapping.
Component wrapping is very similar to OO wrapping, but components, in contrast with objects, must conform to a component model. This constraint enables the component framework to provide the component with quality services. Because component-based modernization is the newest and probably the least known of the approaches illustrated in this survey, this section discusses not only an overview but some implementation details as well.

The component model market consisted initially of numerous proprietary and mutually incompatible solutions. Fortunately, this situation is improving with the emergence of a small set of standard enterprise component models and products. Of these standards, three are of particular consequence:

- Distributed interNet Architecture™ (DNA) is the Microsoft solution and a de facto standard because of Microsoft's weight in the industry.

- The CORBA 3 Component Model is the OMG approach for the enterprise that promises an enterprise component model for CORBA.

- Enterprise JavaBeans (EJB) is the Sun Microsystems solution for Java server-side computing [Johnson 98].

According to press releases from the OMG, it is likely that the CORBA 3 Component Model and EJB will merge into a single standard leaving only two dominant players. The following discussion uses EJB to illustrate component wrapping, but does not necessarily mean that EJB is superior to other competing models or that these solutions cannot be implemented with other products.

Components in EJB are known as Enterprise JavaBeans (we will also refer to them as beans). Each bean encapsulates a piece of business logic. Enterprise JavaBeans are deployed within an application server, or EJB server, that provides the runtime environment for the bean and manages common services such as security, transactions, state management, resource pooling, distributed naming, automatic persistence, and remote invocation. This allows the EJB developer to focus on the business problem to be solved. An Enterprise JavaBean is, in essence, a transactional and secure remote method invocation (RMI) or CORBA object, some of whose runtime properties are specified at deployment using special files called "deployment descriptors."

The first step in wrapping a legacy system using EJB is to separate the interface of the legacy system into modules consisting of logical units—shown in Figure 5 as Function 1 and Function 2. The degree of difficulty in dividing the legacy system into discrete functions will vary depending on the degree to which the separation was defined in the legacy system interfaces and whether new interfaces must be built. Although a black-box approach is preferable, poor documentation and a cryptic legacy system interface may make it necessary to peer into the black-box to better understand the legacy system [Plakosh 99].

The next step in wrapping the legacy business logic is to build a *single point of contact* to the legacy system. It is a good idea to centralize all the communication knowledge in a single software artifact. The communication method used by this artifact depends on the particular situation. Options for communication between the single point of contact and the legacy system include RMI over IIOP, sockets, or even Message Oriented Middleware (MOM), which has the advantage of uncoupling the EJB server from the legacy system and allowing for asynchronous communication. This single point of contact can be implemented as a bean (called *adapter*) or as a *service broker*—a software component placed external to the EJB server. Placing the point of contact inside or outside the server depends mainly on the chosen communication method and some security restrictions. For example, if you need to create a new thread or listen to a socket, the single point of contact must be outside of the application server because the EJB specification prevents Enterprise JavaBeans from being multithreaded or listening to sockets. The final step in wrapping the legacy business logic is to implement a wrapper bean for each module in the legacy system. In Figure 5, this wrapper is shown as Bean 2. These beans forward requests to the legacy system using the single contact point, in a manner similar to object wrapping.

There are several advantages to the component approach for wrapping legacy business logic. First, with relatively limited effort, the advantages of component-based systems are supported. We can, for example, build new Enterprise Java Beans that use the wrapper beans in unanticipated ways, greatly improving system flexibility. Second, wrapper beans are bona fide Enterprise Beans and can be integrated fully with all the management facilities and services included with the application server. Lastly, wrapping legacy business logic provides a roadmap to substitute the old system incrementally. After wrapping the functionality of the legacy system, we can re-implement wrapper beans one at a time (Bean 1 in Figure 5), without having to go through a "big-bang" replacement of the system. This is possible because the system and the clients would not notice any disruption as the re-implemented bean maintains the same interfaces provided by the wrapper bean. In time, it is possible to replace the old system completely.

Wrapping legacy business logic with EJB is not without risk. The EJB specification is porous and portability problems can arise between different vendor's application servers [Comella-Dorda 99]. In addition, the Java programming language is considered by some to be unsuitable for critical applications.

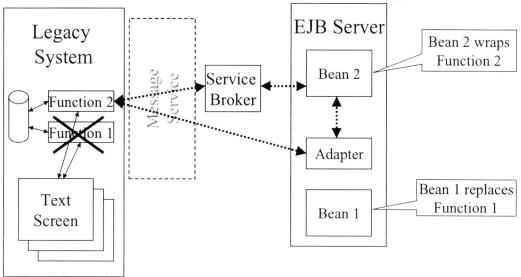

**Figure 5:     Wrapping Legacy Business Logic Using EJB**

## 4. Summary

The modernization of legacy systems is a critical issue that IT departments must face in modern enterprises. Although new technologies such as CORBA and EJB promise to support modernization, it is still a complex task requiring careful consideration and advanced planning. There are different approaches to the modernization of legacy assets including reengineering (white-box) and wrapping (black-box). Before starting any legacy modernization effort, every possible option should be explored and evaluated. This evaluation should cover the technical considerations and consider business and strategic factors outlined in [Weiderman 97b, Bergey 97] to ensure long-term success.

We have presented several techniques to support legacy system modernization. It would be naive to affirm any of these techniques as superior to the others. Each presented technique has strengths, weaknesses, and tradeoffs between cost, flexibility, and other variables. Table 1 summarizes the discussions of each presented technique.

**Table 1:     Comparison of Modernization Techniques**

| | Artifact Modernized | Target | Strengths | Weaknesses |
|---|---|---|---|---|
| **Screen Scraping** | Text-based user interface | Graphical or web-based user interface | • Cost<br>• Time to market<br>• Internet support | • Flexibility<br>• Limited impact on maintainability |
| **Database Gateway** | Proprietary access protocol | Standard access protocol | • Cost<br>• Tool support | • Limited impact on maintainability |

| | | | | |
|---|---|---|---|---|
| **XML Integration** | Proprietary access protocol | XML server | • Flexibility<br>• Tool support (future)<br>• B2B | • Tool support (present)<br>• Evolving technology |
| **CGI Integration** | Mainframe Data or TM services | HTML pages | • Cost<br>• Internet support | • Flexibility<br>• Applicability |
| **OO Wrapping** | Any Enterprise Resource | OO Model | • Flexibility<br>• Easier understanding | • Cost |
| **Component wrapping** | Any Enterprise Resource | Component Model | • Flexibility<br>• Integrated services<br>• Incremen. replacement | • Cost |

# References

[Altman 99]    Altman, R.; Natis, Y.; Hill, J.; Klein, J.; Lheureux, B.; Pezzini, M.; Schulte, R.; & Varma S. Middleware: The Glue for Modern Applications. Gartner Group, Strategic Analysis Report; 26 July 1999.

[Barry 98]    Barry, Doug. "ODMG 2.0: A Standard for Object Storage." Component Strategies. July 1998.

[Bergey 97]    Bergey, John; Northrop, Linda; & Smith, Dennis. Enterprise Framework for the Disciplined Evolution of Legacy Systems (CMU/SEI-97-TR-007). Pittsburgh, Pa.: Software Engineering Institute, Carnegie Mellon University. Available WWW <URL: http://www.sei.cmu.edu/publications/documents/97.reports/ 97tr007/97tr007abstract.html> 1997.

[Bisdal 97]    Bisdal, Jesus; Lawless, Deirdre; Wu, Bing; Grimson, Jane; Wade, Vincent; Richardson, Ray; & O'Sullivan, D. "An Overview of Legacy Information System Migration," Proceedings of the 4th Asian-Pacific Software Engineering and International Computer Science Conference (APSEC 97, ICSC 97), 1997.

[Brodie 95] Brodie, M. & Stonebraker, M. Migrating Legacy Systems: Gateways, Interfaces and the Incremental Approach. Morgan Kaufmann Publishers, 1995.

[Card 96] Card, D.N.; Hissam, S. A; & Rosemeier R.T. "National Software Data and Information Repository." CrossTalk 9, 2. Available WWW <URL: http://www.stsc.hill.af.mil/CrossTalk/1996/feb/national.html> (February 1996).

[Carr 98] Carr, David F. "Web-Enabling Legacy Data When Resources Are Tight." Internet World (August 10 1998).

[Chikofsky 90] Chikofsky, Elliot J. & Cross II, J.H. "Reverse Engineer and Design Recovery: A Taxonomy." IEEE Software, 7 (January 1990): 13-17.

[Cimitile 97] Cimitile, A.; De Lucia, A.; Di Lucca, A.; & Fasolino, A.R., "Identifying Objects in Legacy Systems," Proceedings of the 5th Workshop on Program Comprehension (WPC97), 1997.

[Comella-Dorda 99] Comella-Dorda, Santiago; Robert, John; & Seacord, Robert. "Theory and Practice of Enterprise JavaBean Portability," Proceedings International Society for Computers and Their Applications (ISCA) 1st International Conference on Information Reuse and Integration (IRI-99). Atlanta, Georgia, 1999.

[De Lucia 97] De Lucia, A.; Di Lucca, G.A.; Fasolino, A.R.; Guerra, P.; & Petruzzelli, S. "Migrating Legacy Systems towards Object-Oriented Platforms," International Conference of Software Maintenance (ICSM97), 1997.

[Eichman 95] Eichmann, David. Application Architectures for Web-Based Data Access. Available WWW: <URL: http://www.cs.rutgers.edu/~shklar/www4/eichmann.html>.

[Haft 95] Haft, T. M. & Vessey, I. "The Relevance of Application Domain Knowledge: The Case of Computer Program Comprehension." Information Systems Research, 6. (1995): 286-299.

[JDBC] Introduction to JDBC. Available WWW <URL: http://shrike.depaul.edu/~pgrage/dist_sys/ds520_p1.html>.

[Johnson 98] Johnson, Mark. "A Beginner's Guide to Enterprise JavaBeans." Java World 3, 10. Available WWW <URL: http://www.javaworld.com/javaworld/jw-10-1998/ jw-10-beans.html> (October 1998).

[Karpinski 98]    Karpinski, Richard. "Databases, Tools Push XML Into Enterprise." Internet Week Online. Available WWW

<URL: http://www.internetwk.com/news1198/news111698-3.htm> (November 1998).

[Lakhotia 98]    Lakhotia, Arun & Deprez, Jean-Christophe. "Restructuring Functions with Low Cohesion," Proceedings of the 6th Working Conference of Electrical and Electronics Engineers, 1998.

[Microsoft 95]    Microsoft. "Microsoft Windows Operating Systems and Services Architecture, Chapter 9: Open Database Connectivity (ODBC) 2.0 Fundamentals", Microsoft Corporation. 1995.

[Phoenix Group]    Phoenix Group. Legacy Systems Wrapping with Objects. Available WWW <URL: http://www.phxgrp.com/jodewp.htm>.

[Plakosh 99]    Plakosh, Daniel; Hissam, Scott; & Wallnau, Kurt. Into the Black Box: A Case Study in Obtaining Visibility into Commercial Software (CMU/SEI-99-TN-010). Pittsburgh, Pa.: Software Engineering Institute, Carnegie Mellon University. Available WWW: <URL: http://www.sei.cmu.edu/publications/documents/99.reports/99tn010/99tn010abstract.html> (1999).

[Ransom 98]    Ransom, J.; Sommerville, I.; & Warren, I. "A Method for Assessing Legacy Systems for Evolution," Proceedings of the Second Euromicro Conference on Software Maintenance and Reengineering (CSMR98), 1998.

[Seacord 99]    Seacord, Robert C.; Wallnau, Kurt; Robert, John; Comella-Dorda, Santiago; & Hissam, Scott A. "Custom vs. Off-the-Shelf Architecture," Proceedings of 3rd International Enterprise Distributed Object Computing Conference, University of Mannheim, Germany, September 27-30, 1999.

[Seng 99]Seng, Jia-Lang & Tsai, Wayne. "A Structure Transformation Approach for Legacy Information Systems- A Cash Receipts/Reimbursement Example," Proceedings on the 32nd Hawaii International Conference on System Sciences, 1999.

[Shaw 95]    Shaw, Mary. "Architecture Issues in Software Reuse: It's Not Just the Functionality, It's the Packaging," Proceedings IEEE Symposium on Software Reusability. April 1995.

[Shklar]  Shklar, Leon. Web Access to Legacy Data. Available WWW: <URL: http://athos.rutgers.edu/~shklar/web-legacy/summary.html>.

[Stets 99] Stets, Robert J.; Hunt, Galen C.; Scott, Michael L. "Component-Based APIs for Versioning and Distributed Applications," IEEE Computer, 54-61 (July 1999).

[Sun 99] Sun. J2EE™ Connector Architecture (JSR-000016). Available WWW: <URL: http://java.sun.com/aboutJava/communityprocess/jsr/jsr_016_connect.html> (1999).

[von Mayrhauser 94] von Mayrhauser, A. & Vans, A.M. "Comprehension Processes During Large Scale Maintenance." Proceedings of the International Conference of Software Engineering ICSE. Sorrento, Italy, p. 39-48. May 16, 1994.

[Wallnau 97] Wallnau, Kurt; Morris, Edwin; Feiler, Peter; Earl, Anthony; Litvak, Emile. Engineering Component-Based Systems with Distributed Object Technology Lecture Notes in Computer Science. International Conference WWCA'97 Tsukuba, Japan. March 1997.

[WebMethods 99] WebMethods. B2B Integration: The Drive to Gain and Maintain Competitive Advantage. Available WWW: <URL: http://www.webmethods.com/products/whitepapers/b2b_wpB2Bintegration.html> (July 1999).

[Weiderman 97a]  Weiderman, N; Northrop, L.; Smith, D.; Tilley, S.; & Wallnau, K.  Implications of Distributed Object Technology for Reengineering (CMU/SEI-97-TR-005 ADA326945). Pittsburgh, Pa.: Software Engineering Institute, Carnegie Mellon University. Available WWW <URL: http://www.sei.cmu.edu/publications/documents/97.reports/97tr005/97tr005abstract.html> (1997).

[Weiderman 97b]  Weiderman, Nelson H.; Bergey, John K.; Smith, Dennis B.; & Tilley, Scott R. Approaches to Legacy System Evolution (CMU/SEI-97-TR-014 ). Pittsburgh, Pa.: Software Engineering Institute, Carnegie Mellon University. Available WWW <URL:http://www.sei.cmu.edu/publications/documents/97.reports/97tr014/97tr014abstract.html> (1997).

# Prevention is better than Cure

Mira Kajko-Mattsson
Software Maintenance
Laboratory
Department of Computer and
Systems Sciences
Stockholm University/Royal
Institute of Technology
Electrum 230
SE-164 40 KISTA
mira@dsv.su.se

Gunnar Björkman, Ingegerd
Nyamesah, Anna Sors
Department of Computer and
Systems Sciences
Stockholm University/Royal
Institute of Technology
Electrum 230
SE-164 40 KISTA
[gb, inge-nya, anna-sor]@dsv.su.se

Per-Erik Lundh
Head of Secretariat
The Millennium Commission
SE-103 33 Stockholm
Per-Erik.Lundh@swipnet.se

## Abstract

*Was all the mania leading up to the turn of the millennium warranted or was it just a load of computer maintenance ballyhoo designed to attract attention? In this paper we spot test a selected number of Swedish companies to establish their state of preparedness just prior to meeting the new millennium as well as the effects they have encountered immediately after the turn of the millennium. These are then compared to the list of effects compiled by the Millennium Commission (appointed by the Swedish Government).*

## 1    Introduction

We have been subjected to Y2K (Year 2000) hype and hysteria ad nauseam over the last few years. Dire predictions of havoc and despair have been heard in almost every corner of the world. To come to grips with this common, awe-inspiring adversary, the software community has gathered its troops and raised a substantial armament to defend its sovereignty. Every single country waged war on this common assailant and fought it down to the very last minute. Sweden was no exception. But was all this resistance warranted, or was the threat just a computer maintenance gimmick – a ruse to attract attention and resources [25]?

Just into the second half of 1999, the Millennium Commission[1] declared that most of the companies in Sweden were sufficiently fortified to combat the Y2K assault. To check the merit of this statement, we have spot tested a number of Swedish companies. The

---

[1] The Millennium Commission was appointed by the Swedish Government.

objective was to ascertain their level of fortification (their state of preparedness) to combat their foe (the new millennium) and deal with the immediate damage caused by the encounter (the immediate Y2K effects). These effects were then compared to the results compiled by the Millennium Commission. Immediate effects refer here to the Y2K impact during the first two months of the new millennium.

Solving the Y2K problem requires a high degree of maturity in many facets of the recognised engineering disciplines, such as project management, testing and others [21, p. 126]. During the course of this study, the opportunity was taken to indirectly evaluate the level of engineering maturity within the organisations being studied dealing with complicated problems such as the Y2K problem.

The Y2K problem has led to more than simply the input of a lot of unpaid effort. In this paper, an attempt has been made to compile some of the benefits of the Y2K problem according to the organisations studied and the Millennium Commission.

## 2    Methodology

We have studied a limited number of Swedish companies. As the number is too small to characterise Swedish industry generally, the results of spot testing are compared with the results compiled by the Millennium Commission (see Sections 2.2 and 3.3). The following companies were studied:

1.  *The Ericsson Group*: a world-leading supplier in the telecommunications and data communications industry.

2.  *ABB Automation Products AB (ABB APR)*: a world-leading supplier of process control products.

**Table 1.** Definitions of the Y2K-compliant product.

3. *Svenska Handelsbanken*: one of the largest banks in Sweden.

4. *Länsförsäkringar*: an insurance and development company in Sweden.

5. *Swedbank*: one of the largest banking groups in the Scandinavian region.

6. *SEB Group*: one of the largest financial groups in the Scandinavian region.

7. *Trygg Hansa*: an insurance company in Sweden.

8. *FörsäkringsGirot*: a small transaction administration company in Sweden.

This study consisted of three stages:

**Stage 1**: Defining the level of preparedness within the organisations studied over the final months of the second millennium.

**Stage 2**: Establishing the effects of the Y2K problem for the very first months of the third millennium.

**Stage 3**: Comparing the results of spot testing with those compiled by the Millennium Commission.

The main way of collecting information was by interviewing software professionals. The results of the interviews constitute the data to be analysed. The study has utilised a specifically selected evaluation model, question design and interviewing techniques (the question design and evaluation model are presented in Section 2.1).

## 2.1 Question Design and Evaluation Model

The definitions of a Y2K compliant product as propagated by the Millennium Commission [13] and the IEEE [7] were addressed at the outset of the study. These definitions are presented in Table 1, and appear to be of somewhat limited scope, claiming that a software product is Y2K compliant if it can correctly process date data within and between the 20th and 21st centuries with

| (I) Presentation of the companies | (IV) Measures |
|---|---|
| 1. What is the company name? | 12. Have you attended to all your software systems? |
| 2. What is the number of employees? | • percentage of the attended to systems? |
| 3. What type of business do you run? | 13. What technique have you used (data expansion, windowing, other)? |
| • product, service, product & service? | 14. Have you made all the tests required (unit, integration and system tests)? |
| 4. What is your total annual turnover/annual balance? | |
| **(II) System portfolio** | **(V) Costs** |
| 5. What is the total size of your software systems? | 15. What were your planned costs? |
| 6. What is the age of your software systems? | 16. What were your actual costs? |
| 7. Have you made an inventory of your software systems? | • monetary value |
| | • man-month |
| **(III) Planing** | **(VI) Y2K immediate effects** |
| 8. When did you start attending to the Y2K-problem? | 17. Have you encountered any kind of Y2K-problem at or after the millennium shift and the leap year? |
| 9. Have you made a project plan? | • nr of problems |
| 10. Have you performed prioritisation of your systems? | • problem severity |
| 11. Have you made a contingency plan? | |

**Table 2**. Interview questionnaire.

retained functionality. According to The Millennium Commission [13], the supplier company itself should declare whether its products are Y2K compliant, providing "Yes/No" answers.

As more feedback than this was deemed necessary, a specific evaluation model was designed. Specific measures for attending to the Y2K problem suggested in current literature [3, 9, 19, 20] were incorporated into the design and development of the evaluation model. Interview questions also reflected these measures. The results of the study are of both quantitative and qualitative character.

### 2.1.1 Quantitative Assessment

This quantitative study corresponded to a pure data collection survey. The purpose was to produce quantitative descriptions of the level of preparedness in Sweden and of the immediate post-millennium effects. The interview questions are presented in Table 2. Below is a rationale for the questions chosen:

I **Presentation of the companies**: to provide an overview of the types of the companies studied and their size.

II **System portfolio**: to provide insight into the amount of software systems, their size and distribution by age.

III **Planning**: to find out whether basic Y2K planning has been carried out, and includes the following: the existence of a Y2K project plan, product prioritisation, and the establishment of a contingency plan.

IV **Measures**: to find out the percentage of the programs attended to and the types of technical solutions that have been used to remedy the Y2K problem. The two major techniques suggested are date expansion and windowing [3, 6, 12, 14,

19, 20]. In addition, it was checked whether or not the companies had conducted the basic tests required such as unit, integration, and system tests.

V      **Costs**: to come up with a figure for the cost of the Y2K project and to compare planned costs with actual costs. The costs studied encompass project management, inventory, staffing, analysis and design, programming, testing efforts, training and all other tasks related to the Y2K problem. These costs do not cover the costs after the millennium shift.

VI     **Y2K immediate effects**: to find out whether the millennium shift and the leap year have implied any immediate problems for the organisations studied. Immediate effects here mean the impact of the Y2K problem in the first two months of the new millennium. Efforts were also made to find out the severity of those effects. Hence severity levels were defined as follows:

- *Serious*: Problems implying risk to human life, of business decline, of high financial loss, and/or of undermining of company reputation.

- *Medium*: Problems affecting parts of the software system. Moderately difficult to recover losses.

- *Low*: Problems leading to a minor nuisance. Losses easily recovered.

### 2.1.2   Qualitative Assessment

Regarding the qualitative assessment, efforts have tried to:

1. Evaluate the answers by comparing them to the requirements stated in the current literature dealing with the Y2K problem.

2. Evaluate maturity of the organisations on the basis of our own criteria ( see maturity indicators below).

3. Scrutinise the answers provided by the interviewees for inconsistencies.

Maturity here means the ability of an organisations to manage the Y2K problem. To the best knowledge of the authors of this paper, there are no pre-existing criteria for evaluating organisations in a Y2K context. Hence, new key elements, which are considered pivotal and sufficiently representative had to be identified. Some of our elements however, may overlap with the Capability Maturity Model' (CMM) key elements [4]. The following maturity indicators were identified:

- **Starting date for addressing the Y2K problem**: The sheer magnitude of effort to conduct the Y2K

project necessitates long lead times. Hence organisations were advised to start as soon as possible, preferably in the years 1996-1997 [3, 8, 21]. The longer the organisations waited to address the Y2K situation, the more likely they were to become exposed to its impacts. In other words, they were at more risk.

- **The existence of a Y2K project plan**: Addressing the Y2K problem must be planned. The Y2K problem does not appear to be difficult but requires considerable planning and resources. Given careful planning, the Y2K costs can be reduced [3, 9, 19, 20]. According to the CMM, software project planning is a pivotal prerequisite for performing software engineering and for managing software projects [4].

- **Inventory**: Inventory is a primary source for determining the state of Y2K compliance within organisations [20]. If the organisations have not made an inventory, there is reason for questioning their results.

- **Knowledge of software size**: Numbers of software systems within organisations, and their size (measured in for example, lines of code – LOC, function points – FP and millions of instructions per second – MIPS) is a very important piece of information. Its absence indicates insufficient knowledge for performing basic software engineering. How can effort and cost be estimated without knowing the size of the product to be worked upon [1, 4, 17]?

- **Ability to predict the Y2K cost**: One of the most challenging tasks within software engineering is predicting project costs. Deviations in early estimates are likely to be significant [22]. The aim here was to check the size of those deviations.

- **Prioritisation and Triage**: Assigning priority and triage is a method for minimising damage caused by the Y2K problem. Prudent planning can help to keep the number of "fatalities" to a bare minimum. It was predicted that some companies would be forced to perform triage on their systems due to the time and resource limitations [20]. The Pareto Principle becomes very useful here. The aim is to identify the vital few factors, critical for the business and the trivial many [15]. Hence, a triage approach may be necessary to ensure the continued operation of the organisation.

- **Contingency plan**: Many systems would be overlooked, ignored, or their compliance activities will not be completed in time. Contingency management is intended to minimise the risk related to this problem [3, 20]. We only checked for the

| Network Group Members | Stora Enso |
| Millennium Commission | Swedbank |
| | Sweden Post |
| **Public Sector Authorities** | Telia AB |
| Swedish Armed Forces | Vattenfall |
| The National Board of Psychological Defense (SPF) | Volvo Group |
| The National Social Insurance Board (RFV) | **Other Organisations** |
| The National Tax Board (RSV) | The Association of the Swedish IT and Telecom Industry |
| Swedish Agency for Administrative Development | The City of Stockholm |
| The Swedish Agency for Civil Emergency Planning (ÖCB) | The Federation of Private Enterprises (FR) |
| | The Federation of Swedish County Councils |
| **Business Companies** | Federation of Swedish Industries |
| ABB | Stockholm County Council (SLL) |
| AstraZeneca | Swedish Association of Local Authorities |
| ElectroluxCorporate | Swedish Bankers' Association |
| Ericsson Group | Swedish Employer's Confederation (SAF) |
| Karl-Åke Söderberg Konsult AB | The Swedish Institute of Authorised Public Accountants (FAR) |
| Scania | Svenska Kraftnät |
| Skanska | Svenska Revisorsamfundet (SRS) |
| Statoil | |

**Table 3.** The Y2K network of the Millennium Commission [13].

existence of a contingency plan. We did not check its contents.

## 2.2 Study of the Millennium Commission

The Millennium Commission was appointed by the Swedish Government in January 29, 1998, and dissolved on March 31, 2000. Their role was to constitute a common network for all Swedish organisations for mediating information and experience concerning the Y2K problem [23]. The Swedish organisations involved in this network were Swedish business companies, government authorities, county councils and municipalities. A list of some of them is presented in Table 3. The Millennium Commission did not record any statistics on the Y2K compliant organisations. After the millennium shift, however, they gathered statistics concerning the Y2K effects. These statistics were voluntary to report.

## 2.3 Credibility of Our Results

To the knowledge of the authors of this paper, there is no globally established evaluation model. When designing our evaluation model, we have tried to cover the most important issues necessary for making products/systems Y2K-compliant.

It is difficult to get a total insight into the companies' data. In this study, we rely on the answers of the individual professionals responsible for the Y2K projects. For us, this was the only way available to collect information from several companies. Some of the questions could not be answered for confidential reasons. This is then made evident in the results of our study.

Some of the answers given by the interviewees were very ambiguous. Hence they could be dubiously understood. We remedied this by contacting the interviewees for further clarification.

## 3 The State of Preparedness Level

In this section, we present the results of our study. In Section 3.1, we give our quantitative results. In Section 3.2, we present our qualitative assessment. Finally, in Section 3.3, we present the results of the Millennium Commission.

### 3.1 Data Survey Results

The quantitative results of our study are presented in Tables 4-9. The order of the tables approximately follows the order of our interview questionnaire presented in Table 2.

### 3.2 Results of the Qualitative Assessment

Regarding the qualitative assessment we have tried to find relations between the answers, to evaluate these answers with respect to the requirements stated in the current literature, and finally, to evaluate maturity of the organisations on the basis of the contents of these answers.

#### 3.2.1 Analysing the Answers

**Start Date.** "Money is not the issue, time is" [20, p. 18]. The later a Y2K conversion project starts, the smaller the chance for the organisations to emerge unscathed [8]. This situation is compounded by the fact that the later the job starts, the more staff will be required, and the more project will be delayed. The Brook's law definitely applies here [2]. Every new person on a project adds a number of communication links.

The Y2K problem was the largest collective maintenance project the software industry had ever faced [3, 20]. It was predicted that it might take several years to complete. Long-range preventive steps are highly uncommon in the software industry today [3, 10]. According to [3, 20], 1997 was probably the last year when larger companies, especially those in financial industry, could commence work on their Y2K compliance projects.

Most of the companies studied started attending to the Y2K problem earlier than this. One financial company Länsförsäkringar was exemplary in this case. They already started in 1994. Only ABB APR and Ericsson Group started in 1997. We think that it is still a reasonable point in time, however, at its latest possible. One bank (Svenska Handelsbanken) already paid attention to this problem in 1989. Since then, all newly developed systems were automatically assigned eight-digit dates.

**Planning.** The Y2K problem does not appear difficult but requires considerable planning. Prudent planning might help in decreasing the Y2K project costs [3]. Planning is also a pivotal prerequisite for performing basic software engineering and for managing software projects [4]. It has been predicted that many companies

| Company name | Number of employees | Type of Business | Total annual turnover/ annnual balance | |
|---|---|---|---|---|
| | | | SEC (milliard) | USD (milliard) |
| Swedbank | 11 700 | Service | 720,0 | 84,2 |
| SEB Group | 12 500 | Service | 689,7 | 80,7 |
| Svenska Handelsbanken | 8 500 | Service | 926.5 | 108.4 |
| Länsförsäkringar | 1 500 | Service | 160.0 | 18,7 |
| Trygg Hansa | 1 200 | Service | 5.0 | 0.585 |
| ABB APR | 1 300 | Product and Service | 2,4 | 0,281 |
| Ericsson Group | . 100 000 | Product and Service | 184.5 | 21,6 |
| FörsäkringsGirot | 21 | Service | 0,009 | 0.001 |

**Table 4.** Presentation of the companies.

1) $1=8.55 SEC on December 30, 1999, milliard (BrE), billion(AmE).

| Company name | Total Software system size | Age of Software systems (%) | | | | Made inventory |
|---|---|---|---|---|---|---|
| | | 0-10 | 11-20 | 21-30 | 31- | |
| Swedbank | 15 000 programs | - | - | 5 | 0 | Yes |
| SEB Group | 450 systems (35-40 000 programs) | - | - | - | - | Yes |
| Svenska Handelsbanken | 30 million LOC | 70 | 30 | 0 | 0 | Yes |
| Länsförsäkringar | 12-15 million LOC[1] | 50 | 50 | 0 | 0 | Yes |
| Trygg Hansa | 67 systems | 75 | 20 | 5 | 0 | Yes |
| ABB APR | * | 100 | 0 | 0 | 0 | Yes |
| Ericsson Group | 500 million LOC | 98 | 2 | 0 | 0 | Yes |
| FörsäkringsGirot | # | 100 | 0 | 0 | 0 | Yes |

**Table 5.** System portfolios.

1) concerns old Länsförsäkringar
#) 100 classes per system
*) Difficult to estimate / Not available / Confidential

| Company name | Start attending to the Y2K-problem | Y2K projekt plan | Contingency plan | Prioriti- sation | Necessity for triage |
|---|---|---|---|---|---|
| Swedbank | Autumn 1996 | Yes | Yes | Yes | No |
| SEB Group | Spring 1996 | Yes | Yes | Yes | No |
| Svenska Handelsbanken | Spring 1996 | Yes | Yes | Yes | No |
| Länsför- säkringar | Year shift 1994/95 | Yes | Yes | Yes | No |
| Trygg Hansa | Summer 1996 | Yes | Yes | Yes | No |
| ABB APR | Middle of 1997 | Yes | Yes | Yes | No |
| Ericsson Group | Autumn 1996 | Yes | Yes | Yes | No |
| Försäkrings- Girot | Autumn 1997 | Yes | No | No | No |

**Table 6.** Planning, prioritisation and necessity for triage.

| Company name | Attended all program | Attended to program (%) | Technique used (%) | Made all the tests required |
|---|---|---|---|---|
| Swedbank | Yes | 10 | -Windowing - 100 | Yes |
| SEB Group | Yes | 15 | -Windowing - 99 -Date expansion - 1 | Yes |
| Svenska Handelsbanken | Yes | Missing | -Windowing - 100 | Yes |
| Länsför- säkringar | Yes (own sw) No (purchased sw) | Missing | -Date expansion - 60 -Windowing - 40 | Yes |
| Trygg Hansa | Yes | 10 | -Windowing - 95 -Replacement - 5 | Yes |
| ABB APR | Yes | 12 (products) 15 (support pr.) | -Windowing - 100 | Yes |
| Ericsson Group | Yes | 50-75 | -Own algorithm -Windowing -Date expansion | Yes |
| Försäkrings- Girot | Yes | 100 | -Replacement - 100 | Yes |

**Table 7.** Results of the Y2K problem attendance.

| Company name | Planned costs (SEC) | Actual costs : monetary value (SEC) | Actual costs: man month | Lead time year,month | Cost per LOC | |
|---|---|---|---|---|---|---|
| | | | | | SEC | USD[1] |
| Swedbank | 200 million | Lower than 200 million | 770 | 3 y 4 m | - | - |
| SEB Group | 560 million | 560 million | - | 3 y | - | - |
| Svenska Handelsbanken | 190 million | 190 million | 1380 | 3 y 6 m | 6.34 | 0.74 |
| Länsförsäkringar | 160 million | 140 million | 570 | 4 y 6 m | 5.19[2] | 0.61[2] |
| Trygg Hansa | 30 million | 30 million | 120 | 2 y 9 m | - | - |
| ABB APR | Confidential | Confidential | Confidential | 2 y 3 m | - | - |
| Ericsson Group | 2900 million | 2700 million | 30 000 | 3 y 11 m | 5.80 | 0.68 |
| FörsäkringsGirot | 5.5 million | 5.5 million | 75 | 2 y 2 m | - | - |

**Table 8.** Planned and actual costs of the Y2K problem.

1) $1=8.55 SEC on December 30,
2) Concerns old Länsförsäkringar

| Company name | Millennium shift effects | | | Leap year effects | | |
|---|---|---|---|---|---|---|
| | Serious | Medium | Low | Serious | Medium | Low |
| Swedbank | none | none | minor | none | none | none |
| SEB Group | none | none | none | none | none | none |
| Svenska Handelsbanken | none | none | minor | none | none | minor |
| Länsförsäkringar | none | none | minor | none | none | none |
| Trygg Hansa | none | none | 5 | none | none | none |
| ABB APR | none | none | < 5 | none | none | none |
| Ericsson Group | none | none | minor | none | none | none |
| FörsäkringsGirot | none | none | none | none | none | 1 |

**Table 9.** Immediate impact of the Y2K problem.

might be forced out of business because of the ramifications of not planning for and dealing with the Y2K problem [20].

All the organisations studied have made a Y2K project plan in which the most important phases such as inventory, analysis, planning, coding, conversion, integration and testing, and quality assurance were included. One company FörsäkringsGirot has developed their system from scratch[2]. Hence, they followed the ordinary project planning.

**Inventory**. Inventory is a must when conducting the Y2K projects. It keeps the critical information on hand, identifies lost or invalid code, and helps in tracking update ripples to other linked programs. Inventory is the primary source for determining the state of the Y2K compliance within the organisation [20].

All the organisations studied have made an inventory of their systems. They have even included additional inventory items suspicious of containing six-digit date such as lifts, alarms, and the like.

**Percentage of Programs Affected**. According to [3, 19], 80-90% of all programs would be affected by the Y2K date change[3]. This does definitely not agree with the reality in our Swedish micro context (see Table 7). This could be explained with the fact that most of the programs of the organisations studied are young (less than 10 years old) (see Table 5). Half of the companies (Swedbank, SEB Group, Trygg Hansa, ABB APR) needed to attend to only 10-15% of software programs. Ericsson Group, on the other hand, had to attend to 50-75% of their programs. The remaining companies could not provide this piece of information. They simply did not know.

**Knowledge of Software Size**. Knowledge of size of software systems is pivotal for performing basic software engineering. Half of the organisations studied could specify the size of their software. Regarding the remaining companies, this piece of information was either confidential or not utilised at all.

**Y2K Project Costs**. The Y2K problem is a multi-million maintenance requirement to keep the business running. Across the whole spectrum of systems, the predicted cost per LOC ranged from $0.36 to $3.19 [18, 20].

As depicted in Table 8, the Y2K project has a high price tag. However, not as high as it was predicted by the software community. Some of the Swedish organisations studied ended with a price tag under one dollar a LOC.

When comparing the planned Y2K costs to the actual ones, we could see no difference. Some of the actual costs were even lower than the planned ones. This fact conflicts with all the statements stated in the current software engineering literature claiming that the budget of most software projects is notoriously exceeded. According to [11], the perfect match of the estimated and actual costs will rarely, if ever, be the case. Approximately 80% of all projects are delivered late and over budget [24].

The details on the planned and actual costs made us suspicious. To check their correctness, we contacted the companies studied to confirm their accuracy. We became reassured that these costs were correct.

**Lead Time**. The Y2K problem has an immovable deadline. Historically, software organisations are not disciplined enough to deliver projects on time and within budget [3, 24]. The companies studied claimed that their Y2K projects were completed before the millennium shift. Their lead time varied from 3 to 6 years (see Table 8).

**Techniques Chosen**. Two main techniques could be chosen such as windowing and/or date expansion [6, 12, 14]. As depicted in Table 7, the organisations studied have mainly chosen the windowing technique. Some companies have even chosen windowing in its entirety. For the most part, this is because the date expansion technique is too costly. Only three organisations (Ericsson Group, Länsförsäkringar and SEB Group) have used a date expansion technique. There were also cases when software systems were replaced by rebuilt software. Finally, for some products, Ericsson Group implemented their own algorithm.

**Prioritisation and Triage**. Due to the shortage of time, it has been recommended that organisations should prioritise their systems in order to start attending to the most critical ones, if need arises. The unpopular concept of triage[4] has also been suggested. One must first choose the systems worth saving.

All organisations except for FörsäkringsGirot have made the prioritisation of their systems. However, only ABB APR and Ericsson Group utilised this prioritisation for planning and controlling their Y2K work. The remaining organisations claimed that they did not have this need. For them, all their systems were evenly critical. As depicted in Table 6, triage was definitely not necessary for any of the organisation studied.

**Contingency Planning**. Many companies would experience the ramifications of the Y2K problem due to the delayed or partial solutions to this problem. Hence, contingency planning might partially remedy this [20].

---

[2] FörsäkringsGirot has only one system.

[3] The term "program" is associated with a block of source language statements compiled or assembled as a unit.

---

[4] Triage means that one chooses the most important systems for Year-2000 conversion. Triage also applies to deciding which outside suppliers and customers must be treated first.

The goal would be to control and tackle the immediate damage.

All organisations studied except for FörsäkringsGirot had a contingency plan for the millennium shift. ABB APR's and FörsäkringsGirot's contingency plan did not encompass the leap year for low risk probability reasons. The Ericsson Group's and ABB APR's contingency plan also encompassed supervision of subcontractors.

**Testing**. The systems have been proven compliant through a series of unit, integration, and system tests. Originally, we included regression testing in our questionnaire. Due to the confusion brought forth by the term "regression testing", we left out this question. We understood that this term was differently named and/or understood by the organisations studied. Therefore, we cannot guarantee whether regression testing took place.

**Other Measures**. Some companies such as ABB APR and Ericsson Group decreased the Y2K effort by offering alternative products to customers, for instance, later releases. This is also an efficient way of controlling damage caused by the Y2K problem.

All the organisations mainly used their own staff. In addition, most of them hired consultants. Ericsson Group was even forced to re-employ some of the retired software engineers to attend to some of the legacy systems.

**Y2K Immediate Effects**. As depicted in Table 9, the organisations studied have encountered minor problems. Most of them even claim that after the millennium shift the density of software problems was lower than the average problem density as it used to be at each year shift.

### 3.2.2 Maturity of the Organisations

In Section 3.2.1, we analysed the answers provided by our interviewees. There, we also discussed our maturity indicators. Summing up, we conclude that the maturity of the organisations studied to manage the Y2K problem was fairly good. We motivate this with the following:

- The organisations recognised the Y2K problem early enough. Hence, they managed to complete their Y2K projects in time.

- Planning of the Y2K project was satisfactory. The most important phases were recognised.

- Prioritisation has been made to tackle cases of emergency. Due to good planning and early commencement, triage was not necessary.

- All companies have made inventory necessary for planning, following/following-up of the Y2K project, and for the control of the ripple effects.

- All companies planned to meet the millennium shift by equipping themselves with emergency troops. In

other words, contingency planning has been conducted.

- Knowledge of the software size has not been possessed by all the organisations studied. Some organisations motivated this that it was impossible to measure software size in, for instance, lines of code. We leave this piece of evidence to the software community to judge.

- Planned costs for managing Y2K projects were estimated and compared to the actual ones. The preciseness of the planned costs has taken us aback. Should Swedish companies be better than the other ones? We feel that we would not like to draw any conclusions here. Just as with software size, we leave this piece of evidence to the software community to judge.

- All the necessary testing has been completed. We are not sure however, whether regression testing has been made.

- Finally, the Y2K effects with this preparedness level were not serious at all. They only resulted in minor nuisances.

### 3.3 Results of the Millennium Commission

According to the Millennium Commission, all the companies inherent in the network claimed that they were Y2K compliant.

| Type of organisation | Nr of reported organisations | Y2K immediate effects | | | Nr of reported organisations | Leap year immediate effects | | |
|---|---|---|---|---|---|---|---|---|
| | | Serious | Medium | Low | | Serious | Medium | Low |
| Swedish industry | 26 | 0 | 1 | 42 | 1 | 0 | 0 | 3 |
| Government authorities | 17 | 0 | 0 | 17 | 4 | 0 | 0 | 4 |
| County council | 17 | 0 | 1 | 48 | 3 | 0 | 0 | 6 |
| Munici- palities | 28 | 0 | 1 | 27 | 4 | 0 | 0 | 7 |

**Table 10.** The Y2K effects recorded by the Millennium Commission [13].

The Millennium Commission has collected information on the Y2K effects in a common data repository. Due to the fact that the reporting of the Y2K effects was voluntary, this repository covers the following:

- Data from 88 organisations directly reported after the millennium shift.

- Data from 12 organisations directly reported after the leap year.

These data are presented in Table 10. On their checking, we conclude that few organisations reported on the immediate Y2K effects. This is due to the fact that many organisations did not experience any major problems. Hence, they were of the opinion that reporting to the Millennium Commission was not worth the effort. All the problems reported to the Millennium Commission were of low severity.

## 4 Conclusions

The Y2K problem has become the largest collective maintenance project the computer industry has hitherto had to face. Though it has come to be regarded as complicated, expensive and very boring, companies should most definitely not neglect Y2K problems due to the risk of unwanted consequences arising, the seriousness of which may vary depending on factors such as:

- the level of business dependence on software systems

- the seriousness of the disruption level caused by the Y2K problem

- the degree of preventive measures taken to address the Y2K problem.

Analysts predicted that the Y2K problem would have an impact on most, if not all the organisations in the world [5, 8, 16]. The only problem with these predictions was that the magnitudes of the impacts were unknown. Forecasts varied from minor business disruptions causing annoyance more than anything else, up to major disruptions resulting in business crashes on both a national and international level [3, 5, 8, 19, 20]. The consequences of disruptions would not necessarily be immediate but may even appear long after entry into the new millennium. According to Chikofsky [5], it could take up to ten to twelve years to be sure that the Y2K would not cause problems.

This paper has attempted to establish the level of preparedness within a number of Swedish companies to meet the new millennium and the immediate post-millennium effects. On the basis of the data collected, we conclude that the companies studied here have been sufficiently proactive with respect to the Y2K problem. The basic requirements for Y2K conversion have been fulfilled correctly. The companies studied also claimed to be well equipped to handle the eight-digit date and encountered few problems. Those that were encountered were of low severity.

To achieve a more precise evaluation of the Y2K impact, one should ideally have access to an organisation's reference basis indicating the average level of disturbance encountered daily. Some of the organisations studied claimed that the disturbance level after the turn of the millennium was actually lower than average. As the study did not have access to any of the reference bases, this statement can unfortunately neither be confirmed nor denied.

The only technique that completely remedies the Y2K problem is the data expansion technique. However very few organisations (including those in our spot testing and those who were the members of the Millennium Commission) have adopted it. Most of the organisations appear to have chosen the windowing technique. In many cases the time factor has been a decisive in choosing a technique. Using the windowing method however doesn't completely solve the Y2K problem, but merely postpones the conversion work. Organisations who have chosen this method must continue to convert their systems for a number of years. As a result, these organisations cannot claim to have fully completed their management of the Y2K problem; on the contrary, they have prolonged it.

Addressing the Y2K problem has not only led to unwelcome costs, it has also contributed to substantial indirect returns. The organisations studied here look upon their Y2K work as an investment in the future. The Y2K project provides companies with an opportunity to look constructively at all aspects of their organisations. It has contributed to growing organisational-awareness, through massive education and participation at all levels of organisations. The Y2K problem forced the organisations studied to revise their entire asset inventory including software and hardware products, personnel and other resources, contractors and customers.

The inventory of software products has helped the organisations in the study to identify and remove redundant, duplicated and/or dead code. This removal will definitely save future resources. The inventory of customers has also led to benefits for the Ericsson Group and ABB APR for example, who have now improved knowledge about their customers (the Ericsson Group now possesses knowledge about all their customers, even those in Siberia). This in turn expands business opportunities and improves customer relations in the future. The inventory of contractors has in some cases led to negative effects for the contractors. The Ericsson Group has for instance lost confidence in some of its contractors who have not managed to become Y2K compliant.

In addition to the above, the Y2K project has contributed to the modernisation of computer systems, a growing awareness of the importance of order and discipline, and higher staff qualifications.

## 5 Epilogue

Can the software community be exonerated for making such a loud racket about the Y2K problem? With the benefit of hindsight, perhaps yes. Too many millennium moaners went to town predicting doom, but at least the whole planet was spurred into action in time.

But was all the effort imperative? Well, in some ways yes. By raising a sizeable armament, Sweden has hitherto succeeded in defending its sovereignty against the Y2K's aggressor, and the war damage was insignificant. However what we don't know, is what would have happened otherwise. One will probably never know.

Are there any gains to be harvested yet? One significant gain is that the organisations studied claim that they succeeded avoiding many of the problems associated with the millennium shift. However it is still probably too early to harvest any gains. The real damage might not have surfaced yet [5] and only time will tell. To date some comfort can be found in the old adage *"Prevention is better than cure"*.

## Acknowledgements

We would like to thank all the Swedish industrial representatives who have helped us to conduct this study. They were the following:

- Lennart Flyrén and Peter Wilkens from Swedbank
- Bo Strage from Svenska Handelsbanken
- Cajsa Renman and Gunnar Bjerin from SEB Group
- Christer Baldhagen and Hans Johansson from Länsförsäkringar
- Egon Svantesson from Trygg Hansa.
- Lennart Nilsson (support products) and Roland Revesjö (business mission products) from ABB Automation Products AB
- Jorma Mobrin och Christer Ekengren from Ericsson Group
- Jonas Granström from FörsäkringsGirot

## References

[1] Boehm, B., W., Software Engineering Economics, Prentice-Hall, 1981.

[2] Brooks, F., The Mythical Man Month. Reading MA: Addison-Wesley, 1975.

[3] Butler, J., The Year 2000 Crisis: Developing a Successful Plan for Information Systems, Computer Technology Research Corp., 1997.

[4] Carnegie Mellon University, Software Engineering Institute, The Capability Maturity Model: Guidelines for Improving the Software Process, Addison-Wesley, 1994.

[5] Chikofsky, E., T Minus 10 and Counting, Editor's Message, IEEE Software, November, 1989, p. 8.

[6] Gothard, W., Rodner, L., Strategies for Solving the Y2K Problem, Dr. Dobb's Journal, May 1998, pp. 26-32.

[7] IEEE Standard For Year 2000 Terminology, Std. 2000.1-1998.

[8] deJager, P., Doomsday, Computer World, September 6, 1993, www.basiccomputer.com/doomsday.html.

[9] deJager, P., Bergeon, R., Managing 00, John Wiley & Sons, Inc., 1997.

[10] Kajko-Mattsson, Mira, Preventive Maintenance! Do We Know What It Is?, Proceedings, International Conference on Software Maintenance, San Jose, Oct 2000.

[11] Kemerer, D., L., An Empirical Validation of Software Cost Estimation Models, Communications of ACM, May 1987, No. 5.

[12] Martin, R., A., Dealing with Dates: Solutions for the Year 2000, Computer, March 1997, pp. 44-51.

[13] The Millennium Commission, www.2000-delegationen.gov.se/foretag/ index3.html.

[14] Moore, R., L., Foley, D., G., Date Compression and Year 2000 Challenges, Dr. Dobb's Journal, May 1998, pp. 20-23.

[15] Mosley, D., J, The Handbook of MIS Application Software Testing, Yourdon Press, 1993.

[16] Nearing the Year 2000 : Will Information Managers Be Celebrating?, www.med.virginia.edu/ hlibrary/ newsletter/1996/october/2000.html.

[17] Park, R., E., Software Size Measurement: A Framework for Counting Source Statements, Technical Report, CMU/SEI-92-TR-20, September 1992.

[18] Putnam, L. H., Myers, W., Year 2000 Work Comes Down to the Wire, IEEE Software, Vol. 16, 1999.

[19] Ragland, B., The Year 2000 Problem Solver: A Five-Step Disaster Prevention Plan, McGraw-Hill, 1997.

[20] Shakespeare, N., Year 2000 in a Nutshell, O'Reilly & Associates, Inc., 1998.

[21] Shawn, A., B., Backman, T., Chikofsky, E., de Jager, P., Zvegnitzov, N., Examining Year 2000 Date Challenges from the Maintenance Perspective, Proceedings for International Conference on Software Maintenance, 1996, pp. 126-128.

[22] Sommerville, I., Software Engineering, Addison-Wesley, 1996.

[23] Slutrapport Från 2000-Delegationen, 2000-Säkringen I Sverige, Myt Och Verklighet, SOU 2000:24, Nordstedts Tryckeri AB, Stockholm 2000, ISBN 91-39-21169-6 (In Swedish and English).

[24]    Thomson, B., The New Millennium: A Turning Point?, Computer Software and Applications Conference, 1998, COMPSAC 1998. Proceedings. The Twenty-Second Annual International, p. 524.

[25]    Zvegintzov, N., The Year 2000 as Racket and Ruse, www.westergaard.com:8080/nicholas9704.html.

# Notes

# *Program Analysis*

# C/C++ Conditional Compilation Analysis Using Symbolic Execution

Ying Hu[1], Ettore Merlo[1], Michel Dagenais[1], and Bruno Lagüe[2]

[1]Department of Electrical and Computer Engineering, École Polytechnique de Montréal,
P.O. Box 6079, Downtown Station, Montreal, Quebec, H3C 3A7, Canada
e-mail: huying@casi.polymtl.ca {ettore.merlo,michel.dagenais}@polymtl.ca

[2]Bell Canada, Quality Engineering and Research Group
1050 Beaver Hall, 2nd floor, Montreal, Quebec, H2Z 1S4, Canada

## Abstract

*Conditional compilation is one of the most powerful parts of a C/C++ environment available for building software for different platforms with different feature sets. Although conditional compilation is powerful, it can be difficult to understand and is error prone. In large software systems, file inclusion, conditional compilation and macro substitution are closely related and are often largely interleaved. Without adequate tools, understanding complex header files is a tedious task. This practice may even be complicated as the hierarchies of header files grow with projects. This paper presents our experiences of studying conditional compilation based on symbolic execution of preprocessing directives. Our two concrete goals are: for any given preprocessor directive or C/C++ source code line, finding the simplest sufficient condition to reach/compile it, and finding the full condition to reach/compile that code line. Two different strategies were used to achieve these two goals. A series of experiments conducted on the Linux kernel are presented.*

## 1. Introduction

Software analysis plays an important part of every software development or maintenance project. Preprocessing is the first phase of translation in compiling a program. The C preprocessor provides five separate facilities: defining symbolic constants, inclusion of header files, macro expansion, conditional compilation, and line control, of which conditional compilation is considered as one of the most powerful parts of a C environment available for writing code that is to run on different target systems [7]. Conditional compilation is not restricted to C and C++; its use in other languages such as FORTRAN and COBOL has increased to the point where new standards have been proposed which include conditional compilation [1, 2]. Furthermore, the power of this technique has resulted in published examples of using conditional selection in Ada and Java programs, and has prompted some Pascal and BASIC compiler vendors to retrofit conditional compilation capabilities into their products [5, 12]. Conditional compilation is a flexible code development tool which has many uses including dealing with hardware and software differences, binding features, excluding debug code, safeguarding against multiple header file inclusion, and temporarily omitting code. Although conditional compilation is powerful, it can be difficult to understand and is error prone. Conditional compilation programming errors are easy to make and difficult to detect, mainly because the preprocessor diagnostics are poor. Many errors go undetected until multiple developers attempt to integrate their code, and find that it does not compile, link or execute correctly. Conditional compilation errors can often be difficult to track down because they are hidden, and require analyzing the preprocessor output for clues as to what has gone wrong. In large software systems, file inclusion, conditional compilation and macro substitution are closely related and are often largely interleaved. This may result in overly complex code, hindering program comprehension.

There are many problems associated with the use of C preprocessor and different authors have described some of them, usually from a specific or pragmatic point of view [3, 4, 9, 10, 13]. Many of the problems discussed can be attributed to the lack of programming tools associated with manipulating and managing compilation condition. Other than the preprocessor itself, many programming tools are not able to keep track of the individual threads of compilation and screen out sections of code that aren't being compiled.

The objective of our project is to develop the ability to analyze the conditional compilation of header files. Our analysis of conditional compilation is emphasized on extraction of compilation conditions, which is helpful for programmer to reuse the code. The presented approach is based on symbolic execution of preprocessing directives. Our two concrete goals are: 1) for any given preprocessor directive or C/C++ source code line, quickly finding one sufficient condition to reach/compile it; 2) finding the full condition to reach/compile that code line. Two different strategies were used to achieve these two goals.

## 2. Symbolic Execution

Symbolic execution, sometimes referred to as symbolic evaluation, differs from the traditional sense of executing a program. The traditional notion of execution requires that a selection of paths through the program is exercised by a set of test cases. In symbolic execution, actual data values are replaced by symbolic values. Traditional program execution uses inputs consisting of actual values. Symbolic execution, on the other hand, produces a set of expressions, one expression per output variable [16].

The most common approach to symbolic execution is to perform an analysis of the program, resulting in the creation of a flow graph, which is a directed graph containing decision points and the assignments associated with each branch. By traversing the flow graph from an entry point along a particular path, a list of assignment statements and branch predicates is produced.

The resulting path is represented by a series of input variables, condition predicates and assignment statements. The execution part of the approach takes place by following the path from top to bottom. During this path traversal, each output variable is given a symbol in place of an actual value. Thereafter, each assignment statement is evaluated so that it is expressed in terms of symbolic values of input variables and constants.

At the end of the symbolic execution of a path, the output variable will be represented by expressions in terms of symbolic values of input variables and constants. The output expressions will be subject to constraints. A list of these constraints is provided by the set of symbolic representations of each condition predicate along the path. Analysis of these constraints may indicate that the path is not executable due to a contradiction. This infeasibility problem is encountered in

### Table 1. Preprocessor directives

| #assert | #cpu | #define | #elif |
|---|---|---|---|
| #else | #error | #ident | #if |
| #ifdef | #ifndef | #import | #include |
| #include_next | #line | #machine | #pragma |
| #pragma once | #system | #unassert | #undef |
| #warning | | | |

### Table 2. ANSI C Conditional Compilation Directives

| directive | code is selected under condition |
|---|---|
| #ifdef VARIABLE | VARIABLE is defined |
| #ifndef VARIABLE | VARIABLE is not defined |
| #if EXPRESSION | EXPRESSION non-zero |
| #elif EXPRESSION | EXPRESSION non-zero |
| #else | matching #ifdef, #ifndef, #if statement is not selected |
| #endif | end of conditional compilation |

all forms of path testing.

Partition analysis uses symbolic execution to identify subdomains of the input data domain. Symbolic execution is performed on both the software and the specification. The path conditions are used to produce the subdomains, such that each subdomain is treated identically by both the program and the specification. Where a part of the input domain cannot be allocated to such a subdomain then either a structural or functional (program or specification) fault has been discovered. Symbolic evaluation occupies a middle ground between testing data and program proving.

Symbolic execution can be applied to preprocessing directives to achieve the analysis of conditional compilation. Most preprocessor features are active when enabled explicitly using preprocessing directives. Preprocessing directives are lines in programs that start with '#'. The '#' is followed by an identifier that is the directive name. Table 1 lists preprocessing directives. ANSI C supports six different conditional compilation directives, which are described in Table 2. Conditional compilation directives test for the existence or values of preprocessor symbolic constants. By changing the definition of the preprocessor variables in conditional directives, one can change the way the code is preprocessed. The control flow of the preprocessor directives is similar to but simpler than the one of ordinary programming language. There are macro definitions similar to assignment statements, file inclusions similar to function call statements, conditional directives similar

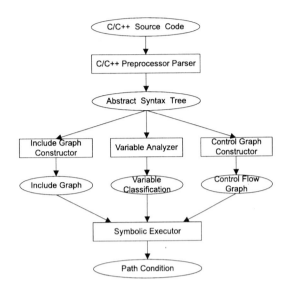

**Figure 1. System architecture of the tool**

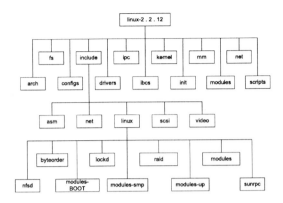

**Figure 2. Directory structure of linux-2.2.12**

to the branch statements, but there is no analogue to loop statements. Furthermore, variables in preprocessor are all global. The basic idea of symbolic execution on preprocessor directives is described in the following example. In executing the code :

```
#ifdef __KERNEL__
code   segment   1
#else
code   segment   2
#endif
```

When __KERNEL__ is either defined or undefined in the execution path, the program splits into two paths, one in which "defined __KERNEL__" is asserted and code segment 1 is executed, and the other in which "! defined __KERNEL__" is asserted, and code segment 2 is executed. If __KERNEL__ is defined, only code segment 1 is chosen to be executed; if __KERNEL__ is undefined, only code segment 2 is chosen to be executed. Symbolic execution represents many different executions.

Effective use of symbolic values requires a capability for the simplification of symbolic expressions, and support for splitting a single execution path into multiple paths when symbolic boolean values are encountered in the conditional statements.

## 3. Tool Design

The system architecture of our tool is shown in figure 1.

The analysis starts by abstracting the source code into an Abstract Syntax Tree (AST). The AST is a

tree-based representation of the tokens contained in the source code. It provides an exact representation of the source code. A JavaCC grammar for the preprocessor was written. Then JJtree was used to build the Abstract Syntax Tree. Finally, JavaCC(Java Compiler Compiler) was used to automatically generate the C/C++ preprocessor parser.

The Abstract Syntax Tree is used to extract control flow, file include hierarchy, and preprocessor variable information for further analysis. An include hierarchy extractor, a preprocessor identifier analyzer, and a control flow graph constructor were implemented.

The next step is to do the symbolic execution along the control flow graph of each compilation unit, and analyze the obtained condition constraints.

## 4. Experimental Results

We have applied our tool to some real software systems. Experiments were conducted on a Pentium III 500MHz with 512MB RAM running Linux.

Here the Linux kernel was chosen as a case study, since it is a large well constructed and widely used system. System header files are in directory linux-2.2.12/include, as shown in figure 2. System header files declare the interfaces to parts of the operating system. Programmers include these to supply the definitions and declarations to invoke system calls and other library functions.

### 4.1. Include hierarchy Graph

Files refer to each other by means of file inclusions. Their relative order is relevant. The presence of numerous conditional directives makes the structure almost impossible to follow. The graphical views provide users with helpful structural information that is

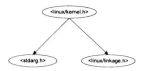

**Figure 3. Include hierarchy of file <linux/kernel.h>**

```
#define BUFSIZE 1020
#define TABLESIZE BUFSIZE
#if TABLESIZE>1024
  cpp context
#endif
```

**Figure 4. Macro identifier indirectly used by conditional directive**

```
1   #ifndef _LINUX_CONFIG_H
2   #define _LINUX_CONFIG_H
3   #include <linux/autoconf.h>
    #endif
```

**Figure 5. Use pattern of preprocessor variable as safe guarder**

usually hidden in the program text. Include directives are analogous to function calls in an ordinary program, and an include hierarchy graph is analogous to a function call graph. The graph simply contains one node for each file that composes the system, and an oriented arc$(f_i, f_j)$ is created when file $f_i$ includes file $f_j$. At the bottom of the graph , one finds low level files that do not include any other files. At the top of the graph, one finds the file that needs to be analyzed. At this stage, the file include graph reflects all file dependencies, and the potential impact of conditional compilation statements (that is #if #ifndef, and #ifdef, etc) are not taken into account. The following information can be provided by such include hierarchy graph: how large the analyzed system is, what header files are involved. The include hierarchy graph stores the index of the files needed to be analyzed further.    Here is an example. Figure 3 shows the obtained include hierarchy graph of file <linux/kernel.h> in linux-2.2.10. There are only three nodes in this graph. The top node is file <linux/kernel.h> itself. From this include hierarchy graph, one knows that <linux/kernel.h> may include <linux/linkage.h> and/or <stdarg.h>, but <linux/linkage.h> and <stdarg.h> do not include any other file. When one analyzes <linux/kernel.h>, only these three files need to be considered.

## 4.2. Preprocessor Identifier Analysis

Conditionals are useful in connection with macros or assertions, because those are the only ways that an expression's value can vary from one compilation to another. A macro is a sort of abbreviation which you can define once and then use later. Each macro has an identifier as name and an associated text string as body. Macros are created using the #define preprocessor directive in C source files or in the header files, or as an option on the compiler command line. When a macro identifier is used in a program, it is replaced with the macro body during preprocessing. Macros may also be undefined, using preprocessor directive #undef.

Macros may be used as:

- constant definition (simple macros)

- function definition (argument macros)

- conditional compilation

In the study of conditional compilation, macros which only serve as constant definition or function definition are not so important, since they will not effect the control flow of compilation. The most important are those macros which appear in the conditional preprocessing directives. These macro identifiers are called preprocessor variables. Another important type of macros are those indirectly used by conditional compilation; an example is shown in figure 4.

Although BUFSIZE does not appear in a conditional directive, it appears in the body of a macro which is used by conditional directives. BUFSIZE is called an indirect preprocessor variable. Also, if a macro identifier occurs in the body of another indirect preprocessor variable (macro), it is an indirect preprocessor variable.

Preprocessor variables have many uses, one of which is as file inclusion guarder. Very often, one header file includes another. It can easily result that a certain header file is included more than once. This may lead to errors, if the header file defines structure types or typedefs, and is certainly wasteful. Therefore, programmers often wish to prevent multiple inclusion of a header file. To prevent the content of an include file from being included twice, the header file is wrapped with conditional logic to test for a previous inclusion.

The standard way to do this is to enclose the entire content of the file in a conditional, like in figure 5.

Variable _LINUX_CONFIG_H indicates that the file has been included once already. When this file is scanned for the first time by the preprocessor, symbol

## Table 3. Statistics of the preprocessor identifier

| measure | linux-2.2.12 | linux-2.2.3 |
|---|---|---|
| $NumIdentifier$ | 19486 | 25718 |
| $NumPPVariable$ | 957 | 1714 |
| $NumIPPVariable$ | 106 | 407 |
| $NumGuard$ | 519 | 1126 |

_LINUX_CONFIG_H is not yet defined. The #ifndef condition succeeds and #include directive is scanned. In addition, symbol _LINUX_CONFIG_H is defined.

When this file is scanned for a second time during the same compilation, symbol _LINUX_CONFIG_H is defined. All information between the #ifndef and #endif directives is skipped.

Symbol name _LINUX_CONFIG_H serves in this context only for recognition purposes. Preprocessor variable _LINUX_CONFIG_H is called a safe guarder. To extract such usage of preprocessor variables, a Pattern Extractor was implemented. By comparing the terminal and nonterminal, one can identify the use of safe guarder pattern. Usually, the preprocessor variables used as safe guarder are not defined at the beginning of the compilation.

Table 3 presents statistics about preprocessor identifiers in linux-2.2.12 kernel and linux-2.2.3 kernel.

The metrics displayed are:

- $NumIdentifier$: number of macro identifiers.

- $NumPPVariable$: number of macro identifiers used in conditional directives.

- $NumIPPVariable$: number of macro identifiers which may be indirectly used in conditional directives.

- $NumGuard$: number of macro identifiers used as safe guarders of multiple inclusion.

From Table 3, one can see that: 5% of macro identifiers in linux-2.2.12 are directly or indirectly used in conditional compilation, 50% of which are safe guarders, which are supposed to be not defined at the beginning. The classification of macro identifiers is very important, it can be used to reduce the variable space of the symbolic execution phase.

### 4.3. Control Flow Graph

A control flow graph (CFG) consists of nodes, which represent single entry, single exit, regions of executable

```
1   #ifndef  _LINUX_CONFIG_H
2   #define  _LINUX_CONFIG_H
3   #include  <linux/autoconf.h>
4   #ifndef UTS_SYSNAME
5   #define  UTS_SYSNAME  "Linux"
    #endif
6   #ifndef UTS_MACHINE
7   #define  UTS_MACHINE  "unknown"
    #endif
8   #ifndef UTS_NODENAME
9   #define  UTS_NODENAME  "(none)"
    #endif
10  #ifndef UTS_DOMAINNAME
11  #define  UTS_DOMAINNAME  "(none)"
    #endif
12  #define  DEF_INITSEG  0x9000
13  #define  DEF_SYSSEG  0x1000
14  #define  DEF_SETUPSEG  0x9020
15  #define  DEF_SYSSIZE  0x7F00
16  #define  NORMAL_VGA  0xffff
17  #define  EXTENDED_VGA  0xfffe
18  #define  ASK_VGA  0xfffd
    #endif
```

**Figure 6. Source code of <linux/config.h>**

code and edges which represent possible execution branches between code regions. In this project, we focus on the preprocessor directives. CFG for preprocessing directives provides a graphic illustration of the use and complexity of conditional compilation in a program.

First, a complete control flow graph was generated for the source code. For each preprocessor directive there is one corresponding CFG node constructed. Also, each non-directive code line is kept as a CFG node for further analysis. Figure 6 lists the the code of <linux/config.h> in $linux - 2.2.3$ with node numbers printed. Figure 7 (a) is the corresponding graphical representation.

As we know, to be portable to different compilers and programming tools, the conditional directives should be left-justified, that is the "#" character must be in the first column followed immediately by the conditional directive, as shown in figure 6. This makes it to be difficult to read and understand. Control flow graphs help programmers see nested structures and relate blocks of code to the associated control statements.

The complete control flow graph of preprocessor directives keeps all the information of the code, which is far more than what we need to do conditional compilation analysis. This dramatically reduces the perfor-

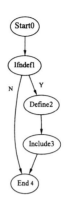

Figure 8. Control flow graph of file <linux/config.h> in linux-2.2.10, the complete one and reduced one are the same

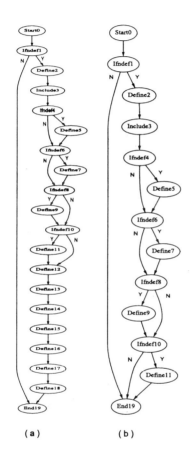

(a)            (b)

Figure 7. (a) Complete control flow graph of file <linux/config.h> in linux-2.2.3, (b)Reduced control flow graph of file <linux/config.h> in linux-2.2.3

mance of the analysis procedure. In some situations, for example in analyzing code with presence of file inclusion, a reduced control flow graph may be sufficient for the included file. However, the complete control flow graph need to be reduced, sufficiently and safely. Here are the rules:

- All the control flow nodes, except macro definitions (#define, #undef), file inclusions (#include) and conditional directives (#if, #ifdef, #ifndef, #elif), can be safely removed.

- Macro definition node (#define, #undef), if the macro identifier is neither a preprocessor variable nor an indirect preprocessor variable, can be safely removed.

- Conditional node (#if, #ifdef, #ifndef, #elif), if neither branch contains other nodes, can be safely removed.

- Include nodes should never be removed.

Figure 7 (b) is the reduced control flow graph for file <linux/config.h> in linux-2.2.3.

It is worth noting that, in some cases, the reduced one is exactly the same as the complete control flow graph, e.g. header file <linux/config.h> in linux-2.2.12, with control flow graph shown in figure 8, corresponding code listed in figure 5. Usually, these files are not complicated, with fewer nodes and fewer branch points.

In some cases, the benefits are significant. The reduced graph is much smaller compared to the complete one, as in header file <linux/linkage.h>. The complete control flow graph is shown in figure 9. There are 30

201

nodes, and 7 branch points, deeply nested. In the reduced control flow graph (figure 10), four nodes and only one branch point are left.

## 4.4. Symbolic execution of preprocessing directives

The symbolic executor traverses the CFG nodes stored in the node stack. Every node has a related macro constant table and a current condition constraint attached. The node stack is initialized with the start node of the tested CFG. Symbolic execution proceeds on each node popped from the node stack, constantly updating the modifications made to the tested unit's macro table, and decorating the corresponding path with the appropriate constraints encountered at branching points along the paths, expanding the node stack with the next possible node in the CFG according to the path selector.

Symbolic execution is time consuming. To improve the performance of the symbolic execution, the following procedures are performed before the symbolic execution phase.

- Finding include hierarchy for the tested file.

- Identifying the preprocessor identifiers directly or indirectly used in the conditional directives for each file in the include hierarchy.

- Extracting the preprocessor variables served as safe guarders for each file in the include hierarchy.

- Undefining safe guarders at the beginning of the symbolic execution.

- Constructing the complete control flow graph for each file in the include hierarchy.

- Constructing the reduced control flow graph for each file in the include hierarchy, according to the classification of the preprocessor identifiers.

Our two goals are: 1) for any given preprocessor directive line or C/C++ source code line, quickly finding one sufficient condition to reach/compile it; 2) finding the full condition to reach/compile that code line. To achieve these two goals, two strategies have been chosen, one is to find the shortest path to any given node by breadth-first expansion, the other is to find all possible conditions to a given node by depth-first expansion. Here <linux/kernel.h> of linux-2.2.12 was chosen as an example. The include hierarchy of <linux/kernel.h> was shown in figure 3.

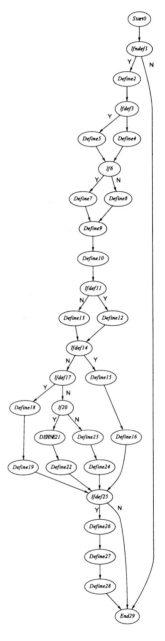

**Figure 9. Complete control flow graph of file <linux/linkage.h> in linux-2.2.10**

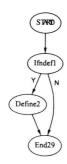

**Figure 10. Reduced control flow graph of file <linux/linkage.h> in linux-2.2.10**

## Shortest path to a given node

To find the shortest path to a given node, the output is sensitive to each execution step, thus the complete control flow information is required. With this strategy, complete control flow graphs are used for all the files in the include hierarchy. Two examples are given below.

Experiment 1: Finding the condition for the first path from the starting node of <linux/kernel.h> to the 5th node of <linux/kernel.h>.
code:        #include   <linux/linkage.h>
path condition obtained is:
        defined    $\alpha_1$
Symbol variable and corresponding preprocessor variable are:
        $\alpha_1$   $\equiv$   __KERNEL__

Experiment 2: Finding the shortest path to the 18th node of $< linux/linkage.h >$.
code:        $\#define$ __ALIGN__ .align 4
path condition obtained is:

$$defined\ \alpha_8\ \&\&\ !\ defined\ \alpha_7\ \&\&\ !\ defined\ \alpha_6$$
$$\&\&\ !\ (defined\ \ \alpha_3\ \&\&\ (\alpha_4 > 2 || \alpha_5 > 7))$$
$$\&\&\ !\ defined\ \alpha_2\ \&\&\ defined\ \ \alpha_1$$

symbol value table:

$\alpha_1$ $\equiv$ __KERNEL__
$\alpha_2$ $\equiv$ __cplusplus
$\alpha_3$ $\equiv$ __i386__
$\alpha_4$ $\equiv$ __GNUC__
$\alpha_5$ $\equiv$ __GNUC_MINOR__
$\alpha_6$ $\equiv$ __STDC__
$\alpha_7$ $\equiv$ __arm__
$\alpha_8$ $\equiv$ __mc68000__

The resulting condition of shortest path strategy is a boolean and-expression with symbolic values, each sub-expression is a constraint. The following metrics are very important to the analysis of constraints, since they are critical to the boolean satisfiability problem solving.

- *NumConstraint*: Number of constraints (sub-expressions) in one path condition.

- *NumSymbol*: Number of different symbols in one path condition.

Figure 11 gives the statistics of number of constraints in shortest path condition for all 90 nodes in file <linux/kernel.h> and its two possibly included files. The average number of constraints per path condition is 4.44. Figure 11 gives the statistics of symbols in shortest path condition. The total CPU time for finding the shortest path to each of these 90 nodes is 3.46s.

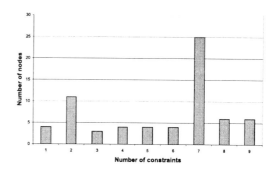

**Figure 11. Statistic of constraints in shortest path condition for kernel.h**

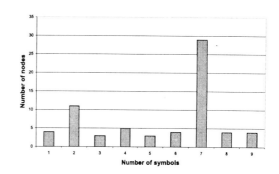

**Figure 12. Statistic of symbols in shortest path condition for kernel.h**

Another two metrics that are also very interesting to programmers are:

- *NumIfBranch*: Number of if-branches (#if,#ifdef,#ifndef) encountered along the shortest path.

- *NumIncludeDirective*: Number of include directives (#include) encountered along the shortest path.

Metric *NumIfBranch* differs from metric *NumConstraint*. In symbolic execution, once one encountering a conditional directive, if the predicate is true after evaluating, it will not contribute to the path condition expression; only if the predicate is undecided, it will become a sub-expression of the current and-expression. Thus metric *NumIfBranch* is always not less than metric *NumConstraint*. The counting of *NumIncludeDirective* does not exclude multiple inclusion of the same file, the prevention of multiple inclusion is implemented by using safe guarder.

Next, experiments were conducted on all the header files under directory linux-2.2.12/include/linux. For each file $f_i$, one can get the set of all the files it may directly or indirectly include: $S_i = \{f_j\}$. For each file $f_j \in S_i$, there is a node set (preprocessor directive line and/or C/C++ ordinary code) associated: $N_j = \{n_k\}$. Totally, for each $f_i$, there are a set of nodes $NC_i = \sum_{f_j} N_j$ associated. The experiments were performed in the following procedures: First, for each file $f_i$, for every node in its corresponding closure set $NC_i$, the shortest path strategy was used to find one sufficient condition to this node, which consists in a path condition set $PC_i$. Then, for each path condition in $PC_i$, metrics *NumConstraint*, *NumSymbol*, *NumIfBranch* and *NumIncludeDirective* were calculated. Finally, for each file, the maximum value and the average value of these four metrics were computed, and the distributions were drawn in figures.

Figure 13 and figure 14 give distributions of maximum and average value of these four metrics for individual files under directory linux-2.2.12/include/linux. Each square represents a file, with its vertical coordinate giving the value of corresponding metric.

**Full condition to a given node**

To find full condition to a given node, we use depth-first-search strategy. Each executing step itself is not important, but the final condition is what is needed. For the file which the target node belongs to, the complete control flow graph is used. But for all the other files in the include hierarchy graph, the complete control flow graph is not necessary, a reduced one is suffi-

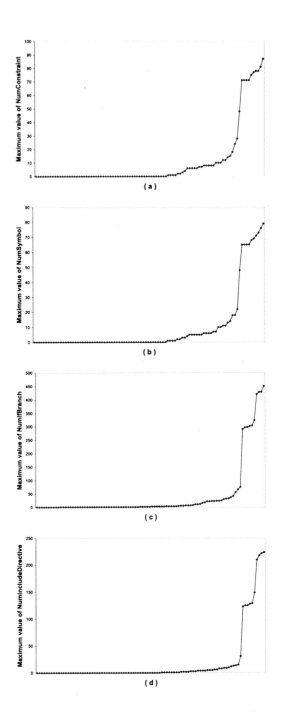

**Figure 13. Distributions of maximum values of four metrics for individual files, sorted by increasing metrics values**

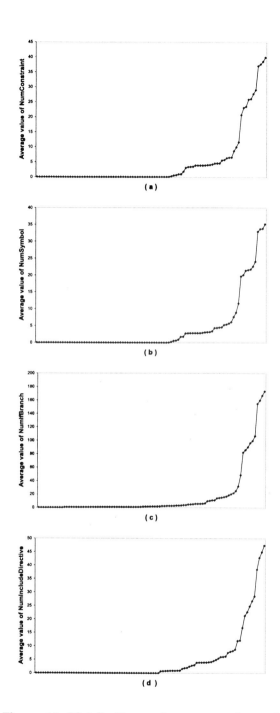

**Figure 14. Distributions of average values of four metrics for individual files, sorted by increasing metrics values**

cient.

Experiment 1: Finding the path condition to code:
 #define FASTCALL ( x ) x
which is the 25th node of $< linux/kernel.h >$.
path condition :
 ! defined $\alpha_2$ && defined $\alpha_1$
symbol value table:
 $\alpha_1 \equiv$ __KERNEL__
 $\alpha_2 \equiv$ __i386__
The condition is in its simplest form, so it does not need to be further simplified.

Experiment 2: Finding the the path condition to
 #define __ALIGN .align 4
which is the 18th node of <linux/linkage.h>.
path condition :

( defined $\alpha_8$ && ! defined $\alpha_7$ && ! defined $\alpha_6$
&& ! (defined $\alpha_3$ && ($\alpha_4 > 2 || \alpha_5 > 7$))
&& ! defined $\alpha_2$ && defined $\alpha_1$ )
||
( defined $\alpha_8$ && ! defined $\alpha_7$ && defined $\alpha_6$
&& ! (defined $\alpha_3$ && ($\alpha_4 > 2 || \alpha_5 > 7$))
&& ! defined $\alpha_2$ && defined $\alpha_1$ )
||
( defined $\alpha_8$ && ! defined $\alpha_7$ && ! defined $\alpha_6$
&& (defined $\alpha_3$ && ($\alpha_4 > 2 || \alpha_5 > 7$))
&& ! defined $\alpha_2$ && defined $\alpha_1$ )
||
( defined $\alpha_8$ && ! defined $\alpha_7$ && ! defined $\alpha_6$
&& ! (defined $\alpha_3$ && ($\alpha_4 > 2 || \alpha_5 > 7$))
&& ! defined $\alpha_2$ && defined $\alpha_1$ )
||
( defined $\alpha_8$ && ! defined $\alpha_7$ && defined $\alpha_6$
&& (defined $\alpha_3$ && ($\alpha_4 > 2 || \alpha_5 > 7$))
&& ! defined $\alpha_2$ && defined $\alpha_1$ )
||
( defined $\alpha_8$ && ! defined $\alpha_7$ && defined $\alpha_6$
&& ! (defined $\alpha_3$ && ($\alpha_4 > 2 || \alpha_5 > 7$))
&& defined $\alpha_2$ && defined $\alpha_1$ )
||
( defined $\alpha_8$ && ! defined $\alpha_7$ && ! defined $\alpha_6$
&& (defined $\alpha_3$ && ($\alpha_4 > 2 || \alpha_5 > 7$))
&& defined $\alpha_2$ && defined $\alpha_1$ )
||
( defined $\alpha_8$ && ! defined $\alpha_7$ && defined $\alpha_6$
&& (defined $\alpha_3$ && ($\alpha_4 > 2 || \alpha_5 > 7$))
&& defined $\alpha_2$ && defined $\alpha_1$ )

symbol value table:

$\alpha_1 \equiv$ __KERNEL__
$\alpha_2 \equiv$ __cplusplus
$\alpha_3 \equiv$ __i386__
$\alpha_4 \equiv$ __GNUC__
$\alpha_5 \equiv$ __GNUC_MINOR__
$\alpha_6 \equiv$ __STDC__
$\alpha_7 \equiv$ __arm__
$\alpha_8 \equiv$ __mc68000__

The complete condition then was submitted to a path condition simplifier. After simplification, the final constraint was given. For example the final one for the above condition is:

defined $\alpha_8$ && !defined $\alpha_7$ && defined $\alpha_1$

The goal of finding the full condition to reach a tested code line seeks to cover all the combination of conditions, thus is of course time consuming. The performance can be largely improved by using the reduced CFG. Another way to tune the performance may be initializing some preprocessor variables in the beginning of the symbolic execution, based on the programmer's knowledge of programs.

## 5. Future Work

The presented technique provides programmers with the following abilities:

- quickly verify the reachability of code

- find conditions of file inclusion

- group the platform dependent code

Two major future research concerns are:

- increase the effectiveness of the tool for larger systems

- add some visualization options

## 6. Conclusion

We have presented an approach to analyze conditional compilation. The approach is based on symbolic execution of preprocessor directives. The system header files in Linux kernel were chosen as examples to explain how the approach worked. To improve the performance of the symbolic execution phase, a series of pre-analysis technologies were proposed. Two strategies were used to achieve our two concrete goals, which are finding the simplest sufficient condition to reach/compile it, and finding the full condition to reach/compile that code line. A tool using this approach was built. Experiments conducted on Linux

kernel were presented. The analysis of resulting path conditions may be used to better understand the program structure and to find practical solutions to refine header file hierarchy.

## References

[1] ANSI Standards X3-J4 COBOL Technical Committee. *X3 Information Processing Systems Minutes*. Post Falls, ID, 1996.

[2] ISO/IEC-JTC1/SC22. *FORTRAN 95*. Draft International Standard IS 1539.

[3] H. Spencer and G. Collyer. #ifdef Considered Harmful, or Portability Experience with C News. In *USENIX*, Summer 1992 Technical Conference, San Antonio (Texas), June, 1992, pages 185-197.

[4] D. Spuler, A.S.M. Sajeev. Static Detection of Preprocessor Macro Erros in C. In *Technical report 92-7*, James Crook University, 1992, 18 pages.

[5] D. Flanagan. *Java in a Nutshell*. O'Reilly & Associates, Inc., Sebastopol, CA, 1996.

[6] K.P. Vo, and Y.F. Chen. Incl: A Tool to Analyze Include Files. In *USENIX*, Summer 1992 Technical Conference, San Antonio (Texas), June, 1992, pages 199-208.

[7] R. Jaeschke. *Portability and the 'C' Language*. Hayden Books, Indianapolis, IN, 1989.

[8] M. Krone, and G. Snelting. On the Inference of Configuration Structures from Source Code. In *Proc. 16th International Conference on Software Engineering*, Sorrento, Italy, 1994.

[9] J.M. Favre. Reengineering-In-The-Large vs Reengineering-In-The-Small. In *first SEI Workshop on Software Reengineering*, Software Engineering Institute, Carnegie Mellon University, May 1994.

[10] J.M. Favre. Preprocessors from an Abstract Point of View. In *Proceedings of the 1996 IEEE International Conference on Software Maintenance*, California, Nov. 1996.

[11] P.E. Livadas. Understanding Code Containing Preprocessor Construct. In *IEEE Third Workshop on Program Comprehension*, Washington, November 1994.

[12] Software Productivity Consortium *Ada '83 Guidelines for Professional Programmers*. Software Productivity Consortium, Herndon, VA, 1992.

[13] T.T. Pearse and P.W. Oman. Experiences Developing and Maintaining Software in a Multi-Platform Environment. In *Proceedings of the 1997 IEEE International Conference on Software Maintenance*, Italy, Oct. 1997.

[14] Sun Microsystems Inc. *Jdk 1.2: Java development kit*.

[15] A. V. Aho, R. Sethi, and J. D. Ullman. *Compilers: principles, techniques, and tools*. Addison-wesley, 1988.

[16] P. D. Coward. A review of software testing. In *Software Engineering: A European Perspective*, IEEE Computer Society Press, Los Alamitos, 1993.

# An Approach to Limit the WYNOT Problem

G. Antoniol*, G. Casazza**, A. Cimitile*, M. Tortorella*

antoniol@ieee.org {gec,cimitile,martor}@unisannio.it

(*)University of Sannio, Faculty of Engineering - Piazza Roma, I-82100 Benevento, Italy
(**)University of Naples "Federico II", DIS - Via Claudio 21, I-80125 Naples, Italy

## Abstract

*Software evolution in a cooperative environment, where a pool of maintainers/developers contribute to the overall system changes, is challanging due to several factors, such as the poor communication among individuals and the high number of produced changes. Conflicting or contradictory changes, unforeseen or unexpected dependencies may result in a non working system. We propose a strategy aimed to reduce the risk of conflicting changes in a maintenance cooperative environment. To evaluate the feasibility of our approach and to attempt to estimate the size of the code to be scrutined per single changed line, we developed a number of tools and tested our approach on 30 release of DDD software system. The preliminary results are encouraging: potentially impacted LOCS per single changed LOC is on the average less than 4.*

**Keywords: cooperative maintenance, software evolution, program comprehensione, object orientation**

## 1. Introduction

Software evolution in a cooperative environment, where a pool of maintainers/developers contribute to overall system changes, poses challenges due to several factors. In particular, the most noticeable are poor communication among individuals and number of produced changes. As Lougher and Rodden pointed out, software maintenance relies on a set of cooperative activities focused on a shared artifact, the system [26]. For this reason, as a development/maintenance team grows up in size and its member composition varies, communication paths enormously increase. Moreover, the single programmer may produce such a high number of changes that it is difficult or even impossible, with currently available tools and conceptual models, to represent and share in real time knowledge of who is actively changing a particular piece of code, rationales of changes, and programming solution adopted.

At University of Sannio we are actively investigating $CM^2$ (Cooperative Maintenance Conceptual Model) [13], a conceptual model aimed to mitigate the outlined difficulties by supporting software maintenance and evolution in a collaborative fashion. COMANCHE (COoperative MAintenance Network Centered Hypertextual Environment), the software environment which reflects the ideas and the concepts of $CM^2$ uses CVS (Concurrent Version System), a public domain widely adopted version control system (available at http://www.sourcegear.com/CVS). CVS allows programmers to edit concurrently personal copies of a revision controlled file. CVS uses the `diff3` 3-way merging engine to assist the merging of the concurrently modified files.

However, an environment aimed at supporting maintenance activities in a collaborative fashion must cope with conflicting or contradictory changes, unforeseen or unexpected dependencies that may result in a non working system causing the WYNOT syndrome. Andreas Zeller [31], the developer and maintainer of the Data Display Debugger (DDD), introduced the WYNOT acronym standing for "my program *Worked Yesterday, NOt Today*". For this reason, it is common sense and a widely accepted practice that a patch (i.e., a set of program modifications), before being incorporated in a product release, has to pass regression testing, and to undergo deep scrutiny of fellow programmers and *guru(s)*, that ultimately decide whether or not the proposed changes should be part of next releases. Indeed, peer review has proved to be one of the most effective way to pinpoint defects [7]; unfortunately, unless the software is an open source software, it is also the most expensive.

Different programming languages, programmer experience, and team size may influence the WYNOT. For example, a claimed benefit of Object-Oriented (OO) approach is that OO developed software should result in more maintainable systems (e.g., class methods tend to be shorter than procedures in a procedural system). Although OO features like inheritance, polymorphism and dynamic binding augment language expressiveness and offer new possibilities

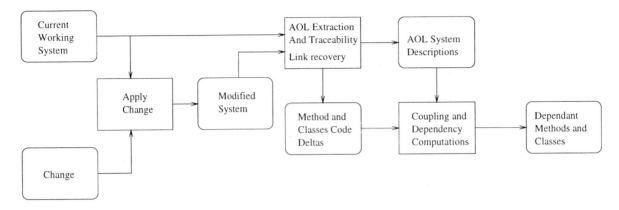

**Figure 1. Coupling/Dependencies Recovery Process.**

to programmers, they also may cause the introduction of complex dependencies promoting WYNOT and posing new challenges to impact analysis [10, 24, 30] and flow analyses [28].

In this paper we present an approach that we believe may help to limit the WYNOT disease in C++ developed systems. As when something of epidemic is likely to spread, two different strategies can be followed: act only when you are in troubles or attempt to limit the contagion by setting practices to avoid getting sick. Zeller in [31] adhere to the former approach: he devised a strategy and developed a prototype tool to help debugging a program when applied changes make the program fail. We advocate the latter strategy: attempt to avoid undesired side effects due to unexpected and unforeseen couplings. Unfortunately, as in everyday physicians practice, we are not able to prevent all sickness, and do not claim the superiority of one strategy over the other. We simply propose to analyze the previous working release of a software system and the modified release to pinpoint possible inconsistencies due to unexpected coupling between modified code (in our case C++ classes) and the remaining of the system.

Our process works as follows: once a change is performed, and already successfully undergone 3-way merging (using CVS functionalities), code deltas between the previous working release and the new ones are computed. Code deltas determine methods impacted in previous release; these methods may be used to define a set of possibly dependent methods/classes according to the coupling taxonomy presented in [12]. These methods and classes could be highlighted to the programmer as possibly unexpected dependencies.

To evaluate the feasibility of our approach and to estimate the size of code to be scrutinized per single line of change, we developed a number of tools. The preliminary results on 30 releases of the DDD systems are encouraging. The size of highlighted LOC per single changed LOC is on

the average below 4: the ratio 1/4 does not account for the cognitive effort required, as it cannot be easily evaluated.

The remainder of the paper is organized as follows: in the next section we present our process in the context of the framework [12], then we describe our tool suite and present results from a case study. In Section 5 we compare our approach with previous work; concluding remarks are given Section 6.

## 2. Process

The proposed process is depicted in the Fig . 1 in its basic elements. It is worth noting that 3-way conflicts are assumed to be successfully handled using CVS (see box *Apply Changes* in Fig. 1 ). The remaining of the process aims to identify dependencies, possibly, unwanted, unexpected and/or newly introduced in the *new* software snapshot.

Fig 2 shows the skeleton of two class hierarchies: the hierarchy on the left uses, by means of aggregation, delegation, association, attributes and data types of the hierarchy on the right. For simplicity's sake, constructors, destructors and other details were omitted.

In the area of OO software metrics there has been a flourishing of contributions related to the themes of cohesion and coupling [6, 11, 15, 16]. Recently, Briand et al. [12] proposed an OO measurement framework which encompasses a coupling taxonomy. The proposed taxonomy can be summarized as follows: whenever a class $C$ or a method $m$ belonging to $C$ references another class, say $D$:

- in an attribute/method type declaration or in the method signature declaration where $D$ is used as type;

- in a method local variable declaration where $D$ is used as type;

- by invoking in a method $m$ of $C$ a method $m'$ of $D$;

```
class c1
{
protected:
  d1 *assoc_c1_d1;

public:
  int mc1(int)
    {assoc_c1_d1->md1(i);};
  int mc2(int)
    {assoc_c1_d1->md2(i);};
};


class c2: public c1
{

public:
  d2 aggreg_c2_contain_d2[2];
  int mc2(int);
};


class c3 : public c2
{
  c2 *assoc_c3_c2;

  public:
  int mc3(d1 *);
  d1* mc3(int );
};


int c2::mc2(int i){
  d1 *lptr = new d2();

  lptr->md2(assoc_c1_d1->md2(i));
  aggreg_c2_contain_d2[1].md2(i);
}
```

```
class d1
{
public:
  int x;
  virtual  int md1(int)
    {x=i; cout << "d1::md1 " << x << endl; return x;};
  virtual  int md2(int)
    {x=i++; cout << "d1::md2 " << x << endl; return x;};
};


class d2: public d1
{
public:
  int y;
  int md2(int)
    {y=i; cout << "d2::md2" <<  endl;  return x;};
};


d1* c3::mc3(int i){
  if (i>0)
    return new d1;
  else
    return new d2;
}


int c3::mc3(d1 *p){

  d2 o;
  aggreg_c2_contain_d2[1].md2(p->x);
  assoc_c3_c2 = new   c2 [o.y];

}
```

**Figure 2. C++ Coupling/Dependencies Code Example.**

- by using/defining attributes of class $D$;

- by passing as actual parameter to a method $m$ of $C$ an object of class $D$ (or an object attributes or methods);

- in a high level relationship such as *aggregation* or *association*;

then, there exist couplings between $C$ and $D$. Since $C$ uses (or defines) $D$ (or attributes and/or methods of $D$), the coupling relation can be expressed, with a compact notation proposed in [12], as $uses(C, D)$. $uses(C, D)$ could be thought of as a dependency relation: any change to $D$ will, possibly, affect $C$.

We are interested in classes somehow changed, thus changed methods and classes have to be located. To capture the $uses(C, D)$ relation we perform the following macro steps:

- recover an annotated design from the two systems;

- compute traceability links;

- identify changed methods and/or classes and compute code deltas;

- recover coupling links.

The first three steps shown in Fig. 1 localize the changes to methods/classes (this is implemented by the box *AOL Extraction and Traceability Link Recovery* in Fig. 1), while the

forth step (box *Coupling and Dependency Computation* in Fig. 1) extracts the dependency sets. In the following each step will be briefly summarized.

## 2.1  Design Recovery

Our process to identify area where changes took place works on a code intermediate representation that encompasses the essentials of a class diagram in an OO design description language: the Abstract Object Language (AOL) [3, 20].

AOL has been designed to capture OO concepts in a formalism independent of programming languages and tools. AOL is a general-purpose design description language, capable of expressing concepts available at the design stage of OO software development. The language resembles other OO design/interface specification languages such as IDL[27] and ODL[25]. More details on AOL can be found in [3, 20].

AOL was conceived as being strictly tied to class diagram, AOL representation was augmented with information required to compute the $uses(C, D)$. Basically, for any given method of a software system, the set of called methods/procedures is captured together with the set of referenced classes and referenced class attributes. Polymorphic calls are resolved associating to the call the superset of methods whose signature is compatible with the actual

209

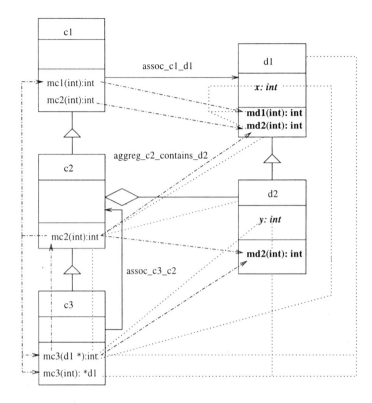

**Figure 3. Annotated C++ Class Diagram.**

method call.

## 2.2 Traceability Link Recovery

The mapping between classes and methods of two releases is contructed/recovered in two steps. In the first step, the AOL representations of the two releases are parsed and a similarity measure between each pair of classes in the two releases is computed. In the second step, the optimum match between classes is inferred by applying the maximum match algorithm [17] to a bipartite graph where nodes are classes of the two releases and edges between nodes are weighted by the corresponding class similarity measures. Only pairs of classes with similarity measures greater than a given threshold are actually considered as matched classes (these classes correspond to cases of class evolution). A threshold value of 75% was chosen to avoid false matching due to the traceability link recovery approach. Such value was empirically derived on the LEDA library and confirmed by the DDD similarity score: classes with similarity value higher than 75% are always to be considered similar; more details can be found in [1]. The unmatched classes of the previous release represent deleted classes, while the unmatched classes of the new release are added classes.

The similarity measure between two given classes is computed from similarity measures defined on properties (attributes/methods) of the classes. First, for each pair of properties of the two classes a similarity measure is computed based on the complemented edit distance [17] between strings. Then, an optimum match between the class properties is inferred by applying a maximum match algorithm [17] to the bipartite graph whose nodes are the properties of the two classes and the edges between nodes are weighted by the corresponding property similarity measures. Again, unmatched properties will be considered either as deleted, if they belong to the class of the previous release, or as added, if they belong to the class of the new release. Finally, the similarity measure between the two classes is computed as the average optimum match between properties, see [1] for details. Once a mapping between classes of different releases has been computed, a detailed mapping between class properties (methods and attributes) is also available: this mapping can be exploited to compute code deltas as detailed in the next subsection.

## 2.3 Code Delta Computation

In the above step similarity has been measured on the basis of string matchings between class names, attributes (including attribute types) and method names (including signatures). Thus we are not guaranteed that, if two classes or two methods obtained a 100 % of similarity, no modification occurred. Due to the available data and data granularity the process was applied to entire releases (i.e. the patch between two subsequent DDD versions); however, the process does not change if applied to smaller changes.

The process goal is to localize possibly unexpected dependencies, in other words if comments are added to a chunk of code or indentation to increase readability is performed we would like to hide such a detail.

The above requirement is achieved by means of the `diff` tool: we identify the number of added, deleted and modified LOC per class and/or method definition; we also consider as added/deleted LOC the code of added/deleted classes and methods.

## 2.4 Coupling/Dependency Links Recovery

The outlined coupling taxonomy has been adopted as general framework. Let $m_i$ be a method of a class $C_i$ in the $i$ release, let $C_{i+1}$ be the $C_i$ evolution and $m_{i+1}$ the $m_i$ correspondent in $i + 1$ release. For any given code delta between $m_i$ and $m_{i+1}$ (as well as between $C_i$ and $C_{i+1}$) we need to recover the set $uses(X_i, C_i)$ where $X_i$ is a generic class of version $i$ such that $X_i \neq C_i$. The $uses(X_i, C_i)$ set recovery is attained in two steps. The first step could be thought of as annotating a class diagram with coupling links as shown in Fig. 3; links represent method calls (the directed dashed line from $c1 :: mc1$ to $d1 :: md1$ means that $c1 :: mc1$ calls $d1 :: md1$) and references (the dotted line between $c3 :: mc3$ and $d2 :: y$ means that $c3 :: mc3$ references $d2 :: y$). The second step constructs, for any given changed method/class, the $uses(X_i, C_i)$ inverse relation by performing a traversal of the annotated class diagram.

Class diagram annotation is accomplished while extracting the AOL representation of methods: for any given method definition the method body is parsed, relevant information collected; any method declaration is linked to method definition; any inheritance relation walked to spot methods/attributes overriding/inheritance. Collected information are:

1. method/function calls (including the actual/formal parameter types);

2. referenced classes and class variables;

3. local variable declaration involving classes as type;

The recovery process is subject to approximation to simplify and speed up computations. Whenever a method or a function invocation is issued via function pointers, or in presence of a polymorphic call, the super set of possible invoked functions/methods is associated to the call based on the signature. Referenced classes and variables may require to walk inheritance, aggregation or association links

to safely identify class definition owning a given attribute. Furthermore, as in the case of methods $c3 :: mc3(d1*)$ of Fig. 2, if an element of a class hierarchy is passed as formal parameter, we are not guaranteed on the actual parameter type e.g., either a pointer to $d1$ or to $d2$ may be passed to $c3 :: mc3(d1*)$.

## 3. Tool Support

A preliminary tool suite, not optimized in terms of performances, was developed to demonstrate the feasibility of the approach and to assess difficulties and bottleneck.

To extract the AOL representation from the source code, we used an augmented version of the `Code2AOL Extractor` tool described in [2]. The augmented `Code2AOL Extractor` capture information required to construct the *uses(C,D)* sets.

Once the AOL of the compared versions (i.e. the current working system and the modified system) are available they can be traversed and similarities among classes are computed. The weights of the computed similarities are used to build a bipartite graph, passed to a maximum match algorithm. The AOL parser and the distance computation have been implemented in Perl and C, while the maximum match algorithm was written in C++.

Finally, we developed a `Dependency-Extractor` tool (written in Perl) to locate the dependent methods and classes by traversing the augmented AOL representation of the source code. Basically the `Dependency-Extractor`:

1. identifies classes and methods that have been modified;

2. extracts the sets of methods calling modified methods;

3. extracts the sets of methods using modified classes;

4. for each modified class identifies the set of dependent classes;

5. evaluates the LOC of the sets identified in the previous points.

At the present level of the experimentation and tool support we were more focused on a proof of concepts rather than on the actual implementation of a fully functional and working system. Consequently, tools rely on the assumption that programmers develop OO code; unfortunately, it is known that C++ can be used either as an OO language or as a procedural language. AOL and AOL related tools disregard the procedural part of the code. We further assumed that encapsulation is enforced by the OO paradigm, thus attributes cannot be directly accessed or modified; however, C++ does not enforce such a strict information hiding.

## 4. Case Study

The goal of the case study was to provide a preliminary estimate of the size of code to be inspected applying our approach, once a change has been applied. The approach was applied to 30 releases of the DDD, Data Display Debugger. DDD is a graphical user interface to GDB and DBX, two popular UNIX debuggers. DDD is a public domain software system developed in C++ at the Technische Universitat Braunschweig, Germany (free software, protected by the GNU general public license and available from http://www.cs.tu-bs.de/softech/ddd/). The DDD distribution comprises several components supporting the DDD core functionalities: libraries (libiberty, pydb, termcap, vslib, etc.), change logs, documentation, icons, bitmaps and patches. We did not analyze such libraries and additional components: our focus was the C++ core functionalities. We analyzed the DDD releases from release 2.0beta1 to 3.1.3; correspondingly we observed a size evolution that doubled the C++ core part (from 52 to 107 KLOC) while the number of classes did not exhibit the same doubling effect (classes increased from 124 to 135).

This preliminary assessment was conducted by mimicking a sequence of evolution changes given the DDD history: each DDD release between the 2.0beta1 and 3.1.2 was in turn considered as the *Current Working System* while the subsequent release was the *Modified System*.

Table 1 summarizes the evolution data, the first column shows the version release upgrade, the second column reports the size of the patch in Kbyte, the third and forth columns contains the number of modified methods and classes. Figures refer to the changes applied to produce the entire release upgrade. Being a patch extracted with a recursive context diff on the entire snapshot trees, the size of a patch is only loosely related with the number of changed LOC (i.e., methods and classes), as it can be deducted from Table 2. The recursive context diff takes into account directories containing documentation, icon files, change-logs, bug-reports and libraries.

Once we identified modified classes and methods, evaluation of dependent LOC, according to the guidelines specified in Section 2, required the extraction from the AOL representation of the *Current Working System* of:

1. all methods directly calling modified methods;

2. all classes dependent on modified classes.

In particular, dependent LOC are obtained summing the LOC of the methods identified at point 1 and the LOC of the class definitions identified at point 2. On average the coupling/dependencies process, depicted in Figure 1, took less than 15 minutes for any given entire upgrade of the DDD history.

| Release | | Changed | |
|---|---|---|---|
| Release Upgrade | Patch size | methods | classes |
| 2.0beta1-2.0beta2 | 114 | 19 | 4 |
| 2.0beta2-2.0beta3 | 765 | 57 | 14 |
| 2.0beta3-2.0 | 343 | 16 | 5 |
| 2.0-2.1beta1 | 2262 | 249 | 17 |
| 2.1beta1-2.1beta2 | 476 | 39 | 8 |
| 2.1beta2-2.1beta3 | 1054 | 54 | 8 |
| 2.1beta3-2.1 | 405 | 5 | 3 |
| 2.1-2.1.1 | 388 | 21 | 2 |
| 2.1.1-2.1.90 | 3007 | 171 | 18 |
| 2.1.90-2.1.95 | 428 | 43 | 9 |
| 2.1.95-2.1.98 | 204 | 14 | 6 |
| 2.1.98-2.2 | 199 | 17 | 5 |
| 2.2-2.2.1 | 810 | 67 | 21 |
| 2.2.1-2.2.2 | 615 | 82 | 11 |
| 2.2.2-2.2.3 | 36 | 25 | 7 |
| 2.2.3-2.99 | 6449 | 211 | 14 |
| 2.99-2.99.1 | 304 | 4 | 2 |
| 2.99.1-2.99.2 | 1223 | 110 | 18 |
| 2.99.2-2.99.9 | 277 | 1 | 1 |
| 2.99.9-2.99.95 | 749 | 41 | 7 |
| 2.99.95-2.99.99 | 238 | 11 | 2 |
| 2.99.99-3.0 | 264 | 12 | 6 |
| 3.0-3.0.90 | 2775 | 12 | 6 |
| 3.0.90-3.0.91 | 449 | 13 | 5 |
| 3.0.91-3.0.92 | 293 | 34 | 9 |
| 3.0.92-3.1 | 963 | 54 | 25 |
| 3.1-3.1.1 | 197 | 19 | 8 |
| 3.1.1-3.1.2 | 403 | 30 | 8 |
| 3.1.2-3.1.3 | 3172 | 2 | 1 |

**Table 1. DDD source evolution: patch size (Kbyte), number of changed methods and classes.**

Table 2 summarizes the case study results: for each release upgrade we counted LOC changed, LOC dependent and their ratio. Changed LOC is given by the sum of the added, the modified and the deleted LOC obtained comparing the *Modified System* versus the *Current Working System*. The average ratio between the changed and dependent LOC is 0.33: for each changed LOC a maintainer should have scrutinized less than 4 LOC of dependent code.

It has to be underlined that this is an approximation of the actual impacted number of LOC: the 1/4 ratio (4 LOC of dependent code for each LOC modified) may or may not completely and fully express of the number of dependent LOC. When suspect couplings are located, the programmer may decide to follow the dependence chains far beyond the direct dependencies identified; at the same time, since we

| Release Upgrade | Changed | Dependent | Ratio |
|---|---|---|---|
| 2.0beta1-2.0beta2 | 301 | 1727 | 17.4% |
| 2.0beta2-2.0beta3 | 430 | 5454 | 7.8% |
| 2.0beta3-2.0 | 336 | 1802 | 18.6% |
| 2.0-2.1beta1 | 5878 | 9577 | 61.3% |
| 2.1beta1-2.1beta2 | 691 | 4030 | 17.1% |
| 2.1beta2-2.1beta3 | 979 | 2560 | 38.2% |
| 2.1beta3-2.1 | 53 | 1484 | 3.5% |
| 2.1-2.1.1 | 532 | 2009 | 15.3% |
| 2.1.1-2.1.90 | 3463 | 8934 | 38.7% |
| 2.1.90-2.1.95 | 1282 | 4128 | 31.0% |
| 2.1.95-2.1.98 | 82 | 1602 | 5.1% |
| 2.1.98-2.2 | 355 | 2674 | 13.2% |
| 2.2-2.2.1 | 556 | 4092 | 13.5% |
| 2.2.1-2.2.2 | 1515 | 7114 | 21.2% |
| 2.2.2-2.2.3 | 38 | 2870 | 1.3% |
| 2.2.3-2.99 | 5501 | 11235 | 48.9% |
| 2.99-2.99.1 | 44 | 710 | 6.1% |
| 2.99.1-2.99.2 | 861 | 7874 | 10.9% |
| 2.99.2-2.99.9 | 3 | 651 | 0% |
| 2.99.9-2.99.95 | 1241 | 5695 | 21.7% |
| 2.99.95-2.99.99 | 339 | 1585 | 21.3% |
| 2.99.99-3.0 | 55 | 1194 | 4.6% |
| 3.0-3.0.90 | 55 | 1209 | 4.5% |
| 3.0.90-3.0.91 | 119 | 1818 | 6.5% |
| 3.0.91-3.0.92 | 471 | 1818 | 14.3% |
| 3.0.92-3.1 | 306 | 4687 | 6.5% |
| 3.1-3.1.1 | 117 | 2802 | 4.1% |
| 3.1.1-3.1.2 | 231 | 4725 | 4.8% |
| 3.1.2-3.1.3 | 43 | 649 | 6.6% |

**Table 2. DDD Case Study Results**

do not distinguish accessor methods from those methods changing class state variables, extra LOC that do not need to be considered may gathered.

## 5. Related Work

Sadly and strangely enough previous works and framework dealing with cooperative maintenance do not provide practical guideline, suggest tools, techniques or methodology to avoid or reduce the WYNOT problem.

Beyond-Sniff, a CSCW software development environment, gives some support to integrate the *current working system* and the *modified system* [9]. In particular, it visualizes the differences between two or more system versions at the class level (added classes, added attributes, added methods, etc.). Our approach identifies such differences, moreover our findings may be used to explicitly highlights potentially WYNOT situations due to these differences.

Chang et al. [14] presented an environment to develop

software in a collaborative fashion. In this approach a kind of *super user* has the responsibility of integrating the code produced by the other members of the development team. However, no automatic support is provided to identify inconsistencies during software evolution.

Commercial CASE tools such as Doors, Rationale Rose, or Together offer very little support, mostly limited to reverse engineer a design from existing code; these tools do not help programmer teams to identify inconsistencies deriving from source code change. Quite often the more sophisticated and expensive tools offer integrated testing environment, thus regression testing suites may be automatically run once changes were applied.

Slicing [19, 23], program merging and integration [8, 22] and impact analysis [4, 5, 10, 18, 29] techniques are to some extent related to our approach.

We were inspired by [10] and we borrowed the proposed taxonomy from [12]. In [10] coupling is used to estimate a change ripple effect in C++ developed system. In other words, given an OO system and a history of system changes, coupling measures are extracted, relevant component identified, and a model of ripple effects constructed; the model attempts to predict coupled classes that will be affected, and possibly changed, if a change to a given class occurs. We do not construct a model of changes, changes already happened. The purpose of our work is to highlight the classes coupled to a given changed class/method.

There are also commonalities with previous work such as [28] dealing with data dependencies and/or reaching definition computation. However, C++ data dependencies subsume at least point-to and inter-procedural computation, sophisticated and computational expensive techniques [21]. We do not perform points-to or polymorphism resolution, nor inter-procedural def/use computation, nor the dependence closure: we assume a super set of def/use and calls. As a result if the inter-procedural closure of dependence is performed, we definitely recover a super-set of the actually *impacted* LOC. There may also be problems related to the imprecision of tools extracting AOL and calls, that in turn may lead to missed dependencies. Missed dependencies will be a severe problem in slicing application. However, in our case missed dependencies may, possibly, cause the WYNOT. This is equivalent of being got sick after attempting to avoid the flu.

There are commonalities with [31], however, as already underlined, the two approaches are applied during different phases: while we attempt to prevent, in [31] a technique to cure is presented.

## 6. Conclusions

We have presented a process that, given a C++ source code change, identifies a set of possibly dependent methods/classes. Once integrated in a more general framework, the process may help to reduce the risk of conflicting changes in a cooperative maintenance environment. Our long term goal is to integrate the developed approach within the COMANCHE environment. COMANCHE encompasses various code visualization and browsing features, that are essential for any foreseeable application of the process presented here.

As when something of epidemic is likely to spread we prefer to follow a strategy aimed to limit the contagion by settling practices to avoid getting sick. Other author's proposed different approaches more focused on removing an already existing disease. Since, as in everyday physicians practice, we are not be able to prevent all sickness, we do not claim the superiority of one strategy over the other, but simply propose to modify the merging procedure just to let programmers being aware of coupling between a change and the rest of the software.

We developd prototype tools to evaluate the feasibility of our approach and provide a preliminary estimate of the size of code to be scrutinized per single line of change. The preliminary results on 30 releases of the DDD systems are encouraging: the size of highlighted LOC per single changed LOC is on average below 4. The ratio 1/4 merely expresses a volume ratio and does not account for the cognitive effort required, which cannot easily be evaluated. Further work is needed to reduce computation time with the present tool set and asses the real process usefulness, if any, in the everyday programmer practice.

## 7. Acknowledgments

This research is supported by the project "Virtual Software Factory", funded by Ministero della Ricerca Scientifica e Tecnologica (MURST) and jointly carried out by EDS Italia Software, University of Sannio, University of Naples "Federico II", and University of Bari.

Moreover, we would like to thank Gerardo Canfora and Andrea De Lucia for their helpfull suggestions.

## References

[1] G. Antoniol, G. Canfora, and A. D. Lucia. Mantaining traceability during object-oriented software evolution: a case study. In *Proceedings of IEEE International Conference on Software Maintenance*, pages 211–219, Oxford, UK, IEEE CS Press, 1999.

[2] G. Antoniol, G. Canfora, A. D. Lucia, and E. Merlo. Recovering code to documentation links in oo systems. *Proc. of the Working Conference on Reverse Engineering*, pages 136–144, Oct 1999.

[3] G. Antoniol, R. Fiutem, and L. Cristoforetti. Using metrics to identify design patterns in object-oriented software. In *Proceedings of 5 th International Symposium on Software Metrics - METRICS98*, pages 23–34, Bethesda, MD, Nov 2-5 1998.

[4] R. S. Arnold and S. A. Bohner. Impact analysis - towards a framework for comparison. In *Proceedings of IEEE International Conference on Software Maintenance*, pages 292–301, Montreal, Quebec, Canada, 1993.

[5] L. J. Arthur. *Software Evolution. The Software Maintenance Challenge*. Wiley-Inter Science, Wiley - NY, 1988.

[6] V. R. Basili, W. L. Melo, and L. C. Briand. A validation of object-oriented design metrics as quality indicators. *IEEE Transactions on Software Engineering*, 22(10):751–761, 1996.

[7] B. Beizer. *Software Testing Techniques, 2nd edition*. International Thomson Computer Press, 1990.

[8] D. Binkley, S. Horwitz, and T. Reps. Program integration for languages with procedure calls. *ACM Transactions on Software Engineering and Methodology*, 4(1):3–35, 1995.

[9] W. Bischofberger, T. Kofler, K. Matzel, and B. Scaffer. Computer supported cooperative software engineering with beyond-sniff. *Proceedings of Software Engineering Environments, Noordwijkerhout (The Netherlands)*, pages 135–143, 1995.

[10] L. Briand, J. Wust, and H. Lounis. Using coupling for impact analysis in object-oriented systems. In *Proceedings of IEEE International Conference on Software Maintenance*, pages 475–482, Oxford (UK), Sep 1999.

[11] L. C. Briand, J. Daly, and J. Wust. A comprehensive empirical validation of design measures for object-orienyted systems. *In Proc. of the Fifth International Symposium on Software Metrics - METRICS98*, pages 246–257, Nov 2-5 1998.

[12] L. C. Briand, J. W. Daly, and J. K. Wust. A unified framework for coupling measurement in object-oriented systems. *IEEE Transactions on Software Engineering*, 25(1):91–121, 1999.

[13] G. Canfora, G. Casazza, and A. D. Lucia. A design rationale based environment for cooperative maintenance. *Technical Report University of Sannio - Faculty of Engineering (Available from authors)*, May 1999.

[14] K. Chang, L. Murphy, J. Fouss, T. Dollar, B. Lee, and Y. Chang. Software development and integration in a computer supported cooperative work environment. *Software - Practice and Experience.*, 28(6):657–679, 1998.

[15] S. R. Chidamber and C. F. Kemerer. A metrics suite for object oriented design. *IEEE Transactions on Software Engineering*, 20(6):476–493, June 1994.

[16] P. Coad and E. Yurdon. *Object Oriented Analysis - Second edition*. Prentice-Hall, Englewood Cliffs, NJ, 1991.

[17] T. H. Cormen, C. E. Leiserson, and R. L. Rivest. *Introductions to Algorithms*. MIT Press, 1990.

[18] A. Fasolino and G. Visaggio. Improving software comprehension through an automated dependency tracer. *Proc. of the Working Conference on Reverse Engineering*, pages 58–65, Oct 1999.

[19] J. Ferrante, K. J. Ottenstein, and J. D. Warren. The program dependence graph and its use in optimization. *ACM Transactions on Programming Languages and Systems*, 3(9):319–349, July 1987.

[20] R. Fiutem and G. Antoniol. Identifying design-code inconsistencies in object-oriented software: A case study. In *Proceedings of IEEE International Conference on Software Maintenance*, pages 94–102, Bethesda, MD, November 16-20 1998.

[21] M. J. Harrold, L. Larsen, J. Lloyd, D. Nedved, M. Page, G. Rothermel, M. Singh, and M. Smith. Aristotle: A system for development of program analysis based tools. In *Proc. of the 33rd Annual ACM Southeast Conference*, pages 110–119, March 1995.

[22] S. Horwitz, J. Prins, and T. Reps. Integrating non-interfering versions of programs. *ACM Transaction on Programming Languages and Systems*, 11(3):345–387, 1989.

[23] S. Horwitz, T. Reps, and D. Binkley. Interprocedural slicing using dependence graphs. *ACM Transaction on Programming Languages and Systems*, 12(1):26–61, 1990.

[24] D. Kung, J. Gao, P. Hasia, F. Wen, Y. Toyoshima, and C. Chen. Change impact identification in object-oriented software maintenance. In *Proceedings of IEEE International Conference on Software Maintenance*, pages 202–211, Victoria,CA, 1994. IEEE Press.

[25] D. Lea and C. K. Shank. Odl: Language report. Technical Report Draft 5, Rochester Institute of Technology, Nov 1994.

[26] R. Lougher and T. Rodden. Group support for the recording and the sharing of maintenance rationale. *Software Engineering Journal*, 7(8):295–306, 1993.

[27] OMG. The Common Object Request Broker: Architecture and specification. OMG Document 91.12.1, OMG, December 1991.

[28] P. Tonella, G. Antoniol, R. Fiutem, and E. Merlo. Flow insensitive C++ pointers and polymorphism analysis and its application to slicing. *Proc. of the Int. Conf. on Software Engineering*, pages 433–443, 1997.

[29] R. J. Turver and M. Munro. An early impact analysis technique for software maintenance. *Journal of Software Maintenance - Research and Practice*, 6(1):35–52, 1994.

[30] N. Wilde and R. Huitt. Mintenance support for object-oriented programs. *IEEE Transactions on Software Engineering*, 18(2):1038–1044, Dec 1992.

[31] A. Zeller. Yesterday, my program worked. today, it does not. why? In *Joint 7th European Software Engineering Conference (ESEC) and The 7th ACM SIGSOFT International Symposium on the Foundation of Software Engineering (FSE)*, Toulouse, France, September 1999.

# ConSIT: A Conditioned Program Slicer

**Sebastian Danicic**,
Goldsmiths College,
University of London,
New Cross,
London SE14 6NW, UK.
Tel: +44 (0)20 7919 7856
Fax: +44 (0)20 7919 7853
sebastian@mcs.gold.ac.uk

**Chris Fox**,
Kings College,
University of London,
Strand,
London, WC2R 2LS, UK.
Tel: +44 (0)20 7848 2588
Fax: +44 (0)20 7848 2851
foxcj@dcs.kcl.ac.uk

**Mark Harman**,
**Rob Hierons**,
Brunel University,
Uxbridge, Middlesex,
UB8 3PH, UK.
Tel: +44 (0)1895 274 000
Fax: +44 (0)1895 251 686
mark.harman@brunel.ac.uk

## Abstract

*Conditioned slicing is a powerful generalisation of static and dynamic slicing which has applications to many problems in software maintenance and evolution, including re-use, re-engineering and program comprehension.*

*However, there has been relatively little work on the implementation of conditioned slicing. Algorithms for implementing conditioned slicing necessarily involve reasoning about the values of program predicates in certain sets of states derived from the conditioned slicing criterion, making implementation particularly demanding.*

*This paper introduces ConSIT, a conditioned slicing system which is based upon conventional static slicing, symbolic execution and theorem proving. ConSIT is the first fully automated implementation of conditioned slicing.*

*An implementation of ConSIT is available for experimentation at* `http://www.mcs.gold.ac.uk/~mas01sd/consit.html.`

## 1. Introduction

Program slicing is a source level code extraction technique that has been extensively applied to many problems in software maintenance, including, debugging [19, 21, 24, 28], re-engineering [7, 16, 23] and program comprehension [17, 18].

Traditionally, slices have been constructed using either purely static or purely dynamic analysis techniques [1, 20, 22, 29]. The traditional static slicing criterion consists of a pair, $(V, n)$, where $V$ is a set of variables of interest and $n$ is some point of interest in the program. Statements which cannot affect the value of any variable in $V$ when the next statement to be executed is at position $n$ in the program are removed to form the static slice. Figure 1 presents a simple C program[1], for which the static slice

with respect to the criterion $(28, \{\texttt{sum}\})$ is depicted in Figure 2. The traditional dynamic slicing criterion augments the static criterion with an input sequence, $I$. Statements which cannot affect the value of any variable in $V$ when the next statement to be executed is at position $n$ *and the input is* $I$ are removed to form the dynamic slice.

Static slices are thus constructed with respect to *no* additional information about the state in which the program is to be executed, while dynamic slices are constructed with respect to complete information about the initial state.

Conditioned slicing is a generalisation of both static and dynamic slicing. The conditioned slicing criterion augments the static criterion with a condition, which captures a set of possible initial states for which the slice and the original program must agree [5]. Definition 1.1 provides a more formal definition of conditioned slice.

**Definition 1.1 (Conditioned Slice)**
A Conditioned slice is constructed with respect to a tuple, $(V, n, \pi)$, where $V$ is a set of variables, $n$ is a point in the program (typically a node of the Control Flow Graph) and $\pi$ is some condition. A statement may be removed from a program $p$ to form a slice, $s$ of $p$, iff it cannot affect the value of any variable in $V$ when the next statement to be executed is at point $n$ and the initial state satisfies $\pi$.

For example, Figure 3 shows the conditioned slice constructed from the program in Figure 1 for the criterion $(\{\texttt{sum}\}, end, \forall i.\texttt{a}_i > 0)$, where $end$ is the end of the program and $\forall i.\texttt{a}_i > 0$ indicates that all values read into the variable a are positive.

Conditioned slicing is of both theoretical and practical importance. It is theoretically important because it subsumes both static and dynamic slicing [5]. It is practically important because of its application to problems in re-use [7, 8, 9, 10], re-engineering [7, 23] and program comprehension [5, 14, 18].

---

[1] This example is Due to Canfora, Cimitile and DeLucia [5]. The figure 28 refers to the exit node of the program.

Currently, there is little work on the implementation of conditioned slicing. Existing proof of concept prototype conditioned slicers, such as that described in [5], are interactive. The human is used to answer questions about conditions which arise during the process of analysis [13]. These prototypes serve to illustrate the importance and application of conditioned slicing. However, for conditioned slicing to achieve its potential, fully automated conditioned slicers must be implemented. Such implementations will need to be able to reason about the effect of the conditions mentioned in the slicing criterion. This paper shows how a traditional static slicer can be combined with a theorem prover and symbolic executor to achieve the goal of implementing a fully automated conditioned slicing system. The implementation, ConSIT, produces conditioned slices for an intraprocedural subset of C, the syntax of which is defined in Figure 4.

The rest of this paper is organised as follows: Section 2 describes the implementation of ConSIT, which relies upon symbolic execution and theorem proving subsystems described in Sections 3 and 4 respectively. Section 5 presents two examples of slices produced using ConSIT. The first is the example used by Canfora, Cimitile and DeLucia [5], which is presented as a 'benchmark' against which ConSIT is compared to prior work in this area. The second illustrates the application of conditioned slicing to business rule extraction. Section 6 concludes with directions for future work.

## 2. The Implementation of ConSIT

The ConSIT system operates on a subset of C, for which a tokeniser and symbolic executor were written in Prolog.

The top level algorithm is quite simple. It is depicted in Figure 5. Phase 1 propagates state information from the condition in the slicing criterion, to all points in the program, using the symbolic execution algorithm described in more detail in Section 3. Phase 2 produces a conditioned program by eliminating statements which are never executed when the initial state satisfies the condition mentioned in the slicing criterion. These are precisely those for which the state information defines an inconsistent set of states. Such statements become unreachable when the program is executed in a state which satisfies the condition of the slicing criterion and are 'sliced away'. The test of consistency of each set of states is computed using the Isabelle theorem prover, as described in more detail in Section 4. Phase 3 removes statements from the conditioned program which do not affect the static part of the conditioned slicing criterion. Phase 3 is implemented using the *Espresso* static slicing system [11].

The architecture of the ConSIT system is illustrated in Figure 6. The system is built from various components written in different languages. For the purpose of rapid prototyping, the symbolic executor and conditioner were written in Prolog. These were developed to work on a bespoke imperative programming language called Haste that includes loops, input statements and conditionals. The conditions of Haste are defined to be a good match for legal Isabelle propositions, and it is easy to parse

```
main() {
    int a, test0, n, i;
    int posprod, negprod, possum, negsum;
    int sum, prod;
    scanf("%d", &test0);
    scanf("%d", &n);
    i = 1;
    posprod = 1;
    negprod = 1;
    possum = 0;
    negsum = 0;
    while (i <= n) {
        scanf("%d", &a);
        if (a > 0) {
        possum = possum + a;
        posprod = posprod * a; }
        else if (a < 0) {
                negsum = negsum - a;
                negprod = negprod * (-a); }
                else if (test0) {
                    if (possum >= negsum)
                        possum = 0;
                    else negsum = 0;
                    if (posprod >= negprod)
                        posprod = 1;
                    else negprod = 1; }
        i=i+1; }
    if (possum >= negsum)
        sum = possum;
    else sum = negsum;
    if (posprod >= negprod)
        prod = posprod;
    else prod = negprod; }
```

**Figure 1. Example from Canfora et al [5]**

using a Definite Clause Grammar within Prolog.

The Isabelle theorem prover [26, 27, 25] is used to check the reachability of a statement. This is written in Standard ML. A wrapper script written in Expect acts as an Isabelle server process. It runs the theorem prover on a pseudo terminal and listens for connections on a socket. When the conditioner requires the services of Isabelle, it spawns an Expect client process which connects to the Isabelle server, via its socket, and requests that the symbolic state be analysed (using Isabelle's auto-tacticals). The server then interacts with Isabelle over the pseudo terminal, returning the result of the query back to the client process. The exit code of the client process is then used to indicate the result of the query.

This architecture means that there was no need to develop the symbolic executor within Isabelle, and that several processors can make use of Isabelle without additional overheads of running several copies of the theorem prover. It also avoids the long delays that would result if the theorem prover process was started every time it was needed. An alternative would be to link the Prolog code with ML via C interface libraries, but such

```
main() {
   int a, test0, n, i;
   int possum, negsum, sum;
   scanf("%d", &test0);
   scanf("%d", &n);
   i = 1;
   possum = 0;
   negsum = 0;
   while (i <= n) {
      scanf("%d", &a);
      if (a > 0)
         possum = possum + a;
      else if (a < 0)
            negsum = negsum - a;
         else if (test0) {
                if (possum >= negsum)
                    possum = 0;
                else negssum = 0;}
      i=i+1; }
   if (possum >= negsum)
      sum = possum;
   else sum = negsum;}
```

**Figure 2. Static Slice of Figure 1 w.r.t.** $(\{sum\}, end)$

```
main() {
   int a, n, i, possum, negsum, sum;
   scanf("%d", &n);
   i = 1;
   possum = 0;
   negsum = 0;
   while (i <= n) {
      scanf("%d", &a);
      if (a > 0)
         possum = possum + a;
      i=i+1; }
   if (possum >= negsum)
      sum = possum; }
```

**Figure 3. Conditioned Slice of Figure 1 w.r.t.** $(\{sum\}, end, \forall i.a_i > 0)$

```
<program>    ::=   main() { <decl-list>
                            <stat-list> }
<decl>       ::=   <type> <var-list> ;
<decl-list>  ::=   <decl> <decl-list> | <empty>
<var-list>   ::=   <var> | <var> , <var-list>
<stat>       ::=   { <stat-list> } |
                   <var> = <expr>; |
                   scanf(<string>,<amp-list>); |
                   if (<expr>) <stat>   |
                   if (<expr>) <stat>
                   else <stat> |
                   while (<expr>) <stat> |
                   ASSERT(<expr>) ;     |
                   <empty> ;
<stat-list>  ::=   <stat> <stat-list> | <empty>
<empty>      ::=
<string>     ::=   "<char-list>"
<amp-list>   ::=   &<var> | &<var>, <amp-list>
<expr>       ::=   <unaryop> <expr> |
                   <expr> <binop> <expr> |
                   <var> | <integer-constant> |
                   ( <expr> ) | <char-constant>
<binop>      ::=   < | > | <= |>= | == | != |
                   || | && | + | * | - | /
<unaryop>    ::=   - | !
<char-const> ::=   '<char>'
```

**Figure 4. The subset of C accepted by ConSIT**

| Phase 1: | Symbolically Execute |
| Phase 2: | Produce Conditioned Program |
| Phase 3: | Perform Static Slicing |

**Figure 5. The Three Phases in Slice Construction**

The slightly contrived acronym ConSIT stands for **Con**ditioned **S**licer using the **I**sabelle **T**heorem prover. The acronym is chosen because ConSIT combines several different systems and languages in concert.

## 2.1. Representing the Slicing Criterion

ConSIT uses a novel technique for representing the slicing criterion and presenting it to the system, which the authors have found to be very effective and worthy of mention. The slicing criterion is effectively *encoded* into the source code of the program to be sliced.

### The Conditioned Part of the Criterion

The condition is inserted into the program using an ASSERT statement, which takes a single boolean argument and asserts that its value is true, allowing considerable flexibility in constructing a slicing criterion. This is because the ASSERT statement can be inserted at *any* point in the program.

To perform a conditioned slice the ASSERT statement will

a solution is not as portable nor as flexible; with the current architecture the resource intensive theorem prover can be run on a separate high-performance server, and the system is dependent on particular versions of neither Prolog nor ML.

A similar client-server approach is adopted with the slicer. However, in this case the slicer and its server process are written in Java, based upon the *Espresso* slicing system [11]. *Espresso* uses a parallel slicing algorithm [12] which takes advantage of inherent CFG parallelism, where each node of the CFG of the subject program is compiled into a separate Java thread.

A pre- and post- processor, written in JavaCup and JLex, are used to translate between C and the internal language Haste.

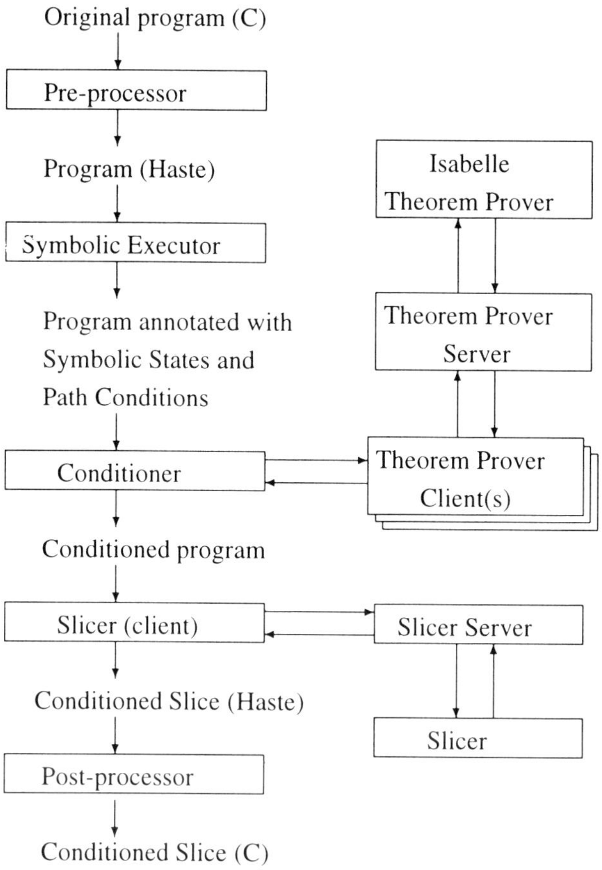
Original program (C)
Pre-processor
Program (Haste)
Symbolic Executor
Program annotated with
Symbolic States and
Path Conditions
Conditioner
Conditioned program
Slicer (client)
Conditioned Slice (Haste)
Post-processor
Conditioned Slice (C)
Isabelle
Theorem Prover
Theorem Prover
Server
Theorem Prover
Client(s)
Slicer Server
Slicer

**Figure 6. The Architecture of ConSIT**

typically be added to the beginning of the program. However, there is no reason why ASSERT statements may not be added to arbitrary parts of the program.

The ASSERT statement is also used to handle conditions on input variables. When defining a conditioned slicing criterion, input variables present a problem because the value of the variable may be read in a loop, causing it to have many values during the execution of the program. Canfora et al [5] address this issue by subscripting the variable name, allowing universal quantification and ranges to be used. For example, the condition in the slicing criterion for the example program in Figure 1 is $\forall i.1 \leq i \leq \texttt{n}.\texttt{a}_i > 0$, specifying that all values read into the variable a are positive.

Unfortunately, this approach becomes inconvenient when it is not easy to specify the range of subscripts of interest. For example, in the code fragment below, it becomes hard to specify that all values read into the variable a by the *second* while loop are positive.

```
while (i>0) {
  scanf("%d",&a) ;
  ...
  i = i-1;
  }
while (j>0) {
  scanf("%d",&a) ;
  ...
  j = j - 1;
  }
```

That is, suppose that the initial value of the variables i and j are dependent upon the input in some arbitrarily complex way. It will not be obvious how many times the first loop executed and therefore difficult to delimit the subscripts which should be applied to the variable a to capture the set of 'occurrences' of interest.

Using the ASSERT statement, this becomes very easy. All that is required, is to add an ASSERT in the second loop, giving:-

```
while (i>0) {
  scanf("%d",&a) ;
  ...
  i = i-1;
  }
while (j>0) {
  scanf("%d",&a) ;
  ASSERT(a>0) ;
  ...
  j = j - 1;
  }
```

¿ From a theoretical point of view, the use of the ASSERT statement does not make for a more general form of conditioned slicing; all ASSERT statements could, theoretically, be moved to the beginning of the program using predicate transformation similar to that proposed by Dijkstra for program verification [15]. However, the ASSERT statement allows for the specification of local constraints in input variables and is thus very helpful from a practical point of view in specifying conditioned slicing criteria.

**The Static Part of the Criterion**

The static part of the slicing criterion is also inserted directly into the program as program code. Recall that the static part of the criterion consists of the set of variables of interest, $V$ and the point at which those variables' values are of interest, $n$. The static part of the criterion is captured by a program variable slice. The user inserts an assignment to this variable at an arbitrary set of points in the program. If the assignment

$$\texttt{slice} = \texttt{f}(x, y, z)$$

is inserted at point $n$ in the program, then the slice must preserve the values of $x$, $y$ and $z$ at point $n$ in the program. This notation allows for multi-slicing [12, 29], in which there may be arbitrarily many slice points in the program, each of which is concerned with a different set of variables of interest.

## 3. The Symbolic Execution Phase

The symbolic states consist of disjunctions of conditional states, each of which in turn is a pair consisting of (in)equalities that arise from conditional expressions and equality statements that arise from assignment and input statements.

In practice, symbolic states are represented as sets of *pairs*. The first element of each pair is a set of bindings between variables and their symbolic values that arise from assignments and input statements. Canfora et al [5] call this the *symbolic state*. The second element of each pair is a set of (linear) inequalities. Canfora et al [5] call this the *path condition*. The intended interpretation is that each pair corresponds to a conditional symbolic state; the variables will have the symbolic values given in the first element of the pair when the (in)equalities in the second element are true. This distinction between assignment of value and other conditions is helpful when dereferencing a variable.

The symbolic executor is derived directly from the semantics of the language. The semantics $\sigma(s)$ of a sequence of statements $s$ is a set of states $\{s_1, s_2, \ldots, s_n\}$. Each symbolic state $s_i$ ($1 \le i \le n$) can be considered as the pair[2]:

$$\langle a_i, c_i \rangle$$

Each $a_i$ is an assignment function from variables to expressions, and $c_i$ is a path condition. $\sigma(s)$ denotes the effect of symbolically executing $s$, replacing each variable reference with its current symbolic value (or a unique skolem constant, indicating an unknown symbolic value).

Each element of $a_i$ is an assignment of the form $\langle v, e \rangle$, intended to mean that variable $v$ is assigned the value of the expression $e$. The conditions $c_i$ indicate the inequalities that must hold between the values of variables and other expressions for the program to be in a state of the form $a_i$. We call $\sigma(s)$ the *symbolic (conditional) states* of $s$.

### 3.1. Arithmetic and Boolean Expressions

Functions are defined to evaluate expressions given an assignment function. The definition of these functions simply propagates the function through the syntax of the expressions in a syntax directed manner. Variables are replaced by their current symbolic values in the state $g$. Some example clauses from the definition of these two functions are given below:

$$
\begin{aligned}
E_g(var) &= g(var) \\
E_g(const) &= const \\
E_g(-expr) &= -E_g(expr) \\
E_g((expr_1 + expr_2)) &= (E_g(expr_1) + E_g(expr_2)) \\
E_g((expr_1 - expr_2)) &= (E_g(expr_1) - E_g(expr_2)) \\
E_g((expr_1 * expr_2)) &= (E_g(expr_1) \times E_g(expr_2))
\end{aligned}
$$

$$
\begin{aligned}
B_g((expr_1 == expr_2)) &= (E_g(expr_1) = E_g(expr_2)) \\
B_g((expr_1 < expr_2)) &= (E_g(expr_1) < E_g(expr_2)) \\
B_g(!\,cond) &= \neg B_g(cond) \\
B_g((cond_1 \,||\, cond_2)) &= (B_g(cond_1) \vee B_g(cond_2)) \\
B_g((cond_1 \,\&\&\, cond_2)) &= (B_g(cond_1) \wedge B_g(cond_2))
\end{aligned}
$$

---

[2] The notation, $\langle x, y \rangle$ is used for pairs in this section, to aid the eye in distinguishing pair constructions from parenthetic sub-terms.

### 3.2. Statements

It is now possible to give a recursive definition of $\sigma(s)$. In general, a statement is executed in the context of a symbolic assignment function; the meaning of a statement depends upon the symbolic values that have been assigned to any defined program variables. In the following, this is modelled with a contextual effect using a $\lambda$-abstracted assignment function $g$. All but one of the following definitions interprets the meaning of a program as a function that expects an assignment function as its argument. The exception is at the top-most level of the program, where no values have been assigned to any variables. The meaning of a program $s$ is thus the meaning of $s$ applied to the empty assignment function $\emptyset$:

$$\sigma(s)\emptyset$$

**Block Statements**

The meaning of a block is the meaning of the sequence of statements it contains.

$$\sigma(\{\ s\ \}) = \sigma(s)$$

**Empty Statements**

An empty statement gives rise to an empty assignment function, and an empty condition set.

$$\sigma(;) = \lambda g.\{\langle \emptyset, \emptyset \rangle\}$$

**Assignment Statements**

An assignment *var=expr* produces an assignment function consisting of variable *var* and the expression *expr* evaluated in the context of the current assignment function $g$. No conditions are created.

$$\sigma(var=expr) = \lambda g.\{\langle \{\langle var, E_g(expr) \rangle\}, \emptyset \rangle\}$$

**Input Statements**

When a `scanf("%d",&x);` statement is evaluated, nothing can be assumed about the value input to the variable x. This is modelled by setting x to some unique symbolic value that, in the semantics, is intended to be interpreted as an existentially quantified variable. That is, the value of the variable is set to some unique skolem constant. It will be unique in the sense that it does not appear in the interpretation of the program leading up to that `scanf` statement. For this purpose, the term $sk_g^?$ will be used to refer to an "unused" skolem constant with respect to an assignment function $g$. That is $sk_g^?$ will be an element of $\{sk_n : n \in \mathbb{Z}^+ \wedge \neg\exists v.\langle v, sk_n \rangle \in g\}$.

$$\sigma(\texttt{scanf("\%d",\&var)}) = \lambda g.\{\langle \{\langle var, sk_g^? \rangle\}, \emptyset \rangle\}$$

**Conditional Statements**

In the case of a conditional, the symbolic execution results in two paths, one where the condition is `true`, and the `then` path

---

220

is taken, and the second where the condition is `false`, and the `else` path is taken.

$$\sigma(\texttt{if (} cond \texttt{ )} s_1 \texttt{ else } s_2)$$
$$= \lambda g.(\{\langle a, c \cup \{B_g(cond)\}\rangle : \langle a, c \rangle \in \sigma(s_1)g\} \cup$$
$$\{\langle a, c \cup \{\neg B_g(cond)\}\rangle : \langle a, c \rangle \in \sigma(s_2)g\})$$

**Statement Sequences**

In the symbolic semantics of sequences of statements, $s_1 ; s_2$, each statement gives rise to a set of pairs of symbolic assignments and path conditions. Considering all the permutations, sequencing two statements results in a set of conditional statements where the total number of pairs of assignments and path conditions is the product of the number of conditional states in the symbolic execution of the constituent statements. As with individual statements, each of the conditional states will be a pair consisting of an assignment function and a path condition. For each combination of elements $\langle a_1, c_1 \rangle$ of $\sigma(s_1)$ in the context of an assignment function $g$, and elements $\langle a_2, c_2 \rangle$ of $\sigma(s_2)$ in the context of an assignment function $g$ updated by the assignment function $a_1$ (formally, $g \oplus a_1$), there will be an element of $\sigma(s_1 ; s_2)$ consisting of $a_1$ updated by $a_2$, paired with the union of $c_1$ and $c_2$: $\langle a_1 \oplus a_2, c_1 \cup c_2 \rangle$. The assignment update operator $\oplus$ is defined by

$$f \oplus h = \{\langle v, e \rangle : \langle v, e \rangle \in h \vee (\langle v, e \rangle \in f \wedge \neg \exists e'.\langle v, e' \rangle \in h)\}$$

Using this, we can formalise the semantics of statement sequencing as

$$\sigma(s_1 ; s_2) = \lambda g.\{\langle a_1 \oplus a_2, c_1 \cup c_2 \rangle :$$
$$\langle a_1, c_1 \rangle \in \sigma(s_1)g \wedge$$
$$\langle a_2, c_2 \rangle \in \sigma(s_2)(g \oplus a_1)\}$$

**WHILE Statements**

With `while` loops, there are various ways of computing a symbolic execution. Perhaps one extreme is just to reset all variables that are assigned to so that it is not possible to infer anything about their values on termination of the loop, other than the fact that the termination condition is met. The other extreme would be to try and build some fixed point construction that models the `while` loop. The first suffers from being excessively weak; no loop invariant could be determined, for example. For the application to conditioned slicing, the second extreme suffers from being excessively complicated; although all relevant information might be encoded in the fixed point construction it is not readily accessible to the automatic theorem proving phase required to infer (relatively simple) theorems concerning boolean predicates.

The ConSIT system adopts a compromise which lies somewhere in between the two extremes. Observe that, either a loop is executed at least once, or not at all. The latter case is trivial, and is accounted for by adding the negation of the loop condition to each of the current conditional states. In the former case, if

the loop terminates, it may have been executed more than once prior to termination, and so the system cannot readily determine the values of any variables. However, it can give the values of the variables derived on the final execution of the loop as a function of the previous values of these variables, although it may have to represent these previous values as being unknown, since they might have been changed by previous executions of the loop body. The loop condition is `true` at the beginning of each iteration, and `false` immediately after the loop.

To implement this, the system uses the set of variables which are defined in the body of the loop. More formally, the set of defined variables, $\nu(s)$ of a statement $s$ is defined as follows

$$\nu(s) = \{v : \exists e \alpha \kappa.(\langle v, e \rangle \in \alpha \wedge \langle \alpha, \kappa \rangle \in \sigma(s)\emptyset)\}$$

The defined variables are those whose values might have been changed on prior executions of the loop. In the symbolic execution, we can take their unknown penultimate values to be unique skolem constants. A unique set of skolemisations, $U_{sk}^g$, of a list of variables, $[v_1, v_2, \ldots, v_n]$, in the context of an assignment $g$, is given by $\{\langle v_1, sk_{g_1}^? \rangle, \langle v_2, sk_{g_2}^? \rangle, \ldots, \langle v_n, sk_{g_n}^? \rangle\}$ where

1. $g_1 = g$

2. $g_i = g_{i-1} \oplus \{\langle v_{i-1}, sk_{g_{i-1}}^? \rangle\}$

where $\oplus$ is the previously defined assignment update operator.

Using $U_{sk}^g$, a unique skolemisation of statements $s$ is given by:

$$U_{sk}^g(O(\nu(s)))$$

where $O$ imposes some total ordering on the set of variables $\nu(s)$, to give a list of variables.

The symbolic states obtained by a `WHILE` loop are then the union of

1. The symbolic states prior to the `while` loop, with the additional constraint that the loop condition is `false` in those states.

2. The symbolic states that result from the execution of the loop body, in the context where all defined variables are uniquely skolemised, with the additional constraint that the loop condition was `true` in the initial states, and `false` in the final states.

$$\sigma(\texttt{while (} cond \texttt{ )} s)$$
$$= \lambda g.(\{\{\langle \emptyset, \{\neg B_g(cond)\}\rangle\}\} \cup$$
$$\{\langle a, c \cup \{B_g(cond), \neg B_a(cond)\}\rangle :$$
$$\langle a, c \rangle \in \sigma(s)(g \oplus U_{sk}^g(O(\nu(s))))\})$$

## 4. The Theorem Proving Phase

The symbolic execution phase takes a sequence of program statements and annotates it with symbolic state descriptions. The implementation seeks to simplify these symbolic states by eliminating those conditional states that are inconsistent from each symbolic state description to determine the paths through the structure of the program code that can never be taken. In 'normal' programs, these paths are unlikely to arise as they would constitute 'bad programming'. However, in conditioned slicing, the program is sliced with respect to an initial condition and the whole point of conditioning is to identify parts of the code which become unreachable as a result. (These are sliced away as irrelevant to the slicing criterion in the same way that statements which have no effect upon the chosen variables are sliced away.)

More precisely, if a conditional state is universally valid, then it will be the only state that can be reached. If all the conditional states of a symbolic state are inconsistent, then that point in the program will be unreachable. The theorem prover is thus used to determine whether the outcome of a predicate *must* be `true` or whether it must be `false` or whether it is not possible to tell. This process is inherently conservative, because there will be predicates which must be `true` and those which must be `false` but for which this information cannot be deduced by the theorem prover. However, this conservatism is safe: if a statement is removed because of the outcome of the theorem proving stage, then that statement is guaranteed to be unnecessary in all states which satisfy the initial condition mentioned in the conditioned slicing criterion.

Using this symbolic execution semantics, each statement in the program is associated with the set of all conditional contexts, $\{\langle a_1, c_1 \rangle, \ldots \langle a_n, c_n \rangle\}$, in which that statement could possibly be executed.

This set of contexts is transformed into a proposition using a function $\mathcal{P}$, where

$$\mathcal{P}\{\langle a_1, c_1 \rangle, \ldots \langle a_n, c_n \rangle\}$$
$$=$$
$$(\mathcal{P}'(a_1) \wedge \bigwedge c_1) \vee \ldots \vee (\mathcal{P}'(a_n) \wedge \bigwedge c_n)$$

and

$$\mathcal{P}'\{\langle v_1, e_1 \rangle, \ldots, \langle v_n, e_n \rangle\} = (v_1 = e_1) \wedge \ldots \wedge (v_n = e_n)$$

If the proposition is inconsistent (`false`), then it is inferred that the statement can never be executed: there is no path to the statement as each of the possible pairs of assignments and path conditions are inconsistent. The program is then equivalent to one in which the statement is replaced by the empty statement. In this way the conditioned program is constructed by considering which statements have inconsistent path conditions.

### 4.1. Checking for Consistency using `Isabelle`

Automatic theorem proving can be of several flavours. The simplest form might repeatedly apply a simple inference rule to the negation of the statement to be proved in the hope that eventually, a contradiction will arise. This can be very inefficient. The kinds of statements that need to be proved involve inequalities. Such transitive relations can lead to a large search space, making computations hopelessly slow.

`Isabelle` adopts a different approach, where more complicated inference rules can be applied in the form of *tactics*. A tactic is applied. If it fails to have the desired effect, then it is undone and a different tactic is attempted in much the same way as program transformation systems apply transformation tactics [3]. In a sense, `Isabelle` can be regarded as an aid to rigorous theorem proving. A collection of tactics is combined into a strategy, or *tactical*. In this application, tactical are used which attempt to perform the consistency check fully automatically.

In the initial system that was developed, a range of different tacticals had to be applied to solve the inequality puzzles. In some cases, it was necessary to temporarily reorder the tactics within a tactical. Given the obvious potential pitfalls of automating the theorem proving with `Isabelle`, the system was designed to be robust; if a theorem cannot be proven, or should an internal `Isabelle` error occur, the conditioning of the program continues, although it might miss a potential simplification. This gives rise to a safe construction of a conditioned slice, but one which is conservative. Nonetheless, as the examples in Section 5 illustrate, ConSIT is capable of reasonable program simplification.

In cases where a boolean condition is neither `true` nor `false`, but contingent upon the values of its variables, `Isabelle` can sometimes derive a simplification of the condition. Future versions of ConSIT may exploit this, substituting the simplified condition when conditioning the program. The intention of this work is to develop amorphous slicing capability [4, 17].

## 5. Examples

### 5.1. The Example from Canfora, Cimitile and DeLucia

Consider again, the example program in Figure 1. Figure 3 shows the conditioned slice produced by the ConSIT system. This is identical to the conditioned slice produced by Canfora, Cimitile and DeLucia using a mixture of automated slicing and manual, human analysis to evaluate conditions.

### 5.2. Checking and Extracting Business Rules

Conditioned slicing can be used as a technique for business rule extraction. For example, consider the simple tax calculation program in Figure 7.

This program represents a computation of tax codes and amounts of tax payable, including allowances for a United Kingdom citizen in the tax year April 1998 to April 1999. Each person has a personal allowance which is an amount of un-taxed income. The personal allowance depends upon the status of the person, reflected by the boolean variables `blind`, `married` and `widowed` and the integer variable `age`. There are three tax bands, for which tax is charged at the rates of 10%, 23% and 40%. The width of the 10% tax band is subject to the status of the person, while the 23% and 40% are fixed for all individuals.

```
main() {
int age, blind, widow, married, income

scanf("%d",&age);
scanf("%d",&blind);
scanf("%d",&married);
scanf("%d",&widow);
scanf("%d",&income);

if (age>=75) personal = 5980;
else if (age>=65) personal = 5720;
else personal = 4335;

if ((age>=65) && income >16800)
{ t = personal - ((income-16800)/2) ;
  if (t>4335) personal = t;
  else personal = 4335;    }

if (blind) personal = personal + 1380 ;

if (married && age >=75) pc10 = 6692;
else if (married && (age >= 65)) pc10 = 6625;
else if (married || widow) pc10 = 3470;
else pc10 = 1500;

if (married && age >= 65 && income > 16800)
{ t = pc10-((income-16800)/2);
  if (t>3470) pc10 = t;
  else pc10 = 3470;    }

if (income <= personal) tax = 0;
else { income = income - personal ;
       if (income <= pc10) tax = income / 10;
       else { tax = pc10 / 10;
              income = income - pc10;
            if (income <= 28000) tax = ((tax + income) * 23) / 100 ;
            else { tax = ((tax + 28000) * 23) / 100 ;
                   income = income - 28000;
                   tax = ((tax + income) * 40) / 100; }
          }
     }

if (!blind && !married && age < 65) code = 'L' ;
else if (!blind && age < 65 && married) code = 'H';
else if (age >= 65 && age < 75 && !married && !blind) code = 'P';
else if (age >= 65 && age < 75 && married && !blind) code = 'V';
else code = 'T';
}
```

**Figure 7. UK Income Taxation Calculation Program**

This set of taxation rules constitutes a governmental 'business system', and the program in Figure 7 represents an attempt to capture these rules in program code.

Conditioned slicing allows us to extract from this program, fragments which correspond to certain taxation scenarios. In so doing, the conditioned slicer is identifying the portions of the code which implement individual business rules. For example, using conditioned slicing, it becomes possible to ask

"what is the personal allowance calculation for a blind widow aged over 68?"

Slicing extracts from the program only the code concerned

with computation on `personal` and from this only that code which is relevant to computations which satisfy the scenario in which the person concerned is blind, over 68 years of age and widowed. Observe that as a *range* of possible inputs is specified by this condition, it is not possible to simply run the program in order to arrive at the answer.

For the blind widow over the age of 68, the conditioned slicing computed by ConSIT is given in Figure 8.

```
scanf("%d",&age);
scanf("%d",&blind);

if (age>=75) personal = 5980;
else if (age>=65) personal = 5720;

if (age>=65 && income >16800)
{ t = personal - ((income-16800)/2);
  if (t>4335) personal = t ;
  else personal = 4335; }

if (blind) personal = personal + 1380 ;
```

**Figure 8. Specialised Personal Allowance**

```
scanf("%d",&age);
scanf("%d",&blind);
scanf("%d",&married);

if (!blind && !married && age < 65)
code = 'L' ;
else if (!blind && age < 65 && married)
code = 'H';
else if (age >= 65 && age < 75
        && !married && !blind)
else if (age >= 65 && age < 75
        && married && !blind)
else code = 'T';
```

**Figure 9. Tax Codes for the Under 60s**

For similar rule-based systems in which source-code effectively captures business rules, this example suggests that conditioned slicing might be effective in recovering business rules in a similar way to the technique proposed by Canfora et al [6].

Another example of a question that can be addressed using ConSIT, is

"What are the possible tax codes that apply to people under the age of 60?"

This computation is captured by the conditioned slice depicted in Figure 9.

The example clearly illustrates the program comprehension advantages of removing 'unnecessary predicates' from a conditioned slice. In deeply nested conditional structures it is helpful

to remove these unnecessary predicate tests, so that those tests which play a part in the computation of interest become more obvious. Doing this produces the further refined conditioned slicing in Figure 10. The slice in Figure 10 satisfies the definition of a conditioned slice and is simpler than one which retains the predicates, and so such a slice would appear to be better from both a theoretical and a practical point of view. The current implementation does not remove these predicates for compatibility with the work of Canfora et al [5].

```
scanf("%d",&age);
scanf("%d",&blind);
scanf("%d",&married);

if (!blind && !married && age < 65)
code = 'L' ;
else if (!blind && age < 65 && married)
code = 'H';
else code = 'T';
```

**Figure 10. Under 60s Without Unnecessary Predicates**

## 6. Conclusion and Future Work

This paper has described ConSIT, a conditioned slicing system which uses symbolic execution, traditional static slicing and the `Isabelle` theorem prover to implement conditioned slicing for a simple intraprocedural subset of C.

The symbolic executor propagates state information to each statement in the program. This information is passed to the theorem prover, which determines (in a conservative and safe manner) which statements have become unreachable under the conditions imposed by the slicing criterion. This forms a conditioned program which is further sliced using traditional static slicing.

ConSIT is the first fully automated implementation of conditioned slicing. However, the language handled by ConSIT is somewhat limited. Pointers and procedures are the most notable omissions. Work is in progress to extend ConSIT to handle fully interprocedural conditioned slicing.

Another problem for future work is the adoption of the technologies used to implement ConSIT so that amorphous conditioned slices [4, 17, 19] can be computed. Amorphous slices share the semantic restriction that they preserve the effect of the subject program on the slicing criterion, but are syntactically unrestricted. In cases where the `Isabelle` theorem prover was unable to decide the truth or otherwise of propositions put to it, it was often able to simplify the proposition as a side effect of its computation. This simplification has a direct counterpart in simplification of arithmetic and boolean expressions which would be useful in an implementation of amorphous conditioned slicing.

Isabelle is a very powerful and general purpose theorem prover. This means that it can take considerable time to produce amorphous slices using Isabelle as the engine for deciding propositions. For instances, the first example presented in this paper, takes about 20 minutes to slice on a Pentium II running at 233MHz. While this may be acceptable for a proof of concept implementation, it is clearly inadequate as a basis for extensive development. However, the kind of propositions which arise in conditioned slicing tend to be rather simple and it could be that great speed improvement can be achieved with a more narrowly focussed technology. To this end, the authors plan to investigate the use of other tools for analysis of conditions, such as the Stanford Validity Checker (SVC) [2]. The hope is that the use of tools like the SVC will dramatically improve performance.

## Acknowledgements

The authors would like to thank Andrea DeLucia and Gerardo Canfora for several helpful discussions concerning conditioned slicing. Lawrence Paulson and Tobias Nipkow kindly made available a development version of `Isabelle` which contained extra features of use in developing ConSIT. This work is supported in part by EPSRC grants GR/M58719 and GR/M78083.

## References

[1] H. Agrawal and J. R. Horgan. Dynamic program slicing. In *ACM SIGPLAN Conference on Programming Language Design and Implementation*, pages 246–256, New York, June 1990.

[2] C. Barrett, D. Dill, and J. Levitt. Validity checking for combinations of theories with equality. In M. Srivas and A. Camilleri, editors, *Formal Methods In Computer-Aided Design*, volume 1166 of *Lecture Notes in Computer Science*, pages 187–201. Springer-Verlag, November 1996. Palo Alto, California, November 6–8.

[3] K. Bennett, T. Bull, E. Younger, and Z. Luo. Bylands: reverse engineering safety-critical systems. In *IEEE International Conference on Software Maintenance*, pages 358–366. IEEE Computer Society Press, Los Alamitos, California, USA, 1995.

[4] D. W. Binkley. Computing amorphous program slices using dependence graphs and a data-flow model. In *ACM Symposium on Applied Computing*, pages 519–525, The Menger, San Antonio, Texas, U.S.A., 1999. ACM Press, New York, NY, USA.

[5] G. Canfora, A. Cimitile, and A. De Lucia. Conditioned program slicing. In M. Harman and K. Gallagher, editors, *Information and Software Technology Special Issue on Program Slicing*, volume 40, pages 595–607. Elsevier Science B. V., 1998.

[6] G. Canfora, A. Cimitile, A. D. Lucia, and G. A. D. Lucca. Decomposing legacy programs: A first step towards migrating to client–server platforms. In *6th IEEE International Workshop on Program Comprehension*, pages 136–144, Ischia, Italy, June 1998. IEEE Computer Society Press, Los Alamitos, California, USA.

[7] G. Canfora, A. D. Lucia, and M. Munro. An integrated environment for reuse reengineering C code. *Journal of Systems and Software*, 42:153–164, 1998.

[8] A. Cimitile, A. De Lucia, and M. Munro. Identifying reusable functions using specification driven program slicing: a case study. In *Proceedings of the IEEE International Conference on Software Maintenance (ICSM'95)*, pages 124–133, Nice, France, 1995. IEEE Computer Society Press, Los Alamitos, California, USA.

[9] A. Cimitile, A. De Lucia, and M. Munro. Qualifying reusable functions using symbolic execution. In *Proceedings of the 2nd working conference on reverse engineering*, pages 178–187, Toronto, Canada, 1995. IEEE Computer Society Press, Los Alamitos, California, USA.

[10] A. Cimitile, A. De Lucia, and M. Munro. A specification driven slicing process for identifying reusable functions. *Software maintenance: Research and Practice*, 8:145–178, 1996.

[11] S. Danicic and M. Harman. Espresso: A slicer generator. In *ACM Symposium on Applied Computing, (SAC'00)*, page To appear, Como, Italy, Mar. 2000.

[12] S. Danicic, M. Harman, and Y. Sivagurunathan. A parallel algorithm for static program slicing. *Information Processing Letters*, 56(6):307–313, Dec. 1995.

[13] A. De Lucia. Private communication, 1999.

[14] A. De Lucia, A. R. Fasolino, and M. Munro. Understanding function behaviours through program slicing. In *4th IEEE Workshop on Program Comprehension*, pages 9–18, Berlin, Germany, Mar. 1996. IEEE Computer Society Press, Los Alamitos, California, USA.

[15] E. W. Dijkstra. *A discipline of programming*. Prentice Hall, 1972.

[16] K. B. Gallagher. Evaluating the surgeon's assistant: Results of a pilot study. In *Proceedings of the International Conference on Software Maintenance*, pages 236–244. IEEE Computer Society Press, Los Alamitos, California, USA, Nov. 1992.

[17] M. Harman and S. Danicic. Amorphous program slicing. In *5th IEEE International Workshop on Program Comprehesion (IWPC'97)*, pages 70–79, Dearborn, Michigan, USA, May 1997. IEEE Computer Society Press, Los Alamitos, California, USA.

[18] M. Harman, C. Fox, R. M. Hierons, D. Binkley, and S. Danicic. Program simplification as a means of approximating undecidable propositions. In *7th IEEE International Workshop on Program Comprehesion (IWPC'99)*, pages 208–217, Pittsburgh, Pennsylvania, USA, May 1999. IEEE Computer Society Press, Los Alamitos, California, USA.

[19] M. Harman, Y. Sivagurunathan, and S. Danicic. Analysis of dynamic memory access using amorphous slicing. In *IEEE International Conference on Software Maintenance (ICSM'98)*, pages 336–345, Bethesda, Maryland, USA, Nov. 1998. IEEE Computer Society Press, Los Alamitos, California, USA.

[20] S. Horwitz, T. Reps, and D. Binkley. Interprocedural slicing using dependence graphs. *ACM Transactions on Programming Languages and Systems*, 12(1):26–61, 1990.

[21] M. Kamkar. *Interprocedural dynamic slicing with applications to debugging and testing*. PhD Thesis, Department of Computer Science and Information Science, Linköping University, Sweden, 1993. Available as Linköping Studies in Science and Technology, Dissertations, Number 297.

[22] B. Korel and J. Laski. Dynamic program slicing. *Information Processing Letters*, 29(3):155–163, Oct. 1988.

[23] A. Lakhotia and J.-C. Deprez. Restructuring programs by tucking statements into functions. In M. Harman and K. Gallagher, editors, *Information and Software Technology Special Issue on Program Slicing*, volume 40, pages 677–689. Elsevier, 1998.

[24] J. R. Lyle and M. Weiser. Automatic program bug location by program slicing. In *2nd International Conference on Computers and Applications*, pages 877–882, Peking, 1987. IEEE Computer Society Press, Los Alamitos, California, USA.

[25] L. C. Paulson. Isabelle: A generic theorem prover. *Lecture Notes in Computer Science*, 828:xvii + 321, 1994.

[26] L. C. Paulson. Isabelle's reference manual. Technical Report 283, University of Cambridge, Computer Laboratory, 1997.

[27] L. C. Paulson. Strategic principles in the design of Isabelle. In *CADE-15 Workshop on Strategies in Automated Deduction*, pages 11–17, Lindau, Germany, 1998.

[28] M. Weiser. *Program slices: Formal, psychological, and practical investigations of an automatic program abstraction method.* PhD thesis, University of Michigan, Ann Arbor, MI, 1979.

[29] M. Weiser. Program slicing. *IEEE Transactions on Software Engineering*, 10(4):352–357, 1984.

# Management I

# Beyond Productivity in Software Maintenance: Factors Affecting Lead Time in Servicing Users' Requests

Taizan Chan

School of Information Systems
Queensland University of Technology
2 George Street, QLD 4001, Australia
taizan@fit.qut.edu.au

## Abstract

*Research on the economics of software maintenance has concentrated on software maintenance productivity. More often than not, maintenance productivity is measured by the number of hours spent in servicing a maintenance request. While this measure captures the cost of an information systems (IS) department, it ignores a potential opportunity cost to the users that is better captured by the lead time taken to fulfill a request. Using detailed data of more than 1,000 maintenance projects collected at a field site over a 6-year period, we examine how the lead time of a request is affected by factors such as the characteristics of the system, the request, and the maintainer responsible for the request. We found that the complexity of a request significantly postpones its lead time. The lead time is also increased by the internal lead time target set by the IS department based on staff availability. We also divided the lead time into the queuing time and the service time components and study how they are influenced by the same factors.*

## 1. Introduction

The huge cost associated with software maintenance has generated considerable research interests in the economics of software maintenance (see for example, [3] [9] [6]). This stream of research suggests means for improving maintenance productivity and for controlling the high maintenance cost that many organizations are experiencing [8] [16]. A central premise of this stream of research is that the IS function, like traditional manufacturing, is a cost center, and thus should aim to *minimize* the cost of fulfilling maintenance requests.

Most IS departments, however, are increasingly charged with other objectives [19]. They are also expected to provide a high level of service to their users. In particular, due to the rapidly changing and increasingly competitive business environments, IS departments are expected to be highly responsive in servicing the request of the users. That is, they need to minimize not only the cost of maintenance but also the opportunity cost to the users for not fulfilling their maintenance requests immediately. Like other servicing processes such as that of a bank teller, the maintenance process involves queues and waiting times. A maintenance request by the users usually has to wait in a queue for a certain period of time before it is being serviced. Unlike other servicing processes which are dedicated, however, the servicing of a request may be interrupted because the server has to attend to other, more urgent requests. Thus, the elapsed service time of a request, from the time its servicing began to the time its servicing is completed, can be quite different from the actual effort spent in fulfilling the request.

The elapsed time between the time a request is initiated by the users and the time it is completed, i.e., the sum of the queuing time and the service time is the lead time experienced by the users. It represents an opportunity cost to the users which could have been reduced if the request was delivered earlier [4]. For example, a speedy implementation of an integration feature that automatically routes customer orders entered in a sales department to the manufacturing department could potentially save many hours spent in fulfilling customers orders and thus increasing customers satisfaction. Indeed, the delay in fulfilling a request can even hurt the ability of an organization to expand its business. Martin and McClure [15] recounted an incident in which an organization had to abandon its plan to acquire a company because its IS department was unable to modify an existing record structure to accommodate the new products' codes in time. Thus, the opportunity costs presented by delayed deliveries of maintenance requests cannot be overemphasized.

Besides capturing user's opportunity cost, lead time is also a good diagnostic of the maintenance process. It measures process response and it often serves as an overall indicator of process control [17]. Long lead times in fulfilling maintenance requests are evidence that a software maintenance process is out of control, and factors affecting the lead time should be identified and controlled for.

Despite its importance, little or no research has been directed at the study of lead time reduction in software maintenance. This paper reports an exploratory study that attempts to bridge this gap in the literature. Based on software maintenance data collected from a field site, we aim to determine the drivers of lead time in software maintenance. In particular, we consider the factors that have been found to be significant drivers of software maintenance effort in other empirical studies [1][7][11][14][16], namely, (i) application characteristics, (ii) nature and complexity of user request, and (iii) programmer's knowledge and constraints, and examine their impact on lead time and its constituent queuing time and service time. Specifically, we aim to answer the following research questions:

1. Do the age and level of deterioration of an application delay the lead time needed to service a request on that application?

2. How does the application familiarity of a programmer influence the lead time of requests serviced by him?

3. Is the complexity of a request a significant driver of its lead time?

4. Can the target lead time set by the IS department predict the lead time?

The rest of the paper is organized as follows. Section 2 describes the conceptual framework for understanding the variables we are considering. Section 3 describes the research site and the data collection procedure. Section 4 presents the statistical results. Section 5 discusses the results and draw implications for software maintenance management. Section 6 concludes the paper by summarizing the main results and highlighting the limitations of this study.

## 2. Conceptual Framework

The software maintenance process is conceptualized here as a service process involving queues and waiting times [12]. The major entities involved in the process are the IS department (which composes of mainly the IS staff), the users, and the application portfolio [19].

The process starts with the initiation of requests by the users. When an application fails to work as intended or does not meet the current needs of the users, requests are initiated. Users may request for corrective, adaptive, or perfective changes and each request may entail a different task complexity [18]. Each request will be evaluated by both the IS department and the users and is selected for servicing only if it adds value to the organization. Once a request is evaluated, it is assigned to a maintainer who will be responsible for its completion.

As the maintainer assigned the new request is likely to be loaded with prior requests, the new request is seldom serviced immediately but has to join the queue of requests waiting to be serviced by the maintainer. That is, a request often has to wait for a period of time before it is serviced. The servicing of a request could begin under one of the three circumstances: (i) when all the requests ahead in the queue have been completed, (ii) when the new request is more urgent than other requests in the queue, or (iii) when the maintainer is unable to continue working with the earlier requests because the material necessary for working with those requests are temporarily unavailable. In this case, the maintainer could begin working on the new request while waiting for the material so that he can continue working with the earlier requests. For the same reason that a request may be serviced before earlier requests were completed, the new request may also be interrupted and put "on hold" during its servicing. As a result, a request usually experiences an elapsed service time that is longer than the actual time-effort expanded by the maintainer on the request.

The elapsed time experienced by a request in a queue, the elapsed time experienced by a request during servicing, and the resultant total elapsed time from approval to completion are the dependent variables of interest in this study. Formally, these dependent variables are defined as follow:

- **Queuing time.** This is the total elapsed time from the date on which the initiated request is approved to the date on which the servicing actually begins.

- **Service time.** This is the total elapsed time from the date on which servicing actually begins to the date on which servicing is completed.

- **Lead time.** This is the total elapsed time from the date on which the initiated request is approved for servicing to the date on which the servicing of the request is completed.

The relationship between the queuing time, the service time, and the resulting lead time of a maintenance request is illustrated in Figure 1.

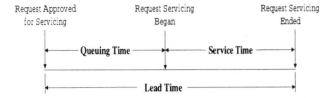

**Figure 1. The queuing time, service time, and lead time of a maintenance service encounter**

Corresponding to the three groups of entities involved in the software maintenance process, namely application portfolio, IS department, and users, we group the relevant factors that might affect the three dependent variables into three broad categories:

1. **Characteristics of the Application**: We consider the following characteristics of the application:

   - **Age**. Old applications are harder to maintain because knowledge of the underlying technologies, business objectives, and data and process models of the application accumulated by staff is more likely to be lost due to staff turnover. Indeed, Lientz and Swanson [14] and Swanson and Beath [19] found that application age is one of the main determinants of the effort required to maintain the application. Thus, we hypothesize that the service time and the lead time of a request will increase with the system age. It is not clear, however, how the age of the application will affect the queuing time. Thus, we make the null hypothesis that queuing time is not affected by the system age. Formally, the hypotheses are as follows:

     *H1a.* Queuing time of a request is not affected by the age of the target application of the request.

     *H1b.* Service time of a request increases with the age of the target application of the request.

     *H1c.* Lead time of a request increases with the age of the target application of the request.

   - **Accumulated number of requests serviced**. On one hand, frequent modifications and enhancements to an application can deteriorate its system structure [10][13] and increase the maintenance effort [7][11]. On the other hand,

frequent modifications on the application by the same group of people also mean that familiarity with the application improves over time, thereby improving maintenance productivity. As it is not clear what is the relative impact of these two factors on service time, we make the null hypothesis that service time is not affected by the accumulated number of requests serviced. Although an increase in the total number of completed requests could potentially imply that a smaller number of requests remained to be serviced and hence shorter queuing time, this is so only if the rate of requests arrival is constant over time. However, given the lack of information on the rate of requests arrival, we could only make the null hypothesis that accumulated number of requests serviced has no impact on the queuing time. Similarly, the resultant lead time may increase or decrease depending on the relative impact of accumulated number of requests serviced on the queuing and servicing time. We therefore assume *a priori* that the accumulated number of requests already serviced has no impact on the lead time. Thus, we have:

*H1d.* Queuing time of a request is not affected by the accumulated number of requests already serviced on the target application of the request.

*H1e.* Service time of a request is not affected by the accumulated number of requests already serviced on the target application of the request.

*H1f.* Lead time of a request is not affected by the accumulated number of requests already serviced on the target application of the request.

2. **IS Staff**: We consider the impact of the following characteristics of IS staff on the queuing, service and lead times:

   - **Application Familiarity**. Chan [5] have shown that familiarity with the application in terms of the number of requests that the staff have accomplished on the application could significantly reduce the effort required to service a request. A programmer with a greater application familiarity is a faster server. Consequently, we expect that the servicing time, the queuing time and the lead time of the request will be reduced by the level of application familiarity of the staff when the request was assigned.

*H2a.* Queuing time of a request assigned to a staff decreases with the level of application familiarity of that staff.

*H2b.* Service time of a request assigned to a staff decreases with the level of application familiarity of that staff.

*H2c.* Lead time of a request assigned to a staff decreases with the level of application familiarity of that staff.

- **Target lead time**. The IS department we worked with set an internal target lead time. This lead time is determined based on an assessment of staff availability. We hypothesized that this internal target is based on an accurate assessment of what can be realistically achieved by the IS department and thus should correlate well with the actual lead time. Hence, we make the following hypotheses:

*H2d.* Queuing time of a request assigned to a staff increases with the internal target lead time.

*H2e.* Service time of a request assigned to a staff increases with the internal target lead time.

*H2f.* Lead time of a request assigned to a staff increases with the internal target lead time.

3. **Complexity of Request.** We consider the following characteristics of a maintenance request:

- **Task complexity**. We use the total effort spent in fulfilling request as a surrogate measure for the complexity of the request. Banker, Datar, and Kemerer [1] have found that task complexity is a major determinant of the effort required to service a request, thereby suggesting the plausibility of using the total effort as a measure for the complexity of the task involved. Besides taking a longer time to complete, a complex request is likely to face more interruptions while servicing. Thus, we expect the elapsed service time to increase with task complexity. Task complexity may increase the queuing time of a request because a maintainer is more likely to service simpler requests first to reduce the length of the queue more quickly. We make the

following hypotheses:

*H3a.* Queuing time of a request increases with its task complexity.

*H3b.* Service time of a request increases with its task complexity.

*H3c.* Lead time of a request increases with its task complexity.

## 3. Research Site and Data Collection

Our research site is the application systems division of the information systems (IS) department of a large non-profit organization in Singapore[1] (hereafter referred to as the "IS department"). The IS department is currently responsible for the maintenance of 23 major application systems. These systems are written in COBOL and run on IBM hardware. The age of an application range from a few months to 14 years old, with an average age of 2.47 years. Thus, the application portfolio is relatively young. The application portfolio supports approximately 1000 users in 11 departments. It is currently maintained by 33 IS staff. The length of service of an IS staff range between 3-6 years. The IS staff are organized by applications. That is, requests for an application is usually assigned to only a small group of people who are mainly responsible for that application. This implies that most of the staff is familiar with their respective applications under maintenance. Eighty-five percent of the staff have either a bachelor or honors degree in computer science or related field.

Raw data are collected at both the application and the individual request level so that all the dependent and independent variables could be computed. They include the following:

### Application Level Data

The year of installation of the application (INSTAL-LYEAR). This is the year from which the application first becomes operational.[2]

---

[1] The IS department has three divisions. The other divisions deal with end-users training and data base support and are thus not relevant to our study.

[2] Another potentially relevant application level variable is the size of the applications. However, the only measure of size available from this field site is the current number of program modules in each application. As the sizes of the modules are not known, and the sizes of the applications have changed over time, these measures would not accurately reflect the actual sizes of the applications at the time the requests were performed. Thus, application size is not included in this analysis.

## Request Level Data

1. Date of initiation (INITDATE). This is the date on which a request was approved for maintenance.

2. Deadline for completion (DEADLINE). This is the date by which the user expected the maintenance request to be serviced. Other things being equal, a closer deadline relative to the INITDATE indicated that the request was more urgent.

3. System code (SYS). This indicates the system for which the maintenance request was initiated.

4. Staff code (STAFF). This identifies the IS staff who was assigned the responsibility of completing the maintenance request.

5. Estimated date of request completion (ESTFINISH-DATE). This is the target date of completion set by the IS department based on an assessment of staff availability.

6. Actual date of starting (ACTSTARTDATE). This is the date on which the servicing of the request actually began.

7. Actual date of completion (ACTFINISHDATE). This is the date on which the request was actually completed.

8. Task complexity (TASK). This is measured as the actual effort in man-days spent in servicing the request.

Based on the above raw data, we compute the following dependent variables:

1. Queuing time, QUEUETIME = ACTSTARTDATE - INITDATE.

2. Service time, SERVTIME = ACTFINISHDATE - ACTSTARTDATE.

3. Lead time, LEADTIME = ACTFINISHDATE - INITDATE.

Obviously, LEADTIME = SERVTIME + QUEUETIME.

The independent variables are derived from the raw data as described below. (Note that the values of the independent variables, such as the age of an application, the cumulative number of maintenance already performed on an application, and application familiarity of a staff, which vary over time, are computed dynamically. This is done to truly reflect the states of the applications and the IS staff at the point the request arrived.)

## Application Variables

- The age of the application (AGE). The age of an application at the time the request arrived is computed on a monthly basis. It is obtained by subtracting the date of installation from the date of request approval. Since only the year of installation was known, it is assumed that the month of installation of each application is January.[3]

- The cumulative number of maintenance already performed on the application (ACCUM). This is obtained by counting the number of requests already serviced on the application by the time the request arrived.

## IS Staff Variables

- Familiarity of STAFF with an application (FAM). This is measured by the cumulative number of requests with which the STAFF had worked on the application.

- Target lead time set by STAFF, TARGETLEAD = ESTFINISHDATE - INITDATE.

## User/Request Variable[4]

- Complexity of request. This is measured by TASK.

## 4. Results

The unit of analysis is a maintenance request. Raw data of 1,003 completed maintenance requests were collected at the field site. The dependent and independent variables were then derived from the raw data. A multiple regression analysis was performed for each of the three dependent variables. Tables 1 and 2 provide a summary statistics of the dependent and the independent variables respectively. Tables 3-5 present the regression results.

We test all our hypotheses at 5% level of significance. The results are discussed below:

### Impact of Application Variables

- *Age.* The regression results indicate that the queuing time of a request decreases with the age of the application, rejecting Hypothesis H1a. On the other hand, both the service and the lead time were not affected by

---

[3] Analysis with a finer-grained measure of AGE in days did not yield any significant difference in the statistical results. Hence, the AGE variable is computed in a more commonly used unit of month here.

[4] Another potentially important user/request variable is the expected lead time of a request, EXPLEAD, which is given by the elapsed time from the initiation of a request to the deadline by which the users expect the request to be completed. That is, EXPLEAD = DEADLINE - INITDATE. EXPLEAD, however, correlates highly with TARGETLEAD and would have resulted in collinearly if it is included in the multiple regression analysis. TARGETLEAD has been included in the analysis instead as it is the most important predictor of all the three dependent variables. The impact of EXPLEAD on lead time, however, is discussed in Section 5.

| Dependent Variables | | | | | |
|---|---|---|---|---|---|
| Variables | Mean | S.D. | Min. | Max. | Median |
| QUEUETIME | 1.54 | 3.46 | 0.00 | 46.00 | 1.00 |
| SERVTIME | 2.01 | 3.37 | 0.00 | 47.00 | 1.00 |
| LEADTIME | 3.54 | 5.20 | 0.00 | 52.00 | 2.00 |

**Table 1. Summary statistics of dependent variables**

| Independent Variables | | | | | |
|---|---|---|---|---|---|
| Variables | Mean | S.D. | Min. | Max. | Median |
| AGE | 34.70 | 20.36 | 0.0 | 173 | 36 |
| ACCUM | 76.90 | 68.17 | 0.00 | 318.00 | 61.00 |
| FAM | 9.35 | 13.28 | 0.00 | 61.00 | 4.00 |
| TARGETLEAD | 2.09 | 3.70 | 0.00 | 42.00 | 1.00 |
| TASK | 7.76 | 20.29 | 0.10 | 273.00 | 3.00 |

**Table 2. Summary statistics of independent variables**

| Dependent Variable: QUEUETIME | | | |
|---|---|---|---|
| Independent Variable | Coefficient | t-value | Significance |
| Intercept | 0.8515 | 5.6237 | < 0.0001 |
| AGE | -0.0106 | -2.9780 | 0.0030 |
| ACCUM | -0.0030 | -2.7486 | 0.0061 |
| FAM | -0.0131 | -2.4944 | 0.0128 |
| TARGETLEAD | 0.7362 | 38.5341 | < 0.0001 |
| TASK | -0.0169 | -4.8758 | < 0.0001 |
| F Value | 326.13 | | |
| $Pr > F$ | < 0.0001 | | |
| $AdjustedR^2$ | 0.6187 | | |

**Table 3. Multiple regression results on QUEUETIME**

| Dependent Variable: SERVTIME | | | |
|---|---|---|---|
| Independent Variable | Coefficient | t-value | Significance |
| Intercept | 0.3456 | 1.7912 | 0.0736 |
| AGE | 0.0056 | 1.2331 | 0.2178 |
| ACCUM | 0.0009 | 0.6449 | 0.5192 |
| FAM | 0.0267 | 3.9847 | 0.0001 |
| TARGETLEAD | 0.3167 | 13.0115 | < 0.0001 |
| TASK | 0.0628 | 14.2154 | < 0.0001 |
| F Value | 106.38 | | |
| $Pr > F$ | <0.0001 | | |
| $AdjustedR^2$ | 0.3446 | | |

**Table 4. Multiple regression results on SERVTIME**

| Dependent Variable: LEADTIME | | | |
|---|---|---|---|
| Independent Variable | Coefficient | t-value | Significance |
| Intercept | 1.1970 | 5.6517 | < 0.0001 |
| AGE | -0.0050 | -1.0056 | 0.3149 |
| ACCUM | -0.0021 | -1.3774 | 0.1687 |
| FAM | 0.0136 | 1.8465 | 0.0651 |
| TARGETLEAD | 1.0529 | 39.3977 | < 0.0001 |
| TASK | 0.0459 | 9.4631 | < 0.0001 |
| F Value | 407.18 | | |
| $Pr > F$ | < 0.0001 | | |
| $AdjustedR^2$ | 0.6696 | | |

**Table 5. Multiple regression results on LEADTIME**

the age of the application, thus rejecting hypotheses H1b and H1c.

- *Accumulated number of requests serviced.* Contrary to our hypothesis H1d, the queuing time decreases with the accumulated number of requests already performed on the application. This suggests that perhaps the rate of requests arrival is relatively constant over time. Consistent with our hypothesis H1e, the service time of a request is not significantly affected by the accumulated number of request serviced. The accumulated number of request serviced also does not appear to have a significant impact on lead time. Thus hypothesis H1f is not rejected.

**Impact of IS Staff Variables**

- *Application familiarity.* Consistent with hypothesis H2a, application familiarity helps to reduce queuing time of a request. Contrary to hypothesis H2b, the servicing time of a request *increases* with the application familiarity. The lead time is not significantly affected by the application familiarity of the staff, rejecting hypothesis H2c.

- *Target lead time.* Target lead time appears to be the single most important predictor for all three dependent variables. All three variables increase with the target lead time, supporting hypotheses H2d-f.

**Impact of User/Request Variable**

- *Task complexity.* As expected, the service and lead times are significantly increased by the task complexity. Thus hypotheses H3b-c are supported. Contrary to our hypothesis H3a, however, queuing time decreases with the task complexity.

## 5. Discussion

Our results suggest that neither the age nor the amount of system deterioration has a negative impact on the total elapsed time required to deliver a request. Indeed, these two factors were found to have positive impact on the constituent queuing time. On the other hand, application familiarity, which has been found to improve maintenance productivity, appears to have negative impact on the service time (although this impact is not significant enough to influence the resultant lead time).

These results suggest that factors that have been found to influence maintenance productivity do not necessarily affect the elapsed time and may even have opposite impact on the elapsed time involved. It should be cautioned, however, that this does not necessarily mean maintenance productivity has no impact on the lead time of a request. A plausible explanation for the lack of significant influence of application characteristics on lead time is that, by organizing the maintenance staff according to applications, each staff is very likely to be familiar with the respective application they are responsible for, thereby significantly reducing the impact of these application characteristics on their performance [5]. Furthermore, the negative impact of application familiarity on the service time is likely due to the fact that a maintainer who is more familiar with an application would tend to be assigned more requests on that application and therefore experience more interruption in servicing the requests.

A further analysis of the impact on lead time of another independent variable, the expected lead time, which is the elapsed time from the initiation of a request to the deadline by which the users expect the request to be completed, as an alternative to TARGETLEAD, reveals that it also has a significant impact on the lead time ($coef. = 0.6143$, $t - value = 9.7307$, $sig. = 0.0001$).[5] However, as it can be observed, its impact on the lead time is not as strong as that of TARGETLEAD. Furthermore, it is also found that a large number of requests were not completed in time (64.4% of the requests were not completed by the deadline set by the user, with the mean delay of 2.6 days).

Thus, despite the IS department's attempt to increase maintenance productivity and users' satisfaction by organizing its staff by applications, the delivery of requests does not seem to meet users' expectations. This, however, does not imply that the IS department ignores users' need. The problem seems to lie in the inability of the staff to complete servicing the request in time. We conjecture that this is due mainly to the fact that the staff are overloaded and are therefore unable to pay enough attention to any particular request, resulting in a prolonged service and lead time. Furthermore, the significant impact of the internally

| Period | Yr.1 | Yr.2 | Yr.3 | Yr.4 | Yr.5 | Yr.6 |
|--------|------|------|------|------|------|------|
| Jan | 310 | 542 | 620 | 1562 | 2644 | 4726 |
| Feb | 294 | 553 | 1191 | 1866 | 2773 | 4862 |
| Mar | 342 | 846 | 1175 | 2002 | 3362 | 5223 |
| Apr | 350 | 768 | 1214 | 2188 | 4067 | 5546 |
| May | 343 | 822 | 1326 | 2389 | 3922 | 5136 |
| Jun | 365 | 799 | 1413 | 2191 | 3708 | 5810 |
| Jul | 353 | 832 | 1516 | 2530 | 3799 | 5291 |
| Aug | 377 | 939 | 1524 | 2557 | 4081 | 5016 |
| Sep | 453 | 950 | 1576 | 2546 | 4489 | 4438 |
| Oct | 477 | 984 | 1643 | 2583 | 4627 | 3958 |
| Nov | 537 | 719 | 1557 | 2629 | 4539 | 3927 |
| Dec | 548 | 609 | 1522 | 2599 | 4606 | 3651 |

**Table 6. Cumulative backlogs of unserviced requests (in man-days) by months**

set target lead time on all the time variables indicates that the IS department indeed strives to meet the more realistic targets that take into account the resource constraint and availability faced by the department.

An analysis of the backlog of unfulfilled requests in man-days over the period of data collection[6] (shown in Table 6) as well as the mean load of a staff at any one time (mean = 4.6 requests, standard deviation = 4.4) supports the above view. The results reveal that the current IS department is indeed under-staffed relative to the volume of requests that arrived from the users. This finding suggests that an IS department must reduce the average load of each staff if meeting users' expectations is a high priority. This could be accomplished by either having a group of "backup" programmers to relieve the load of the staff when it is too high, or hiring more people permanently. The first strategy is more flexible when the patterns of requests arrival for the various applications fluctuate over time and are seasonal. Its drawback is the associated lower productivity due to unfamiliarity of the programmers. The second strategy gains in productivity but is less desirable because the IS department is tied with a greater number of personnel. Either way, it is clear that there is a fundamental tradeoff between the costs that the IS department has to bear and the level of users' satisfaction. Thus, better service to the users does not come free. One way to resolve this dilemma is to charge the users a fee for servicing their requests.

Consistent with the results of Banker, Datar, and Kemerer [1], task complexity (as measured by TASK here) is a main determinant of the elapsed time spent in servicing the request and the lead time. The parameter estimate for the variable TASK in the regression analysis of servicing time suggests that an increase in the task complexity of one man-

---

[5]This variable is not included in the main model as it is highly correlated with TARGETLEAD.

[6]The values in each cell is obtained by summing up the total efforts of all requests that were initiated earlier but have not begun servicing yet in that month.

day (8 hours) increases the elapsed servicing time by 1.5 days. This suggests that the servicing and therefore the lead time could be improved if the task complexity of each request is reduced. This implies that the IS department should try to identify the possibility of dividing up a large maintenance project into several independent tasks that could be performed simultaneously by a number of staff. This could greatly reduce the service and the lead time. However, note that this might be done at the expense of the scale economies that a large project could provide [2][3]. This suggests that to meet users' expectations, it may be necessary to forgo the possibility of productivity gain.

## 6. Conclusions

In conclusion, we have found that system factors such as system age and deterioration, that were found to impact maintenance effort, do not necessarily prolong the service and lead time. On the other hand, application familiarity, which was found to be an important driver of software maintenance productivity does not help in improving service and lead time if the staff are overloaded. Our analysis highlights a potential tradeoff between maintenance effort (and hence cost to the IS department) and users' opportunity cost. By considering the costs from the IS department's perspective alone will not reduce but actually shift the costs from one department to another. This shifting of cost may be suboptimal from an organizational wide perspective.

Our study has some limitations. While our sample is large, the data were collected from only a single site. Greater generalizability could be achieved if a larger sample of organizations is involved. We are planning to conduct a comparative analysis of different IS departments on their cost-saving strategies and the associated impacts on users' opportunity cost.

## References

[1] R. D. Banker, S. M. Datar, and C. F. Kemerer. A model to evaluate variables impacting the productivity of software maintenance projects. *Management Science*, 37(1):1–18, January 1991.

[2] R. D. Banker and C. F. Kemerer. Scale economies in new software development. *IEEE Transactions on Software Engineering*, 10(10):1199–1205, October 1989.

[3] R. D. Banker and S. A. Slaughter. Project size and software maintenance productivity: Empirical evidence on economies of scale in software maintenance. In *Proceedings of the Fifteenth International Conference on Information Sysems*, pages 279–289, Vancouver, Canada, 1994.

[4] B. W. Boehm and P. N. Pappacio. Understanding and controlling software costs. *IEEE Transactions on Software Engineering*, 14(10):1462–1477, October 1988.

[5] T. Chan. *Three essays on the economics of software maintenance*. Unpublished phd dissertation, National University of Singapore, 1998.

[6] T. Chan, S. L. Chung, and T. H. Ho. An economic model to estimate software rewriting and replacement times. *IEEE Transactions on Software Engineering*, 22(8):580–598, August 1996.

[7] V. R. Gibson and J. A. Senn. System structure and software maintenance performance. *Communications of the ACM*, 32(3):347–358, March 1989.

[8] R. J. Glass. Help! my software maintenance is out of control! *Computerworld*, pages 87–91, February 1990.

[9] D. K. Gode, A. Barua, and T. Mukhopadhyay. On the economics of the software replacement problem. In *Proceedings of the Eleventh International Conference on Information Sysems*, pages 159–170, Copenhagen, Denmark, 1990.

[10] V. Gurbaxani and H. Mendelson. Software and hardware in data processing budgets. *IEEE Transactions on Software Engineering*, 13(9):1010–1017, September 1987.

[11] D. Kafura and G. Reddy. The use of software complexity metrics in software maintenance. *IEEE Transactions on Software Engineering*, 13(3):335–343, March 1987.

[12] L. Kleinrock. *Queueing Systems Volume II: Computer Applications*. John Wiley and Sons, New York, NY, 1976.

[13] M. Lehman. Programs, life cycles, and laws of software evolution. In *Tutorial on Software Maintenance, Proceedings of IEEE*. IEEE Computer Society, Los Angeles, CA, 1983.

[14] B. Lientz and E. Swanson. *Software Maintenance Management*. Addison-Wesley, Reading, MA, 1980.

[15] J. Martin and C. McClure. *Software Maintenance: The Problem and its Solution*. Prentice-Hall, Englewood Cliffs, NJ, 1983.

[16] J. T. Nosek and P. Palvia. Software maintenance management: Changes in the last decade. *Journal of Software Maintenance*, 2(3):157–174, September 1990.

[17] R. Schonberger and E. Knod. *Operations Management: Continuous Improvement*. Burr Ridge, Irwin, Il, fifth edition, 1994.

[18] E. B. Swanson. The dimensions of maintenance. In *Proceedings of the Second International Conference on Software Engineering*, pages 492–497, 1976.

[19] E. B. Swanson and C. M. Beath. *Maintaining Information Systems in Organizations*. John Wiley and Sons, New York, NY, 1989.

# Techniques of Maintaining Evolving Component-Based Software

Ye Wu
Information and Software Engineering Department
George Mason University
Fairfax, VA 22030
wuye@ise.gmu.edu

Dai Pan and Mei-Hwa Chen
Computer Science Department
SUNY at Albany
Albany, NY 12222
(daip and mhc)@cs.albany.edu

## Abstract

*Component-based software engineering has been increasingly adopted for software development. Such an approach using reusable components as the building blocks for constructing software, on one hand, embellishes the likelihood of improving software quality and productivity; on the other hand, it consequently involves frequent maintenance activities, such as upgrading third party components or adding new features. The cost of maintenance for conventional software can account for as much as two-thirds of the total cost, and it can likely be even more for maintaining component-based software. Thus, an effective maintenance technique for component-based software is strongly desired. In this paper we present a technique that can be applied on various maintenance activities over component-based software systems. The technique proposed utilizes a static analysis to identify the interfaces, events and dependence relationships that would be affected by the modification in the maintenance activity. The results obtained from the static analysis along with the information of component interactions recorded during the execution of each test case are used to guide test selection in the maintenance phase. The empirical results show that with 19% effort our technique detected 71% of the faults in an industrial component-based system, which demonstrates the great potential effectiveness of the technique.*

## 1 Introduction

Component-based software development facilitates software reuse and promotes quality and productivity. Such a building-block approach has been increasingly adopted for software development, especially for large-scale software systems. Much work has been devoted to developing infrastructure for the construction of component-based software[3, 14, 23, 25, 26, 35]. The aims of component-based software development are to achieve multiple quality objectives, such as interoperability, reusability, evolvability, buildability, implementation transparency and extensibility, to facilitate fast-paced delivery of scalable evolving software systems. To this end, a component-based software often consists of a set of self-contained and loosely coupled components allowing plug-and-play. The components may be implemented by using different programming languages, executed in various operational platforms distributed across geographic distances; some components may be developed in-house, while others may be the third party off-the-shelf components of which the source code may not be available to the developers.

When a component in a component-based software is modified or upgraded, a maintenance activity occurs. Due to many of the characteristics of component-based software, difficulties could be encountered when traditional maintenance approaches are applied. For instance, in a component-based system, many third-party packages are adopted and the source code of these components is often unavailable. A traditional code-based approach that relies on the analysis of program code may not be applicable. Moreover, since component-based systems may be heterogeneous, some faults that are related to interoperability could be encountered. However, most traditional approaches do not take interoperability into consideration.

Software maintenance activities can be classified into corrective, perfective and adaptive maintenance. In this paper we present a technique that can be applied on various maintenance activities including corrective, adaptive and perfective maintenance. In the maintenance phase, testing involves two issues: (1) test selection from an existing test suite for re-conforming program behaviors as those before the modification, and (2) test generation for validating new features introduced. In this paper we present a technique for test selection in maintaining component-based systems; the technique for test generation can be found in [43]. Our technique utilizes both static and dynamic information to efficiently select an effective regression test suite. The static analysis identifies the collaborative relationships among components that are affected by the modifications. The collaborative relationships include the direct interactions among components and the dependence relationships among components, which can be derived from the function dependence relationships. A component interaction graph is proposed to depict the collaborative relationships and the affected dependence relationships. To capture the dynamic behavior of each test execution, we use an interface and event execution graph illustrating the interaction activities among the components for each test case. The interface and event execution graph can be used to determine more precisely, whether a test case will cause the software to execute the affected interfaces, events or collaborative relationships, which therefore needs to be retested. When a component is upgraded or the environment is changed, perfective and adaptive maintenance are needed. Our methodology will first identify all affected interfaces, events and collaborative relationships among interfaces and events. Based on the criteria we proposed for corrective maintenance, test cases are selected from the original test suite. If the criteria cannot be fulfilled, new test cases are needed; then we can use the technique developed for testing component-based software [?].

The remainder of the paper is organized as follows: In Section 3, we discuss several issues addressing the need of a new technique for component-based software maintenance, as well as a fault model that depicts the potential pitfalls of component-based software. The methodology we propose is described in Section 3, and in Section 4 we present an empirical study to demonstrate the potential strengths of the methodology. We conclude this study in Section 5.

## 2 The Pitfalls

Several issues[6, 16, 17, 38] have been addressed and used to suggest that the existing techniques are not adequate for maintaining component-based software. To investigate the weaknesses of the existing techniques and develop a stronger one, we analyzed the common characteristics of component-based software and developed a fault model that classifies potential faults in the software into three categories: inter-component faults, interoperability faults and traditional faults.

When developing and maintaining component-based systems, each individual component can be tested and maintained separately. When integrating a set of components, the evaluation of the interactions among the components will be the central issue. Faults, related to the interactions among components, can be classified into coding related, which are inter-component faults, and non-coding related faults, which are interoperability faults. Other faults which reside within one component can very often be processed by using the traditional methodologies and therefore are classified as traditional faults.

*Type I* - **Inter-Component faults:** In a component-based system, even though each individual component has been evaluated separately, when combining them together, failure may be encountered. Those coding related faults, which are associated with more than one component will be considered as inter-component faults. For example, in the following code, after adding the line $i = 0$ into $I_1$ of Component $C_1$ and testing $I_1$ and $I_2$, we cannot detect any problems. But when the component $C_1$ is deployed and $I_1$ is invoked followed by $I_2$ in Components $C_2$ and $C_3$, a failure, which is divided by zero, occurs in $C_3$.

$C_1$:
$$I_1 \rightarrow i = 0;$$
$$I_2 \rightarrow \text{return } i;$$

$C_2$:
$$I_3 \rightarrow C_1 :: I_1();$$

$C_3$:
$$I_4 \rightarrow j = 1/C_1 :: I_2();$$

*Type II* - **Interoperability faults:** Many characteristics of component-based systems, such as heterogenerity, source code unavailability, resuability and etc, will generate different types of interoperability problems in a component-based system. The interoperability problems can occur at different levels. From low level to high, they may be classified into system level, programming language level and specification level interoperability faults.

**System level interoperability faults** : In a component-based system, different components may be built under different infrastructures, for instance, different operating systems or different sets of system libraries. The incompatibility among the operating systems and libraries may cause this type of fault. For example, integers can be represented by 2 bytes or 4 bytes in different operating systems, unaware the difference may cause the failure.

**Programming level interoperability faults** : When components are written in different programming languages, the incompatibility among the programming languages may cause the failure. For example, one of the incompatibility problems which is often encountered is due to the different floating point processing of Visual C++ and Visual Basic.

**Specification level interoperability faults**

Specifications may be misinterpreted by the developers, and there are many different ways that the specifications may be misunderstood.

- Data misunderstanding. Data passing through the interfaces are misunderstood. For example, misunderstanding of types and values of the input parameters, misunderstanding the return value and etc.

- Control misunderstanding. The patterns of the interactions may be misinterpreted. This includes the misunderstanding of execution sequences of the interfaces. For example, many components have an initiating interface which has to be invoked prior to any invocation of other interfaces, failing to do so may cause the failure. Or, misunderstanding the interaction mechanism, for example, if an interface requires an exception handler when exceptions are generated, the software will crash when the exception handler is missing.

*Type III-* **Traditional faults and other faults:** For those faults which can be isolated within one component, traditional testing and maintenance techniques can be adopted. These faults will be identified as traditional faults. Other faults, such as those faults related to the distributed characteristics, will also be classified into this category.

## 2.1   Empirical Study I

To investigate the presence of faults in real component-based applications, we conducted an empirical study on an industrial system, obtained from a company located in New York City. The system we used in this experimental study is a subsystem of a trading assistant system. Adopted by more than 100 companies and 4000 individual users, this system provides various models to help users in summarizing, visualizing, analyzing and predicting the stock data. The math libraries of the system were implemented by using both C and C++, while its GUI was implemented using C++ and Visual Basic. In addition, many third party components are used in the system. Currently, this subsystem has two versions: the first version was delivered more than one year ago, the second is on the production line. Version 1 has total of 18 components, 1037 interfaces and exposes 2245 different events. This information is summarized in Table 1. We analyzed the test report of the system, which records that during the system test phase 1388 test cases were executed and 95 faults were detected. Version 2 of the system was obtained after several modification activities and upgrades of the third party components. The data for version 2 is summarized in Table 2. Version 2 not only corrected

| # of Components | | | # of Interfaces | # of Events |
|---|---|---|---|---|
| System | MFC | 5 | 46 | 4 |
| | ATL | 5 | 316 | 124 |
| | Visual Basic | 1 | 34 | 1876 |
| | SubTotal | 11 | 396 | 2004 |
| Third Party | | 7 | 641 | 241 |
| Total | | 18 | 1037 | 2245 |
| Total Test Cases | | 1388 | Total Faults | 95 |

**Table 1. Version 1.0 Summary Information**

| # of Components | | | # of Interfaces | # of Events |
|---|---|---|---|---|
| System | MFC | 5 | 46 | 4 |
| | ATL | 9 | 382 | 137 |
| | Visual Basic | 1 | 54 | 3310 |
| | SubTotal | 15 | 482 | 3451 |
| Third Party | | 7 | 709 | 300 |
| Total | | 22 | 1191 | 3751 |
| Total Test Cases | | 1388 | Total Faults | 24 |

**Table 2. Version 2.0 Summary Information**

some faults in the first version, but also enhanced the performance by adding and replacing some components. There are 154 new interfaces and 1506 new events added into the system.

To assure that modifications won't adversely affected the Version 2, the original 1388 test cases were re-applied and 24 faults were uncovered. Moreover, to validate the new features of the version 2, 755 new test cases were generated and detected 39 faults. Our methodology will focus on selecting test cases to validate the original functionalities, validation of the new features can be performed by using the methodology of testing component-based systems. The detailed information about the 24 faults is summarized in Table 2.

Table 3, which summarizes the distribution of the four types of faults in Version 1 and 2, shows that about 20% - 35% faults belong to *Type I*; 40% - 66% are *Type II*, and 13% - 25% are *Type III* faults.

**Some Observations**

| | Type I | Type II | Type III | Total |
|---|---|---|---|---|
| Version 1 | 33 | 38 | 24 | 95 |
| Version 2 | 5 | 16 | 3 | 24 |

**Table 3. Number of Faults detected**

1. From the data shown in Tables 1 and 2 we can see that third party components play a significant role in the component-based system. Usually, the source code of the third party component is unknown, and therefore, many traditional testing and maintenance methodologies are not appropriate.

2. Faults related to the interactions among components are the majority faults. From the table we can see, Type I faults and Type II faults, which related to the interactions among components occupy 83% of the total faults. The ability of an methodology to detect those types of faults are crucial.

## 3  Methodology

Based on the analysis of the types of faults that can be encountered during the integration of component-based software and the observations of the empirical study, we developed a technique that uses minimal effort yet preserves the quality of the system.

To maintain each individual component, many existing techniques can be applied [1, 30, 31, 32, 42]. When maintaining component-based systems at integration and system level, the component-based system characteristics produce a lot of difficulties for the adoption of the existing techniques. The trivial method which simply retests all original test cases may guarantee good quality of the software, but due to the cost and time constraint, it is very often impractical. In addition, this method won't be able to help generate new test cases when needed. Alternatively, maintenance techniques, such as data-flow-based techniques, slicing-based techniques etc., can provide more precise analysis; however, when the source code of certain components is not available, the technique may not be adequate, and when we apply those methods on heterogeneous component-based systems, complexities of dealing with different programming languages and different platforms are encountered.

However, from our fault model and the results of the empirical study, 67% of the faults are related to the incorrect interactions among the components. Once these faults are identified, we can significantly improve the quality of the software. In addition, in a component-based system, the interactions among components are only fulfilled through the interfaces and events. Therefore, even though when the source code for some components is not available, their interfaces and events, which are always available, can be utilized to analyze the interactions among components.

In this paper, we present a methodology that utilizes a graphical representation to describe the interactions among components. Once one or more components are modified or updated, the affected interfaces and events will then be identified. When affected interfaces, events and different combi-

nations are validated, the direct interactions among components will be evaluated and many Type II faults will be identified. In order to pick up Type I faults, which are related to the data dependence relationships, further investigation of the dependence relationship among interfaces and events are provided. Besides the affected interfaces and events, the affected dependence relationships among the interfaces and events will be identified, and are utilized to identified Type I faults. Based this, we propose a group of coverage criteria to satisfy different quality requirements. When a coverage criterion is selected, in order to verify whether it has been satisfied or not, we suggest a wrapper-based methodology to trace the dynamic interactions among interfaces and events. This mechanism can be easily adopted despite the availability and the heterogeneity of the components.

In this section, we will first present the interaction information of a component-based system by depicting the different kinds of communication among interfaces and events. We then further consider the data dependence relationships among interfaces and events. Based on the interactions and dependence relationships among interfaces and events, maintenance techniques are proposed.

### 3.1  Component Interaction Graph

Each individual component is self-contained and relatively independent. When a number of components are integrated, the interactions among components are performed through interfaces and events. *Interfaces* are the named services, which provided by the component, as well as the parameters to those services. *Event* is the invocation of one or more interfaces. Events can be classified into the following three categories:

Interface invocation. In one interface, in order to utilize a service provided by another interface, a message will be sent to that interface, and the message sending will be considered as an event.

User actions. For example, when clicking a mouse button or pressing a key, certain GUI related events will be generated.

Exceptions. Such as files can not be opened, divided by zero and etc.

The interactions among interfaces and events can be classified into the following four categories:

1. One interface when invoked generates an event. For example, an interface which is to close the window, when invoked, a close_window event will be generated.

2. When one event is generated, it invokes an interface of a component. For example, when pushing a button, an event is generated and certain interfaces are invoked.

3. One interface of a component invokes another interface of the same component or a different component. This is will be considered as an interface which will generate an event first and then that event will invoke another interface.

4. When one event is generated, it will trigger another event in the same or a different component. For example, in a situation where a window component contains a sub_widow component, when a resize event is generated for the main window, it triggers the resize event of the sub_window.

The above relationships among interfaces and events depict the control flow information of a component-based system. We can use the following Component Interaction Graph(CIG) to represent the relationships.

In a Component Interaction Graph G=(V,E), V = VI $\bigcup$ VE. $v_i \in$ VI stands for an interface of a component, while $v_i \in$ VE stands for an event which may be generated in the component. $e_{ij}=(v_i,v_j)$ denotes one of the above relationships. A path (or subpath) in CIG is a finite sequence of vertices $(v_0, v_1, ..., v_k)$ such that $e_{i,i+1} = (v_i, v_{i+1}) \in$ E for $i = 0, 1, ..., k - 1$. A loop free path is a path $(v_0, v_1, ..., v_k)$ such that for any $i$ and $j$, $i \neq j$ and $v_i \neq v_j$.

In the CIG, the out-degree of a node is the number of edges leaving it and the in-degree of a node is the number of edges entering it. For every node $\in$ VE, its in-degree and out-degree are greater than 0. The in-degree of an event is greater than 0 because every event is generated by some interface. If the out-degree of an event is 0 while the event has to be processed, then it is considered a fault in the system; otherwise, the event will not be included in CIG, since the event will not have any effect on the system. Therefore, the out-degree of every event is greater than 0.

## 3.2 Interface and event dependence relationships

CIG provides an overview of the interactions of a component-based system. Data dependence, on the other hand, can provide additional information to further understand more precisely about the effect of the update on the system. When an interface is invoked, a group of methods or functions will be executed. Therefore, function dependence relationships, which have been shown to be effective in object-oriented class testing[8] and in regression testing[44], can be utilized to identify interface and event dependence relationships.

The function dependence relationship is defined as follows: A function $f_1$ **depends on** a function $f_2$ if the value of a variable defined in $f_2$ is used in $f_1$.

**Interface dependence:** Interface dependence describes the data dependence relationships among the interfaces. Interface dependence relationships can be classified into two categories: intra-component interface dependence and inter-component interface dependence.

**Intra-component interface dependence:** Two interfaces $I_1$ and $I_2$ of component C have a dependence relationship if one of the following conditions holds:

1. Source Code Available:

   (a) $I_1$ directly invokes $I_2$ i.e. in CIG,there are edges $e_1 = (v_{i1}, e), e_2 = (e, v_{i2}) \in$ E; where $v_{i1}, v_{i2} \in$ VI and $e$ is an Interface invocation event; or $I_2$ directly invokes $I_1$

   (b) $I_1$ indirectly invokes $I_2$, i.e. if there exists a loop-free path $n_0, n_1, n_2, ..., n_k$ in CIG such that $n_0 = v_{i1}$ and $n_k = v_{i2}$, $n_i \in$ V for i=1,2,...,k-1, and $e = (n_i, n_{i+1}) \in$ E for i=0,1,...,k-1; or $I_2$ indirectly invokes $I_1$

   (c) $I_1$ calls a member function $f_1$ which depends on another function $f_2$ which is called in $I_2$;

2. Source Code not Available:
   If we do not have any information other than the interfaces, we have to make a conservative approximation in which every pair of interfaces is considered as having a dependence relationship.

**Inter-component interface dependence:** Interfaces $I_1$ of component $C_1$ and $I_2$ of component $C_2$ have a dependence relationship if one of the following conditions holds:

1. $I_1$ directly or indirectly invokes $I_2$; or $I_2$ directly or indirectly invokes $I_1$;

2. $I_1$ directly or indirectly invokes interface $I_1'$ while $I_2$ directly or indirectly invokes interface $I_2'$ and $I_1'$ depends on $I_2'$.

3. A variable is passed into $I_1$ by reference and the same variable is passed into $I_2$ either by reference or by value under the condition that the invocation of $I_1$ is followed by the invocation of $I_2$.

Besides the data dependence relationships among interfaces, events also involve data dependence relationships. Event $e$ *directly triggers* interface $I$ if edge $e = (v_e, v_i) \in$ E, and event $e$ *indirectly triggers* interface $I$, if there is a loop-free path $n_0, n_1, n_2, ..., n_k$ in the CIG, such that $n_0 = v_e$ and $n_k = v_i$, $n_i \in$ V for $i = 1, 2, ..., k - 1$, and $e = n_i, n_{i+1} \in$ E for $i = 0, 1, ..., k - 1$;

**Event dependence:** Event $e_1$ depends on event $e_2$ if: $e_1$ directly or indirectly triggers an interface $I_1$ while $e_2$ directly or indirectly triggers an interface $I_2$ where $I_1$ depends on $I_2$.

## 3.3 Maintaining evolving component-based system

As we have shown in the previous section, when one component is modified or upgraded, there are many potential interoperability problems in a component-based system. If a maintenance technique targeted to provide a safe approach, which guarantees the selection of all modification-revealing test cases[31], the technique has to select all test cases which execute any of the modified components. Such an approach is often impractical because it will include too many test cases to be retested. Alternatively, other approaches, such as coverage-based techniques, won't guarantee the safeness, instead, they are intended to spend less effort, while obtaining relatively high reliability. There are many coverage-based maintenance approaches[5, 19] for traditional systems. These methods can be based on block & branch coverage or def-use pair coverage and etc. When source code of the components is not available, these coverage criteria are not adequate, because those components without source code won't able to be verified. On the other hand, as shown above, interactions among interfaces and events, with further assistance of the dependence relationships among interfaces and events, can be helpful in identifying faults. Therefore test case selection strategies based on this information will be more appropriate than traditional approaches.

In this section, we will first describe how we perform corrective maintenance, where one or more components are modified. First of all, affected interfaces and dependence relationships are identified and then test case selection strategies are provided, according to the availability of the source code. Next, we further extend this strategy to perform perfective and adaptive maintenance.

### 3.3.1 Affected interfaces and events

After modifications have been made to the system, we need to identify the effect of the modifications on the interfaces and their dependence relationships.

An interface $I$ is considered as *affected* if it is either

1. when source code is available;

   (a) the interface $I$ is modified; or

   (b) the interface *uses* a variable $x$, and the value of $x$ may be affected by the modifications. An interface *uses* a variable means the value of the variable is referenced in an expression or is used to decide a predicate in the interface.

2. when source code is not available; We will make a conservative estimation. If an interface is modified or upgraded, all other interfaces in the same component will be considered as affected. If one parameter of an interface is affected, then the interface is considered as affected.

An event is considered as *affected* if one of the following holds:

1. Interface invocation. In one interface, when invoking another interface, if any of the parameters is affected, the interface-interface invocation event is considered as affected.

2. User actions. If a user action event is generated by a component, which contains affected variables, the event will be considered as affected.

3. Exceptions. When any portion of the code, which may generate the exception, contains at least one affected variables, the exception will be considered as affected.

The dependence relationship between $I_1$ and $I_2$ is considered as affected if $I_1$ depends on $I_2$ and both $I_1$ and $I_2$ are affected.

To identify the affected interfaces, we need to identify the affected variables of each component. The algorithm described in [44] can be adopted, which will first construct the control flow graph for the components with source code, and mark the modified variables as affected variables. An iterative procedure is then performed to find out whether new affected variables are identified. The iterative procedure will terminate when no more affected variables are identified. We have shown that this algorithm will correctly identify all affected variables [44]. After all affected variables are identified, for each interface, we can traverse the source code the interface may execute, and determine if it will use any affected variable, thus, deciding if the interface is affected. The complexity of finding all affected variables has been shown to be $O(\mathcal{N}_v * \mathcal{N}_{lc})$, where $\mathcal{N}_{lc}$ is the lines of code and $\mathcal{N}_v$ is the number of the variables and functions in the system. Let $\mathcal{N}_{Interface}$ be the number of interfaces in the system, then the complexity to find all affected interfaces is $O((\mathcal{N}_v + \mathcal{N}_{Interface}) * \mathcal{N}_{lc})$. After affected interfaces are identified, affected events and affected interface dependence relationships can be identified within $O(\mathcal{N}_{Interface}^2 + \mathcal{N}_{Event})$, where $\mathcal{N}_{Event}$ is the number of events in the system.

### 3.3.2 Interface and event execution graph

In order to perform regression testing on the component-based system, the execution history for each test case needs to be recorded during the execution. According to the features of the component-based system, using an interface and event execution graph to record the interaction among interfaces at run time is appropriate.

An Interface and Event Execution Graph(IEEG) G' = (V',E') for each test case is a subgraph of the CIG, that is, V' $\subseteq$ V and E' $\subseteq$ E. An edge $e = (v_i, v_j) \in$ E' if:

1. $v_i \in$ VI, $v_j \in$ VE and $v_i$ generates event $v_j$;

2. $v_i \in$ VE, $v_j \in$ VI, and event $v_i$ triggers interface $v_j$;

3. $v_i, v_j \in$ VE and event $v_i$ triggers another event $v_j$;

The advantages of using IEEG are:

1. *Easy and efficient recording.* Due to the fact that a component-based system can be implemented by different programming languages, and source code may not be available, it may be very difficult to instrument code into the system. In order to record the interactions among interfaces, we can wrap all components and these wrapped components will provide the same services, regardless of the programming language of the component and the availability of the source code. During the execution, when one interface of the component is invoked, the wrapper will record the request and then forward the request to the original component. Thus, it is feasible to obtain the IEEG of each test case, and it won't affect the performance too much.

2. *Compact saving of execution sequences.* The execution information, for traditional maintenance techniques, is usually $O(\mathcal{N}_{lc})$ per test case, which could be a huge number[31]. By using IEEG, it is bounded by $O((\mathcal{N}_{Interface} + \mathcal{N}_{Event})^2)$. But usually IEEG is a sparse graph, the real storage is much smaller.

3. *Precise representation of execution sequences.* The execution information, recorded and used by the traditional maintenance technique, is usually a bit string, which indicates whether a statement is executed or not. Such an approach does not depict the relationships among statements, while IEEG can precisely represent the relationships among interfaces and events, and provide more information for further analysis.

### 3.3.3 Test case selection without source code

To assure that the modifications won't adversely affect the quality of the software, it is necessary to apply regression testing on the modified software. Retesting all test cases in the original test pool is a safe method to reveal faults introduced by the modifications, but it is too expensive to be practical. As shown before, it is very difficult to obtain a safe regression testing methodology, therefore, we provide the following criteria to guide our test case selection.

*all-affected-interfaces:* all the affected interfaces have to be retested at least once.

*all-affect-events:* all the affected events have to be retested at least once.

*all-affect-edges:* every edge in CIG, which connects to at least one affected interface or affected event, must be retested at least once.

*all-affected-dependences:* every affected dependence relationship, where $I_1$ depends on $I_2$ and the execution of $I_1$ is followed by the execution of $I_2$, must be retested at least once.

*all-affected-paths:* every affected dependence relationship, where $I_1$ depends on $I_2$ and the execution of $I_1$ is followed by the execution of $I_2$ must be retested at least once. In addition, from the entry node of CIG, every path to $I_1$ and to $I_2$ must be retested at least once.

When using these criteria to select test cases for retesting, there is always a trade off: that is, the stronger the selection criterion, the more the faults of the program are likely to be exposed, and the more test cases are need to be retested. Therefore, in order to decide the criterion to be used in selecting test cases, we have to consider other factors such as the budget, the schedule, the cost, the size of the program etc. Let C be a set of entities need to be tested in order to satisfy one of the criteria described above, the following selection algorithm can be applied.

Algorithm: Test case selection.

Input: IEEG of every test case and C;

Output: Test cases to be retested.

Step 1: Utilize the algorithm discussed in the previous section to identify all affected interfaces, events and affected interface dependence relationships.

Step 2: According to the selection criterion, construct a set C which includes all the entities need to be covered.

Step 3:
    T = $\phi$;
    For each test case $t$ in the original test pool
        If (IEEG of $t$ contains any element of C)
        Then
            T = T $\bigcup$ t;
            Remove those elements, which occur in both C and IEEG of $t$, from C;
        Else Discard $t$;
    T will contain all the test cases which need to be

retested

As shown in the previous section, the complexity of the step 1 is $O((\mathcal{N}_v + \mathcal{N}_{Interface}) * \mathcal{N}_{lc})$. The complexity of Step 2 and Step 3 depends on the complexity of C. If C is based on *all-affected-interfaces* criterion, then C will contain $O(\mathcal{N}_{I\_Affected})$ elements, where $\mathcal{N}_{I\_Affected}$ is the number of affected interfaces. Because Step 1 already obtains all the affected interfaces, thus, Step 2 can finish within $O(\mathcal{N}_{I\_Affected})$ time. In Step 3, the *for* statement will loop $\mathcal{N}_t$ times, where $\mathcal{N}_t$ is the number of test cases in the original test pool. During each iteration, it will check the occurrence of content in C, therefore, step 3 can be finished within $O(\mathcal{N}_t * \mathcal{N}_{I\_Affected})$ time. Similarly, when choosing C as *all-affected-events* and *all-affected-edges* criteria, the complexity of step 2 will be $O(\mathcal{N}_{Event\_Affected})$ and $O(\mathcal{N}_{Edge\_Affected})$ correspondingly, where $\mathcal{N}_{Event\_Affected}$ is the number of affected events and $\mathcal{N}_{Edge\_Affected}$ is the number of affected edges. Furthermore, the complexity of step 3 will be $O(\mathcal{N}_t * \mathcal{N}_{Event\_Affected})$ and $O(\mathcal{N}_t * \mathcal{N}_{Edge\_Affected})$ correspondingly. Therefore when we use *all-affected-interfaces*, *all-affected-events* or *all-affected-edges* criteria, the selection algorithm is very efficient.

If C is based on the *all-affected-dependences* criterion, the size of C is bounded by $O((\mathcal{N}_{I\_Affected} + \mathcal{N}_{Event\_Affected})^2)$ and the complexity of step 2 and step 3 will be $O((\mathcal{N}_{I\_Affected} + \mathcal{N}_{Event\_Affected})^2)$ and $O(\mathcal{N}_t * (\mathcal{N}_{I\_Affected} + \mathcal{N}_{Event\_Affected})^2)$ accordingly. Thus, based on *all-affected-dependences* criterion, we can still derive a relatively efficient selection algorithm.

When C is based on the *all-affected-paths* criterion, theoretically, the size of C is exponential to the number of interfaces and events in the CIG. In real systems, the number could be less, but it is still a huge number. Therefore, the selection algorithm based on *all-affected-paths* criteria is inefficient.

### 3.3.4  Test case selection with source code

After one or more components are modified, all the affected interfaces will be identified. For some components, whose source code is not available, the previous selection approach can be applied. In many cases, the source code of all the affected interfaces is available, then we can apply a more accurate maintenance technique.

When all affected interfaces are implemented in the same environment and using same programming language, traditional maintenance techniques [1, 30, 31, 32, 42] can be applied. But there are many disadvantages to those traditional maintenance techniques, under the circumstances described below.

1. As described in section 4.3.2, recording a bit-string for each test case may not be viable, therefore, many traditional maintenance techniques may not be adequate.

2. Applying traditional maintenance techniques, may either require more overhead or not be precise. Methods which are based on the program analysis will be inefficient due to the rapidly growing size and complexity of the component-based systems. For the methods, which perform less analysis and make conservative estimations, may select too many test cases to be retested.

Our previous work[44] has shown that function dependence relationships can be utilized in maintaining object-oriented software. Stemming from this work, we obtain the following approach to maintain component-based software. Our objective in selecting all test cases, when executed, will generate different output, i.e. modification-revealing test cases, and therefore the approach is safe. This technique is a two-step procedure. First step is a static analysis for the affected interfaces. Then a dynamic analysis for each test case will decide which test cases need to be retested.

### Static Analysis

Static analysis will statically identify all affected interfaces and behavior affected interfaces.

Affected interfaces are described in section 4.3.1. An interface is considered as a behavior-affected interface if the interface is affected and will change communications between the component and external entities. For example, when the interface is invoked, it changes the output to the screen or the files in the disk, etc.

To obtain the behavior-affected interfaces, we first identify all affected variables and interfaces, as described in section 4.3.1. Once all affected variables are identified, one more traversing of the program will find all the statements, which when executed, will change the behavior of the system. If an interface will execute at least one of these statements, it will be identified as a behavior affected interface.

### Dynamic Analysis

Dynamic analysis will dynamically analyze the IEEG of each test to determine whether the test case needs to be retested.

For each test case, if it contains an execution path which executes at least one modified interface and then executes a behavior affected interface, the test case needs to be retested.

### 3.3.5  Discussion

When one or more components are upgraded, or their execution environment has been changed, issues of perfective and adaptive maintenance arise. When the execution environment of certain components changes, all the interfaces,

243

events and dependent relationships are considered to be affected. When a component is updated, where perfective maintenance is necessary, if the source code of the component is not available, all the interfaces, events and dependent relationships are considered to be affected as well. If the source code of the updated component is available, further program analysis can be applied to the component, and we can determine whether an interface or an event is affected. For the dependence relationships, we can also determine whether there are new dependence relationships, absence of the original dependence relationships or changes in the existing dependence relationships, all these dependence relationships will be identified as affected. After all the affected entities are identified, the same test case selection algorithm can be applied. If the selected test cases won't be able to cover the affected dependence relationships, new test cases need to be generated.

## 4 Empirical Study II

To demonstrate the effectiveness of our strategy in maintaining component-based systems, we apply the technique on the the component-based system, used in the empirical study, described in Section 3.2.

### 4.1 Experiment

As described in Section 2, in the system test phase, 1388 test cases were executed, and 95 faults were detected. Version 2 of the system was obtained after a number of corrective activities were applied to remove the faults and several perfective activities performed to enhanced the system. To ensure the quality of the software, not only does the correctness of new added features need to be validated, it is also necessary to verify that the modifications will not adversely affect the other portions of the system. Therefore, the original 1388 test cases were re-applied on the new version of the systems and 24 new faults were detected caused by the modifications.

By using our strategy, first, affected interfaces, events, and all kinds of dependence relationships were identified. Among them, some belong to components with source code and others reside within components without source code. Therefore, coverage-based maintenance technique had to be adopted. In the experiment, when we selected 62 test cases from the original test pool to cover all affected interfaces, 4 faults were detected. To cover all the affected events, 80 test cases were selected, which revealed 6 faults. To fulfill the all-edges criterion, 101 test cases were chosen from the 1388 test cases and 7 faults were uncovered. Finally, the all-affected-dependences criterion was adopted and 258 test cases were selected, which revealed 17 faults. The detailed information is summarized in Table 4.

|  | # TC | I | II | III | Total |
|---|---|---|---|---|---|
| Retest All | 1388 | 5 | 16 | 3 | 24 |
| All-Affected-Interfaces | 62 | 2 | 1 | 1 | 4 |
| All-Affected-Events | 80 | 3 | 1 | 2 | 6 |
| All-Affected-Edges | 101 | 3 | 1 | 3 | 7 |
| All-Affected-Dependnences | 258 | 5 | 9 | 3 | 17 |

**Table 4. Faults detected after modifying the original system**

From the data shown above, we derived the following observation:

1. Maintenance component-based software at integration level is necessary, after some components are modified or upgraded, and validated individual. In Version 2, even though all the faults detected in the first version were corrected, the modifications introduce 24 new faults. Therefore, more testing effort is needed.

2. Test case selections based on the *all-affected-interfaces*, *all-affected-events* and *all-affected-edges* criteria are simple and efficient, whereas they can only provide a certain level of reliability. To further improve the quality of the system, *all-affected-dependences* are necessary. Even though *all-affected-path* criterion can be used to detect more faults, the inefficiency is a major concern when adopted in reality.

## 5 Conclusions and Future Work

We have presented a new approach for maintaining evolving component-based software. Our empirical studies show that validating evolving component-based software is necessary yet expensive. The technique we proposed provides several criteria for determining test adequacy. The all-affected-dependences criterion used only 19% of test cases, yet detected 71% of the faults; even the weakest criterion, the all-affected-interfaces, used 5% of test cases and detected 16% of the faults. Therefore, the strengths of the technique can be expected. Our method, which can be applied on all types of component-based systems, does not rely on knowledge of the source code. For applications whose source code is available, our technique provides a safe, efficient and precise test selection methodology, while for those whose source code is not available, our technique provides a means for improving the quality of the evolved component-based software.

Our on-going research directions on this topic are to develop a tool supporting automation of the technique and to enhance the technique for resolving problems caused by a distributed characteristic, such as synchronization.

# References

[1] K. Abdullah and L. White. A firewall approach for the regression testing of object-oriented software. In *Software Quality Week Conference*, San Francisco, 1997.

[2] M. Arnold, M. Hsiao, U. Kremer, and B. G. Ryder. Instruction scheduling in the presence of java's runtime exceptions. In *Proceedings of the 12th Workshop on Languages and Compilers for Parallel Computing (LCPC'99)*, August 1999.

[3] D.J. Barrrett, L.A. Clarke, R.L. Tarr, and A.E Wise. A framework for event-based software integration. *ACM Transaction on Software Engineering and Methodology*, 5(4):378 – 421, 1996.

[4] A. Beugnard, J. Jezequel, N. Plouzeau, and D. Watkins. Making components contract aware. *IEEE Computer*, 32(7):38–45, July 1999.

[5] D. Binkley. Reducing the cost of regression testing by semantics guided test case selection. In *Proceedings of International Conference on Software Maintenance*, October 1995.

[6] U. Buy and et al. A framework for testing object-oriented components. In *First International ICSE Workshop on Testing Distributed Component-Based Systems*, Los Angeles, 1999.

[7] R. Chatterjee and B.G. Ryder. Data-flow-based testing of object-oriented libraries. Technical Report DCS-TR-382, Rutgers University, 1999.

[8] M. Chen and M. Kao. Effect of class testing on the reliability of object-oriented pro rams. In *Proceedings of the Eighth International Symposium on Software R liability Engineering*, May 1997.

[9] J. Choi, D. Grove, M. Hind, and V. Sarkar. Efficient and precise modeling of exceptions for the analysis of java programs. In *Proceedings of the ACM SIGPLAN and SIGSOFT workshop on Program analysis for software tools and engineering*, pages 21–31, 1999.

[10] P.C. Clements. From subroutines to subsystems: Component-based software development. *The American Programmer*, 8(11), 1995.

[11] J.E. Cook and J.a. Dage. Highly reliable upgrading of components. In *International Conference on Software Engineering*, pages 203 – 212, Los Angeles, 1999.

[12] G.S. Fowler, D.G.Korn, and K.Vo. Principles for writing reusable libraries. In *Proceedings of the 17th International Conference on Software Eng ineering*, pages 150–159, 1995.

[13] P. Frankl and E.J. Weyuker. An applicable family of data flow testing criteria. *IEEE Transactions on Software Engineering*, 14(10):1483–1498, 1988.

[14] E. Di Nitto G. Cugola and A. Fuggetta. Exploiting an event-based infrastructure to develop complex distributed systems. In *The 20th International Conference on Software Engineering*, Kyoto, Japan, April 1998.

[15] D. Garlan, R. Allen, and J. Ockerbloom. Architechtural mismatch or why it's hard to build systems out of ex iting parts. In *Proceedings of the 17th International Conference on Software Eng ineering*, pages 179–185, 1995.

[16] S. Ghosh and A.P. Mathur. Issues in testing distributed component-based systems. In *First International ICSE Workshop on Testing Distributed Component-Based Systems*, Los Angeles, 1999.

[17] M.J. Harrold, D. Liang, and S. Sinha. An approach to analyzing and testing component-based systems. In *First International ICSE Workshop on Testing Distributed Component-Based Systems*, Los Angeles, 1999.

[18] M.J. Harrold and G. Rothermel. Performing dataflow testing on classes. In *Proceedings of the Second ACM SIGSOFT Symposium on Foundations of Software Engineering*, pages 154–163, December 1994.

[19] M.J. Harrold and M.L. Soffa. Interprocedural data flow testing. In *Proceedings of the Third Testing, Analysis, and Verification Sym posium*, pages 158–167, December 1989.

[20] M.J. Harrold and M.L. Soffa. Selecting data flow integration testing. *IEEE software*, pages 58–65, 1991.

[21] M. Heimdahl, J.M. Thompson, and B.J. Czerny. Specification and analysis of intercomponent communication. *IEEE Computer*, 32(4):47–54, April 1999.

[22] D. Kung and et al. Developing an object-oriented software testing and maintenance environment. *Communications of the ACM*, 38(10):75–87, 1995.

[23] G. Larsen. Designing component-based frameworks using patterns in the uml. *Communications of the ACM*, 42(10):38–45, 1999.

[24] K. Maruyama and K. Shima. New class generation mechanism by method integration. In *Fifth International Conference on Software Reuse*, 1998.

[25] M. Mezini and K. Lieberherr. Adaptive plug-and-play components for evolutionary software development. In *Proceedings of the conference on Object-oriented programming, systems, languages, and applications*, pages 97–116, 1998.

[26] O. Nierstrasz, S. Gibbs, and D. Tsichritzis. Component-oriented software development. *Communications of the ACM*, 35(9):160–165, 1992.

[27] S. Rapps and E.J. Weyuker. Selecting software test data using data flow information. *IEEE Transactions on Software Engineering*, 11(4):367–375, 1985.

[28] M.P. Robillard and G.C. Murphy. Analyzing exception flow in java programs. In *Proceedings of the 7th European Engineering Conference held jointly with the 7th ACM SIGSOFT symposuim on Foundations of software engineering*, pages 322–337, 1999.

[29] D.S. Rosenblum. Adequate testing of component-based software. Technical Report TR97-34, University of California at Irvine, 1997.

[30] D.S. Rosenblum and E.J. Weyuker. Using coverage information to predict the cost-effectiveness of regression testing strategies. *IEEE transaction on Software Engineering*, 23(3):146–156, 1997.

[31] G. Rothermel and M.J. Harrold. A safe, efficient regression test selection technique. *ACM Transactions on Software Engineering and Methodology*, 6(2):173–210, April 1997.

[32] G. Rothermel, M.J. Harrold, and J. Dedhia. Regression test selection for c++ software. Technical Report TR99-60-01, Oregon State University, 1999.

[33] B.G. Ryder and et al. A static study of java exceptions. In *9th International Conference on Compiler Construction*, March 2000.

[34] S. Sinha and M.J. Harrold. Analysis of programs with exception-handling constructs. In *IEEE International Conference on Software Maintenance*, Bethesda, Maryland, November 1998.

[35] K. Sullivan and D. Notkin. Reconciling environment integration and component independence. In *Proceedings of the fourth ACM SIGSOFT symposium on Software development environments*, pages 22–33, 1990.

[36] C. Tai, R.H. Carver, and E. Obaid. Debugging concurrent ada programs. *IEEE Transactions on Software Engineering*, 17(1):45–63, 1991.

[37] R.N. Taylor, D.L. Levine, and D.D. Kelly. Structural testing of concurrent programs. *IEEE Transactions on Software Engineering*, 18(3):206–215, 1992.

[38] J. Voas. Maintaining component-based systems. *IEEE Software*, 15(4):22–27, July/August 1998.

[39] N.J. Wahl. System-level testing of distributed systems. In *Proceedings of the 22nd annual ACM computer science conference on Scaling up: meeting the challenge of complexity in real-world computing applications*, pages 46–51, 1994.

[40] G. Wang and L. Ungar. Component assembly for oo distributed systems. *IEEE Computer*, 32(7):71–78, July 1999.

[41] E.J Weyuker. Testing component-based software:a cautionary tale. *IEEE Software*, 15(5):54–59, September/October 1998.

[42] L. White and H.K.N. Leung. A firewall concept for both control-flow and data-flow in regression integration testing. In *Proceedings of International Conference on Software Maintenance*, pages 262–271, 1992.

[43] Y. Wu and M. Chen. Testing and maintaining component-based software. Technical Report TR00-02, State University of New York at Albany, 2000.

[44] Y. Wu, M. Chen, and M. Kao. Regression testing on object-oriented programs. In *Proceedings of the Tenth International Symposium on Software R liability Engineering*, November 1999.

# Software Maintenance Types—A Fresh View

Ned Chapin
Information Systems Consultant
InfoSci Inc., Box 7117
Menlo Park CA 94026–7117, USA
NedChapin@acm.org

## Abstract

*Compatible with the recently proposed ontology of software maintenance, the paper proposes a fresh view of the types of software maintenance. The paper offers a classification based not on people's intentions, but upon objective evidence of activities based on documentation that may include the source code. The classification includes taking into account evidence of: 1) changes in the character and use of the documentation, 2) changes in the properties of the software, and 3) changes in the in the functionality of the software. The paper provides a hierarchic summary guide to the proposed fresh view of the types of software maintenance.*

Keywords: software maintenance; enhancive maintenance; adaptive maintenance; corrective maintenance; performance maintenance; evaluative maintenance; empirical studies; maintenance terminology

## Introduction

The significant new work proposing an ontology of software maintenance [1], done by a multinational mostly European team, has stimulated a next step from the other side of the Atlantic—proposing a fresh view of the types of software maintenance.

The motivations include those of the ontology team, namely:

- providing a context for the study by researchers of specific questions about software maintenance,
- helping in the interpretation of the reports of empirical studies of maintenance,
- offering a common ground for a cogent reporting of empirical studies of maintenance, and
- supplying a framework for organizing and categorizing the reports of empirical studies of maintenance.

The additional motivations are:

- providing a realistic and practical terminology to facilitate communication about and the management of software maintenance among researchers, practitioners, and their managers,
- basing the terminology on objective evidence ascertainable even in the absence of the personnel who may have been involved with the maintenance,
- recognizing that software maintenance efforts typically encompass a variety of tasks and activities that both practitioners and their managers, and researchers, want to capture in order to record them as meaningful data, and
- focusing on the more commonly encountered software maintenance situations and circumstances.

Practitioner concerns were the focus of early published work. Thus, in 1972, Canning [2] summarized these in his well known piece, "That Maintenance 'Iceberg'." Canning reported that practitioners saw maintenance narrowly as correcting errors, and broadly as expanding and extending software functionality. Some practitioners also included accommodating to changes in the underlying system software or hardware. For the benefit of practitioners and researchers alike, E. Burton Swanson in 1976 offered a typology to rationalize the practitioners' varied recognition of types of software maintenance [3]. His typology was based on the system's owners'/users' dominant objective or intention in requesting or undertaking the maintenance work—i.e., what was seen as the cause or purpose of the maintenance, or why was the maintenance to be done [1,4]. On a mutually exclusive and exhaustive basis [5], Swanson pointed to three intentions for software maintenance:

- to perfect the system in terms of its performance, processing efficiency, or maintainability ('perfective maintenance'),

- to adapt the system to changes in its data environment or processing environment ('adaptive maintenance'), and
- to correct processing, performance, or implementation failures of the system ('corrective maintenance').

These intentions, like beauty, exist primary in the eye of the beholder, and unless specifically recorded by the personnel involved at the time of the event, cannot be reliably and consistently determined after the fact from available objective evidence. Intentions reflect the organizational and political context in which the system operates as well as the character of the maintenance work. The requester may consider something as "corrective" but the person with approval authority may regard the requested change as "perfective". If approved and done, the Information Technology manager may treat the change as part of an "adaptive" maintenance project. However, an intentions basis for a maintenance typology is appropriate for and can be used in some kinds of valuable research, as has been well demonstrated, for instance, by Lientz and Swanson [5].

## Current state of the field

Among researchers, Swanson's typology has been influential [6]. Many researchers have adopted the terminology ('corrective', 'adaptive', 'perfective'); however, few researchers have used the typology with Swanson's definitions. Instead, they have redefined the terms, and not agreed among themselves on the meanings. While this diversity has made for variety in the reported research, the lack of agreement on the meaning of commonly used terms has added to the chaos in the literature making it difficult for researchers to build upon each other's work. The IEEE put out a glossary [7] that includes the terms 'corrective maintenance', 'adaptive maintenance', and 'perfective maintenance'. Interestingly, the IEEE *Glossary* definitions are partially inconsistent with Swanson's definitions [3,7], and with the definitions in the IEEE *Standard for Software Maintenance* [3,7,8] . Most researchers have made modifications, especially to the definitions. Some have done so explicitly, such as [9,10,11,12] but most implicitly or tacitly such as [13,14,15,16], even when retaining the use of the terms 'corrective', 'adaptive', and 'perfective'. Non-researcher authored materials have followed a similar pattern, such as [17,18].

Such extensively observable variations in definitions and terminology suggest that the time is ripe for a fresh classification of the types of software maintenance to meet the needs of researchers, and of practitioners and their managers. The next section summarizes this paper's objectives in proposing a fresh classification of software maintenance types. The third section presents the proposal, and the closing section provides some discussion.

## Objectives

The objectives in proposing a fresh classification for types of software maintenance have been to make the classification be:
- based on objective evidence of activities ascertainable from documentation including the source code, rather than be based on intentions,
- independent of hardware platform, operating system choice, design methodology, implementation language, organizational practices, and the availability of the personnel who were or are involved in the maintenance or its management,
- applicable to a large proportion of the situations encountered by researchers and practitioners and their managers, but not try to fit all of the situations of every researcher, practitioner or manager,
- practical to use for a large proportion of researchers and of practitioners and their managers, but not try to meet all of the needs of every researcher, practitioner or manager,
- an evolutionary refinement and/or redefinition of existing terminology and practice, and
- an extention and enrichment the contributions from the proposed ontology of software maintenance [1].

## Proposed classification

### Criteria decisions

Changes made, observed or detected on three aspects of the software maintained or the being maintained, serve as the criteria for groups or clusters of types:
- the software as a whole,
- the source code, and
- the customer-experienced functionality.

The classification is based on changes in these entities as a result of the activities of doing software maintenance. Evidence is obtained by comparing the relevant parts of the software as of *before* the alleged maintenance, with the relevant parts of the software as of *after* the alleged maintenance. None of the evidence requires or depends upon personnel's statements or recollections of intentions about, or the causes of, or the reasons for, or the purposes of, the software maintenance. For personnel using intention-based classifications, the objective evidence can sometimes be used to find out or infer causes or purposes or intentions or reasons or stated requirements for work done.

As pointed out in the ontology [1], software maintenance

commonly involves several to many processes or activities that may result in from none to many changes in the software. Within each grouping of processes or activities noted from applying the criteria, detailed types of software maintenance can be distinguished by applying type decisions. From the set of all changes made, observed, or detected as attempted from the evidence, a dominant process or activity, or a grouping of processes or activities, typically emerges, with supporting or associated processes or activities usually also present. Relevant management and quality assurance activities are considered to be included within each type. The classification proposed here is defined to be exhaustive with mutually exclusive types, where any instance of maintenance work may involve a mix or aggregate in any order of some or all of the types, even though one type may be deemed or observed as dominant.

## Type decisions

The use of the criteria decisions to identify the grouping or clusters of types, is followed by the use of the type decisions to identify the type within the group or cluster. Table I summarizes this in a hierarchic pattern. Note that the groups or clusters and the types within the groups or clusters increase in their software maintenance significance from top to bottom in Table I.

The first column in Table I lists the three criteria, with their associated criteria decisions shown immediately to the right. The second column indicates the response choices for the associated criteria decisions. The third column lists the decisions, type and criteria, to be made from the evidence, or in order to provide the hierarchic structure, directs the nesting of the applicability of the criteria decisions. The fourth column provides two kinds of data. At the left margin, it lists the group or cluster identifying names. Indented under those names it lists the types within the group or clusters. The types apply only when the response to the associated type decision to the left is "yes".

To use Table I, the starting point is criterion decision # 1: "Did the work change the software?" The choice ("yes" or "no") dictates the type decisions to ask or provides direction to the next criteria decision. Within the choice, each type decision is asked in turn from top within the choice to bottom within the choice. A "yes" response to any type decision leads to the cluster and type shown to the right. Note that typically software maintenance work involves many activities. In some situations, the type for each should be identified. In other situations, only a single overall type is wanted, even when many types have been identified. In such cases, the applicable type that is lowest in Table I is used.

Consider an example of using Table I. Suppose that the available evidence indicates that the software maintenance work in question resulted in changing a small part of a user manual. The assigned programmer-analyst made the changes after studying the existing user manual and the associated other documentation, and conferring with the user. The first criteria decision is "Did the work change the software?" Conferring with the user did not change the software, but gives a "yes" on the type decision "Was the software the basis for consultation?" identifying the *consultive* type. Studying the existing user manual and associated documentation did not, but gives a "yes" on the type decision "Was the software evaluated?" identifying the *evaluative* type. Making changes to the user manual did change the software, and hence directs us to the second criteria decision "Was the source code changed?" Since the response here is "no", the first type decision in the documentation cluster is "Did non-code documentation change make it meet stakeholder needs?" Since the response is "yes", the type is *reformative*. Hence, three types of software maintenance were done, *consultive*, *evaluative*, and *reformative*. Even though most of the time may have been spent on activities of the evaluative type, if a single type is wanted, then *reformative* is the type, since it the lowest in Table I of the relevant types.

In general, most maintenance work examines and tests more source code and other documentation than gets changed. The changes that do get made in source code may change its characteristics or properties, many of which are transparent to the user or customer. The ones that are not transparent are usually instances of the *performance* type, like increasing the response speed. The most important category of changes to the source code that are visible to the user or customer or other stakeholders, are the changes in functionality. Such software changes may causes the system to do more for the customer, or alter what the customer sees or does or can do. These almost always involve implementing changes to the business rules embedded in the software.

## Type summary

Each group or cluster of types is distinct and different. The **support interface cluster** concerns changes in how information systems or technology personnel interact with stakeholders and others with respect to the software. In the *training* type, common activities are presenting training to stakeholders about the system implemented by the software. In the *consultive* type, common activities are making time and cost estimates for proposed maintenance work, serving on a help desk, assisting a customer in preparing a maintenance work request, and making specialized knowledge about the software or resources available to

**Table I. Summary of proposed evidence-based types of software maintenance**

| Criteria | Choice | Decisions to be made from the evidence, or directions | Cluster and Type |
|---|---|---|---|
| 1 | | Did the work change the software? | |
| | | | Support interface |
| | No | Was the software the subject of stakeholder training? | Training |
| | | Was the software the basis for consultation? | Consultive |
| | | Was the software evaluated? | Evaluative |
| | Yes | Ask criterion decision # 2. | |
| 2 | | Was the source code changed? | |
| | | | Documentation |
| | No | Did non-code documentation change make it meet stakeholder needs? | Reformative |
| | | Did non-code documentation change make it conform to implemented? | Updative |
| | Yes | Ask criterion decision # 3. | |
| 3 | | Was the customer-experienced functionality changed? | |
| | | | Software properties |
| | No | Did change in software properties improve elegance or security? | Groomative |
| | | Did change in software properties facilitate maintainability or future use? | Preventive |
| | | Did change in software properties alter performance characteristics? | Performance |
| | | Did change in software properties utilize different technology, resources? | Adaptive |
| | Yes | | Business rules |
| | | Was customer-experienced functionality removed, restricted or reduced? | Reductive |
| | | Was customer-experienced functionality made more correct or fixed? | Corrective |
| | | Was customer-experienced functionality replaced, added to or extended? | Enhancive |

others in the organization. In the *evaluative* type, common activities are very diverse and include studying the source code and other documentation, tracing how a proposed change might ripple, preparing and running tests, examining the interactions between operating system features and the software to be maintained, searching for needed data, and debugging.

The **documentation cluster** concerns changes in the documentation other than the source code or its machine language equivalents. In the *reformative* type, common activities are improving the readability of the documen-

tation, modifying the documentation to incorporate the effects of changes in the local standards manual, preparing training materials, and adding entries to a data dictionary. In the *updative* type, common activities are replacing obsolete documentation with accurate current documentation, preparing UML models to document existing source code, and incorporating test plans into the documentation.

The **software properties cluster** concerns changes in the properties and characteristics of the software, but not changes in the functionality of the software. In the *groomative* type, common activities are replacing algorithms or components with more elegant ones, changing data naming conventions, doing backups, modifying access authorizations, and recompiling source code. In the *preventive* type, common activities are making modifications to improve maintainability, and putting in place a base for making a future change to some new technology. In the *performance* type, common activities have results that affect the user (but not the functionality) and are such activities as improving system up time, and replacing algorithms or components with faster ones. In the *adaptive* type, common activities are porting the software to a new platform, increasing COTS utilization, and moving to object-oriented technologies.

The **business rules cluster** concerns the functionality experienced by the customer—i.e., how the software and the customer personnel work together to get the customer's work done. In the *reductive* type, common activities are eliminating data from output received by the customer, reducing data flows into or out of the software, and reflecting a customer's narrowed business plan. In the *corrective* type, common activities are fixing detected bugs, adding more defensive programming, and changing the handling of exceptions. In the *enhancive* type, common activities are adding or replacing business rules to extend or expand the system's functionality accessible to the customer, and adding data flows into or out of the software.

## Discussion and conclusion

Evidence for many of the twelve types of software maintenance can be observed for most software maintenance work. This is such a common situation that the question is, what type of maintenance is dominant for any specific maintenance task?

On a person-hours spent basis, the *evaluative* type is usually dominant, because it includes comprehending what the software does and how it does it, and preparing and using diagnostic tests. Practitioners and their managers are usually loath to report or advertise *evaluative* as their dominant type of software maintenance because that fails to communicate clearly about the contribution information systems or technology makes to the stakeholders. The more obviously significant work is nearer the bottom of the list in Table I.

Consider an example. A programmer-analyst was assigned to work a change request. The programmer-analyst examined some software seeking the parts that would be relevant, and making an estimate of the time and cost to do the work. After some conferences with the customer personnel and the programmer-analyst's own supervisor, the programmer-analyst got the go ahead. The first task was to

build a protected test environment, a regression test suite and associated test plan, and run the tests diagnostically. Then came designing the data layouts, the patches to add the new functionality, and the revised database access. To forestall a warned about possible future complaint, the programmer-analyst replaced an existing procedure with a faster one before attempting to test run with the compiled patches in place. After debugging and having to add a defensive trap, the programmer-analyst prepared the software for regression testing. After passing that testing, and updating both the user manual and the UML, the programmer analyst secured SQA's signoff, and with the supervisor's approval, scheduled and put in some on-site time to help transition the customer personnel to using the changed software when it was put into production.

Question: what type of software maintenance was this? The evidence indicates that nine types were done, but with *preventive*, *adaptive*, and *reductive* apparently not done. Even though comprehending the code and testing appeared to have accounted for the most person-hours, what appeared to stand out most is the increase in functionality gained by the customer. Therefore, within the business rules cluster, we seek the process that yields the best fit with the evidence that is lowest in Table I. In this example, that puts *enhancive* in the position of being the dominant type. Note, however, that both practitioners and their managers, as well as researchers, may find value in knowing about all of the types individually identifiable in order to gain insight and management opportunities.

The choice of names for the types of maintenance has been a matter of concern. Following the lead of Swanson [3], words ending in ...ive have been usually used. Only one freshly coined term, "groomative", has been proposed as an adequately descriptive adjective for grooming the documentation. "Perfective" has been dropped in order to make the proposed classification more precise and useful both to practitioners and their managers, and to researchers. Previous attempts at terms redefinition have not been warmly received and widely used, as for example [7,9,19]. Nonetheless, two terms used by Swanson [3], "adaptive" and "corrective", have been redefined by deleting the intention component from both and by narrowing their applicability to software properties and business rules respectively. These two redefinitions are urged for three reasons:

- the likely acceptance of two newly coined terms for these types of maintenance would likely gain even less acceptance,
- the terms help provide some continuity with popular usage, as noted earlier, and
- the two types, *corrective* and *adaptive*, along with *enhancive*, get the most attention.

The proposed types of software maintenance are

independent of the "scenarios" concerns addressed in the ontology report [1]. The types proposed here bypass not only the scenarios discussed in that report, but also nearly all others. The possible exceptions are total outsourcing of software maintenance, or the combination of total retirement and replacement.

In closing, a look at a major limitation is appropriate. As a detailed analysis can easily show, the use of the proposed criteria decisions in their three levels can be followed by far more than just a dozen type decisions to yield more than a dozen types of software maintenance. Some persons (more likely managers than researchers) may argue that the field does not need to recognize even a dozen types of software maintenance at all. Just two, they say, are and will be sufficient: "too much" and "none".

## Acknowledgments

The author thanks the ICSM reviewers for their advice to shorten and condense the paper as submitted. This has been done here.

## References

1. Kitchenham BA, Travassos GH, Mayrhauser Av, Niessink F, Schneidewind NF, Singer J, Takada S, Vehvilainen R, Yang H. Toward an ontology of software maintenance. *Journal of Software Maintenance* 1999, **11**(6):365–389.
2. Canning RG. That maintenance 'iceberg'. *EDP Analyzer* 1972, **10**(10):1–14.
3. Swanson EB. The dimensions of maintenance. In *Proceedings 2nd International Conference on Software Engineering*. IEEE Computer Society Press: Long Beach CA, 1976; 492–497.
4. Chapin N. Do we know what preventive maintenance is? In *Proceedings International Conference on Software Maintenance*. IEEE Computer Society Press: Los Alamitos CA, 2000; in press.
5. Lientz BP, Swanson EB. *Software Maintenance Management*. Addison-Wesley Publishing Co.: Reading MA, 1980; 214 pp.
6. Swanson EB, Chapin N. Interview with E. Burton Swanson. *Journal of Software Maintenance* 1995, **7**(5), 303–315.
7. IEEE. *IEEE Standard Glossary of Software Engineering Terminology, IEEE Std 610.12-1990*. Institute of Electrical and Electronics Engineers: New York NY, 1991: 83 pp.
8. IEEE. *IEEE Standard for Software Maintenance, IEEE Std 1219-1998*. Institute for Electrical and Electronic Engineers: New York NY, 1998; 47 pp.
9. Kemerer CF, Slaughter SA. Determinants of software maintenance profiles: an empirical investigation. *Journal of Software Maintenance* 1997, **9**(4):235–251.
10. Martin J, McClure CL. *Software Maintenance: The Problem and Its Solution*, Prentice-Hall, Inc.: Englewood Cliffs NJ, 1983; 472 pp.
11. Parikh G. *Techniques of Program and System Maintenance, 2nd Edition*. QED Information Sciences, Inc.: Wellesley MA, 1988; 463 pp.
12. Perry WE. *Managing Systems Maintenance*. Q.E.D. Information Sciences, Inc.: Wellesley MA, 1981; 371 pp.
13. Arthur LJ. *Software Evolution*. John Wiley & Sons, Inc.: New York NY, 1988; 254 pp.
14. Bendifallah S, Scacchi W. Understanding software maintenance work. *IEEE Transactions on Software Engineering* 1987, **SE–13**(3):311–323.
15. Gustafson DA, Melton AC, An KH, Lin I. *Software Maintenance Models*, Technical Report. Department of Computing and Information Sciences, Kansas State University: Manhattan KS, 1990; 14 pp.
16. Martin RJ, Osborne WM. *Guidance on Software Maintenance, NBS Special Publication 500-106*. National Bureau of Standards: Washington DC, 1983; 66 pp.
17. Grady RB. 1987. Measuring and managing software maintenance. *IEEE Software* 1987, **4**(9):35–45.
18. Reutter J. Maintenance is a management problem and a programmer's opportunity. In *AFIPS Conference Proceedings of the 1981 National Computer Conference, Vol. 50*. AFIPS Press: Reston VA, 1981; 343–347.
19. Chapin N. Software maintenance: a different view. In *AFIPS Conference Proceedings of the 1985 National Computer Conference, Vol. 54*. AFIPS Press: Reston VA, 1985; 328–331.

# Management II

# Leveraging Software Reengineering Systems for Heterogeneous Distributed Computing Environments

Chia-Chu Chiang


Allen Systems Group, Inc.
Software Development
4343 E. Camelback Road, Suite 205
Phoenix, AZ 85018, USA
E-mail: Chia-Chu_Chiang@viasoft.com

## Abstract

*ASG's Existing Systems Workbench (ESW) is a comprehensive, integrated tool set that supports the software reengineering process. These software reengineering tools were originally developed for centralized environments. With the widespread use of object-oriented and client-server technologies, customers are expecting ESW to take advantage of these new technologies and also cooperate with their heterogeneous distributed computing environments. In this paper, we propose a distributed object computing architecture for allowing ESW to operate in a heterogeneous distributed environment. The architecture was implemented with CORBA technology. The leverage of this new architecture enhances the product value and adapts the product to customer expectations.*

**Keywords:** Common Object Request Broker Architecture (CORBA), Existing Systems Workbench (ESW), Legacy Integration, Object Request Broker (ORB), and Software Reengineering

## 1. Introduction

Currently, ASG's ESW for software reengineering operates in a centralized environment. With today's demand from high-tech industry, distribution and scalability are very important to a software tool, especially when it is part of an enterprise information system. The migration of ESW built on centralized environments for distributed environments using the Intranet/Internet and multi-tier client-server architecture greatly enhances the product connectivity, performance, robustness, distribution, and scalability.

With the widespread use of object-oriented and client-server technologies, customers are expecting ESW to take advantage of these new technologies and also cooperate with their heterogeneous environments. There are two approaches to modernizing ESW: *convert* or *facelift*. The first approach is to *convert* ESW from older computing environments to modern computing languages, platforms, and architectures. ESW could be thoroughly analyzed and then transformed into a completely new product. This approach is more than just converting code from one language to another. It is the conversion of entire system architectures, including the user interfaces and database structures. The second approach is to *facelift* ESW by means of middleware [11] such as CORBA [4, 5, 8, 10] or COM/DCOM [6, 7, 9, 12]. Although some functionality can be added by using this approach, most of the inherent deficiencies of the product remain. This approach is generally only a stopgap solution, rather than a strategic one.

Generally, the first approach may not be suitable for ASG to convert ESW. ASG has already made significant investments in the product; the company is usually unwilling to pay the cost of conversion if the new version of ESW does not improve the output results to benefit the customers. From an economical point of view, the second approach is a cost-effective way of wrapping ESW by means of middleware without major changes in ESW.

The approach we propose in this paper is a blend of both approaches. To support highly interactive user interfaces, ESW has been designed and tuned so that the complex analysis tasks are done in the Analytical Engine and the results are stored in a repository. The interactive tools mainly deal with presentation details. The migration of ESW to a client-server environment is therefore made possible by converting only the user interfaces. This approach is a slightly more invasive than facelift, but less drastic than a total conversion. This approach benefits the customers and ASG for using and maintaining ESW for software reengineering tasks. The main goals of this approach are: 1) preserving and leveraging ESW for software reengineering, 2) keeping ESW operational in the customer's site, and 3) promoting batch mode in ESW to highly user interactive mode.

## 2. Organization of the paper

The remainder of this paper is organized as follows. Section 3 describes ESW for software reengineering in centralized environments. In Section 4, we describe the legacy integration of ESW into heterogeneous distributed computing environments. The design of the proposed architecture is discussed in Section 5. The implementation of the architecture with CORBA technology is discussed in Section 6. The overall description of the project is given in Section 7. Section 8 briefly discusses the quality attributes of the architecture. Finally, the paper is summarized in Section 9.

## 3. ESW for software reengineering

ESW is a comprehensive, integrated tool set that facilitates the software reengineering process as shown in Figure 1 [2].

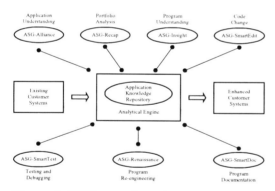

**Figure 1: ESW repository based architecture**

ASG-Alliance is the application understanding component that identifies all the entities of an application, the relationship between those entities, and how proposed changes will affect the application. The entities may include programs, files, databases, JCL, load modules, copybooks, and data items. ASG-Recap is an application measurement tool used to determine program complexity. ASG-Insight provides interactive facilities to investigate and answer programming questions that accommodate 'What if?' inquiries. ASG-SmartEdit provides interactive program analysis capabilities in a syntax-sensitive source editor. It also checks for syntax errors to ensure a clean compile for the code. ASG-SmartTest is a

program testing component that allows the user to step through the code one statement or paragraph at a time, run to breakpoints, and execute entire perform ranges with a single command. ASG-Renaissance , a program reengineering tool, splits large, complex programs callable modules. ASG-SmartDoc is a static analysis tool that generates documentation about programs.

ESW's repository-based technology stores comprehensive information about programs and applications. This information is extracted by the Analytical Engine and stored in the Application Knowledge Repository (AKR). Together, the Analytical Engine and the Application Knowledge Repository give the facilities of ESW access to the specific needed information in performing the software reengineering task on legacy systems. ESW runs on IBM MVS for reengineering legacy systems designated for the same platform as shown in Figure 2. The legacy systems may contain programs, JCL, and load modules. The programs may be written in COBOL, Assembly, PL/I, DB2 SQL, IDMS, and IMS.

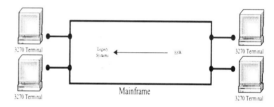

**Figure 2: A centralized environment for ESW**

## 4. Legacy integration into heterogeneous distributed computing environment

The proposed architecture allows ESW to take advantage of a customer's heterogeneous systems. By incorporating the respective powers of both centralized and decentralized computing resources, client-server models of computing use the data storage and processing power of centralized database systems and decentralized presentation of information on desktop systems. A scenario of the integration is shown in Figure 3.

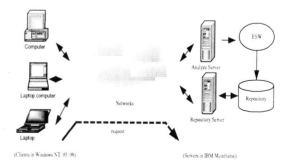

**Figure 3: The scenario of ESW integration**

255

There are two kinds of servers: Analyze and Repository. The Analyze Server receives the requests from the clients and invokes the Analytical Engine to fulfill the requests. The Analytical Engine stores the analysis results in the repository. The Repository Server retrieves the results of the program/application analysis from the repository. In the following sections, the Repository Server will not be covered as we discuss the implementation of the architecture.

The main goal of this project is to transit ESW into a distributed computing architecture. The architecture should be designed to decouple the clients and the servers within ESW. The implementations of the clients and servers should also be hidden from each other.

## 5. Overview of the architecture

There are three blocks as a fundamental basis to design and implement the architecture for leveraging ESW into the heterogeneous distributed computing environments as shown in Figure 4. The blocks are client-side proxy, Analyze Server, and Work Controller that will be described below. Note that the Repository Server will not be discussed in Section 5 and 6.

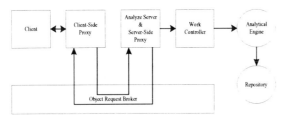

**Figure 4: An overview of the architecture**

Object Request Broker (ORB) serves as the foundation of the architecture. When a system is made up of heterogeneous distributed cooperating components, those distributed components need a way to communicate. The ORB component is responsible for coordinating communication, such as forwarding requests, as well as for transmitting results and exceptions. In this architecture, the clients should not have to know where the Analyze Server is located. The Analyze Server can be moved without affecting client access. The ORB component was added to decouple the clients and the Analyze Server. The Analyze Server registers with the ORB and the clients access the Analyze Server by sending requests to the ORB. The ORB's tasks include locating the Analyze Server, forwarding the request to the Analyze Server and transmitting results and exceptions back to the client. By using ORB, the client can access the Analyze Server simply by sending message calls to the Analyze Server, instead of focusing on low-level inter-process communication.

Client-side proxy can be considered as a local representative for the Analyze Server. The client talks to the Analyze Server using the client-side proxy. However, the client code needs to include the client-side proxy, more code will be brought in the client code. To reduce the complexities of the client code, the client-side proxy was designed as a separate component in the architecture. Whenever there is a change in the implementation of client-side proxy, only the client-side proxy component needs to be recompiled.

The Work Controller component was added to decouple the Analyze Server and the Analytical Engine. When the clients send the requests to the Analyze Server, the Analyze Server invokes the Analytical Engine to perform the program/application analysis. The Analyze Server only transmits the requests to the Analytical Engine. How can the Analyze Server be shielded from the complexity of the interfaces of the Analytical Engine? The Work Controller component was added to encapsulate the Analytical Engine functionality and makes the Analyze Server's interfaces simpler. It reduces coupling between the Analyze Server and the Analytical Engine. The Work Controller provides an interface to the Analytical Engine while hiding the implementations of the Analytical Engine from the Analyze Server. Reducing complexity of interfacing to the Analytical Engine for the Analyze Server is the primary motivation for using the Work Controller component in this architecture.

## 6. Implementation

### 6.1.1. Implementation of the analyze server component

ORB serves the foundation for the interoperability. The architecture was able to get the clients and the Analyze Server talking by using CORBA technology. The architecture allows the client-side proxy component in Windows NT or Windows 95/98 to transmit requests from the clients to the remote Analyze Server in the IBM mainframe through an ORB. The Analyze Server is responsible for analyzing the programs/applications in COBOL, JCL, DB2 SQL, IDMS, CICS, and IMS and storing the information in a repository. The Analytical Engine is operational on the IBM MVS mainframe. The scenario is shown in Figure 5. The clients send requests to the Analyze Server through ORB. The Analyze Server sends results back to the clients through ORB as well. In Figure 5, there are two additional components not shown in the figure. The client-side proxy component is between the clients and the ORB. The Work Controller component is between the Analyze Server and the Analytical Engine. These two components will be explained in detail in the following sections.

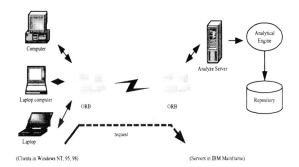

**Figure 5: The scenario of the implementation**

Interoperability in CORBA, as shown in Figure 5, is based on ORB-to-ORB communication. The clients do nothing different for a remote invocation compared to the local case. The ORB takes care of the details of interoperability among a heterogeneous network with different data formats such as byte ordering. The clients do not have to know whether the Analyze Server is local or remote.

Figure 5 shows a request passing from a client to the Analyze Server in the architecture. CORBA requires that the Analyze Server's interface be expressed by an Interface Definition Language (IDL) interface. The interface definition specifies the methods the object is prepared to perform, the input and output parameters they require, and any exception that may occur during the operation. The clients only know the Analyze Server's interface without knowing how the Analyze Server is implemented. The following is a part of the Analyze Server IDL specification as shown in Figure 6.

```
module AnalyzeServer
{
  // global type declarations start here
  typedef long WorkID;
  struct Info {
      ...
      ...
      int rc;    // return code
      int abend; // reason for abnormal termination
      ...
      ...
  };

  interface AnalyzeServices
  {
  // local types and data structures start here
   ...
   ...
   // methods start here
   WorkID CobolAnalyze(...);
   Info GetCobolAnalyzeInfo(in WorkId handle);
   ...
   ...
  }
}
```

**Figure 6: Partial IDL specification of the analyze server**

The Analyze Server's IDL specification is compiled using the IDL compiler for generating client-side proxy and server-side proxy. Client-side proxy is placed in between clients and the ORB. This additional component provides transparency in that the Analyze Server appears to the client as a local one. The client-side proxy also allows the hiding of implementation details from the clients such as inter-process communication, memory allocation and deallocation, and marshaling of parameters and results. Server-side proxy is generally analogous to client-side proxy. The difference is that they are responsible for receiving requests, unpacking incoming messages, unmarshaling the parameters, and calling the appropriate services. They are used in addition for marshaling results and exceptions before sending them back to the client. When results and exceptions are returned from the Analyze Server, the client-side proxy receives the incoming messages from the Analyze Server, unmarshals the data and forwards it to the client.

In this architecture, the client-side proxy is included in a separate DLL executable component. Without this component on the client side, the client code has to include the client-side proxy and more code will be brought in the client code. The result is likely to be a large and complex client code that is hard to understand and maintain. Figure 7 shows the components interacting with ORB.

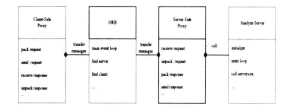

**Figure 7: Components interacting with ORB**

The clients send requests to the client-side proxy component that transfers the requests to the ORB component. The ORB handles low-level communication and forwards the requests through the networks to the server-side proxy. The proxy then transfers the requests to the Analyze Server. The same scenario occurs when the Analyze Server sends the results back to the clients.

### 6.1.2. Implementation of the client-side proxy component

Without making the client-side proxy as a component, the client code needs to bring in the client-side proxy. Whenever a new client-side proxy is generated, the client code needs to be recompiled and relinked. The addition of the component to the architecture decouples the clients and the Analyze Server. Figure 8 shows the components interacting with the client-side proxy component.

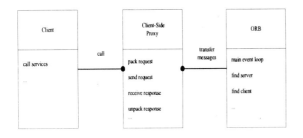

**Figure 8: Components interacting with the client-side proxy**

The client-side proxy component was implemented using the Envelope/Letter idiom [3]. The Envelope class and the Letter class are related by inheritance, with the Letter class derived from the Envelope class. The client code deals exclusively with the Envelope. The implementation is held in the Letter class. Letters are both contained and referenced from Envelopers. Figure 9 shows the diagrammatic representation of the relationships involved in applying a client-side proxy abstraction to the Envelope/Letter idiom.

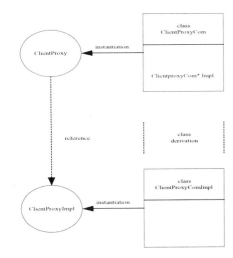

**Figure 9: Structure of the client-side proxy component using the envelope/letter idiom**

The ClientProxy is an instantiated object of the ClientProxyCom class; the client code accesses the ClientProxy object only. The ClientProxyImpl object is an instantiation of ClientProxyComImpl class derived from the base ClientProxyCom class. When the ClientProxy object is created, the ClientProxyImpl object is also created, though this fact is hidden from the client code.

Figure 10 shows the partial declarations of the ClientProxyCom and ClientProxyComImpl classes.

```
class ClientProxyComBase {
};

class ClientProxyCom {
  public:
        ClientProxyCom(void);
        ClientProxyCom(int argc, char** argv);
        virtual ~ClientProxyCom(void);
        virtual long VCobolAnalyze(…);
        …
  protected:
        ClientProxyCom(ClientProxyComBase* t);
  private:
        ClientProxyComImpl* m_Impl;
};

class ClientProxyComImpl: public ClientProxyCom {
  public:
        ClientProxyComImpl();
        ClientProxyComImpl(int argc, char** argv);
        ~ClientProxyComImpl();
        long VCobolAnalyze(…);
        …
        …
  private:
        VAnalyzeServer::VAnalyzeServices_var vas_var;
        int Initialize(int argc, char** argv);
};
```

**Figure 10: Partial declarations of the ClientProxyCom and ClientProxyComImpl classes**

Clients call operations on a ClientProxyCom instance, ClientProxy. In turn, the ClientProxy forwards the request to a ClientProxyComImpl instance, ClientProxyImpl, to carry out the request. The ClientProxyCom and ClientProxyComImpl were built into a DLL executable file.

### 6.1.3. Implementation of the work controller component

The Work Controller component helps to simplify much of the interfacing between the Analyze Server and the Analytical Engine. However, it is unreasonable to let the client wait for the results given by the Analytical Engine, since the analysis of programs/applications may take hours. In order to have an asynchronous modeling of the Analyze Server and the Analytical Engine, a Work Controller was implemented to manage, schedule, and handle the work orders. The Analyze Server's responsibility is to receive the requests from the client and immediately forward the requests to the Work Controller. The view of the Analyze Server and the Work Controller is given in Figure 11. There is a message queue between the Analyze Server and the Work Controller. The Analyze Server operates in the IBM OMVS environment. The Work Controller and the Analytical Engine are operational in the IBM MVS environment.

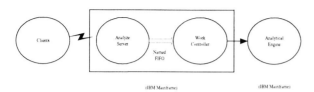

**Figure 11: The Relations between analyze server and work controller**

As the Analyze Server receives a request from the client, the Analyze Server creates a work order containing the information for analyzing programs/applications and stores it in a persistent file. After that, the Analyze Server returns a unique work id to the client and only forwards the work id to the Work Controller through a named pipe (also called a FIFO because data are retrieved in a first-in-first-out manner). The Work Controller is in a loop that reads the named FIFO. If the named FIFO is empty, the Work Controller goes back to sleep. As long as there is a work id, the Work Controller reads the work id from the named FIFO. Then the Work Controller reads the work order from the persistent file in terms of the work id. Based on the information in the work order, the Work Controller dynamically creates the required data sets and invokes the Analytical Engine to analyze the programs/applications. The Analytical Engine writes the information about the programs/applications to a repository. It also writes the execution results to a data set that shows whether the analysis completed normally or not.

After the Analyze Server forwards the work id to the Work Controller, the Analyze Server continues its task without blocking. The Work Controller then looks at its work load and forks children to work on the work orders. The Work Controller immediately goes back to listen the named FIFO for work orders. If there is no work order in the named FIFO, the Work Controller goes to sleep and wakes up when a work order arrives. In Figure 12, the code shows how the Work Controller handles the concurrent processing of multiple work orders.

```
for (count = 0; count < num_of_children; count++)
{
 if (pid = fork()) < 0)
   perror("fork() error\n");
 else if (pid == 0) // child
 {
  while (1)
  {
   // read work id from the named FIFO

   // get the work order by the work id
   switch (workorder.type)
   {
    case COBOL:
        ...
        break;
    ...
```

```
    ...
    case JCL:
        ...
        break;
    default:
        break;
   }; // switch
  }; // while
  exit(0);
 };
}; // for loop
```

**Figure 12: Partial implementation of work controller**

The customer may preset certain number of processes (*num_of_children*) to handle the work orders. However, in some situations, some of the requested processes may not be forked successfully because of the lack of available resources. The Work Controller only tracks the processes that are forked successfully. Figure 13 shows the components interacting with the Work Controller.

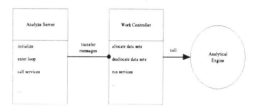

**Figure 13: Components interacting with the work controller**

In this architecture, multiple Work Controllers were designed and implemented to handle the multiple work orders concurrently. As long as a Work Controller completes its assigned work order, it goes back to get the next work order in the FIFO. If there is no work order, the Work Controller goes to sleep and wakes up when a work order arrives. Figure 12 shows the implementation of multiple Work Controllers handling multiple work orders simultaneously.

## 7.  Overall description of the project

The entire project was divided into three subprojects including User Interface, Analyze Server and Repository Server. User Interface subproject focuses on the interactions between the clients and the servers. Since the old architecture for ESW was built on the IBM mainframe, the users usually run ESW through TSO and ISPF. The new architecture for ESW allows the users to invoke ESW from their desktops on Windows 95 or NT. The Analyze Server receives the work orders from the clients and forwards the work orders to the Work Controller that is responsible for invoking the Analytical Engine for completing the work orders. The Repository Server is responsible for retrieving the information stored in the repository and displaying the information on the client's desktop. The design and implementation of the User Interface and the Repository Server are not covered in this paper. In this section, we mainly describe the Analyze Server. The entire project was initiated in 1998. The team has 11-13 members including managers, engineers, and technical writers. Currently, the implementation of the Analyze Server includes 19 files in .cpp, .h, .i, idl, and Pascal, totally approximate 16073 lines. The client-side and server-side proxies in C++ are automatically generated from the IDL. The implementation of the Analyze Server's services was also written in C++. The implementation of the Analyze Server is operational in the IBM OpenEdition environment. The Work Controller implemented in C++ operates in the IBM MVS environment. The Analyze Server listens the client's work orders in the IBM OpenEdition system and forwards the work orders to the Work Controller in the IBM MVS environment, which invokes the Analytical Engine in the same environment as the Work Controller.

## 8. Evaluation of the architecture

Bass, Clements, and Kazman provide several quality attributes for analyzing a software architecture [1]. We discussed response time, security, modifiability, portability, and interoperability here. The architecture was designed to allow a client to send a work order to the Analyze Server and continue his/her task. Since the analysis of programs/applications may take several hours, it is unreasonable to block the client to wait for the results. The architecture supports fast response time by allowing the Analyze Server to return a work id to the client after the client sends a work order to it. After the client received the work id, he/she can continue the task without being blocked by the server. The work id is unique and corresponds to a work order. The work order is then immediately forwarded to the Work Controller that is responsible for invoking the Analytical Engine to perform the task according to the work order. Currently, the client does not receive notification from the Analyze Server when the work order has been completed. The client needs to use the work id to query the status of the work order.

Modifiability, portability, and interoperability are the main motivators behind the use of middleware technology in the architecture. The separation of client and server code, the use of IDL to describe interfaces to CORBA components, and the use of standard mapping from IDL to programming languages such as C++ help the architecture support modifiability, portability, and interoperability.

The performance of the entire architecture heavily counts on the performance of the Analytical Engine. The

analysis of programs/applications may take several hours for completion. The old architecture of ESW allows the users to submit an analysis job in the batch mode so that the users can still work in the foreground mode. The response time for the users was taken into account in the design of the new architecture. It is unreasonable for the users to wait for the analysis results. The new architecture allows the users to send a work order to the server and receive a work id for this work order from the Analyze Server. Once the client receives the work id, the client can continue his/her task without waiting for the Analytical Engine to accomplish the analysis. The client then uses this work id to check whether the work order is completed or not. The response time for the users is just the time for the work order sent to the Analyze Server, the time the Analyze Server allocates a unique word id for the work order, and the time for the work id travels back to the client. The new architecture did improve the performance of the Analytical Engine. The new architecture allows the users to submit an appropriate work order to the Analytical Engine only for the information they concern. If the clients need more detailed information, the clients may send another work order to have the Analytical Engine work on it. The design of analysis level setting may reduce the analysis time for the Analytical Engine. Nevertheless, the design of the new architecture is mainly for flexibility and connectivity. The clients can perform the analysis of programs/applications and view the results from their desktops without logging on IBM Mainframe due to the benefits of connectivity in the heterogeneous computing environment.

Currently, the architecture does not have the ability to resist unauthorized attempts at usage and deny service while still providing its services to legitimate users. For example, users may delete someone else's work order by accidentally supplying a wrong work id. However, this kind of unauthorized access can be avoided by checking the user id and its authorities.

## 9. Summary

Existing commercial tools for software reengineering are mostly designed for centralized environments. These tools are usually inflexible and non-scalable. In addition, with the widespread use of object-oriented and client-server technologies, customers are expecting their software reengineering tools to take advantage of these new technologies and cooperate with their heterogeneous systems and environments.

There are two approaches to modernizing centralized software reengineering products: *convert* or *facelift*. The first approach is to *convert* the products from older computing environments to modern computing languages, platforms, and architectures. The second approach is to *facelift* the products by means of middleware without major changes in the products. This approach is generally only a stopgap solution, rather than a strategic one. From an economical point of view, the second approach is also a cost-effective way of modernizing existing commercial software reengineering products by means of middleware. The approach discussed in this paper is a blend of two traditional approaches. The approach made the products have highly interactive user interfaces. The migration of the products to a client-server architecture is made by converting only the presentation layer of the products. The approach is a slightly more invasive than facelift, but less drastic than a total conversion.

ASG's Existing Systems Workbench® (ESW®) is a comprehensive, integrated tool set that supports the software reengineering process. In this paper, a distributed computing architecture was presented that allows ESW to cooperate with a customer's heterogeneous systems. The legacy leverage avoids to rewriting or converting ESW, but has modernized ESW to have the capability to cooperate with the customer's heterogeneous environments. The architecture enhances the product value and adapts the product to customer expectations.

There are three components – client-side proxy, Analyze Server, and Work Controller as a fundamental basis for designing the architecture through using CORBA technology. The ORB serves the foundation for the interoperability. Using the ORB, the client can access the remote Analyze Server simply by sending service calls to the Analyze Server without concerning the details of communications. We also added a client-side proxy component between the client and the Analyze Server to reduce the complexity of the client code. The component was implemented using the Envelope/Letter idiom. The client deals exclusively with the Envelope. The addition of the component to the architecture also decouples the client code and the Analyze Server code. We also added the Work Controller between the Analyze Server and the Analytical Engine. The Work Controller component was added to decouple the complexities of interfacing to the Analytical Engine. It provides interfaces to the Analytical Engine while hiding the implementations of the Analytical Engine from the Analyze Server. Multiple Work Controllers were designed and implemented to handle multiple work orders concurrently. The Analytical Engine is invoked to analyze the customer's legacy systems in COBOL, JCL, CICS, DB2 SQL, IDMS, and IMS. The Analytical Engine then writes information about the programs/systems to a repository. The Repository Server allows the customer to query the results of the analysis. During analysis, the customer is free to cancel the request.

## Acknowledgements

I am much indebted to referees for their valuable comments in improving the quality of the paper. Enthusiastic support from Mr. Frank Antal, Director of ASG made this paper possible. In addition, I want to thank Mr. Chien Yueh, Principal Engineer of ASG, who provided advice and technical review. I also would like to thank Mr. Ken Richardson for his editorial assistance and valuable comments.

## References

[1] Len Bass, Paul Clements, and Rick Kazman, *Software Architecture in Practice*, Addison Wesley, 1998.
[2] Chia-Chu Chiang, "Reengineering Enterprise Systems for Y2K Compliance," *Proceedings of the 23rd Annual Conference*, The Chinese-American Academic and Professional Association in Southeastern United States (CAPASUS'99), pp. 29-38, July 1999.
[3] James Coplien, Advanced C++: Programming Styles and Idioms, Addison-Wesley, 1992.
[4] Robert Orfali, Dan Harkey, and Jeri Edwards, *Instant CORBA*, John Wiley & Sons, 1997.
[5] Randy Otte, Paul Patrick, and Mark Roy, *Understanding CORBA*, Prentice Hall PTR, 1996.
[6] Rosemary Rock-Evans, *DCOM Explained*, Digital Press, 1998.
[7] Dale Rogerson, *Inside COM*, Microsoft Press, 1997.
[8] Ben-Natan Ron, *CORBA – A Guide to Common Object Request Broker Architecture*, Mcgraw-Hill, 1995.
[9] William Rubin and Marshall Brain, *Understanding DCOM*, Prentice Hall PTR, 1999.
[10] Jon Siegel, *CORBA – Fundamentals and Programming*, John Wiley & Sons, 1996.
[11] Clemens Szyperski, Component Software – Beyond Object-Oriented Programming, Addison-Wesley, 1998.
[12] Nathan Wallace, *COM/DCOM*, The Coriolis Group, 1999.

# A Deployment System for Pervasive Computing

Jesper Andersson
Department of Computer and Information Science
Linköpings universitet
jesan@ida.liu.se

## Abstract

*Software has for a long time been used for controlling different systems. Today, there is a trend towards integrating more software in consumer electronics, home appliances, cars etc. Suddenly, software is moving from traditional environments, such as the desktop computer into new and unknown territory. This will influence many aspects of the software engineering process, above all several new problems arise in the domain of software deployment. How can software be effectively deployed in these environments? Current deployment strategies are not directly applicable. This paper discusses problems with current deployment models and proposes a new, modified model. A deployment model for pervasive computing must support component based development, different delivery models, and installation and activation strategies. Support for dynamic installation and activation (i.e. making modifications without de-activating the software), is especially important. We introduce a prototype implementation, the Java Distributed Run-time Updating Management System (JDRUMS), which we have used as a vehicle for eliciting requirements for our deployment model.*

## 1 Introduction

In the last few years mass-produced, cheap, single-chip computers have been included in different "devices", such as consumer electronics, home appliances, and vehicles. Implementing core functionality in software instead of hardware is a more flexible and cost-effective approach. New developments in communication technology, especially in the area of mobile and short-range digital communication will be available on the market within a year or two. This technology, integrated in different "devices", opens up a new software market. Several companies claim that network connectivity and new types of application software will add significant value to their products, something that will be decisive in the marketplace, where every com-

petitor will face increasing competition and reduced profit margins.

Pervasive computing, the latest buzz word for this technology, focuses on the opportunities associated with this new computing model as well as the problems it entails. The "intelligent household" with "smart" refrigerators and "personal assistants" which combine mobile phone technology and palm-top computing are some examples of the applications involved.

This new computing model, require changes in the software life cycle and several problems wherein current software engineering practice is not directly applicable can be identified.

One of the most radical changes, compared to traditional desktop systems, concerns how a device's software is to be deployed, i.e. packaged, delivered, installed, configured, activated, repaired, and adapted to changing user needs. These devices will have no dedicated system administrator, i.e. personnel that is responsible for the overall proper functioning of a device. Most devices, will not even have a suitable interface were users can perform these tasks.

Our research focuses on software deployment in "a world of devices". We see that without such system administrators many of the existing deployment models will not work. Most end-users will not be interested in installing a new piece of software for their refrigerator, especially not if the refrigerator is only one out of many such devices in the household. It doesn't matter if the software is distributed via surface mail or downloaded from the Internet. At the same time the other major actor in this play, the manufacturer, will not be excited about having non-professionals attempting installation, repair or modification of their appliances' software. Alternatives, when a change to the software is necessary, are to send qualified personnel to the end-user's site or to call the various devices in to a service workshop. However, the potential number of devices involved and the variety of vendors who will supply them make this a severe logistical problem and neither of these approaches will be found to be cost-effective.

At the same time, a number of the devices will be mobile which will introduce additional complications due to the variability in locations the device is to be found at, at any one time. New strategies wherein functionality is downloaded on demand will have to emerge. This is similar to, but more automated than the "plug-in" approach used today in many web-browsers. When a device needs a specific functionality which it currently lacks, it will – automatically or semi-automatically – download, install and activate it itself. In a mobile scenario, this type of updating will probably include some de-installation of some other functionality, due a lack of internal resources supplied with the device. Current deployment strategies are seriously inadequate in coping with these new environments.

To deal successfully with this situation we need a different deployment model; a model that transfers the responsibility for installation, maintenance, repair, adaptation, and enhancement from "end-users" to either the devices themselves or ti the device suppliers, and that utilizes via network connectivity the flexibility of independently deployed components and dynamic updating of systems.

In this paper we outline a deployment model that we believe is better addressed to this new computing model. Hereby systems administration responsibilities can be transferred to either the devices or device manufacturers. We present a prototype implementation that supports our model, the Java Distributed Run-time Updating Management System (JDRUMS). This Java based system initially focused on dynamic updating of component based software, but additional subsystems that handle other aspects of our model have been introduced.

The remainder of this paper is organized as follows. Section 2 discusses existing delivery models and why these do not work well in the context of pervasive computing. Continuing in Section 3, we discuss the requirements for a pervasive computing deployment model. In Section 4, we present our prototype environment JDRUMS. Related work is surveyed in Section 5. Finally, in Section 6 we evaluate our model with respect to the requirements we foresee and to other deployment systems, before we conclude with a discussion of future work.

## 2 Software Deployment

In the last few years, software has become an integral part of many devices. This is an accelerating trend and today, it is difficult to imagine all future systems that will use software for adding value to a product. Increased use of software in different devices gives rise to several questions; one is how all this software should be administrated in order that updated versions and new functionality can be made available to the device. This will affect software deployment, i.e. how software is packaged, delivered, installed, and activated on devices.

Existing models for content delivery, discussed more in depth below, will not work well for these new types of systems for the following reasons.

- A majority of the devices will have no user-interface from which a user can perform system administration tasks.

- Even if there is a suitable interface, it is impossible to require that device owners take on the administrative responsibility for all the numerous devices they will utilize.

- In many cases the application software in the devices will consist of several composed software components. These components will come from different component manufacturers and integrated with the in house developed components by the device manufacturer.

- The newer types of applications will require a new system for managing upgrades, one which is more flexible. It must have tha capability to work at the single component level as well as at the integrated assemblage level.

If we look at current practice for software deployment we see three widely used approaches by commercial vendors. One approach is that used for private desktop machines including most computers in an office environment. Another approach is the "semi-automated" one wherein servers install "images" on machines. This is increasingly used in office environments. And the third, approach is that used for systems administration of distributed systems.

### 2.1 Current Deployment Models

The most widely used deployment model involves the new software being transported to the user, either over a network or via some media (e.g. CD-ROM). The user installs the software on secondary storage and configures it prior to execution. In this model there are several variations. For instance, it could be a system administrator instead of an ordinary user who carries out the work, the software could be installed on a server. etc. In all cases the deployment is heavily dependent on the involvement of on-site people in order to work.

In some companies an automated approach to deployment is being used. Every machine in the company network has a "software profile", stored locally or on a central server. This profile is used to create machine specific software images that are downloaded and installed on a machine, for practical reasons most often during non office hours. This approach is an improvement compared to the first as the current software configuration is available and much of the work can be automated. But the approach is too coarse-grained to be directly applicable in a pervasive computing environment. It is also not an approach easily conductible to the situation where there are great numbers of widely distributed devices, some connected via unreliable network connections, to be dealt with.

In a distributed system environment, the remote systems administration approach is widely accepted. Here, a central command center supervises systems, and sees to it that a correct configuration is running on all nodes. Tools are used for content delivery and installation of new packages. Some distributed infrastructures also provide for dynamic updating of components. This approach is also offers steps in the right direction, but it needs some significant change to fit the needs of pervasive computing.

## 2.2 Recent developments

As previously mentioned, several deployment systems are available. The increased usage of the Internet has influenced these products. For instance, "Installation wizards" the de-facto standard on Windows-based systems does not contain all the content required anymore. Instead it works as a "content deliver proxy" that downloads the content needed from the "nearest" server on the Internet, based on the component requests specified by the user in the wizard..

In the Linux world, automated routines for download and installation of software are used in several distributions. These schemas are based on complete descriptions of the software that is currently installed on the system.

A survey of different approaches to software deployment and available systems for different deployment activities is presented by Hall [7].

## 3  A Deployment System –Requirements

A deployment model for pervasive computing has to satisfy several requirements. In the discussion below we have chosen to divide the requirements into three groups.

- Component Based Systems. This implementation technique has grown in popularity the last few years, and we believe that components and component infrastructures will be a fundamental element in pervasive computing.

- Flexible Content Delivery. The varieties of separate systems in the totality of a pervasive computing environment require that a deployment model support different ways of delivering software. In pervasive computing several actors can take part in the delivery activity, users, devices, and manufacturers; which all require different support in terms of content delivery.

- Flexible Installation and Activation. Traditional installation where software packages and systems are de-activated before installation of new content is inappropriate in many situations. Some devices have a high-availability requirement, which means that we must minimize downtimes, others are mobile and work autonomously. For these types of systems, dynamic installation and activation will be a fundamental requirement.

## 3.1  Component Based Systems

Component based system development is the most recent star in "the software engineering canopy of heaven". Components have been on the agenda since McIlroys paper from 1968 [10]. But owing to recent advances in component technology, such as CORBA, DCOM, and Java Beans, components have started to gain much greater utilization.

Szyperski [12], foresees a market for software components that are self-contained, binary and independently deployable. Device manufacturers that use a component strategy when developing their applications, can choose to develop all components in-house, but the greater likelihood is that they will combine product specific components developed in-house with procured components.

This new development strategy will have a great impact on how software extensions and upgrades should be managed. The problems related to component based applications differ depending on whether or not the perspective of a device manufacturer, of a component developer, or of a device user, is taken.

From a device manufacturer's perspective, software systems will be composed of components from multiple component manufacturers. New releases of these components will appear from time to time. Some of these releases will be regarded as more critical than others which means that there will be a prioritized hierarchy of upgrades to implement with those at the top being of the greatest importance and, in most cases requiring, immediate deployment. Other components that are less critical can be held back to be part of a major upgrade package distributed later. So the optimum model will be one wherein individual components can be separated out and deployed as the situation demands. Very few deployment systems (or run-time systems) support this level of granularity. Typically, a manufacturer needs to deploy superfluous content, in order to deliver a single, newly released, component. For instance, if the bandwidth is limited big chunks of data that effects other communication is not desirable.

The current software configuration resident in a device must be accessible to the remote systems administration function, so the operating components' versions can be compared to those of a new configuration to be implemented. Some deployment systems support this, others attempt to detect the versions and configuration as a pre-installation activity.

How components are assembled and deployed should be transparent to developers. This will increase the number of candidate components to use. A deployment system should have minimal influence on the implementation of components.

The majority of device users have no interest in which software versions are currently running in their devices and definitely no interest if the software to be delivered is a component or some other type of software package. Consequently, component wrapping (and unwrapping) should be transparent as far as users and developers are concerned. The wrapping of components is not transparent to the user in many deployment system today. For instance some systems require certain functionality that unpacks compressed files before the installation program can be started.

- Components should be packaged as self-contained "deployment-units", hiding how components are packaged and what it is that makes it "deployable". This will make the deployment activity transparent to both device users and component developers and result in deployment being principally a responsibility for device suppliers.

- Manufacturers need support for packaging content spanning the range from single components to complex composites containing components from different component producers.

- An accurate remotely accessible description of the current software configuration operating in a device is an absolute necessity for use in the decision process when components are packaged.

## 3.2 Flexible Content Delivery

Beside the problems related to components, the sheer number of devices that a deployment system will serve is another dimension of the total problem. Potentially hundreds of thousands of devices may have been sold and the software running in these all needs to be attended to. Different devices will require different delivery models. A household will have devices from several manufacturers and, some of these will be mobile, other users prefer maintaining their devices by themselves. A manufacturer will require that the deployment system provide sufficient support for handling the full gamut of cases to be encountered.

In order to fully support this diverse set, we have formulated three delivery models that should be supported. Below, we describe two "pull" models where a user or a device initiates and controls the deployment. Then we describe a

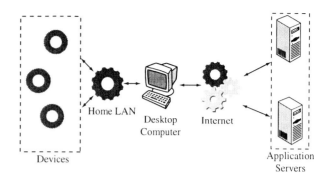

**Figure 1. Upgrades managed from a desktop computer**

model based on a "push" strategy. Here the device supplier is responsible for the deployment.

Existing deployment systems, typically support one or two of these models (or something similar to them). But we argue that all are equally important in a pervasive computing environment.

### 3.2.1 Two "Pull" models

The "pull" strategies are based on a scheme where deployment of software content is initiated at the "user-side". Packages are downloaded directly from application servers and installed on the device.

In the first "pull"-delivery model, a user initiates and controls upgrades from a terminal, typically a personal computer. The model, depicted in Figure 1, supports more advanced users wanting to have control over the software that is downloaded and installed on their devices. In this model, the user needs some application that can be used to survey which devices are on-line, query for deployment-units available for these devices, and capable of delivering the necessary software to the devices. The application must be able to handle devices from different suppliers and compare current software and their component configurations with versions available on different application servers. This delivery model has the advantage of being able to handle several devices and components coming from different manufacturers. Another advantage is that every device is treaded uniformly. The drawbacks include the need for detailed standardization of device interfaces and application servers, so applications can interact with devices from different manufacturers and different application servers.

- Possibilities to locate and establish communication with devices that are online in a specified domain.

- An administrative tool will interact with servers were deployment-units are stored.

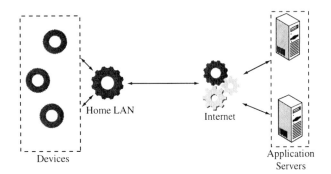

**Figure 2. Devices initiate and manage upgrades**

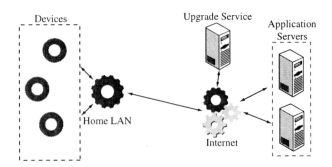

**Figure 3. Update service manage upgrades**

- Automation of the deployment is important, i.e. hide details and minimize the risks of wrongdoing.

Our second model, based on a "pull" strategy, is outlined in Figure 2. Here, the functionality for delivery, installation, and activation is implemented in the devices themselves, hence it is fully automated. Every device is responsible for checking different application servers for available upgrades, downloading the proper packages and installing and activating them. In this model the devices will communicate directly with applications servers. This delivery model is particularly useful if the devices need some form of "functionality on demand", for instance, a mobile device with a positioning system. When such a device moves around in an environment it can add and remove functionality depending upon where it is. When the device enters the "automated bank" the device downloads and installs the bank's components, and executes it. Prior to that it must free resources, so it "de-installs" some components that are not directly needed in this environment, for instance the GPS-map software.

Compared to the previous model this model requires limited standardization which means that device manufacturers can develop optimized implementations for their devices. The disadvantages include providing extra functionality in the devices which can be quite problematical since many devices have limited resources.

- Devices should be capable of carrying out the deployment.

### 3.2.2 A "Push" model

The "push" strategy is based on a scheme where deployment is initiated at the "supplier-side". The manufacturer keeps a record of devices and "pushes" deployment packages from application servers to devices. This strategy is similar to the approach often used for deploying software in a distributed system.

In Figure 3, we present a schematic view of a "push" system. Typically, there is a dedicated "upgrade service" or deployment application, which automates the deployment. The deployment application keeps a record of the devices, with an address and the current software configuration. When a new package is made available, it deploys this to all devices. This model is probably the most preferred, from a supplier perspective. Manufacturers will have full control. A deployment model supporting this delivery strategy must meet a certain set of requirements.

- The delivery system must keep track of devices and their current configuration.

- Device suppliers need to have the possibility of communicating, directly or indirectly, with a large number of devices and component servers, when pursuing deployment of new software.

### 3.3 Flexible Installation and Initiation

The delivery models discussed above, all depend on devices providing support for installation and activation. There are two strategies for these activities. The first one is similar to the one used on desktop computers where the software is de-activated, a new version installed, and finally the new software instance is re-activated. The second strategy, dynamic updating, is used in many mission critical applications, where high availability is required. For instance, many command and control applications and communication systems utilize some form of dynamic updating. Dynamic updating is discussed more in depth in Section 5. If we look for dynamic updating support in existing deployment systems it is difficult to find any system that offers this functionality. Some few systems do offer such functionality, but most often these are domain specific systems that are difficult to use in other domains.

A deployment model for pervasive computing should support both these strategies. The "dynamic deployment strategy" will be useful in different applications, especially when deployment is controlled at the supplier-side. Then it is difficult, if not impossible to decide whether some piece of software can be closed down or not, without interfering with the usage of the device. Another situation where dynamic updating is preferable is when software is deployed on a context dependent basis. When a device moves around in the world, changes to the software configuration should be fully transparent to a user. Finally, some devices, will be devices with a high availability requirement, e.g. fire- and intruder-alarms where dynamic updating is an absolute requirement. We present a more detailed list of requirements below.

- Installation and de-installation of components and applications.

- Activation, de-activation, and re-activation of applications and components.

- Replacement of running component instances with new versions, with the application state preserved.

- See to it that dynamic deployments are made persistent. Dynamically deployed software should be used the next time an application is activated.

# 4 JDrums

The Java Distributed Run-time Updating Management System — JDRUMS [3], is a prototype implementation of a flexible framework for software deployment for pervasive computing. Previously, we discussed several requirements for such a deployment system. Initially, in this prototype, we have focused on basic support for component-based systems, different delivery models, and dynamic updating.

The prototype is based on and restricted to Java. One important factor for choosing Java as the implementation platform, is the JINI technology [4]. Directed towards small, embedded systems, JINI simplifies many tasks, for instance communication between different system components and registration of devices. Another reason for choosing Java was the strong component model of Java Beans.

## 4.1 System Architecture

The JDRUMS system architecture consists of three elements depicted in Figure 4 and described below. First, there is the JDRUMS devices, where user applications are executed. In our current implementation a device is represented by a modified Java Virtual Machine (JVM). Modifications include support for dynamic updating and network awareness. Second, the JDRUMMER tool that functions as the command post for deployment activities. Third, there are component servers (JSTOREs) . These servers works as component warehouses and JDRUMS devices and JDRUMMER tools interact with these when carrying out deployment.

The communication between the components is JINI based. All components register as services in a JINI lookup service. When a component requires a service, it queries the lookup service, then it can connect to any of the services available using RMI [8]. JINI offers a clean Java solution and has built in security policies, which is advantageous in a network environment.

### 4.1.1 The JDRUMS - JVM

In order to fully prototype our deployment model, we needed something that simulates the "devices". In a Java environment, the choice of a JVM as the basis for the simulation of devices comes naturally. The JDRUMS-JVM is a modified virtual machine with extra functionality, providing for dynamic updating of classes and registration of the JVM as a JINI service.

Dynamic upgrades works on a class[1] level [2]. When a "deployment-kit" is delivered to the JVM, it is unwrapped and installed. Later, when objects that are instances of an obsolete class version are referenced, an instance of the new class version is created, the object state is migrated from the "old" object to the "new" object, and then the reference that "triggered" the migration is changed to reference the newly created object. The object migration is controlled by a conversion class, which is packaged together with the new class release. The conversion class consist of a set of mapping functions. The functions transfers or converts information from the old object.

The contents of a deployment package vary. For small upgrades, the new version of a class and the conversion class are sufficient. But, more complex upgrades – ones which include more than one class require more classes to be included in the package.

The JVM also keeps version information for all installed classes. This information is used when deciding the specific contents of the deployment packages that are to be delivered.

### 4.1.2 The JSTORE

The JSTORE component has one main responsibility, that is to store several releases of different components. It also keeps version and dependency information for all releases. The JSTORE can use information from the JVM or directives from the JDRUMMER, when creating deployment packages.

---

[1]The terms component and class are interchangeable in this description.

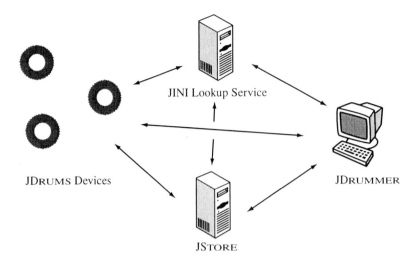

**Figure 4. The** JDRUMS **System Architecture**

### 4.1.3 The JDRUMMER tool

To assist system administrators with deployment, the JDRUMS environment includes a tool, the JDRUMMER. It is a GUI based tool, in which you can easily combine one or more deployment packages from different JSTOREs and deliver these to a specified set of devices. The tool, also includes lists of running JDRUMS-JVMs' and JSTOREs in the neighborhood. Using these lists, an administrator can query running JVMs for their current class configuration, find out if new releases are available at the component stores, and select JVMs as targets for deployment.

## 4.2 A deployment scenario

In the environment there is at least one JSTORE, component storage running and registered in the JINI lookup service. When, a device is started it also registers in the JINI lookup service. The device can be given a startup directive to download the latest available software directly from storage or use the software that is already available on the device. When a system administrator thinks it is time to administrate the running devices, he starts up the JDRUMMER tool. The JDRUMMER looks up running devices and JSTOREs and displays this information. Then the maintainer begins by assembling deployment packages and deploying these to target devices. In the process, he queries devices for the current software configuration and the component stores for available packages. As deployment packages arrive in the devices, they are automatically installed. When the components have been installed, objects are migrated and state transfered when the object handle is dereferenced by the virtual machine. Eventually, all objects in the running application are migrated to the new class representation. The work being done, the administrator exits the tool.

## 5 Related work

### 5.1 Deployment systems

As we previously mentioned there are several commercial deployment systems available on the market. Spanning the range of simple systems, supporting delivery of software from one site to another, to complex systems supporting enterprise wide installations and updates. Many of these systems work well when complete applications with very few inter-application dependencies are deployed. But they suffer from severe problems in a pervasive computing environment.

The Software Dock [7] is a research project, wherein a framework for software configuration and deployment is being developed. The deployment framework uses a client-server architecture in combination with a event system. At the manufacturer or supplier-site, there is a server (release dock) with release information. On every user-site, a client (field dock) works as an interface with the release dock. There is a registry containing all information on releases available at release docks and configurations in field docks. Software Dock uses an event system for signaling changes in the registry and agents for controlling certain deployment tasks such as delivery, installation, and activation.

### 5.2 Dynamic updating systems

Dynamic deployment systems are by no means a new field for research, especially if we go into the domain of distributed systems and large mission-critical software packages. Several strategies for dynamic updating, both hardware and software based, have been proposed, although none have revolutionized dynamic updating by offering a solution cheap or practical enough for anyone to use. They all have some shortcomings. The special case with object-oriented systems, has limited or no support in existing approaches. More details and in depth descriptions of different types of such systems can be found in the works of Segal and Frieder [11] and Gupta [6].

There are hardware-based solutions that allow dynamic reconfiguration of applications by replacing the running system with an updated one. Here, a secondary system is used wherein the new release is activated, then the system switches to the secondary system and de-activates the "old" release. Such a system is often operated in conjunction with a hardware-based system for fault-tolerance, but it is still difficult and expensive [11] to provide the functionality for migrating states between machines. The cost of duplication hardware in a device disqualifies this approach for pervasive computing.

The software-based approaches presuppose that programs consist of a number of independent building blocks, or modules. To reconfigure the system, no modifications are necessary to the individual modules, since the connections between them are handled by the manager rather than hardcoded references. The main drawback is that special knowledge is demanded from both programmers and system administrators. This violates our transparency requirement. Other variants of a module based approach use procedures and ADTs as modules, e.g. the dynamic type replacement system proposed by Fabry [5].

Other module-based approaches are based on the client-server architecture, often used in distributed systems. The client-server model works much in the same way as that for abstract data-types, only on a bigger scale. The granularity of components is increased from data-types to server-modules. The interfaces to the server never change only the implementation of the different services it provides. A general drawback using systems which follow this approach, is the size of the components being replaced. Even a small change will lead to an entire server being unavailable for some time during the duration of the update. Darwin [9] is one example of a configuration language for distributed systems. Darwin provides support for dynamic reconfiguration at run-time in the form of a reconfiguration manager. A supervisor can send directives in a script language to the system that invokes dynamic reconfiguration. In a Darwin implementation, every element can be added, removed, or replaced dynamically.

## 6 Conclusions and Future work

We have proposed a flexible deployment model for pervasive computing environments. Furthermore, we have described JDRUMS, a Java based deployment system prototype that provides support for component based applica-tions, flexible delivery, and dynamic updating. Below we evaluate our model and prototype with respect to the requirements listed in Section 3 and other approaches to software deployment.

With our model, component designers do not have to consider how a component is deployed. The deployment system handles everything. This transparency is favorable, since it will make components less product specific and widen the potential market. There is one exception though, when a component is targeted for dynamic updating. There is a need for additional functionality describing how an object should be migrated to the new class representation. Here, we see a clear violation of our transparency requirement. But, on the other hand, the component developer can probably develop a conversion class along with the new version without straining the project budget. For some components, the conversion class could be generated automatically using some reflection technique. Components are packaged into upgrade-units that contain one or several components and other required parts. The JDRUMS-JVM keeps information on the current component configuration, the device or some other component in the system having access to this.

Our model supports the three delivery models. But here more research and hands-on work is needed to fully implement all models in the prototype system and to evaluate these. Our prototype relies on JINI, and devices and other components are registered in a lookup-service. Here, devices can lookup component storages, deployment tools can find devices etc.

The prototype supports dynamic updating of Java components, which has been our main objective. More work is needed here also, such as improved support for complex upgrades, performance optimizations, and the introduction of a true "first-class" representation of the software architecture configuration.

Compared to other deployment system, such as Software Dock and other, commercial systems, our work has a different focus. Our system is intended for fine-grained deployment, at the component level. We emphasize dynamic updating where new functionality and updates can be integrated into an active application transparently.

To summarize, the goal of this project is not to provide a fully functional, industrial strength, deployment system. Our prototype is solely used as a vehicle to verify and elicit requirements for a model of a deployment system and as a "proof-of-concept". We believe that the model we have presented and the prototype meets most of the requirements for deployment in a pervasive computing environment. It is flexible in the sense that we can easily adapt to new or modified requirements. It supports component based applications, different delivery models, and is flexible in terms of installation and activation is a key success factor for pervasive computing.

Future work in this area will focus on context and quality-criterion based configuration. We will look into problems concerning how to model, implement, and maintain applications were the architecture changes. These changes are due to certain events such as hardware failures and "a mobile device entering a room". A more detailed description is provided by Andersson [1]. We will also look into how to provide support for "large-scale" deployment. Here, others, for example the Software Dock project, will influence our work.

# 7 Acknowledgements

This material is based upon work sponsored by the Swedish National Board for Industrial and Technical Development (NUTEK), Växjö universitet and the ECSEL program at Linköpings universitet. I would like to thank Marcus Comstedt, Pär Danielsson, Torbjörn Hultén, and Tobias Ritzau, for their contribution to this work. Thanks also to Richard Olson for useful comments on both language and contents.

# References

[1] J. Andersson. Towards Reactive Software Architectures. Technical report, Linköpings universitet, May 1999. Licentiate Thesis. In Linköping Studies in Science and Technology, No. 769.

[2] J. Andersson, M. Comstedt, and T. Ritzau. Run-time Support for Dynamic Java Architectures. In *Proceedings of the ECOOP'98 workshop on Object-Oriented Software Architectures*, 1998. Technical report 13/98 University of Karlskrona/Ronneby.

[3] P. Danielsson and T. Hultén. Java Distributed Run-time Updating Management System. Master's thesis, Växjö universitet, 2000. Under preparation.

[4] W. Edwards. *Core JINI*. Prentice Hall PTR, 1999.

[5] R. Fabry. How to Design A System in Which Modules can be Changed on the Fly. In *Proceedings of International Conference on Software Engineering*, pages 470–476. IEEE-CS Press, 1976.

[6] D. Gupta. *On-line Software Version Change*. PhD thesis, Department of Computer Science and Engineering, Indian Institute of Technology, Kanpur, November 1994.

[7] R. Hall. *Agent-based Software Configuration and Deployment*. PhD thesis, University of Colorado, 1999.

[8] *Java Remote Method Invocation - Distributed Computing For Java*, March 1998. Available at: http://java.sun.com.

[9] J. Kramer and J. Magee. Dynamic Structure in Software Architectures. In *Proceedings of the fourth ACM SIGSOFT symposium on Foundations of software engineering (FSE'96)*, pages 3–14. ACM, ACM-Press, October 1996.

[10] M. D. McIlroy. Mass produced software components. In *Software Engineering, Report on a conference sponsored by the NATO Science Committee*, 1969.

[11] M. E. Segal and O. Frieder. On-the-fly program modification: Systems for dynamic updating. *IEEE Software*, 10(2):53–65, 1993.

[12] C. Szyperski. *Component Software – Beyond Object-Oriented Programming*. Addison-Wesley, 1997.

# Support for System Evolution through Separating Business and Technology issues in a Banking System

John Edwards, Ian Coutts and Stuart McLeod

*The R.E.D. Group, Department of Manufacturing Engineering, Loughborough University,*
*Loughborough, Leicestershire LE11 3TU, UK,*
*Email j.m.edwards@lboro.ac.uk*

## ABSTRACT

*It is commonly accepted that there is a need to create IT systems that adapt easily and indefinitely to changing business requirements. Contemporary software design approaches often mix business issues with IT implementation issues to form monolithic systems that are no more responsive to change than their predecessors.*

*This paper introduces an approach which seeks to separate a description of the business system from the technological issues within an IT implementation. Such a separation can serve to handle legacy IT systems today, while providing a strategy for migrating towards systems where business and IT issues are de-coupled and thereby provide improved conditions for system maintenance.*

*The paper demonstrates how a model of the business, software design patterns, contemporary tools and emerging object standards can be used to create the separation. It provides detail of the many issues raised when moving from laboratory based proof of concept systems to a system integrated with existing IT in a prestigious financial institution in the City of London.*

## Keywords

Design Patterns, Legacy Systems, Migration, Financial Systems, Object Standards, Technology Transfer

## 1 INTRODUCTION

In a drive to create systems that can move forward in an evolutionary manner the principals of object oriented design have been employed when building new financial software systems. Projects often use financial software development environments. These are typically billed as a software platform and suite of financial trading applications, but are effectively a toolkit comprising a set of finance specific base classes sitting above a data model. Use of such products gives undeniable advantage over bespoke coding. However, this only leads to a system which provides better support for change, primarily because the IT department can re-write code faster. It does not create a system where change is inherent [2].

The use of such tools relies heavily on inheritance from the toolkit base classes when building higher level business applications. The class hierarchies produced often mix business issues (the business logic) with IT implementation issues (distribution, database management etc.). This leads to the creation of inflexible systems that are tied to a set of vendor supplied object classes that can change following a new vendor software release. The approach described in this paper enables the creation of business applications whose implementation are effectively separated from the underlying software technology. Under these conditions the business system can evolve at its own pace, driven by business needs of the global financial market, while the IT system can evolve at its own pace governed by technological innovation.

## 2 SEPARATING BUSINESS ISSUES FROM TECHNOLOGY ISSUES

The overall approach being developed in the project is based on the use of a live business model that is semantically and dynamically aligned with the financial domain [1,3]. The model is expressed in a form that can enable the reconfiguration of business process support functionality to suit the changing business requirements of the bank. This overall approach is reported in [3].

The success of such an approach relies on the ability to link the semantic banking entities which form the building blocks of the model to the existing technology in the collaborating companies IT systems. In order to ease the replacement of IT technology in the future, a primary objective of our work is to create and maintain a flexible link between the live business model and the underlying IT system.

The authors contend that the critical problem with IT business solutions that are built today is the confusion that results from mixing business and technological issues. The need for the business to evolve separately from the technology is clear, investment banking has little in common with computing technology. Establishing a separation between business processes and technology is a major step to avoiding legacy system dependency.

Our approach uses deconstruction of the underlying IT infrastructure together with emerging object standards [4] and design patterns [5] to create a set of translation objects which provide reusable services. These objects will effectively surround the banks central IT system and enable controlled replacement of functionality over a period of time. The following sections of the paper detail how the design and implementation of these flexible translation objects has been achieved and how they are being moved out of the laboratory at Loughborough into the collaborating company.

## 3  ISSUES TO BE ADDRESSED

Our approach is based on the notion that the business model will be built on a banking ontology comprising fundamental atomic elements of banking. Given this, the translation objects which the final system must posses must also be based on these semantics of the banking world, and as such, the following issues must be addressed:

- What should the banking services look like;
- How can the services be mapped onto the existing IT system;
- Can this mapping be constructed in a flexible manner to allow future IT systems to be accommodated.

Addressing the first issue requires both the expertise of the financial domain and experience of implementing IT systems within this domain. As a starting position for this research we have adopted the standards of the OMG Financial Domain Taskforce, due to their members experience in implementing IT systems within the financial sector and the commitment expressed by a number of important financial system vendors to adhere to the OMG's output. We have also used our own banking model derived from both the literature and the experience of our collaborating company. Finally we have also used the industry standards that are agreed within the international financial domain.

## 4  TECHNIQUES INCORPORATED

### Interface Definitions
In order to specify the services provided by a system component, OMG's Interface Definition Language (IDL) is used. An IDL interface describes the functionality that will be provided by an object. This description is needed to develop clients that make use of objects which support the interface. An interface typically specifies attributes and operations, and includes the parameters of each operation. In order to achieve this, IDL posses its own programming language independent data types and supports the creation of new data types.

### Object Oriented Design
Given that the work is adopting the OMG specifications and that there is a requirement to encapsulate the mechanisms involved with mapping financial domain services onto legacy IT systems, it was natural to choose object oriented design.

In order to support the abstractions specified by the OMG and retain some flexibility in how they are mapped onto the underlying IT system, the service abstractions (relating to the business world) and the IT implementations must be kept separate within the system design. Some clearly defined means to distinguish these concepts must be employed.

### Design Patterns
An object oriented approach has a number of advantages including the provision of numerous fundamental (fine grained) building blocks. However, it doesn't provide the system designer with support for many of the larger grained system issues.

Design patterns have been adopted in our work to provide a means to tackle different aspects of the design problem e.g. overall system structure or managing a large number of system configurations. In particular, the Bridge pattern has been useful in supporting the separation of business issues from the issues associated with a particular underlying IT implementation. Also the Abstract Factory pattern has been used to ensure that the bridging between the business and IT implementations is flexible and supports multiple and changing IT implementations.

The following provides a definition of the Bridge pattern, which gives an impression of why it is an appropriate approach to solving our problem. The intent is to "de-couple an abstraction from its implementation so that the two can vary independently". The intent of the Abstract Factory pattern is to "provide an interface for creating families of related or dependant objects without specifying their concrete classes" [5]

### Example Design Fragment
To illustrate the design decisions described above, consider the following design fragment. The concept of Money is supported by a class hierarchy which provides a range of concepts from fixed price (maybe the value associated with an enacted transaction) to a fluctuating spot price (maybe a share price from a real time financial price feed such as Reuters). Issues relating to how such values are obtained from current IT systems must not taint the pure business considerations that relate to this hierarchy. Some means of instantiating a monetary value must exist, but knowledge of the mechanisms employed should be hidden. This leaves the designer free to consider how these classes should support the services specified by the OMG money specification. The issues associated with actually providing for the storage and retrieval of such information, which can be complex when interfacing with legacy applications, can be addressed within a separate class hierarchy. As such, if appropriate, these issues can be resolved by a separate designer who has experience and skills in a particular legacy application.

## Separation

The concept of a monetary value is separate from how monetary values are mapped onto the underlying IT systems. This is in line with the OMG value based semantics for money, in essence objects that support the Money interface are intended to be passed as parameters between business utilities. Therefore the implemented class hierarchy contains a number of relatively simple Java classes which contain no mechanisms to relate them to the underlying IT systems within the Bank as shown in Figure 1.

**Figure 1** Application of the Bridge Pattern in Design

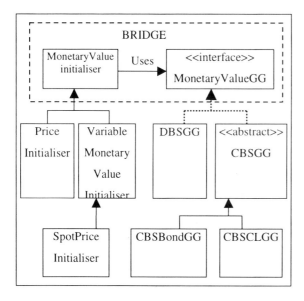

The task of relating these simple classes to the underlying IT systems falls to the MonetaryValueInitialiser bridge. The Java class `MonetaryValueInitialiser` provides an implementation independent abstraction which couples particular instances of Java classes, which implement the Money interface, with the underlying IT system.

The abstraction `MonetaryValueInitialiser` can then be refined through inheritance without regard to any implementation issues. For example `PriceInitialiser` defines an abstraction that relates to mapping fixed monetary values (represented by the Price abstraction) to the underlying IT system. However the assumption contained within `PriceInitialiser` are de-coupled from the mechanisms required to actually instantiate its monetary value.

Conversely the class hierarchy which implements the `MonetaryValueGG` interface can be designed without regard to the semantics of classes such as Price. Objects can be instantiated using the methods defined by the Money interface only. This allows this class hierarchy to focus on

the particular requirements associated with access to information stored in various underlying IT systems. This will include issues such as interpreting database schema, accessing database tables, screen scraping, interposition, remote access methods etc. These issues are being resolved with respect to our collaborators systems, as part of our work, and will be reported separately from this paper.

Once the two separate hierarchies associated with business and IT concerns are implemented the issue of which particular implementation class must be referenced by a given MonetaryValueInitialiser must be resolved. To aid clarity to the design and to externalize such decisions within a separate abstraction, the Abstract Factory pattern has been adopted. A class which implements the factory interface can construct the association between the two sides of the bridge at runtime, given some contextual information on which to base the decision. How these runtime decisions are resolved can be encoded using different strategies within different class declarations.

A Price object can then be instantiated by the client without any regard of how it related to the underlying IT system. This de-couples the client code from underlying IT system issues allowing for separate evolution of both the financial business systems which must closely follow the market and the underlying IT systems which generally follow a more step wise evolutionary model.

## 5 THE APPLICATION

### Requirements

The application used to trial these concepts in the collaborating company provides support for foreign exchange spot deal trading. It was designed and built in two phases, both phase 1 and phase 2 systems were designed and tested in the laboratory at Loughborough before being integrated with the companies IT systems in their premises in the City of London.

The Phase 1 system comprised a basic foreign exchange (Forex) spot deal application capable of: taking input from a "price feed" for Forex rates; handling four currencies (Sterling, Dollar, Yen and Euro); allowing the user to input the source currency and amount, and allowing the user to input the target currency.

Screen inputs are checked by ensuring that input of source currency, amount and target currency are mandatory fields (a simple error message is generated if they are not entered). The appropriate exchange rate, determined by the source and target currencies, is extracted from the "price feed". The target amount is calculated and displayed using the exchange rate.

The system will output the exchange rate, source / target currencies and amounts. This output is via the translation object technology that in this case is capable of switching between two separate existing legacy sysems in the bank:

The phase 2 system is an upgrade that includes new features for displaying the spot date, derived from a data warehouse in the companies IT systems, it also includes the provision of a search facility.

## Solution

This section provides a brief description of the major system components and summarizes the broad technological and implementation decisions taken. It includes the rationale behind the architectural decisions that have been made when structuring the system as depicted in Figure 2.

**Figure 2** Relationships between Major System Components

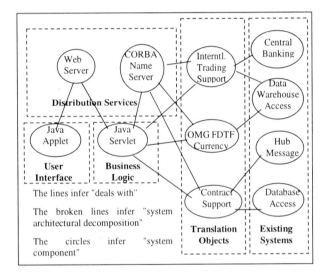

The lines infer "deals with"

The broken lines infer "system architectural decomposition"

The circles infer "system component"

### 1) User Interface

The UI is implemented as a Java Applet which comprises thin client. Java has been used rather than conventional HTML based implementation to provide richer functionality and security support.

### 2) Java Servlet

This contains the "Business Logic" i.e. the behavior of the system as defined by the set of calls to business objects supported by the Currency Support, Contract Support and International Trading Support components. Servlet technology has been used to provide an improved server side development environment in comparison with CGI (Common Gateway Interface).

### 3) Web Server

This hosts the byte code for the Java Applet that is downloaded to a browser. It also hosts the Java Servlet.

### 4) CORBA Compliant Name Server

This server allows the system components to locate required system services by name.

### 5) OMG FDTF Currency Support

This is a suite of Java classes implemented to support the OMG financial domain task force currency specification (finance/98-03-03) Version 3.0. There are abstractions for Currency, Money and ExchangeRate, plus abstractions to manipulate these including ExchangeRateManager CurrencyBook, MoneyCalculator and MoneyFormatter. These classes fulfill the role of a translation object, providing a mapping from the concepts in the standard to the concrete implementations in the companies IT systems.

### 6) Contract Support

This is a suite of Java classes implemented to support the concept of financial contracts e.g. buying and selling foreign currency. The specification of these classes has been derived from the Banking Model, which is being created by an associated PhD student working though both literature and discussion with members of the bank. These classes fulfil the role of a "translation object", providing a concrete mapping from concepts of contracts within the banking domain onto the existing IT implementation within the company.

### 7) International trading support

This is a suite of objects that support dealing in international currencies. Again these are translation objects, in this case the objects manage the information regarding "working days" for various currencies and the calculation of spot dates for a given combination of currencies.

### 8) Partial Hub Message

This is a partially completed message designed to convey the essence of a simple Forex deal as defined in the existing Hub message record for incoming Forex Trades.

### 9) Database access

This populates a database with the Deal Currency and Deal Amount, Dealt Exchange Rate and Other Currency and Other Amount, information. Access to the database is via a JDBC interface.

Figure 2 provides an overview of the relationships between the system components described above.

## 6 EVALUATION

The system described in this paper is currently running in the bank as a demonstration and evaluation system. Research staff from RED have transferred the technology used into the bank through a series of demonstrations and associated workshops with the development team in the bank. The bank's senior development staff have been involved throughout the project for both requirements specification and for their experience of the domain when modeling the bank. Additional flexibility is inherent in the separation within the design and implementation of the system. However, following the workshops the development staff evaluated the system in terms of those issues that are also of particular importance to them. It is important that these issues are considered and that the new system does not compromise these issues while striving for improved flexibility.

The feedback highlighted the following issues:

- Performance - how much is the speed of response effected by the added layers of abstraction; how does this effect the network load
- Robustness - how well does error handling percolate through the layers; are there policies for handling server failure
- Deployment and subsequent change control - how is role-out and change control effected by the additional complexity inherent in a system based on reduced system component granularity
- Scalability - The Forex Spot Desk system includes 26,468 lines of Java (in 252 files), 725 lines of IDL (in 9 files). Are there any implications concerned with scaling up the design approach to a complete Foreign Exchange support application which could be in the order of 2.5 M lines of code
- Tool Support - What effects would the use of such an approach have on the skills of the IT development department in terms of supporting a greater range of tools and techniques within a single system.

Additional concerns included the fact that the system did not explicitly handle security and transaction management. However these concerns were considered of less significance as it was never the intention to handle these issues as they are normally handled through existing general system facilities.

To continue the transfer of Translation Object technology into the bank a further phase of work is taking place which will investigate these issues during the design and implementation of a mission critical application at the heart of the banks IT systems

## 7 THE FINAL PHASE OF TECHNOLOGY TRANSFER:ADOPTINGTRANSLATION OBJECTS WITHIN THE COMPANY

In order to assess the concept and feasibility of adopting translation objects for mission critical systems the company has commissioned a pilot project. This project is being specified, managed and implemented by the company, with the authors serving in an advisory role with specific responsibility for closely supervising the architectural phase of the design. The project involves creating an application to manage the correlation of client information held within the companies underlying IT systems with information issued by the authority which manages a international electronic payment system.

This application provides an opportunity to evaluate the feasibility of translation objects as the application itself deals with information translation. The information issued by the electronic payment authority is a stable de-facto industry standard that we use to define the interface offered by the translation objects. The client information is held on various banking systems which present a range of legacy and integration issues which can be handled in a flexible manner through the de-coupling provided by the translation objects.

## 8 CONCLUSIONS

This paper has addressed the need to create business support applications using business abstractions, without having to consider issues relating to the underlying IT technology. To support this need the paper has demonstrated how translation objects implemented using the object oriented design patterns Bridge and Abstract Factory can be used to separate issues relating to the two different domains.

The paper has described how various techniques have been combined and transferred from the laboratory to the collaborating company through an intermediate trial/evaluation application that has been integrated with the companies IT systems. A number of relevant issues have been raised during the trial/evaluation work which are being considered during the final phase of technology transfer as the translation object concept is used to structure the architecture of a new mission critical application within the company.

The incorporation of emerging financial domain object standards together with agreed international banking standards plus the RED groups own banking models will be of benefit when using translation objects to map to next generation component based systems which adhere to standard business object specifications based on domain semantics.

## 9 ACKNOWLEDGEMENTS

The work described in this paper is supported by the EPSRC, IT and Computer Science Directorate, as part of their managed program "Systems Engineering for Business Process Change" (SEBPC).

## 10 REFERENCES

[1] Coutts97: Coutts, I., Edwards, J.,"Model Driven Distributed Systems",IEEE Concurrency, Vol. 5, No. 3, 1997, pp55-62.

[2] Coutts98: Coutts, I., Edwards, J.,"Support for Component Based Systems:Can Contemporary Technology Cope?", Intelligent Systems For Manufacturing, Edited by L.M. Camarinha-Matos et. Al., Kluwer Academic Publishers, 1998, ISBN 0-412-84670-5, pp279-288."Basys paper"

[3] Edwards98: Edwards J, Millea T, McLeod S, Coutts I, "Agile System Design and Build" IEE, Informatics Division, Colloquium. "Managing Requirements Change: A Business Process Re-engineering Perspective". Digest No: 98/312, June, 1998.

[4] OMG94: OMG (1994) "The Common Object Request Broker: Architecture and Specification", Object Management Group Inc., 492 Old Connecticut Path, Framingham, MA., USA.

[5] Gamma94: Gamma E, Helm R, Johnson R and Vlissides J, (1994) "DesignPatterns", Addison-Wesley.

[6] OMG98: CORBAFinance: Financial Domain Specifications Version 1.0, December 1998

[7] IBMBusinessFrameworks97: San Francisco project tech. overview, IBM Systems Journal, Vol 36, No. 3,199

# Index of Authors

Revised 9 November 1999